LAJOS BÁRDOS

SELECTED WRITINGS
ON MUSIC

LAJOS BÁRDOS

SELECTED WRITINGS
ON MUSIC

EDITIO MUSICA BUDAPEST

Translated by Alexander Farkas (Chapters I-VII, IX)
and Kata Ittzés (Chapter VIII)

Responsible for publishing: The Director of Editio Musica Budapest
Responsible Editor: Lilla Fantó. Technical Redactor: Andrea Richter
Technical Manager: Mrs. Béla Tóth
Z. 60049 (1984)
Published in 43,97 A/5 gatherings
Printed in Hungary by Editio Musica Budapest
Responsible Manager: Imre Kormány

CONTENTS

SINGING INSTRUMENTS

"Whoever wishes to fully understand
our music to its very roots must
approach it with a Glareanus-like
esteem for single-voice melody."

(Zoltán Kodály: *Hungarianness in music*)

Through all of Zoltán Kodály's pedagogical work, through his entire life's work as well, runs one leading thread: *Make music by singing!* Specifically: only through singing, from the songs of the people, may we learn our Hungarian musical mother-tongue—a broadly based musical culture may only be built upon a broadly based vocal culture—one who cannot sing is no musician—a musician may not merely strike keys nor draw a bow upon his instrument, but should rather sing through his instrument, and so forth.

Let us make music by singing! In Kodály's compositions this principle is realized in two ways. Firstly: a substantially greater and, from the point of view of the nation's music education, more significant proportion of his works is comprised of vocal music. Secondly: his purely instrumental music is developed from the seeds of enduring vocal melodies.

This is naturally accepted as a fact and widely recognized as such from those of his works which are based on folk melodies.

In this regard, how do matters stand with the great instrumental masters of earlier periods?

The natural parent of more highly structured, multivoiced instrumental works is the choral music of the Renaissance. The organ ricercars of Palestrina would make acceptable motets, only a text need be set under the lines.

In the subsequent course of development, would we perhaps have lost all trace of this?

Do the later descendants no longer bear any resemblance to the physiognomy of their ancestors?

To explore this matter in detail would be a delightful but very long assignment. Here, just a few random examples which come to mind will serve to illustrate that probably much more remains, and at a much deeper level, of the ancient vocal vocabulary in the language of instrumental works than we generally think.

We offer a few examples.

BACH: PASSACAGLIA

Bach's greatest work in variation form is the Passacaglia in *c*-minor for organ. Unlike so many of his significant works for organ, it is not a setting of a chorale melody, and yet if we listen to its theme, somehow a vocal line comes to mind:

Ex. 1

This melody—although primarily intended as a harmonic background—is still a melody: as if asking to be hummed, it is an easily and readily singable melody.

Its rhythmic formula is strikingly that of a sung verse. One of the most characteristic meters of European verse, the *iambic*, pulsates throughout the entire line. The line is cut midway, after the half-cadence, divided thus into 8 + 7 tones. Let us examine these two segments of the line separately.

a) *Four-part (TETRAPODIC) iambic*: the iambic dimeter of antiquity. This means *two* measures, for to the Greeks, with their fine musical sensitivity, one iamb in itself was not perceived as a measure. To be sure, to the concept of measure belongs one accented and one unaccented beat. Therefore, two iambs, the one heard as more accented, the other as less accented, coupled together created the measure.

Bach's theme is modelled most exactly after this pattern. The first iamb (*c-g*) is strongly accented, the following iamb (*e♭-f*) less strongly accented, and so on. Actually—just as in Beethoven's movements in a fast 3/4 meter—we hear two written measures as one measure of six units.

Ex. 2

a)   ∪   ╵ | ∪   ╵ | ∪   ╵╵ | ∪   ╵

     Jam   sur - git   hu - ra   ter - - ti - a

d)

c)

    A   pün - kösd - nek   je - les   nap - ján

b)

After the disappearance of the Greco-Roman culture, St. Ambrose, in the fourth century A. D., brought this type of meter back into fashion.

8

He created—perhaps after precedents found in folk style—the poetry of Western hymnody, eight-syllable iambic lines forming a four-line verse. This form acquired unusually widespread popularity. Beyond serving as hymn-poetry, it became woven into the treasured fabric of both chorale and folksong, and penetrated the area of secular poetry as well.

In our diagram the prosodic formula printed as *a)* may be read in musical notation as *b)*. This form of scansion—short and long syllables sung in 1:2 proportion—is called *metric*. Its later popularized and simplified form *d)*, in which there is no longer any difference in value between arsis and thesis, is referred to as *rhythmic*. (These technical terms of poetic meter should sooner or later be revised as they give rise to much confusion. There is certainly rhythm in the "metric" pulsation, and meter in the "rhythmic" loosened form, even if only of the simplest possible order.)

The Ambrosian line has a characteristic dynamic structure: the tension creates a certain crescendo through the first five syllables—the climax occurs on the sixth syllable—there is afterwards a decrescendo to the cadence.

Bach realizes this principle as well with crystalline exactness: the climax of the dimeter—indeed of the entire theme—occurs in the third measure on the *a♭*, namely on the sixth syllable of a probable text! This is true not only in the melody, but in the harmonic possibilities as well: this tone will bear the weight of the heavily stressed deceptive cadence with the VI chord or with absolutely any subdominant inversion.

b) *Three-and-one-half-part iambic*: the Anacreontic line. This is none other than a dimeter whose last member has been replaced by a rest (or whose seventh member has been lengthened). The Greeks referred to this type of line as catalectic, or truncated verse.

The two lines taken together as one whole present seven-and-one-half iambs. Its complete ancient name: *tetrameter iambicus catalecticus*.

It is a splendid form, as the masculine cadence of the antecedent part is answered by the lovely variant of the consequent part's feminine cadence. How monotonous it would be to have an isometric-isorhythmic cadence pair extending through the long succession of the variations!

After the appearance of so many vocal characteristics, we must examine the chorales of Bach. If we calculate on the basis of the 389 pieces of the Richter collection (Breitkopf), no less than 31 different chorales with their 46 variants, altogether 77 *vocal* melodies begin with the meter of our passacaglia; that is to say one out of five. And among these are some of the most famous! I have written under the music several of these texts which may be sung through to the end of the theme. (I have also quoted two Hungarian verse texts which bear witness to the widespread use of this form.)

```
23 Am  Was-ser- flüs- sen  Ba- by  - lon, da    sas- sen  wir  mit  Schmer- zen.
31 Aus  tie- fer  Not schrei ich zu   dir, Herr  Gott  er- hör' mein  Ru  - fen !
74 Ein'  fe -ste  Burg  ist  un- ser  Gott, ein'  gu - te  Wehr und Waf - fen.
288 O   Trau-rig- keit,  o  Her- ze - leid !  Ist  das  nicht  zu  ,be-  kla - gen ?
338 Was Gott thut, das  ist wohl- ge - than, es   bleibt ge - recht sein Wil - le.
(Petőfi: A  szé- gyen  és  a    fáj- da - lom  ket - tős  kö - nyű- je    áz - tat.
Arany: Jaj  an - nak, mely már tün- dö - költ, an - nak   kö - zelg ha - lá  - la.)
```

It is understandable why this rhythm is so close to Bach's heart. The popular practice of wearing down the metrical rhythm and reducing each tone to a uniform quarter-note value was already true for some time. But it is as if Bach had said to himself: if the gathered congregation is not capable of varying the rhythm, at least when no one is singing, I will give to the meter that which is the meter's, and to the iambus that which is the iamb's...

The melody is sounded in the pedals. The singular profusion of variation begins, already the pure soul of the instrument brimming over with rhythms, chords, and linear flourishes. But amidst all this the melody rings through as a song, as if the instrument were proclaiming:[1] even though a hundred strings may sound, even though a thousand reeds may pipe, I shall not forget that I may thank the ancient line of song for my music!

1 The work, originally intended for use in the home, was prepared and published for pedal harpsichord. However, the organ version is even more closely tied to vocal practice, which further reinforces the strength of the vocally rooted underlying concept behind it.

THE SONATAS OF BEETHOVEN

A moment ago we referred to the great popularity of the eight-syllable Ambrosian verse line. Let us now look through Beethovens's sonatas, satisfied for the time being to examine the first 15 from this point of view. Do these works no longer bear any relation to the metrical folksongs of the Middle Ages?

An examination yields surprising results.

A) Metrical dimeters. The natural scansion of the rising rhythm, the 1:2 mora-proportion, is clearly found in the following examples:

4. Demonstratively large leaps in each of the four iambs: not only a rising rhythm, but a rising melody as well!—The central sixth syllable is quite conspicuous: the $g\flat$ is the high point of the example.—The harmonic order, that of a period, renders the dimeter character: the dominant of the fourth tone is answered by the tonic of the eighth tone. This elemental rhythm continues without letup through the entire Trio.

5. Instead of large instrumental-type leaps, we find a melody quite in

the nature of a chorale. The intervals of prime and second create a closely-formed melody resembling the dimetrical lines of Josquin or Lassus. Its beginning conceals the upbeat, the anacrusis having been moved to stressed position. This is also characteristic of Josquin (Ave vera virginitas etc.). An iambic melody of this type survives among our people as well, the Whitsuntide melody heard on the lips of Hungarian children in the countryside. *(Ex. 2 c.)* There is a further intensification of this otherwise unvaried scansion: the rhythmic reversal in the second measure, the long and short values changing places. This is reminiscent of the ancient Greek "nodding" verse, the scazon. As in the preceding example, the principal syllable is similarly the *fa* of the key—in fact, the two melodies closely resemble each other, both resting on the melodic tones 3–2–4–3. If we take into consideration that the melody can emphasize the stressed syllable principally by means of a more accented, higher, or longer musical tone, then we can easily assess in our two examples, and in numerous other instances as well, the generous advantage granted to the sixth syllable: the *g♭* and the *g* are more accented, longer, and higher than the other tones. It is as if to say that the importance of these tones warrants a three-dimensional delineation.

6. A basically instrumental concept: the rhythm is divided between the lines played by the two hands — nonetheless an iambic melody is heard from the example. Yet another animating device: the long syllables of the third and fourth feet are broken up each into decorative intervalic figures. This is similar to the appearance in verse form of the tribrach (three short syllables) which may take the place of the iamb:

> auf Flü- | geln des | Ge- san- | ges
> Fort nach | den Fluren | des Gan- | ges
> *(Heine)*

The original slurs of the phrase markings confirm this view as do also the unbroken, smooth complementary iambs of example *6 b*, the beginning of the three-voiced middle section of the Trio. The period-type D-T rhyme is also found here.

7. The first period of the Scherzo of the *F*-major Sonata likewise begins with a fragmented line and then flows smoothly. Why do we hear iambs in the continuous quarter-note motion of the first part? Is this not a forced interpretation of the "moving" verse-foot? In one respect the second part of the line subsequently explains the first part by projecting back onto its dissected rhythm. (This phenomenon also occurs in verse forms.) But if this is not sufficiently convincing, let us listen to the harmonies implied in the first four measures. The first and second quarters of these measures

12

are always a broken interval which thus delineates the underlying harmony (note the dotted slur marks). The third quarters, however, always lead to the new function at the beginning of the next measure with a strong authentic-type movement, either the upward V–I harmonic movement or the melodic leading-tone movement of VII–I. The iambic scansion is thus precisely revealed by the hidden harmonies. The leading syllable of each dimeter stands out: in the first due to the only appearance of the subdominant, in the second the cadential $^6_4$ gives stress to the thesis of the third foot.—The fragmentation in *Ex. 7 b* is also a typical verse characteristic: the iamb of the third foot has been replaced by an anapest, or more specifically the normal 1:1:2 proportion has been replaced by the three-mora $1/_2:1/_2:2$ proportion, the so-called cyclical anapest. The Hungarian poet Arany employed the anapest:

Van-e ott | folyó
Legelő- | in fű

(The Bards of Wales)

Furthermore, of the 8 iambs of the two dimeters, the first six ascend in the melodic line. Only the final two iambs descend creating the cadence in the strictest sense of the word (i.e. a melodic fall).

8. A reversed situation: at the outset the accompaniment establishes the basic rhythm, while the tribrachs of the melody *(8 b)* may then subdivide the iambs. Let us not fail to recognize them. The ostinato of the accompaniment, on the other hand, moves along on the "walking" feet. The sixth syllable, in an exceptional manner, falls on a melodic lowpoint in *Ex. 8 b*, but this is also a way of showing emphasis.

B) Rhythmic dimeters. Leaving scansion aside, we find considerably more of the simplifying "rhythmic" iambs with a mora-ratio of 1:1 in these sonatas, just as among the chorales there are many more of this (so-called measured) type than those of the scanned three-quarter measures.

13

9 a. Simple as the rhythm of a folksong. It calls to mind the Swiss song which Beethoven used similarly as the theme for a set of variations *(9 b)*. In both instances the melody of the first three feet ascends and only the fourth foot cadences downward (see explanation for *Ex. 7*). The principal syllable here is also well stressed, if not quite as conspicuously as in the Swiss melody.

10 a. The simplest possible iambic rhythm. Rising seconds and fourths, the characteristic elements of authentic interval-turns, form the melody *(cf. Exs. 7 a, 9 a)*. The decisive syllable is emphasized by the S function at the beginning of the cadence.–An earlier theme of the same movement is more fragmented *(10 b)*: the beginning is scanned, while the melody of the third and fourth feet is in smaller units. –The principal syllable is again

14

not stressed melodically, but the harmony more than adequately compensates for this: leaving *b*-minor, the melody modulates to *f♯*-minor. The sixth syllable arrives exactly above the cadential $^6_4$ of the new key.

11. The same type of chord accents the sixth tone in one figure of the *C*-major Sonata, final movement. The c^1 is the melodic lowpoint just as in *Ex. 8 b.*

12 a. Also the most simple rhythm, only the plain measured line is begun with the more iambic iamb of the half-length first tone.

12 b and c. An interesting rhythmic weave. In the first the left hand, and in the second the right hand produces three iambs. However, the motivic segment of an imitative nature in the other hand extends the total number from six to eight, and therefore once again we have an Ambrosian line. In both cases the melody of each foot moves upward.

13 a. The significant leading-tone movements (*e-f, d-e♭*) here give evidence of the iambic feeling.

13 b. The coda derived from the principle theme of the same movement, with authentic intervals of upward leaping fourths in the bass, stresses the iambic pulsation. The embellishment of the fourth foot is delicate and clever: the fourth-leap also appears here but now displaced to an unstressed eigth. This maneuver allows the sixth tone (*g*) to maintain precisely its dominant significance.

14. As in examples *12 b* and *12 c*, the right hand here presents only three iambs, but the dimeter of the organically related bass figure completes the motive. The melody ascends in each of the four feet. The sixth tone is significantly accented.

15. While the former example began with an ascending octave, this example begins with a descending octave. Here also the cadential $^6_4$ emphasizes the principle tone.

16 a. An extremely strong example of sixth-tone emphasis. Not only is this note heavier, higher and longer than the others, but also receives extra dynamic stress by virtue of the accent mark.

16 b. In the secondary theme of this movement the melodic direction is reversed, therefore the intensity of the principal tone loses something—it almost appears that the accent of the former example redoubled as a sforzato and the tension of the altered dominant ninth (*f♭*) would like to balance out this missing quantity.

C) Extended iambs. The above group of examples do not show notevalue differences between stressed and unstressed tones. Other examples on the contrary stress these differences. In the following group we find the 1:3 mora-proportion in place of the metrical 1:2 proportion:

Ex. 17   Ex. 18   Ex. 19

Molto allegro e con brio   **Molto allegro e con brio**   **Allegro**

c, Op. 10/1   c, Op. 13   Ibid.

17. Very sharply delineated iambs: beside the extended iambs there are large upward leaps (as in *Ex. 4*).

18. Standing out from among the outer non-scanned iambs, extended formulas climbing to the $g\flat$ give the motive its character.

19. A variant of the former theme within the Rondo. The sixth syllable receives a certain weight as it falls on the only dominant which breaks through the surrounding tonic areas.

D) Bimeter with bisected lines. A mid-point division often demonstrates a $4+4$ construction of the eight syllables:

Ex. 20

a) **Presto**   6   b)   F, Op. 10/2

Ex. 21

a)   **Molto allegro e con brio**   b)   E♭ Op. 7

Ex. 22

a)   **Allegro, ma non troppo**   b)

T—D   D—T

Ex. 23

c)   D, Op. 28   **Allegretto**   B♭, Op. 22

T - D D-T

16

As in the mid-line rhymes of Arany's verse:

> Földet, folyót, | legelni jót,
> Körötte csend, | amerre ment,
> Szó bennszakad,| hang fennakad
> *(The Bards of Wales)*

20. In the Presto of the F-major sonata, every principal and closing theme has this type of construction. The sixth tone is strongly prominent in the first theme.

21. We find a similar construction in the second group of themes of the E♭-Major sonata: in *Ex. 21 a* we hear a sequentially built theme (just as in *Ex. 20 a*), and in *Ex. 21 b* a varied repetition (as in *Ex. 20 b*).

22. From the Rondo of the Pastorale Sonata, one of the richest storehouses of iambic formulas, we quote three such themes. The first theme (*22 a*) is of a periodic nature: a D-T answer to a T-D question. Here the sixth tone dominates by virtue of a stressed suspension. The second theme remains entirely in the tonic, while the third theme (*22 c*) twice presents the play of question and answer through a diminution of the functional structure of *22 a*. (In this regard it is identical to *Ex. 21 b* as well!)

23. Under the richly built melody the harmonies clearly maintain, or explain as it were, the dimeter rhythm of the theme. The chord structure insures the prominence of the sixth tone: in place of the former analogous c-minor[6], a C-Major[6] appears, signifying a new key.

Other examples of bisected lines from the preceding group of examples: *4, 7 b, 12 a, 12 b, 13 a, 15*, as well as the examples of the following groups (*24-29*).

E) Lines of separated verse feet. In addition to bisected lines, there also appear examples of lines divided into four parts, that is to say lines in which each foot is sharply separated, strengthening even more our thesis: that the influence of the iamb is apparently indestructible even in instrumental music.

Ex. 24   Ex. 25

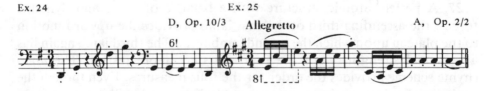

Once again Arany comes to mind:

> Ha, ha!   mi zúg?   mi éji dal...
> *(The Bards of Wales)*

24. Two separate iambs, then the third and fourth iamb joined by small steps. The rarely used device of a suspension in the bass calls attention to the main stress of the sixth tone.

25. Exactly the same articulation as in the previous example, even the manner, place and rhythmic function of the segments is identical.

Ex. 26

26 a. A reverse play: the first half in one unit, the second half in separated feet. We could sing to it such a line of verse as:

Mint egy veled | a rög | s a föld
(Kosztolányi: Ever closer)

26 b. The middle section of the piece however, reestablishes the full continuity of the dimeter.

Even with all four iambs entirely separated by rests, the unity of a dimeter is created, proclaiming loudly the truth of our thesis:

Ex. 27   Ex. 28

Just as Petőfi wrote:

Mi kék | Az ég! | Mi zöld | A föld!

(*Ex. 28*, with its dialogue of higher and lower voices, is a particularly suitable model of this type.)

27. A perfect atomic structure with a balance of static and dynamic forces: the ascending third of the first iamb provides the upward motion to the plateau upon which the second iamb rests. The third iamb again has a tensional strength, while the fourth is once more restful. The *abab* rhyme scheme provides the order for the four measures. Even though the sixth tone has lost height in comparison to the second, still it has a certain stress and tension due to the appearance of the dominant.

28. Identical in thought to the former example, but with altogether sharper inner divisions: in place of the triplets there are two sets of four thirty-second notes. The sixth tone here stands out by virtue of the change of harmonic function, only instead of the D the much rarer S gives a more individual flavor to the sequence.

Ex. 29

D, Op. 28

Allegro, ma non troppo

29. The variant of *Ex. 22 b*: in place of the continuous legato there are rests, and the ornamentation of the arses is achieved by the use of chromatic alterations.

At this point we must realize that these and other similar inner divisions, always in an unstressed position, bring to light the innermost essence of the iamb. Indeed, they achieve this aim better than the spoken word. In general we are rather content with the definition:

"an iamb is a verse foot rising from the unstressed

short to the stressed long syllable",

but does this really tell all about the iamb? What lies within this description of its outward appearance?

When I raise my foot something begins to happen. Movement is initiated, energy is exerted. This is the first part of the iamb, the arsis.

When I put my foot down, the event reaches its end. The movement is finished, the production of energy is completed. This is the second member of the iamb, the thesis. (Let us not forget that the iamb formerly flourished together with dance!)

Thus the iamb is not only a matter of short-long and unstressed-stressed quantities, but also of movement-rest, tension-relaxation, and dynamic-static qualities as well. Inhalation and exhalation, wave-height and wave-depth as well. That is to say a two-phased unity without which there is no movement on earth, neither light, nor sound, nor electric current—no life of any kind.

The arses of these Beethoven examples, in which an unstressed part is broken into small units, point up exactly this intensity of movement, which in turn intensifies the magnetic attraction so apparent in the direction toward the point of rest. Let us play or think through several times in succession the second iamb of *Ex. 28* and we will realize what is in question. In addition to the last three examples, let us look back over examples *7 b, 10 b, 12 c (!), 15, 18,* and *25.* How many times and in what significant manner the artistry of the genius discloses to us the internal nature of the iamb!

19

Conclusion:

a) an elemental vocal basis is probably much more significant in the thought processes of composers of instrumental music than is generally realized,

b) among the forms of instrumental music the iamb is most significantly pre-eminent,

c) among iambic forms *the iambic dimeter* appears with greatest frequency,

d) we may find, within *each* of the first 15 sonatas of Beethoven, motives of just such rhythmic types. Moreover they are among the most important themes, often the opening theme of a movement. (On an average we find three such themes in each sonata, one such theme appears in almost every movement!),

e) the treatment of these themes from the standpoint of meter, rhythm, melody, phrasing, and even harmony generally corresponds to the ancient patterns of vocal verse, even to the Ambrosian heightening of the sixth syllable.

It would be an enormous assignment, but certainly an enticing one, to trace the forms of other vocal meters through the entire literature of instrumental music. Besides the scientific value, such research would perhaps bring us to the point at which instrumental musicians would have a deeper respect for vocal music and would make music with a more singing heart.

And this would help to realize Zoltán Kodály's dream of an ever more musically cultured Hungary.

(Zenetudományi tanulmányok, I.
Budapest, 1953)

ORGANICISM

When analyzing musical forms, we speak of motivic and thematic work, by which we mean the further development of shorter or longer units of thought.

But how shall we designate a melodic fabric, a musical construction in which there is not one generative unit which could rightfully be called a motive but only an element of a few tones, in itself quite insignificant, which, by virtue of highly varied transformations, creates a musical work of clear integrity?

It would be advisable for us to introduce the term *organic work*, understanding by this the creation of a fully developed melody—or an entire musical composition—which has sprung from one modest little seed.

The devices of musical organicism are transposition, recapitulation (in rare instances: repetition), but mainly every imaginable type of variation.

There are four areas which provide occasion to examine this particular process of musical composition:
a) Gregorian melody,
b) the music of Bach,
c) Hungarian folk music,
d) a choral work of Zoltán Kodály.

A) GREGORIAN MELODY

Let us begin with an example of old music, the Sanctus of the Ninth Mass (dated fourteenth century):

Ex. 1

San - - ctus, San - ctus, San - - - ctus,

It was Alfonz Nádasi who realized that the entire melody is comprised of small three-member cells which each share one common characteristic: three tones moving in one direction. (We do not count the repeated tones directly joined to these units as they do not alter the direction.) In what follows, I have simply related Nádasi's observations with the occasional addition of some of my own comments.

Brackets have been superimposed onto the score to indicate these single-phrase ternions. These appear one after another in two different ways: either joined together by a common tone (the brackets coincide), or separately one after the other (there is a space between the brackets). This corresponds to the treatment of the ancient Greek tetrachords: the synemmenon and diazeugmenon (overlapping and separated) types of linkage.

Four formulas of the same basic principle dominate the melody: descending thirds, ascending thirds, descending seconds, ascending seconds. All are developments of the initial triad by inversion or intervalic diminution (projection). The variants which occur:

Ex. 2

The occurrences and frequency of each formula:

a) under brackets 1, 11, 21, 31, 41 5
b) 5, 20, 37, 40 4
c) 2, 15, 22, 34, 35 5
d) 3, 4, 13, 14, 23, 33, 39 7
e) 6, 8, 18, 24, 28 5
f) 9, 26 2
g) 7, 10, 17, 27, 30, 38 6
h) 16, 25, 29 3
i) 12, 19, 32, 36 4

Total: 41

The precision of the regular re-appearance of the first form at place-numbers 1, 11, 21, 31 and 41 is indeed surprising. Intentional? Instinctive? Merely by chance? Who can say? (Nádasi found a similarly surprising regularity in the occurrence of the *do, mi, so* pillar-tones: each one is sounded precisely for the length of 29 eighth-notes in the course of the melody!)

There are yet other hidden triads which also reinforce the organic construction:

the d) formula (*mi-re-do*) appears as a sycopation extending
between brackets 19–20;

the e) type (*do'-ti-la*) between brackets 9–10, 26–27 and E–38;

the f) ternion (*ti-la-so*) between units 18–A and 28–29.

The numbers indicating the occurrences of the individual figures do not in the least imply a literal reiteration. Deep within the lines of this melody lies an instrinsic elasticity, a constant plasticity. In almost every instance, extremely fine differentiations of rhythm, accentuation and phrasing are shown in the variants of the basic idea. Furthermore, different effects are achieved depending on whether separate syllables occur on two neighboring tones (syllabic style), or whether an inflection of such neighbor-tones is used to decorate one syllable (neumatic style). See, for example, the occurrences of the principal formula at nos. 11 and 21 in the score *(Ex. 1)*.

23

As a case in point, let us examine in detail the variants of the d) formula descending trichord:

Ex. 3

Here the beams denote the stressed group of tones belonging together (their first tone receives the pulsating accent of the ictus), the slurs show how the tones fit within the phrasing. Let us isolate just one small detail: the middle tone of the ternion, the *e = re*, where it is an unstressed passing-tone (3, 4, 39, 14), where the stressed beginning of a neuma (13,33), or where, because it is a repeated tone, it has become accented as the ca-dential tone which slows down the movement (23). Thus it may equally be a beginning, middle or closing tone of one elemental measure-cell. It would be instructive to place the variants of the other eight types one next to the other and examine them in this way—but due to lack of space I entrust this task to the interested reader.

By pushing just a little further, we may discover four other places where a pentatonic ternion, comprised of second and third, lies hidden:

Ex. 4

These are retrograde-inversions of each other, thus strengthening the organicism here as well. The disjunct movement of the minor third calls to our attention the infrequent appearance of the *g = fa* in the melody: of 131 tones it is heard altogether only four times! And then it is always as the *fa-mi-re* climacus, the fifth-answer to the high *do'-ti'la*. This is probably a manifestation of the basic Gregorian six-tone system (here the *do-so-re-la-mi-ti* hexatonic fifth-crystal).

There are altogether only five places in the course of this long melody which break the rule of the ternions proceding in only one direction. These are designated in *Ex. 1* by the upper case letters:

A = a solitary third-flexa,

B = a changing-note resting point (torculus),

C = disjunct changing-note,

D = seemingly a fifth-answer to the previous, with rhythmic trans-formation,

24

E = the variant of B with a new, free-standing beginning-tone after a break.

There exists between these elements an organic relation which is significant with respect to form. Taken in pairs, they each have their respective fifth-answer:

Ex. 5

In each pair, the dominant-tonic relation is evident. This may remind us of the similarly-related cadential order of one of the ancient psalm melodies—or on the other hand it could be a foreshadowing of the classical period-type rhyme-order which was to take shape in the centuries to come.

Similar nearly-functional relations also appear elsewhere. Along with the above-mentioned E-F pair:

Ex. 6

These element-pairs, of question-answer type, seem to create a certain free four-membered shape. Referring once more to *Ex. 1:*

   I = brackets 1–13,
  II = 14–19, with an outward extension to bracket 23,
 III = 24–33,
 IV = 34 to the end.

Four loose quasi-periods in "prose"-structure—each of them moving toward a melody-type characterized by rhyming half-cadence and full cadence.

And in conclusion a request: let us not leave the structure like this, broken apart in small pieces. Let us put it together again, which means singing through to the end without interruption. Let us feel and enjoy, throughout the melody, its free lilt, its varied undulation, bearing in mind that we owe all of this to three tones.

25

B) BACH

The unsurpassable giant of organic musical creation is Johann Sebastian Bach. Let us consider for example those preludes which have no motivic material of a clearly melodic nature or well-defined rhythm but which, throughout their entire duration, are put together by the continuous organic weaving of altogether one single figuration. True, these pieces do rest on an unusually solid harmonic texture. But the music which is heard is nonetheless an evenly flowing succession of tones without any clearly delineated melody or rhythm. An organic blossoming from one single basic germ.

Examples of purely harmonic figuration:

A peak of bravura marks the above-quoted Prelude in *d*-minor: the basic formula, broken triads almost throughout, consists of but three tones (just as does the Ninth Sanctus discussed above). Even richer is the opening figuration of the famous Prelude in *C*-major: the chords are divided into a $5 + 3$ grouping.

The *F*-major Prelude (Vol. II), with its long lines, is built purely on melodic figurations:

Trichords and tetrachords bridge the gaps between the chord-tones. (Kodály made us study this piece in great detail when we were students in his composition class.)

In a mixed figuration, disjunct movement between the chord-tones alternates with step-wise movement of changing-notes:

26

But when the music is further enriched by an integral melody and rhythmic formula, we may still marvel at the organic role of the simple four-member formula, whether it be a main voice or an accompanying part as for instance in the mighty opening movement of the St. John Passion:

Ex. 10

And so forth without interruption throughout the entire 153 measures of the movement. And even though we may hear it six hundred times, either in one voice or simultaneously in several voices, why is it that we never find it boring?... (It just so happens that this quaternion corresponds to the mirror-inversion of the basic four-tone group found in Kodály's Norvég leányok. It serves to illustrate that a small group of given tones, turned in any direction, may become, in an almost limitless number of ways, living, poetic music.)

Then, under the beautiful, heart-stirring vocal lines of the counter-theme, the figure assumes the more modest role of an ostinato bass:

Ex. 11

But we shall not continue our detailed examination of Bach's writing here. His music is accessible to all. We merely recommend a measure-by-measure analysis of his works which display such an organic conception. Those who decide to do this will find in them the wonders of a power shaped into musical composition.

C) FOLKSONG

It is less generally held, or perhaps until now not at all recognized, that a portion of our Hungarian folksongs likewise employ, here intuitively, the technique of organic melody-construction. We need only look about, search a bit, and surprising things will appear before us.

Of the many interesting examples, let us choose one, the melody of Ablakomba... (Bartók was very fond of this melody. He published it, furnished with an accompaniment, in the famous volume entitled Hungarian Folksongs which—together with some of Kodály's harmonizations—first broke through the wall of Hungarian popular "taste" around 1906.)

Let us look at the song:

Tura, Harasztpuszta

Ab-la-kom-ba, ab-la-kom-ba be-sü-tött a hold-vi-lág.
A-ki ket-tőt, hár-mat sze-ret, so-sincs ar-ra jó vi-lág.
D.C. Ez az ál-nok bé-res-le-gény csal-ta meg a szí-ve-met.

Lám én csak e-gyet sze-re-tek, még-is de so-kat szen-ve-dek,

Da Capo

Into my window shone the moon light.
He who loves two or three will never have a good life.
Alas I love but one, yet I suffer greatly,
This false lad has deceived my heart.

The text follows the well-known Hungarian verse-form: four-syllable measures with a three-syllable cadence at the end of the line. A lovely, natural order: the three tones of the strong (masculine) cadence serve to brake the flowing (feminine) groups of four tones. One of the characteristics of the AABA form: the third line among four is not closed but remains open.

Let us examine the melody. What happens to these groups of four tones?

The essential feature of the first melodic-molecule is the *up-down-down* (pes subbipunctus) movement. The initial momentum of a rising third, then a more gently sloping return. In itself this is a formal unity.

The second measure? It presents something significantly new. A higher register, augmented note-values, larger intervals. But here we also find essentially *up-down-down*! Clearly, it has sprung from the first measure, the details of which have been enriched in three ways. The four diatonic tones of the first measure are projected into the pentaton. Measured in half-steps we find the dimensions 3–1–2 (first measure) and then 5–2–3 (second measure). These two proportions correspond to each other exactly (according to the Golden Section) in their two respective systems. What is more, the melody reflects the poetic truth of the verse. If we do indeed repeat a word (ablakomba), its repetition ought to be justified, ought to be intensified. (As similar phenomena occur in numerous Hungarian folksongs, could we not investigate the possibility that Bartók's feeling for projection technique, variation, etc. did not perhaps find its origins in our folk music also?)

29

The third measure ... once again, of course, *up-down-down*! After the height of the second measure, it leads the melody back down toward the finalis.

The final measure of the line falls outside the circle of our four-tone groups. We may nevertheless mention its formal pertinence to our melody: it inverts the rising, open third of the first measure back to a falling third of a closing character. In other words, even this measure is organically linked to those preceding!

And now let us examine the implied functions of the first four measures:

Ex. 13

Measures 1, 2 and 4 give shape to the tonic triad concealed within them. Their primary tones coincide with the consonant *la-do-mi*. And the third measure? It "deliberately" stresses the otherwise neglected *re* and *ti*. It is difficult to know whether we should assign a dominant or a subdominant significance to these two tones. (Bartók, in his above-mentioned harmonization, uses both possibilities. He first accompanies the melody with the natural VII degree which, in modal context, is of dominant character, and then later the subdominant triads on degrees IV and II are woven together into one and the same chord.) From a purely melodic viewpoint we may designate this *re-fa* tone-pair as being antitonic. I may not fail to mention that this is the measure which is unlike the other—the third among four! Or we may simply say that it falls under the principle of the Golden Section! With regard to the latent functions, we find within this selfsame line the *aaba* structure in miniature. While obviously only a fortuitous occurrence, we may still marvel at the treatment of the prosody: in each instance it is the third measure which contains the predicate: besütött (= shone in), sosincs arra (= will never have), csalta meg (= has deceived).

Nor should we refrain, in our investigation, from examining, with respect to the hidden harmonic structure, the foreign or embellishing tones of each measure. The passing- and changing-tones marked by an asterisk in *Ex. 13* lend greater melodic interest to the line which would otherwise consist of excessive disjunct motion. (See Bach's mixed figuration in

30

Ex. 9.) And where are these tones to be found within the four-tone measures? We are no longer amazed (or perhaps all the more so?)—in the third among four places. The third measure however "knows" that it must say something else, something of a contradictory nature: thus in retrograde, it is the second eighth-note of the measure which is the foreign-tone within its *re-ti* antitonic surrounding. The negative Golden Section is used in place of the positive.

What do we find in the third line? Something entirely new, truly worthy of the B designation it holds within the AABA formula. The melody, having until now remained with the compass of one octave, immediately shoots up to the tenth. But of course the song turns here to something very personal. After the first line, which describes a phenomenon of nature, and the general subject of the second line: "én" (= I)! Alas, behold, I ...! The directions, as compared to the first lines, are also changed. But wait! Let us look for the retrograde-mirror[1] inversion of the first quaternion:

Ex. 14

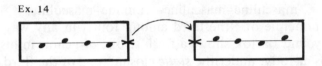

And here is the surprise. The seemingly new quaternion at the beginning of the B line is also derived from the very first measure of the melody. (We may still, despite this fact, rightfully use a B designation in our analytic

1 The retrograde-mirror is generally considered to be a two-fold inversion since the basic formula is rotated about both the horizontal and vertical axes. I do not know whether it is a widely held view, but in my opinion this is still an inversion achieved through only one single operation. Let us imagine that we place a rod through the center of the basic form as it appears in the score, and that we then rotate the page about this rod through 180 degrees. We thus obtain the retrograde-mirror. (The rod of course is not really necessary. We need only turn the book upside-down in order to see that from the original "up-down-down" line there now appears the "down-down-up" of the retrograde-mirror.) How is it then that the retrograde-mirror is still generally considered a two-fold inversion? Precisely because we notate our score on a two-dimensional page which has only the width and length readily acknowledged as belonging to written notation. But our space has also the third dimension of depth. It is through this dimension that, with one single motion, we have rotated the score about the (imaginary) rod and thus obtained the same retrograde-mirror inversion as would have been achieved through the other two processes. (It would be good if someone were to find a simpler term for the compound "retrograde-mirror" to describe this type of rod-inversion.)

formula as the line has such a very new character. At most we may provide the letter B with a small A index: B^A.)

Nor does the continuation of this line refuse the total organicism of the melody. Both the second and third measures vary the *down-down-up* direction, intensifying the returning, descending motion toward the finalis. Even the fourth measure begins with a *down-down...* but then the fourth tone, instead of turning upward, continues the downward slope in order to bring the lone to a close. (Kodály was known to say more than once during his composition classes: to reiterate a sequential figure three times is quite enough!) But then, at the end of this line, we find once again, just as in the outer lines, the closing *do-la* third. Does it not weaken the form to close each of the four lines on the first degree of the scale? We may be sure that our folksongs are generally characterized by a richer cadential order. But we do find such melodies of this rhyme-ending type. Be that as it may, an extemely fine difference is to be found in the way the melody closes the third as opposed to the other lines: the closing *la* is heard only once and in an unstressed position. The cadential order of the four lines is thus:

masculine–masculine–feminine–masculine.

Nor is the principle of "the third among four" in any way repudiated here. (The young Bartók shows a fresh stroke of genius in his harmonization of this melody: under the *static* closing tone of the third line he sets the *most dynamic* chord, the diminished seventh on the raised fourth degree!)

Let us now turn back to the score *(Ex. 12)* and compare the measures as written one beneath the other.

The first measures (of both the first and third lines) contain exactly the same set of tones with the octave difference (of the third line) providing a lyrical outburst, a melodic climax. In the second measures the difference of register disappears: the quaternions are both drawn from the same pentatonic triad. (But we never feel this while singing the melody!) The third measure of the B line provides something new, but only with its first and fourth tones. The two middle tones (*mi-re*) are identical in both the inner and outer lines. The first tone, the upper *la*, appropriately stresses the word *mégis* (= yet); the last tone of the measure is one which has not yet been heard: the very expressive minor-sixth, the *fa* degree. (It is as if one had realized: which scale tone has not been used up to this point? I will place it in the third measure of the third line...)

As for the fourth measure, it will suffice to say that it combines the period-like rhyming thirds which close each of the two halves of the first line. Let us illustrate:

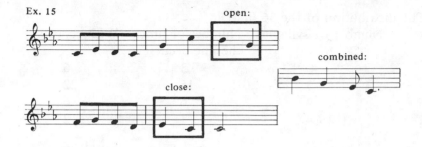

Ex. 15

Thus no matter how great the differences between lines A and B may appear, the organic connection between analogous measures of the two lines is total.

Lastly, the most surprising (at least in my opinion) observation: the appearance of the recurring "third among four" in three different orders of magnitude:

1. *measure-wise* in the principle line: the third tone is, in comparison to the main *la-do-mi* tones, relatively speaking a foreign tone;

2. *line-wise*: the third measure among four presents new melodic elements in contrast to the other measures;

3. *the entire melody*: the AABA construction of the lines.

D) THE NORWEGIAN GIRLS
(NORVÉG LEÁNYOK)

THE UNUSUAL CONSTRUCTION OF AN UNUSUAL WORK

In 1940, Zoltán Kodály composed one of his most poetic and most original works, the Norwegian Girls. When the work first appeared we all felt that its creation was a show of sympathy for the northern country which had at that time been overrun by the Germans.

THE POETRY
This poem of Sándor Weöres shows the characteristics of the Hungarian folk-verse idiom: measures of four syllables with cadential formulas of three syllables. (The same was true for the text of the folksong discussed in the previous section.)

33

The distribution of the 36 lines:

Number of syllables	Number of times the line occurs	With repeats
4	3	6
4 + 3	15	22
4 + 4	6	= 6
2 + 4	1	2

Total: 36

In other words, the four-syllable verse-measure occurs at least once in every line—in six cases even twice.

The composer also took this as his basis for creating the rhythm of the melody.

If we then dissect the piece into its molecular units, we must first examine the four-syllable units.

THE MUSIC

Let us look at the melody of the first stanza:

Ex. 16

This principal melody is essentially the further development of a small formula formed by the first four tones. The second measure also presents the same formula with the first tone placed a second lower and the rhythm varied. The third measure offers the basic formula in a mirror-inversion. (We shall hereafter designate this basic formula as "A".) The sixth measure is also an "A"-mirror one degree higher, and finally in the eighth measure the basic formula is heard once again. We should also note the *fi-mi-fi* in the second half of the first measure. It is a mirror of the basic form with the fourth tone left out. (Left out? it appears immediately at the beginning of the second measure!)

34

It is precisely at the mid-point of the melody that we find two new elements: the quarter-note pair (worthy of the text in length, height and content) over the word "mindig" (= always), and the descending tetrachord which follows immediately afterward. This latter has a melodic function: to fill in the preceding fifth-leap (motus interpositus), and to lead the line back to the natural middle-range of the sixth measure. The closing ternion is sung three times. In measure 4 it is an open half-cadence, and its appearance as a secondary dominant in measure 7 prepares the dominant *f*♯-minor verse-ending of measure 9.

The music composed for the remaining five stanzas of the poem *is developed entirely from the musical material of the first verse.* (Altogether only two new elements appear: the "csillog-villog", sparkle-and-glitter measure and the raindrop music. But this is comparatively nothing more than when Bach, that giant of musical organicism, interpolates a free improvisatory roulade or a prolonged dissonant chord under a fermata in one or another otherwise clanging-type prelude.)

From the second stanza of this work of Kodály we quote only the beginning melody:

Ex. 17

Pu - ha pá - ra bo-rul rá a he-gyek - re,

Let us but compare this with the first four measures of *Ex. 16* to see how the most significant elements of this preceding section have been compressed! We meet first with the "A" formula in augmentation (Puha pára). Of further interest: the "kacskaringós tenger" of measure 16 (once again derived from the "A", see meas. 15–17), the already-mentioned rain-music (meas. 20), as well as the "sparkle-glitter" of measure 25 *(Ex. 42)*. However, the connective tissue throughout the stanza is again nothing but the "A" quaternion. It is heard ten times in the principal melody alone. At one point it takes a new form: in the second half of measure 22 it is sung in a retrograde-mirror inversion: the *mi-re-do-re* of "esik eső" (= rain is falling).

The key phrase of the third verse (measures 29–43): "Szálldogál a szél" (= The wind is flittering). At the end of the stanza the ambling of the girls walking arm in arm: restful quarters (measures 41–43). The "A" quaternion appears here also ten times in the principal melody and several times in the accompanying voices as well.

The first secion of the fourth stanza (measures 44–54) springs organically from the tetrachord of meas. 5: "kéklő szemük" (= their blue eyes). Agreeably fresh but still capable of leading back to the familiar material is the line-pair of measures 45–48. However, here as well, the final word is given to the "A" quaternion of the first measure and its three-member closing formula.

The fifth (measures 55–60) and sixth (measures 61–67) sections, with regard to both music and text, serve to bring the piece around to the recapitulation, now presenting the material of the first two stanzas in reversed order.—The coda gently reminds us of the constant rain.

With this piece (73 measures in all!), Kodály, relying on the successive organic development of modest elements from beginning to end, has created fresh, original music of a personal, poetic mood, and using a motive of not more than four tones. In this regard I do not know whether other such feats may be found elsewhere among our newer musical literature...

THE BASIC MATERIAL

Let us take stock: how are the basic individual elements used? (The letters S, A, T, B designate the voices of the mixed chorus; the T sounds one octave lower.)

I. The appearance of the initial basic formula beginning on the main (I, IV, V) tonal degrees:

Ex. 18

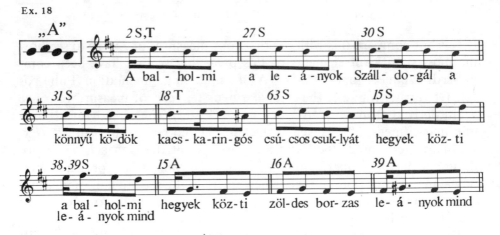

36

Placed at the lower second:

Ex. 19

he-gyek köz- ti   de so - ha - se   vil - log   a bal - hol- mi
ki- kö - tő - ben

Transposed by a third (three times at the upper, once at the lower third):

Ex. 20

he-gyek köz- ti   kacs -ka- rin- gős   he-gyek köz- ti
a bal - hol- mi

The initial step widened to a third:

Ex. 21

le- á - nyok mind   Száll a fe-hér   e - sik e - ső   de so- ha- se

Containing a leap of a fourth:

Ex. 22

Zöl- des bor- zas   a ten- ge- ren   a ten- ge- ren   de so - ha- se

In augmentation, with "walking" quarters:

Ex. 23

Pu- ha pá- ra (bo)rú -   (ra)(bo)rú -   (ra)

37

With anticipations in a neumatic figuration:

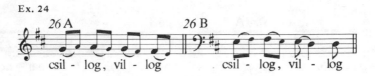

Ex. 24

csil - log, vil - log   csil - log, vil - log

(It has been my own idea to show the noteheads in differentiated sizes, in part for the sake of lucidity, and in part as advice to the singers.)

Among my students at the Liszt Academy of Music, many have insisted that there is another appearance of ''A'' above the broken organpoint in measures 42–43:

Ex. 25

(sé)tál -   -   (nak)

Thus there are altogether 35 variants of the basic ''A'' form—with repeats and with the recapitulation actually 45 in all.[2]

II. Mirror inversion. The classical principle of ''unity in diversity and diversity in unity'' is also served by the various inversions of ''A''. We arrive at the mirror form by rotating about the horizontal axis.

Beginning on degrees I, IV and V:

2 The reader has no doubt realized that the basic four-tone set (the up-down-down) of the folksong Ablakomba... corresponds exactly to the main formula of the Norvég leányok. And as we have already mentioned, the quaternions of the St. John Passion also belong to the same family. Yet what enormous differences exist between all of these! In rhythm, intervalic variation, in the overall melodic weave etc., the differences derived from the very same basic cellular-unit are so nearly inexhaustible, that we perhaps do not even recognize the common form. But that is only if we do not thoroughly examine the material. (Composers! Students and skilled masters! Who will try to emulate this work? To take almost nothing, the barest motive of three or four tones, and from it, using the tools of organicism, create an ample melody or an entire choral work. And something at least as beautiful as our examples!)

With displacement at the interval of a second:

Ex. 27

At the third below or above:

Ex. 28

It is debateable whether the following should be included in our discussion here, but among my students many claimed that this bass measure is pertinent, saying that it is also *"down-up-up"*:

Mirror inversions occur altogether in 27 variants, and with repeats in 36 instances.

III. Retrograde. Although a less frequent occurrence, the four-member basic formula does appear rotated about the verticle axis:

Ex. 30

In augmentation, and augmented by a factor of four also:

Ex. 31

In the "sparkling" neumatic form:

Ex. 32

(See explanation following *Ex. 24*.)

Fitting between repeated tones, and overlapping with the three-member closing formula:

Ex. 33

Even this extended form follows the *"up-up-down"* direction:

Ex. 34

Retrograde inversions occur altogether in 13 variants, with repeats in 15 instances.

IV. Retrograde-mirror. I list the appearances of this fourth type of moving eighth-note configuration as it occurs at successively higher scale degrees:

Ex. 35

In the "walking" quarter augmentation:

Ex. 36

sé - tál - (nak)

Nor is the "sparkle" variant omitted from this group:

Ex. 37

csil - log, vil - log

There are altogether 10 retrograde-mirror variants, with repetitions and recapitulation it is heard 17 times.

Summarizing the various appearances of the "A" cellular-unit:

basic form 45
mirror 36
retrograde 15
retrograde-mirror 17

total   113

One hundred thirteen instances in barely fifty-five measures!

The closing ternion

If the poet himself has already chosen to employ the three-syllable ending typical of our folksongs for the rhythmically closed lines, the composer has also considered as most suitable the *ti-ta-ta* measure-long rhythm which emphasises melodically the main syllable and which, along with the repeated tones, strengthens the line-closing.

As it appears in the piece (we show only the soprano voice of the main melody):

Ex. 38

vi- sel - nek,   hegyek - re,   ten-ger - re,   szi - tál - nak,

ne - vet - nek.   ne - vet - nek.   vib-rál - nak.   sé - tál - nak.

bo-rú- ra,   fi- ú - ra,   is túl- ra.   ne-vet - nek.

We find here only one instance of mirror inversion (the penultimate of the above examples).

And such an artistic economy of means. The melody descends only *one single time*, at the end of the last line of verse, to the closing b^3 tonic. This corresponds to what we may call in certain old melodies the characteristic "unprepared finalis": the closing tone does not previously occur in the melody, appearing only at the very end. It is worth our while to consider and analyze this: how is it possible that the one and only appearance of this tone achieves the effect of a total, final closing?

Examples of the "unprepared finalis"-type among Kodálys's folksong settings: A citrusfa, Vasárnap bort inni, Túrót eszik a cigány, Ifjúság, mint sólyommadár—among the ballads Görög Ilona, Barcsay, Molnár Anna etc. Among Kodály's original melodies of this type it will suffice to mention the principal theme of the Psalmus Hungaricus (Mikoron Dávid).

Returning to the closing three-note unit of the Norvég leányok, beside the already listed instances, we meet with syncopated forms as well:

Ex. 39

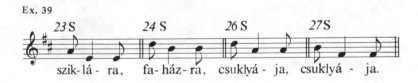

23 S   24 S   26 S   27S

szik-lá - ra,   fa-ház-ra,   csuklyá - ja,   csuklyá - ja.

Line endings of this type are frequently found among our Hungarian folk-songs, many of which have been arranged by Kodály.

---

3 It is certainly only coincidental that Mendelssohn's Hebrides Overture and the Norvég leányok are both in the key of *b*-minor. But then who knows?... The two topographies are indeed closely related to each other. Jagged, broken coastline, perpetually humid, foggy, rainy climate... Geographically they are neighbors: the Gulf Stream progresses from the Celtic islands directly to the Norwegian coast.

SECONDARY ELEMENTS

In this category belong one *porrectus* (valley-shaped line) and a *scandicus* (three rising tones), the latter appearing four times:

Ex. 40

I have already referred to the first as the abbreviated form of the "A" mirror inversion *(Ex. 16)*. Similarly, the ascending trichords appear to be catalectic variants of the "A" retrograde. All of these are indisputably linked organically to the basic quaternion.

If we allow only a slight extension of our imagination, the *tetrachord* may also be considered as having stemmed from the "A" formula: there are three places where four tones procede in one constant direction. They balance out the abridged figurations of the preceding illustration:

Ex. 41

Occurring only once, and entirely independent, is the four-tone "sparkle-glitter" figuration:

Ex. 42

The tone *e''* is perfectly suited to the twin-words "csillog-villog". (In singing this measure, we should minimize the difference between the primary and secondary stress. We should feel instead two measures of $\frac{2}{4}$ rather than one measure of $\frac{4}{4}$.)

44

The four-tone groups already referred to in *Ex. 34:*

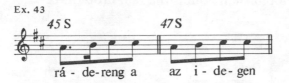

Ex. 43

45 S   47 S

rá - de- reng a   az i - de- gen

are also somehow linked to the tetrachord. Indeed they seem to combine the "A" retrograde inversion and the four-member scale segment:

Ex. 44

retrograde: tetrachord: combined:

−1   +1   =

. The step down and the step up are equalized by the repetition of the third tone. The binding link between the two is the unvaried trichord. Looking at it in this way we see the entire composition in yet a more organic light.

Two-member elements. Within the linear construction of the poetry there occurs only once a phrase which shows a 2 + 4 division of the syllables. Not without good reason is it cast in this way. The broad value and great stress of the word "mindig" (= always) demands such treatment:

Ex. 45

6 S

Min- dig   mo- so- lyog-nak,

The fifth-flexa placed mid-way in the first stanza is most appropriate. But for the recapitulation at the end of the piece the melody is smoothed out:

Ex. 46

65 S

Min - dig mo - so- lyog-nak,

by now it is not of the first experience that we sing but only of a gentle re-membrance.

The other notable ambiom is the rain-drop third:

Ex. 47

This effective tone-painting (heard together with the complementary counter-rhythms of the other voices) is self-explanatory. But let us not fail to notice how, in following the internal laws of the composition, it is linked to the "A" retrograde-mirror inversion. The *g-e* third of measure 22 is followed by the *f♯-e* second and as the verse then continues, we scarcely notice—so smoothly does it happen—that already we are once again deal-ing with one of the primary elements. The legerdemain of organicism!

Summary. Leaving aside the three-syllable closing measures, it appears that the melodic cells of even-numbered (two and four) syllables are all organically related to each other. The "sparkle-glitter" measure alone shines through the mono-chromaticism of the grey landscape.

A composer's signature... We have seen that a mass of seconds charac-terizes the entire melody of this composition. And then, at the very end:

Ex. 48

Yes, we have been singing of a distant land, of girls in strange dress, of fog, gloomy clouds, of the eddying sea... But who has sung of all this? A Hungarian poet and a Hungarian composer. Thus the final word may be none other than our typical, eloquent pentatonic melody-line with its descending octave and miniature fifth-change. The mark of the composer.

(Magyar Zene, IV [1972], II [1973]
Budapest)

47

MODAL HARMONIES IN THE WORKS OF LISZT

Three roads stand open before one who wishes to speak in a new musical language. He may apply in a new way the commonly used elements of his own contemporary style—or he may introduce new elements pointing in the direction of the future—but he may also be innovative by enriching his language with the forgotten vocabulary of a former age. Just as the stone of an ancient period, unexpectedly found during excavation, may be fitted into a new building, the unique harmonic-system of Josquin, Palestrina and Lassus is built into the Romanticism of the nineteenth century. There is danger neither to the structure, the content, nor even to the style of the new creations. The old material may be joined excellently to the new bricks, indeed may even be used as impotant cornerstones and support beams, while at the same time gracing the new style of construction with new lines.

Modal harmony does not die out with Palestrina's generation. Even though during the seventeenth century it is driven more and more into the background by the emerging new order, the functional major-minor system, yet even on Bach's palette—primarily in his movements of a chorale-like nature—the modal colors are there. Perhaps only in the works of the Viennesse masters does the functional chord-system achieve absolute reign. But already in the later works of Beethoven which point in the direction of Romanticism (the masses, String Quartet in a-minor, etc.) we find one or two figures from the old modes. It is probably the Requiem of Berlioz which takes the first step toward their wider, more systematic use, for afterwards Romanticism embraces definitively this tonal domain as well.

Within this realm Ferenc Liszt moves with extraordinary versatility. Let us attempt—even if only in a very selective manner due to the unsurpassed abundance of the material—to glance into the secrets from the workshop of the great master of harmonic innovation which deal with this area.

The great bulk of modal harmonies is made up of (for the most part) root-position major- and minor-triads. But then triad-chords exist likewise in the works of Händel and Haydn also. When is their use functional,

48

when is it modal? In the interest of stylistic differentiation it is necessary for us to clarify certain basic elements, and to introduce an appropriate system of measurement and the tools which it requires.

Measurement of distances, pillar of fifths. The color strength and the degree of tension of major- and minor-triads (*i. e.* the consonant triads) may be most suitably measured with the aid of the dual fifth-pillar. With this device, any chord may be taken as the tonic of a major- or minor-key designated by name, the uppercase letters indicating major-triads (and keys), the lower case indicating the minors. The plus-minus signs show the direction of increasing sharps or flats, the numerals the fifth-distance from the central point. This being understood, we may say, for instance, that *E* is higher than *C* by four, or that *g*-minor is lower by five than *f♯*-minor, or rather *A*-major, etc.

$$
\begin{array}{rcl}
+\ 2\ \text{D} & & \text{b} \\
+\ 1\ \text{G} & & \text{e} \\
0\ \text{C} & & \text{a} \\
-\ 1\ \text{F} & & \text{d} \\
-\ 2\ \text{B} & & \text{g}
\end{array}
$$

etc.

Measurement of progression, pillar of thirds. In seven-tone systems, any chord—not counting repetitions—may be joined to the chords of six other degrees. The uniform measurement of all progressions may be aided if we consider that the more substantial the progression, the more new tones (or the fewer common tones) will be found in the new chord. This, however, depends on the number of thirds through which the harmony moves to the new chord:

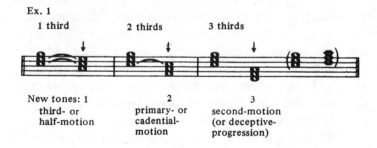

Ex. 1

| 1 third | 2 thirds | 3 thirds |

New tones: 1 — third- or half-motion
2 — primary- or cadential-motion
3 — second-motion (or deceptive-progression)

These three possibilities exist in both directions (and these are the only possibilities since four thirds downwards = three thirds upwards, etc.). Since we feel the descending direction by thirds as being authentic, we must designate the opposite direction as being plagal. Thus all six structural possibilities may be measured by a system of uniform measurement. The measuring tool for this is the seven-tone pillar of thirds to whose central member we may relate all the others:

Ex. 2

This formula (the "progression-measurer") does not depend on whether the illustrated chords be of major or minor quality, diatonic or altered chords, nor upon what degrees of which key. In comparison to the number of new tones, consideration of their quality is truly of secondary importance. But since we must secondarily count the possible varieties, we must introduce an additional, important pair of concepts.

Structure, quality (coloration). We will refer to the intervalic arrangement of any tonal-area (scale, chord, etc.) as being the structure, without regard to the accidentals, and will refer to the variants of similar structure, but now taking into consideration the finer differences of expression achieved by the accidentals of the interval (perfect, diminished, augmented, major, minor, etc.) as being the quality (or coloration). There is a difference of structure, for example, between a $\frac{4}{3}$- and a $\frac{6}{5}$-chord, and a difference of quality between a dominant- and an augmented- $\frac{4}{3}$ chord.

Functional progressions: most usually the cadential (V–I pattern) or authentic primary motion, but for the most part with dominant-tonic function, namely with leading-tone motion. (In major, the III–VI motion is cadential in structure but not functional in quality. For this reason, in functional music, the first chord in such a relation occurs ever so much more frequently as a major or secondary-dominant.) Equally characteristic is the authentic (upward moving) progression of a second, but here also primarily as the leading-tone VII–I type (we are now not speaking of root-position triads). Less frequent are the plagal motions, with the exception of the question-like inverted motion of the two previous types: the I–V and I–VII leading-tone progressions in the negative sense. Even less common are the other plagal fifth- and second-motions (*e. g.* II–VI, III–II) while the plagal third-motions (VI–I, III–V, etc) are almost entirely absent.—Let us add that in general, the diatonic root-position triads of the secondary degrees are rarely used.

Modal progressions. In its harmonic polyphony[1], the area of the Palestrina-style which is of concern to us here, each of the six progression-types occurs with almost equal importance. We must consider as characteristically modal—if we mean to make a contrast between functional and modal style—those progressions which do not coincide with the typically functional relations described above. They are:

a) cadential motion without the leading-tone (*e. g. a-d*),

b) primary plagal movement, if not of the leading-tone I–V type,

c) plagal second-progression between consonant triads (thus not of the major or minor I–VII types),

d) plagal third-motion (*e. g. e-G*),

e) a series of authentic third-motion which is hardly used in functional music (*e. g.* V–III–I).

Here also there are no more than six possibilities. The great richness which the consonant triads can provide (in much greater abundance than can the root-position triads of functional music), is verified by the variegated coloration of the progressions.

Modal tone- and chord-groups. In order to measure this variety, we must become familiar with the tone-group of the Palestrina-style, a collection of tones set forth in a line of fifths:

Ex. 3

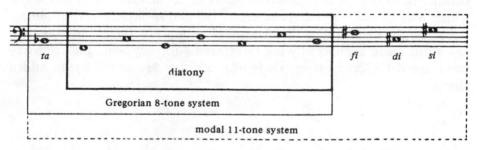

Palestrina confines himself to this 11-member tonal-system with exceptional, self-imposed exactitude. If he often notates these tones in a transposition with one flat (one perfect-fourth higher), their function within the tonal-system (that is their relative solmization names) do not change.

It is important to realize that this set of tones is not tied to any specific tonality, but instead may be turned equally in the direction of any of the possible modes. For example, the *ta* may be the VI degree in the dorian, the V in the phrygian, the III in the mixolydian, the II in the aeolian, or

1 See Bárdos, Lajos: Modal Harmony (Editio Musica, Budapest, 1979).

51

the VII degree in the ionian mode—in the lydian it often all but displaces the diatonic *ti*. (The system of alterations in functional music is radically different: thus, for example, the neapolitan tone is the lowered second degree of both the major and the minor. In this case then, the number of the degree is fixed and the solmization changes: *ra, ta*.)

In the age of Palestrina, the following consonant triads were constructed from this eleven-degree (11°) system (naturally we are not taking into account the great chromatic stylist Gesualdo who worked at the end of the century):

In Common-tonality:			*Generalized*:	
E-major	—	+4	*Mi*-major	—
A-major	—	+3	*La*-major	—
D-major	—	+2	*Re*-major	—
G-major	e-minor	+1	*So*-major	*mi*-minor
C-major	a-minor	0	*Do*-major	*la*-minor
F-major	d-minor	−1	*Fa*-major	*re*-minor
B♭-major	g-minor	−2	*Ta*-major	*so*-minor

From eleven tones, eleven consonant chords, the triads in exactly the same arrangement as the order of the individual tones. The most stable core is comprised of the six perfect-fifth chords of the diatonic area (the series which may be built on the members of the major-hexachord), of almost equal importance, filling in the ranks alongside these, are the two *ta*-chords made available by the Gregorian 8-tone system, and relatively rarer are the altered major-triads whose thirds are raised by an added sharp:

Ex. 4

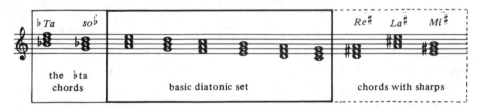

Now then, what purpose does the differentiation of structure and coloration serve? Authentic primary motion—this simply means one type of structure. The skeleton. The coloration provides the flesh:

Ex. 5

Structure: Coloration variants:

V   I   F-major   f-minor   f-aeolian   F-mixolydian   locrian
                F-lydian   f-dorian

Plagal   Its   +1 −1   +4   +2   −3   −1
2-motion   colorations:

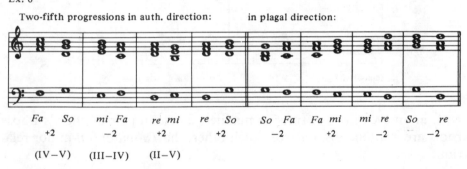

Among the characteristically modal progressions there are four which are pre-eminent and for which we have indicated in *Ex. 5* the measurement-number of their chords. Among them are both motion by second and by fourth. What then is common to each of these? The fifth-distance. In each of the four cases the difference of their measurement-number = two. If we consider the opposite direction, there are eight such "two-fifth" progressions. Illustrated in the common-tonality:

Ex. 6

Two-fifth progressions in auth. direction: in plagal direction:

Fa	So	mi	Fa	re	mi	re	So	So	Fa	Fa	mi	mi	re	So	re
+2		−2		+2		+2		−2		+2		−2		−2	

(IV−V)   (III−IV)   (II−V)

One or another among these may be identical to a common functional progression, but only in relation to a particular position within the major or minor (see the Roman degree-numbers under the solmization names). —The 11° system provides the possibility for a single chord to be placed in several positions. For instance, the typical minus-two-fifths *So-Fa* type also occurs within the frame of *Do-Ta, Re-Do, La-So* and *Mi-Re*.

Modal cross-relation. The eight-tone system, constantly extending the diatonic, in the works of the old masters provides the possibility for a certain type of cross-relation: the displacement of one major-third interval through the distance of a minor-third. The consonant triads thus give rise to four types of progressions:

53

Ex. 7

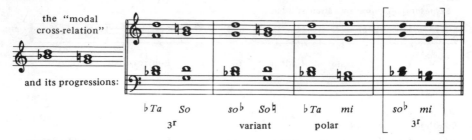

the "modal
cross-relation"

and its progressions:

♭*Ta*   *So*   *so*♭ *So*♮   ♭*Ta* *mi*   *so*♭ *mi*

3ʳ   variant   polar   3ʳ

These may occur in the opposite direction—and in other voicing positions as well.

Each of these entails a displacement of three fifths. Among them is the polyphonic-modal forerunner of third-related harmonies (indicated above as 3ʳ).

Ex. 8

Lassus: Super flumina

(a-aeolian)   *So* ♭*Ta*

and, in an even more surprising manner, a certain pair of chords whose roots are a tritone distant from each other, the *Ta*-major/*mi*-minor relation:

Ex. 9

Josquin: Ave Maria (1502)

no - stra   fu - it pur -   ga - ti - o.

(C-ionian)   ♭*Ta* *mi*

54

which we may most suitably refer to as a *polar* distance, relation or progression since, on the enharmonic circle of fifths, the two members of the tritone (the half of the octave) appear in polar opposition to each other.

LISZT AND PALESTRINA

Now, after all this, having properly outfitted ourselves for the course of our expedition, let us look about in the enormous realm of Liszt's harmonic-world and search for the modal elements.

Diatony. While, on the one hand, Liszt was one of the greatest to show the further development possible within the chromatic-enharmonic area—he was also able to produce a significantly new environment using the modally-woven cloth of pure diatony. The effect is all the greater precisely because of this contrast:

Ex. 10

Christus (1866), Second Movt.

Into this mixolydian excerpt is condensed almost every modal characteristic which the diatonic permits within its harmonic realm: the wide use of minor-degrees, the third-pendulum (I–VI–I), plagal motion (second: II–I, third: VI–I, fourth: VII–IV), progressions of the two-fifth type (*re-mi, mi-Fa, Fa-So*), and finally the non-leading-tone "subtonal" cadence.

Nor was Liszt's imagination able to exclude the other classical modal tonality, the dorian:

Ex. 11

Christus, I

ff con maesta

d-dorian

55

in which the modal *Do-re-Do-re* provides the equivalent to the functional/leading-tone VII–I–VII–I.

Even pieces in major-mode may at any time take on a modal color. And this is perhaps more profoundly characteristic of the new modal feeling:

Ex. 12

Missa solennis (1865), Credo (beginning)

It is precisely the non-functional I–III–I pendulum-motion which sets forth the concise main idea of this colossal movement.

The triumphant major sound of the now widely-sung "Ünnepi dal" (composed for the formal opening of the Budapest Opera House, but remaining at that time an unperformable hymn to the Hungarian king because of its "rebellious" nature) prominently features the minor-degrees:

Ex. 13

Syncopated V–III–V pendulum, plagal progression of two fifths at the climax—this is not the sound of the functional major.

The accumulation of movement by two fifths has an increasingly modal effect:

Ex. 14

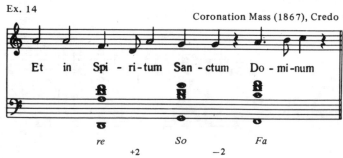

Coronation Mass (1867), Credo

56

Ex. 15

Pater noster (mixed voices, 1869)

A -   men.

III   II   V   II   III   I
−2   +2   −2   +2

In the same manner also the rising, therefore plagal succession of thirds:

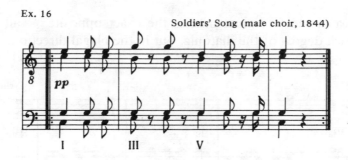

Ex. 16

Soldiers' Song (male choir, 1844)

pp

I   III   V

The following excerpt is quite unique:

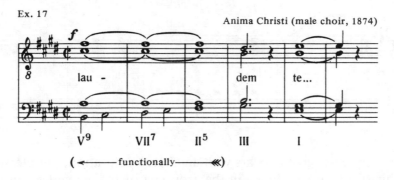

Ex. 17

Anima Christi (male choir, 1874)

f

lau -   dem   te...

V^9 VII^7 II^5 III   I

(⟵———— functionally ————⟫)

It is not only that the bass line bridges plagal thirds, but also that the chords remain in place and thus in contrast to the natural widening tendency of functional music to descend in thirds (II–VII[7] or VII[7]–V[9])—everything is exactly reversed: the rich ninth-chord "decomposes" to a seventh-chord and then to a triad. Out of the very great tension of the

57

dominant comes a cool, restful subdominant, and then, unexpectedly, with a two-fifth-type progression, by means of the most ethereal diatonic chord, the *mi*-minor, with but one modal third-shift we arrive at the tonic which was promised by the dominant ninth.

To the extent that it is characteristic of functional music—especially in the Baroque style—the diatonic circle of fifths, of course by cadential movement, in the authentic direction:

Ex. 18
"Baroque circle of fifths"

Liszt's idea, a most original one, is the exact opposite = all the way through each degree of the diatonic, but in the plagal direction:

Ex. 19   Christus, XIV

(True, the *Ti*-degree appears with an altered coloration, but please forgive this slight disorderliness in the grouping of the examples, since this excerpt, with regard to its special structure, otherwise seems to belong among the plagal phenomena of the diatonic.)

Elsewhere the three types of plagal-structure progressions are freely mixed:

58

Ex. 20   St. Elizabeth (1855), Sixth Movt.

Eight chord-changes one after another, all plagal! Two changes by second, two by fourth, and four by third render the exclamatory statement
modal in a most concentrated manner.

Eight-tone system. A diatonic system extended to include one neighboring fifth-member provides a very characteristic station along the historical
route of tonal-system development. The entire, greater Gregorian system
is of this type—Guido developed his three-hexachord system within this
frame:

Ex. 21

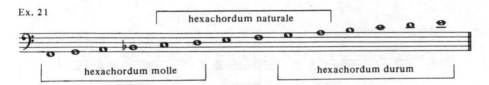

the remembrance of which is maintained to this very day by the fact that
there are (in the European ordering) eight single-letter absolute names:
b(bb!)-f-c-g-d-a-e-h(b!), in which is preserved (the names differentiating
the coloration of *b* and *h*) the terminology of major and minor. The true,
larger middle-realm of Palestrina's music is this eight-tone system which
lies between the inner diatonic sphere and the frontier zone which en-
compasses the sharped degrees. And that this fifth-extension is one of the
most natural, acoustically-based developmental routes is verified by our
folk music, which from its pentatonic core, moves out into systems of six
and seven tones,—and, if it should then take one step further beyond diatony, it does not seek in most cases just any fifth-member at whatever distance, but instead hunts down the neighboring fifth-member and builds
for itself a continuum of fifths (in other words, the many such songs
which fill our collections may be notated with the above eight single-letter
absolute names).

Liszt also worked within precisely this area. In many of his modal tex-

59

tures, it is only this *ta* which extends the diatonic, giving rise to two consonant triads: the *Ta*-major and *so*-minor triads (see *Ex. 4*). In the aeolian, for example, this means the lowered II degree:

Ex. 22

d-aeolian   ♭*Ta*

(We might also consider this to be a root-position neapolitan chord, but the preceding non-functional second-motion directs the line onto a modal plane.)

In major, the *ta* "sterilizes" the two most functional degrees, making the V and the VII non-dominant degrees:

Ex. 23

Do   ♭*Ta*   *so*♭   *re*

The extent to which the use of this unique coloration is intentional in Liszt's works is shown by the extreme dynamic markings given to the accented and climactic points of the Sonata's secondary theme:

Ex. 24

I (schematic)   VI   IV·   II   ♭*Ta*

60

In one of his compositions, the *entire* set of tones is exactly this modal—folk eight-tone system. The harmonic elements of the piece are the following:

Ex. 25

In Farewell (1855?)

On the one hand complete fidelity as implied in the chosen folksong's set of tones, on the other hand the melancholy atmosphere of separation, —how perfectly the modal *g*-minor complements, as a fourth element, the many *a*-, *d*- and *e*-minor chords! Minor, minor... here and there but barely does a major chord gleam forth, as on the day of farewell a few rays amid the clouds of twilight.—Josquin comes to mind, as he laments of the "most bitter cup of bile":

Ex. 26

Josquin: In flagellis (1503)

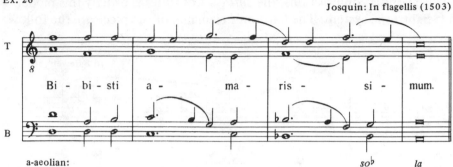

T

Bi - bi - sti a - ma - ris - si - mum.

B

a-aeolian:

so♭ la

Modal cross-relation. Upon hearing the *B♭-G* pair of major-chords *(Ex. 27)*, we may think to recognize the third-relation of Romanticism. At this point the sixteenth and nineteenth centuries do truly meet. The lengthy *Ta*-major triad immediately prior to the *Do*-cadence, however, calls to mind the older modal cross-relation:

Ex. 27

Licht! Mehr Licht! (male choir, 1849)

Licht! Mehr Licht! Mehr Licht! Mehr Licht! Mehr Licht!

C-major

♭Ta So Do
(S? D T)

The other offspring of the *b♭-b* cross-relation is the polar *Ta-mi* progression (see *Ex. 7*). Liszt was also acquainted with this device, turning the direction toward the plagal in a true Romantic manner:

Ex. 28

a) St. Elizabeth, 5

b) B-minor Sonata (1853)

a)

b)

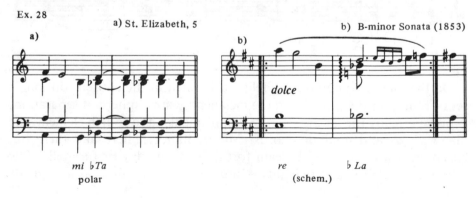

dolce

mi ♭Ta
polar

re ♭La
(schem.)

62

The two chords are exactly the same as in the Josquin hymn *(Ex. 9)*, only now it is Liszt that is creating music with them.

Eleven-tone system. Let us now step into the outer circle of the modal dominion. Brighter, raised tones now balance out the duller effect of the *ta* and with their brilliance change the three diatonic minor-chords to major *(Ex. 4)*. Of such type are the *A*-, *D*- and *G*-major chords of an *F*-major movement in which they do not appear as functional secondary-dominants but rather are imbedded in modal progressions of the two-fifth type:

Ex. 29

a)

Soli

Christus, XII

PP pa- ra- di- si glo - ri - a. *(sim.)*

Mi ♯ *Re* ♯ *Do*

Coro

Soli

3ʳ *La* ♯ *So* ♯

Fa 3ʳ

b)   Palestrina: Stabat Mater

(d-dorian)

The circle will then be complete if the *ta* is also included beside the sharped tones:

Ex. 30

Ave Maria (A-major, 1852)

The set of tones is typical, but even more so the manner in which they are treated, the non-functional pendulum-motion by third and major-second:

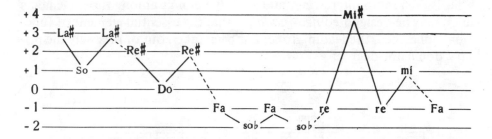

NEWER EXTENSIONS OF MODAL PRINCIPLES

The examples cited up to now have illustrated—even though employed in a personal manner,—the faithful adoption of elements from the Palestrina-style. Liszt does not stop here, but instead enriches his style with newly derived words, grammatical complements and sentence structures from, and in the spirit of, the older, traditional vocabulary.

New cadences. Each one of the modal progressions is woven in and about the choral works of the Renaissance, but one must know that at the *cadences*—the leading-tone is already always present, signifying the first sprout of the soon-to-blossom functional concept:

Ex. 32

Principal voice-leading of Palestrina's cadences:

| lydian | ionian | mixolydian | dorian | aeolian | phrygian |

Only the phrygian is different. On the one hand, the descending *fa-mi* leading-tone insures a secure binding, and on the other hand the subsemitonium would here be the *ri* which has not yet been accepted into the style.

In Liszt's compositional technique, progressions without a leading-tone often and characteristically take the place of leading-tone cadences. He has raised every type of progression-structure to the rank of cadence: Liszt has become more Palestrina-like than Palestrina himself! Let us examine the various types:

It is not necessary for us to quote examples of the *IV–I* primary plagal motion, as we are familiar with its expanded use in the Romantic era, as

65

opposed to the nearly exclusively authentic cadences of the preceding era. What is even more interesting, and already belongs among those elements which may be designated *neo-modal*, is that the essential element of functional adherence, the leading-tone, has been taken out of precisely the primary dominant degree:

Ex. 33

Coronation Mass, Credo

d-dorian   V   I

(♯ missing)   (third missing)

This again may call Josquin to mind. Although we cannot be certain whether his singers placed the sharp into progressions of this type, we may rightfully deduce that this coloration was still present in the modal harmonies of his works. Palestrina—taking the significant step in the direction of a functional conceptualization, or rather feeling—sifted this element out of the style of the earlier master.

The *VII–I*, with leading-tone, ranks second in the functional order. The de-functionalization of this progression belongs among the most characteristic traits of the neo-modal style: the finalis is approached by a major-second instead of from the leading-tone. We may refer to this type of cadence, already introduced in *Exs. 10, 11* and *25*, as a *subtonalis cadence*. This principle of bass-line writing, in concept more melodic than harmonic, is rendered even more melodic when preceded by the VI degree, the rising trichord mirroring the descending melody-close. In phrygian this is still in keeping with Palestrina's modality:

Ex. 34

Ave Maria (A-major)

Je -   sus!

Mi ♯   re   Do   re   Mi ♯
I   VII   VI   VII   I

but in the other modes belongs among the neo-modal innovations:

Ex. 35

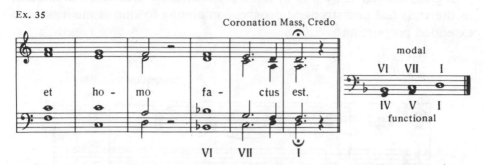

Coronation Mass, Credo

et · ho - · mo · fa - · ctus · est.

VI · VII · I

modal

VI · VII · I

IV · V · I

functional

This substantial, characteristic progression-set is so firmly established in the new style that we are obliged to view it as the equivalent of the functional IV–V–I. And in truth, the chords, which substitute for one another, are in a parallel relation one to another, thus they indicate degrees of similar tension—the new cadence in the same way may define the tonality unambiguously through the articulation of all the seven degrees on the tone-ladder, as does the former—in the end the tonic is circumscribed, in a S–D–T meaning, by touching on the –1 and + 1 lines of fifth-distance, in the same manner as the basic functional cadence:

Ex. 36

Cadences of S-D-T function'

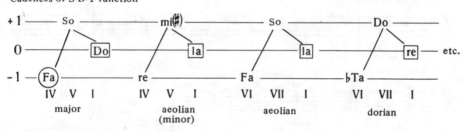

+ 1 —— So —————— mi(#) ————— So —————— Do ——

0 ——— Do ——— la ——— la ——— re — etc.

–1 — Fa ————— re ————— Fa ————— bTa ——

IV · V · I   IV · V · I   VI · VII · I   VI · VII · I

major   aeolian (minor)   aeolian   dorian

(Aside from the fact that this first effort in collecting material should like to present historical, aesthetic, psychological and other viewpoints— it is impossible for us not to consider what the composers of today would do without this cadence which has by now become such a common occurrence. It is only fitting for us to acknowledge our debt to Liszt.)

The *III–I* progression is among the weakest of the authentic-type (a displacement of one third, one new tone). It is almost entirely missing from the greater functional style, where the composers might at least have assigned to it some strength as a closing figure. For this reason it is a chord all the more desirable to Liszt, the innovator. He even inserts it after a V degree, arrived at by way of the truly functional secondary-dominant, as the verly last and strongest progression aiming to close a movement of extended proportion:

Ex. 37   Coronation Mass, Graduale

Another typically functional extended cadence—the IV–II–V–I progression is also made modal when the dominant role is enstrusted to the gentler III-degree triad:

Ex. 38

Christus, II

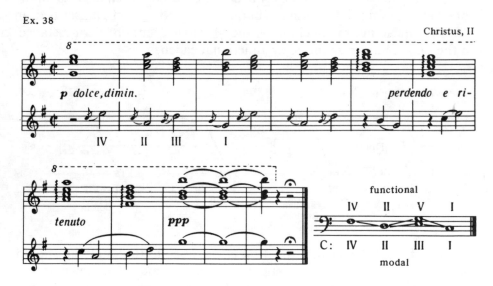

A floating register, an ethereal orchestration and the easily adaptable III-degree serving the programmatic intent of the music.

(But for what reason do we sense the *mi*-degree as the most floating, most disembodied among the diatonic triads? Does this secret in some way perhaps lie hidden in the order of fifths, in the *lü* of the Chinese?

Ex. 39

The "specific weight" of the consonant diatonic triads:

Is it only personal, or do others also share my feeling: that in weight, density and gravity nothing surpasses the *Fa*-chord, and as we progress upward along the fifth-pillar everything becomes lighter, airier, and that at the very top floats the most ethereal, the *mi*-minor?...)

Liszt's versatility is of course capable of providing another color to this degree. To close a victorious hymn for male voices—he finds the median degree suitable for this purpose as well:

Ex. 40

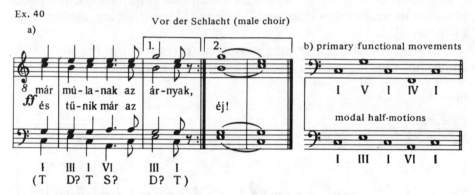

The two neighboring thirds to the tonic present an interesting new variant of the principal neighboring fifth-order. In a Romantic-modal fashion the fifth-leaps are replaced by the half-distance thirds *(Ex. 40 b)*.

Once again a truly typical example: the iambic *so-do* upward leap is accompanied not by the V–I cadential motion, but instead by the *mi-Do* half-motion, strongly repeating a favored type of cadence:

Ex. 41

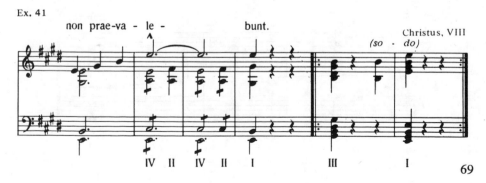

69

Liszt readily combines these cadences with the sharped tones of the Palestrina-style:

Ex. 42   Tantum ergo (women's choir, 1869)

The proximity of the *D*-major and *Bb*-major chords suggests a third-relation. The interpolated *d*-minor chord would seem to be a symbolic, binding link between the old and the new, between Palestrina and Liszt.

Ahead of us still are the two least functional progressions, the plagal bass-line movements by third and by second. Liszt does not neglect either of these.

The final statement of a long movement rings forth in the special ceremonious, old but yet new cadence on the VI–I degrees:

Ex. 43   Christus, VI

Liszt even dares utilize this VI–I progression in such a place where there is need of a cadence capable of bearing weight: at the point of introducing a change of key:

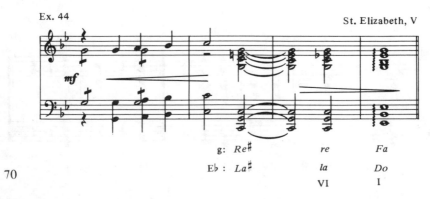

Ex. 44   St. Elizabeth, V

A functional modulation could easily present itself for the shift from *g*-minor to the major on the lower median. Viewing the succession from the direction of both keys, we may behold a truly modal modulation-type. The *C*-major chord appearing in *g*-minor gives a dorian coloration to the departing key—the sharped VI degree of the new tonic is this *c-e-g* after which the *la-Do* modal progression confirms the tonality of the subsequent longer *E*♭-major area.

The progression on the II–I degrees in some way exerts an extreme influence within the six possibilities (see our measurement of progressions, *Ex. 2*). In the plagal direction we find it to have the greatest number of possible new tones. More surprising and of greater significance is the fact that in the functional sense it does not exist among the progression-types of diatonic structure. Liszt concludes one of his longest motets, a movement leading through numerous chromatic, enharmonic progressions and modulations, with this concise, simple type of new cadence (see *Ex. 57*, end).

The end of the movement, a description of St. Elizabeth conveyed by its gentle, meek atmosphere, repeats the secondary-degrees with Liszt's characteristic coda-technique:

Ex. 45   St. Elizabeth, V

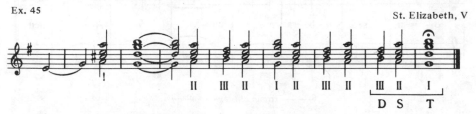

Even more daringly modal however is that which occurs in this excerpt before the diatonic pendulum-motion: a II degree of major coloration resolves to the I, and at the point of the movement's main cadence. Thus the *G*-major basic key is given—even though only for a moment, albeit an important one—a lydian coloration.

The alternations of *la*-minor and *La*-major, *re*-minor and *Re*-major provide coloration in a modal manner to the end of this movement which ascends on high *(in excelsis)*, and which likewise closes with the II–I cadence:

Ex. 46

The expansion of chords into new keys. In a manner derived from the Palestrina style, a new, organic further development, yet in an individual type of construction, changes one or another colorful modal chord by means of broadening it onto the plane of a new key. The characteristic *so*-minor chord expands to a *so*-minor excursion immediately before the final cadence of a piece in major. A harmonic direction reflecting a radically modal concept:

Ex. 47

Pater noster

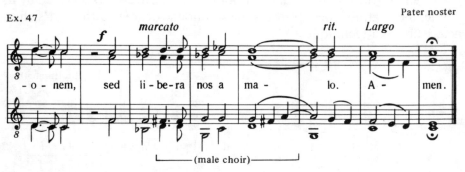

Liszt uses his palette to paint the color of *Ta*-major in an even more extended manner in yet another piece similarly in a major tonality:

Ex. 48

Pater noster (mixed choir)

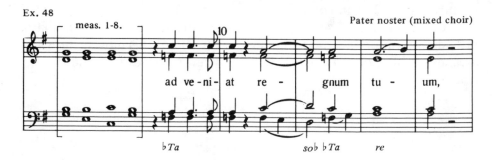

After eight initial measures in *G*-major, then another eight measures
which broaden out—with the typical two-fifth progression, thus consequently with modal solemnity—into the subdominant *F*-major area. And
once again with a deliberativeness of the highest order: the progression to
the *D*-major chord, expanding out of the long sustained *F*-c^2 bass-soprano
track, emphasizes both by its melody and the chordal illumination precisely that word (in *caelo*) which is the most deserving of such treatment.
What could be more prosaic, as we know from countless pieces in *G*-ma-
jor and the even more numerous V degrees which they contain, than a
D-major triad! But if, in this way, for the first eighteen measures of the
piece, the *f♯* leading-tone is scrupulously avoided (a characteristically anti-
functional concept)—the simple dominant triad of meas. 19 has a truly
surprising and touchingly Romantic effect. (All of this is still merely
words. But for one who first knew the piece from having sung it rather
than having analyzed it, the reality of an experience is confirmed. If the
reader is not able to bring together a small quartet for the purpose of singing the excerpt through a few times—I ask then that without fail he at
least play the excerpt on the piano singing in turn the soprano, the bass,
and the voice which is most responsible for the change of tensions, the
alto.)—Our recommended tool, the pillar of thirds, serves well for
measuring this phenomenon. After the depth of the preceding measures,
how vividly is the high plateau of the *caelo* brought into relief! (See the
graph at the end of *Ex. 48.*)

The expansion of a set of chords. Liszt's neo-modal style does not come
to a halt at the borders which limit the 11-tone system of the Palestrina-

style. In a favored widening gesture, going beyond the former boundary of the *Ta*-major, the harmonic motion reaches even further downward to the subdominant of this *Ta*:

Ex. 49

Vor der Schlacht (male choir)

ff Es ru-fet Gott uns mah - nend zu der geweih-ten Schlacht.

Do ♭Ta ♭Ma

This *Do-Ta-Ma* formula may be found in many of his works. But even this is not sufficient. With yet one more downward leap of a fifth we reach the lowered *La*-degree, in major the triad on the VI degree of the parallel minor, from where we generally swim back to shore through functional waters, such as the minor-subdominant. Schematically:

Ex. 50

a) Dominus conservet (c. 1880), harmonic sketch b) functional cadence

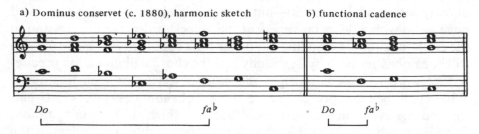

Do fa♭ Do fa♭

The functional composer generally links the minor-triad on the IV degree directly to the tonic, and indeed the strongest cadential bond joins the two chords together:

Ex. 51

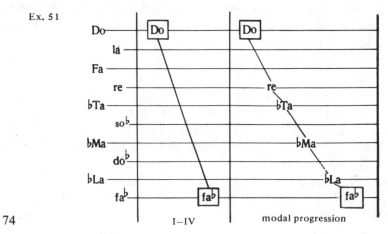

And still even further downward! We need only extend, in a similar spirit, the *Do-Ma-Ta* formula by two fifths in the negative direction and we arrive in modal fashion at the neapolitan degree, the *Ra*-major which is lower than the tonic by five fifths:

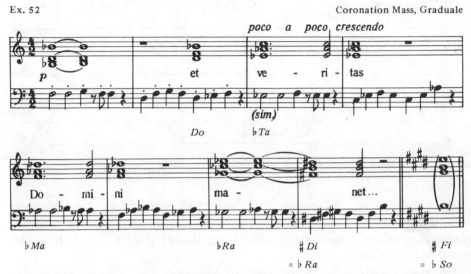

Our example, however, does not even stop here, since the following tonal area, written as *E*-major has actually an *F♭*-major meaning. In this way, almost without our realizing it, the line has moved along to the lowered V degree, traversing the polar distance to the *So*-major with extraordinary ease and yet with festive dignity. The excerpt also provides an example of another aspect which falls under the principle of expansion: the modal progressions are brought into being among the $^6_4$-chords which were rendered capable of standing on their own only during the Romantic era.

A constant plagal direction may also lead, in its own way, to the polar degree which is found 6 fifths lower:

Let us compare the two sub-polar itineraries:

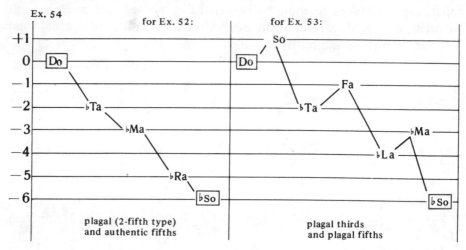

Ex. 54

for Ex. 52:

for Ex. 53:

plagal (2-fifth type)
and authentic fifths

plagal thirds
and plagal fifths

As opposed to the plagal progression-by-seconds of the previous example, here are the two other possibilities: the sequence of primary plagal motion and plagal motion-by-thirds leads from *F♯* to *C* with an unusual wave-action.

Liszt also widens the boundaries of a minor-area. The earlier lowest point, the *so*-minor, now descends to the *do*-minor—and, on the other side, the *mi*-minor, until now the highest point, is now outdone by the *ti*-minor with two sharps:

Ex. 55

Coronation Mass, Graduale

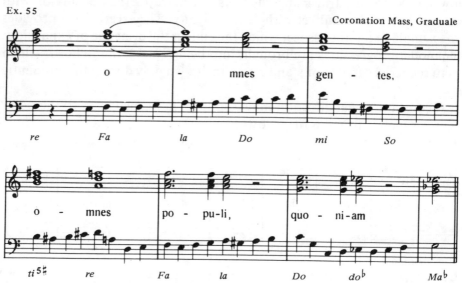

This imposing, grandiose section (tutti, solo quartet, chorus, orchestra, organ) is also at the same time an example showing the compilation of the least-functional progression, a rising chain of thirds. The following is a sketch of the 12-member pillar of thirds built on the base of a plagal outline:

Ex. 56

the root-tones of the plagal order of thirds:

The uppermost member of the modal set of chords was the *Mi*-major chord. We have already seen in *Ex. 19* that Liszt extends this upper limit to *Ti*-major. On the other hand he also organically builds into his style the parallel minor of *Mi*-major, the *di*-minor of four sharps. (Let us not forget our point of departure: these measurement-numbers do not indicate a specific key with a specific key-signature, but rather the distance from the presiding tonic of any altered chord.)

Ex. 57

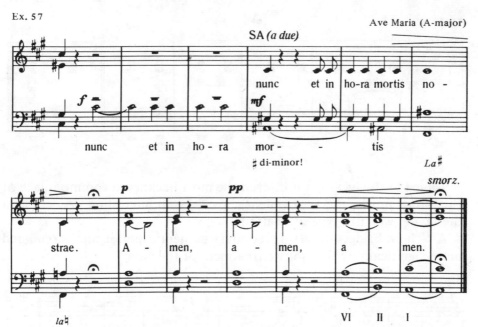

This special color-effect perhaps first struck our ears in the Rákóczi March of Berlioz (the two measures preceding the returning member of the three-membered principal idea). But there it is only a brief flash, and immediately we swing back from the *c♯*-minor chord, passing through the

77

E dominant, into *a*-minor. How differently, how profoundly exploited is this chord, a minor which shares a common third with the tonic, as it appears in Liszt's work! A special effect: one would normally except that some minor-subdominant, neapolitan chord, or else some color pulling deeply in the flatted direction be assigned the word *mortis*. But Liszt paints this word in the color of the more penetrating *di*-minor, higher by four sharps, with a startling effect. This is accompanied naturally by the bass tumbling a tenth (into the grave), the other voices beating the muffled drums of mourning in low registers ("the knock of fate"), and also the unexpected cessation of the forte "in the hour of our death". The modal daring of this color-area is intensified by its having been placed directly before the *A*-major cadence which ends the movement. It is as if the profiles darkened by the black ink of death would be smoothed by the peace of pure diatony and would become accepting in their final rest.

Seventh-chords. A newer principle of neo-modal expansion: the intensification of modal-type triads to seventh-chords. The frequent leaping-seventh of the tenor voice in Bach Chorales arises also in the dorian "dominant" without leading-tone:

Ex. 58

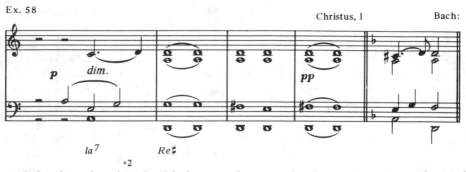

Joined to the picardy third, even the most hackneyed commonplace of functional music, the V[7]–I cadence, receives an interesting new color in the *la/Re* two-fifth type of relation.

A $^4_2$-chord bridges the III–I secondary authentic motion and is rendered more significant by the motivic treatment of the bass:

Ex. 59

78

(The bass motive moreover is descended from the ethereal, high theme of the solo violin at the beginning of the movement:

Ex. 60

the sound of which is one of the most poetic, heart-warming manifestations of Liszt's Hungarian character.)

The triad on the II degree may also expand to a seventh-chord:

Ex. 61

a)

Christus, X

b)

Salve Regina (c. 1885), conclusion

or may appear above a tonic organ-point, resulting in a deceptive $^4_2$-chord:

Ex. 62

Christus, VII

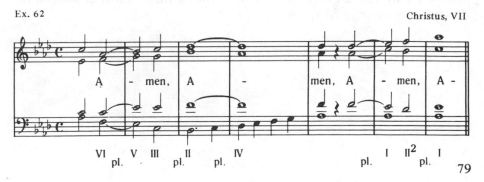

Modality and enharmonic relations. If the modal frame has once been widened, even to a distance of six fifths, the other basic principle of the era, the enharmonic relation, may bring the circle to completion. From *C* it is a long way to *F*♯, and in the other direction to *G*♭. On the enharmonic globe, however, we arrive at exactly the same point if we travel a half-circle distance in one direction or a half-circle distance in precisely the opposite direction. How would it be possible for Liszt to leave out this "round-the-world" path? And in truth, in the process of collecting these examples, a remarkable number of such modal-enharmonic circles have revealed themselves. We offer just a few by way of whetting the appetite. The following, for example, is a sketch of all the harmonic events of the Cecilia-antiphon:

Ex. 63

Cantantibus organis (1879), harmonic sketch

pl. +2   − 2   − 2   − 2   − 5 pl. pl.

The very beginning of the piece rises most lavishly through three fifths to the *E*-major chord, thus actually not 12 but 15 fifths will have to be added in order to arrive back at the closing tonic (written as *G* but in its true meaning *A*♭♭). And nowhere is there a third-relation or some other strong chromatic progression. Every step fits purely within Palestrina's store of devices. Beside the five cadential-type motions, the typically modal progressions dominate: motion by two fifths, plagal seconds, thirds, closing fourth.

This piece, written for the 1883 dedication of the great organ in Riga, descends to a depth of nine fifths rather than six. In place of the lower polar *C*♭-major, the *c*♭-minor is used as the turning-point, at least in the flat-to-sharp change of the notation:

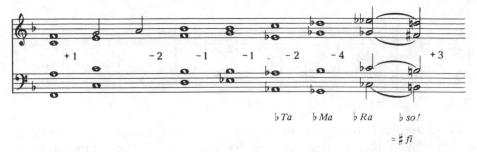

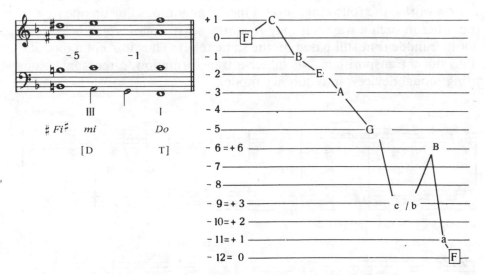

Exactly the same lavishness as in the preceding example. With the arrival to b-minor, we have come rather close to the target, for surely a directly functional "landing" could be achieved through the G or C. But no, the polar degree is transformed for coloration to B-major, and we have sprung through a half-arc back to the area of the sixth fifth, from which we may take a bravura nose-dive through five fifths in order to arrive at the favorite median degree. From here then the brake of the passing $^6_4$-chord allows a safe crossing to the finish line. All of this is described exactly on the fifth-graph *(Ex. 64)*.

The circle will be more quickly completed if third-related chord-movement (4-fifth type) is mixed among the modal progressions. The old and the new are welded into one by the force of a great creative personality. Thus six steps are sufficient for Liszt to spin round the entire enharmonic circle:

Ex. 65
a)

St. Elizabeth, 5

b) ibid. illustrated without enharmonic equivalencies

$$-1 \quad -2 \quad +1 \quad -4 \quad -2 \quad -4 = \quad -12$$

Hetero-modal transformations. Among the expansion techniques which adhere to modal principles, we also find, rather abundantly in Liszt's works, the following: several modal alterations line up one next to the other in such a way that they form the set of tones which belongs to another mode (but still based on the same tone). Thus it is not a modulation, not a transposition, but rather a transformation, a reorganization, using modal devices, into another mode.

Ex. 66

Christus, X

This often appears in functional music as the *maggiore-minore* exchange. An *e*-minor area in an *E*-major movement, or vice-versa. Except that this is not functional, and not *e*-minor. The *D/C* two-fifth chord-pair creates a characteristically *e*-aeolian section before we meet once again with the dominant. Liszt then uses a neo-modal equivalent of the major-minor variant-exchange phenomenon.

The colors of several modes meet together in one of the most deeply affecting of Liszt's motets:

82

Ex. 67

Ave verum (1871)

Lento

A - ve   ve - rum   Cor - pus   Chri - sti

re⁶   So   re⁶

beginning:

A   -   men,   a   -   men.

end: Fa⁶   ♭Ta   Fa⁶

The initial statement starts out in *d*-aeolian—beginning, in the best Romantic tradition, on the subdominant. Indeed, the first gentle chord-movement conveys immediately a modal surprise (please sing the alto line!) —*g/C* is a typically dorian progression of the two-fifth type, especially when the slow pendulum swings back to the point of departure. (Without these returning motions we could consider it to be an *F*-major cadence, in the sense of the II⁶–V primary functional motion.) The last third of the piece—after a passionately intensifying, chromatic-enharmonic middle section—brightens into *D*-major, and now the opening thought appears once again, within this new frame, as a conclusion, serving as a perfectly organic codetta to this piece which follows the true ABC motet principle and does not otherwise contain a recapitulation. True to form, in the second measure of this codetta, appears the very same *C*-major chord which gave a dorian coloration to the beginning. Due to its presence, the otherwise functional-sounding major area receives a mixolydian color. Minor and major, aeolian, dorian and mixolydian—diatony, chromaticism, enharmony—modal, functional and Romantic harmonies all contribute to form the picture of this work which tells us so much about Liszt's harmonic richness and innovative powers.

Ultra-modal phenomena? We are most apt to use this designation for those most daring ideas which, even though they spring from modal soil, progress entirely beyond the circle of the Palestrina-type elements. For

83

example: the relation of triads at a diminished-fourth distance from each other, progressions of six and more fifths distance (polar and ultra-polar), the locrian mode (considered "unsuitable for polyphony") and the appearance of other, non-diatonic folk modes, etc. Several examples:

Ex. 68   St. Elizabeth, 3

The previously-introduced *di*-minor chord comes into direct relation with the VI degree of the relative minor, the *Fa*-triad (as does the relative minor of the dominant major-triad in any minor key). As commonplace as is the descending fifth of the melody, it has an entirely fresh effect when accompanied by these chords. An idea for further organic blending: using the final chord of this motive as the initial chord of the next motive, it is possible to repeat the spirited shout of the Christian knights at the minor-second above. It is of little consequence that an *e* and *b* are written under the *a*♭, since we hear this chord, analogous to the previous *E*♭-triad, as an *F*♭-major, the motion in the bass once again perceived as a diminished-fourth leap.

Minor $^6_3$-chord appear next to each other with the distance of a diminished-fourth between them—maintaining a surprisingly strong connection even across a break in the sequence:

Ex. 69   Christus, XI

"Sorrowful is my soul unto death"... Would it be possible to create the atmosphere in this vocal prologue with any more modest means than these

84

writing minor-chords? The basic key is c♯-minor. The very first chordal-motion brings forth the neapolitan minor—to which the a♯-minor chord, higher by eight fifths, answers with its respective neapolitan minor on b. And this is no different than Palestrina's so-minor chord from which point, traversing the *Ta-Fa-Mi* plagal series, the tonal circle of c♯-minor is closed.

A torturous presentiment of death? Elsewhere a transfigured solemnity may shine forth from the very same progression! We need only exchange the minor-harmonies for major, leave out the painful suspensions, and re-verse the direction of the diminished-fourth and the neapolitan motion:

Ex. 70   Missa solennis, Credo

The diatonic melody soars triumphantly—three times in succession, ever stronger, with ever more sound until the grand tutti of the entire en-semble. And beneath it the harmonies! Is it possible not to tire of triadic chords? After being used for half a millenium, is it still possible to say something new with them?—Well, we are by now not simply eager tour-ists, but workaday cartographers who, with instruments in our hands, must chart the snowy peaks as yet untrodden by human feet. Let us take up our tools. Four fifths down, eight up, nine down, five up:

Ex. 71

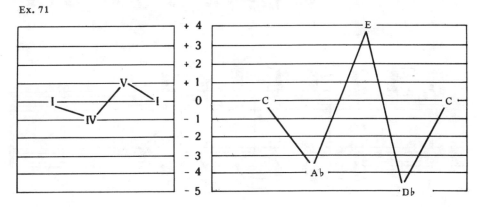

85

Where are we now in relation to the old basic cadence? It is as if an electrocardiagram were to show our hearts beating dangerously fast from the emotional tension.

New tonalities. We are still faced with the question of new modes. New?... Locrian, *ti*-ending melodies occur plentifully in Gregorian music (however much traditional analysis does not wish to know about them). The *ti/ta* oscillation in the old phrygian polyphony may bring about areas of locrian character:

Ex. 72

Josquin: Qui velatus (1503)

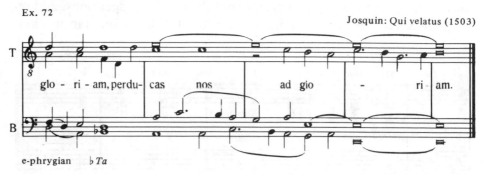

e-phrygian ♭ *Ta*

But to use the cadential V–I motion of the *ti*-mode as the closing progression of a movement when "there is no such tonality"? To whom else would it have occurred if not to Liszt?

Ex. 73

Conclusion of the B-minor Sonata:

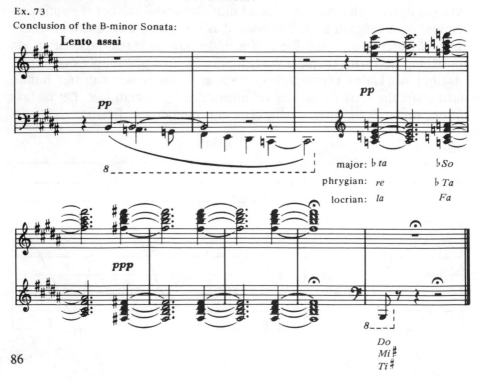

Unexpected at the end of the *B*-major coda is a section of close-fitting, touching effect whose set of tones is filled exactly from Palestrina's eleven-tone system:

Ex. 74

phrygian:

the occurrence is nonetheless modal, on the one hand because it joins to-gether the two outer links of the 11-member chain, the *ta* and the *si*, and on the other hand because at the last chord-change the final word is given to the characteristic diminished-fifth of the "non-existent" locrian mode:

Ex. 75

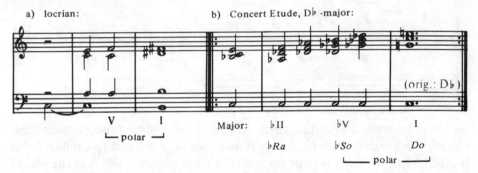

A worthy companion to these last examples is the end of the first move-ment of the Dante Symphony, where also the *g♯*-minor and *d*-minor chords are woven together (even repeated several times) in a polar relation.

Liszt's modal style, his pursuit of neo-modal reforms, hetero-modal and ultra-modal daring, the virtuosic facility with which he handles polar and ultra-polar progressions, his Sonata in *b*-minor, the Eastern Euro-pean folk-scales of his Roumanian Rhapsody, his new type of multiple-chords—all these lead directly to the world of Bartók and Kodály. We would, however, need a separate book to speak of this matter.

In any event, Count Wittgenstein was correct when he said:

"Liszt cast his lance much further into the future than Wagner. Gener-ations will pass before we may be able to comprehend his true worth..."

(Zenetudományi tanulmányok, III.
Budapest, 1955)

HEPTATONIA SECUNDA
A UNIQUE TONAL SYSTEM AND ITS MODES IN THE WORKS OF ZOLTÁN KODÁLY

(PREPARED IN HONOR OF THE COMPOSER'S EIGHTIETH BIRTHDAY)

Among the first great Kodály experiences of our youth and commonly considered to be among his greatest works is the first (and for a long while the only) section of the Mountain Nights. The unusual murmuring of the accumulated seconds (*f-g-a-b*), the melody bursting out from the depths of the soul, passion intensifying to white heat... then the quieting down, the end disappearing into the night...

But how does this end occur?

Ex. 1

We were students at the Liszt Academy of Music, and, not content merely with a deep personal experience, we also wished to analyze. But our tender knowledge was of no avail. In what possible key was the piece? Perhaps it was actually the whole-tone scale? (That was still something terribly new at the time!) True, five of its tones are there. But how then to explain the *d* and the *e*? Or were we perhaps dealing with the "mysterious" locrian scale? The unusual coloration of the *c♯* in the closing harmony however contradicted this possibility. And even earlier:

Ex. 2

88

We were soon to meet this *c♯* among the mournful sounds of the Epitaph:

Ex. 3

Seven Piano Pieces, Op. 11, IV

Later, as a chamber-music player, I was bewitched by the unusual change of coloration wrought by the long-held *f* on my viola over the *c♯* tones of the cello:

Ex. 4

Second String Quartet, Op. 10

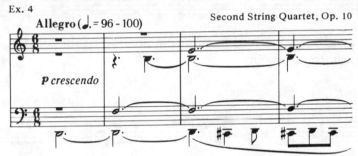

Try as I might, the *D♭-f* major-tenth resounded constantly within me, and with such strong acoustical presence as may only be achieved by that plasticity which is built into the sound of the stringed instruments. A *D♭*-major excursion within a *d*-dorian frame? (At that time I was not yet acquainted with the common-third triads of Schubert...)

Elsewhere, in a longer diatonic line, one single *c♯* disturbs the normal coloration of the home-tonality:

Ex. 5

Duo, Op. 7, I

89

Indeed, this was already sufficient cause for us not to understand the tonality of this section when prepares the *a*-aeolian second theme.

Still elsewhere this *c*♯ would seem to be "in place" in a probable *A*-major motive. But in the harmony the *f* is stubbornly reiterated:

Or in a sound-scape derived from a combination of the melodic *d*-minor and the pentatonic system:

Also in the fragrant spring clouds of the *A*-mixolydian motive with two sharps:

And yet our constant remains: an otherwise white-key scale, but with a
c♯ in place of c!

This number of examples—and many more—can not be mere coincidence. It slowly became clear: we were dealing with elements of a well-
defined *tonal system* as yet unknown to us. In place of the familiar "three
whole, one half, two whole, one half" diatonic order of seconds, we find

$$4 + \frac{1}{2} + 1 + \frac{1}{2}$$

giving rise to:

...A—B—C♯/D—E/F—G—A—B—C♯/D—E/F—G—A...

But if this is a tonal order (that is: in some way or another a well-defined set of tones, irrespective of the scales which may be derived from it)
—than it also has its own modes. And of course there will be as many modes as there are member-tones. This is also a seven-tone system. Let us
therefore see: how do these seven modes appear? *(Ex. 9)*

We find to our surprise that the melodic minor is part of this group.
Could, however, the above-quoted Kodály example (and we could find
hundreds more) all be squeezed into the procrustean frame of the melodic
d-minor scale?

It is of course a purely arbitrary choice to put the minor first in the above
arrangement. We shall soon see from the following discussion that these
scales are all equally independent, all of equal value. In the meanwhile,
for lack of something better, we have chosen the above diagram according
to the principle of "from the known to the unknown." We shall maintain
the same order in our discussion, but by no means do we wish to imply
that this system—which may also be referred to as a *heptatonia secunda*—
developed from the melodic minor.

Ex. 9

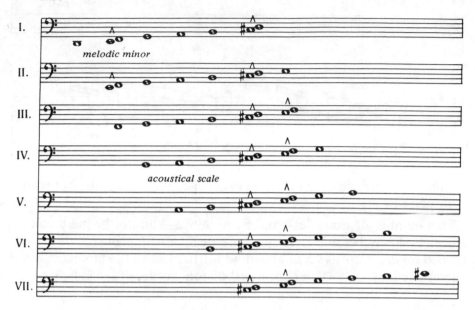

I. The melodic minor. An original creative talent is capable of building something new based upon traditional material:

Ex. 10

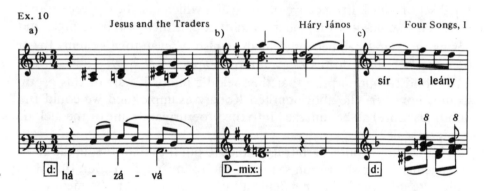

The melodic minor does actually appear in the section quoted from Jesus and the Traders. The passing and changing *G-b-d* chords above the *A* organpoint do indeed create a pleasant effect. (Just as in the "pentatonic dominants" of Chopin.) In the next instance the *D*-mixolydian provides coloration within context of the parallel minor *(Ex. 10 b).* Here it is also the free-standing ninths and sevenths which render the sound-texture accompanying the fourths of the melody more "Kodály-like". In its construction the VII–I progression in *d*-minor, which we hear in the first of

92

the Four Songs *(Ex. 10 c)*, conforms to the expected rules of harmony. The *fi* (here the *b*), which was formerly only an ascending passing-tone, has now become an independent member of an already concretized tonal-system: the *fi-mi* *(b-a)* voice moves down from the seventh of the *c♯*-chord. This is not a classical *d*-minor progression! The construction is traditional, the coloration belongs to the new tonal-system.

The following also bears a strong resemblance to the classical *d*-minor:

Ex. 11

103   Hungarian Folk Music, I, 4

re - mény-ség táp- lál ez- u - tán is:

The major-subdominant of the first measure provides fresh color above the drone-bass, as does the major-sixth affixed to the tonic triad in measure 3. The frame is old, the picture placed into it is new. Thus also in the following excerpt the *c♯* is not only a customary leading-tone but also (in measure 2) a suspension resolving to the *b* previously mentioned as a coloring tone:[1]

Ex. 12

Organ Mass, Kyrie

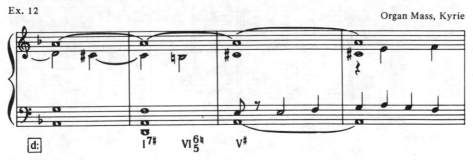

d: I 7♯ VI 6♮/5 V♯

1 A remembrance from our student days. During one of his classes, Prof. Kodály casually said that "the first seventh-chord of the minor key, the *d-f-a-c♯*, is not used. Only in the case..." And here, as was his custom, leaving off in the middle of a sentence, he looked out into the dusty, foggy air of Király Street for a long while. It was as if he had in the meanwhile reconsidered: it would not be worthwhile to disturb the study of the classical style by mentioning the later possibilities. And how valuable were these interrupted words! We became accustomed to thinking through the unspoken sentences with our own minds.

II. The neapolitan dorian. We may perhaps use this designation for the minor-third line which combines the dorian major-sixth with the minor-second of the neapolitan-phrygian *(Ex. 9 II)*. If this is joined to a pentatonic melody we then find a fourth way of placing the two pien-tones. In our Hungarian folk music we can find numerous instances of melodies which, by way of tonal enrichments, become dorian, aeolian and phrygian even though they are basically pentatonic. What the folk sensitivity instinctively leaves out is precisely that which is then discovered by the consciousness and regenerative daring of composed music. In pentatonic melodies with *E-la* there may appear the dorian $f\sharp + c\sharp$, the aeolian $f\sharp + c$, or the phrygian $f + c$ (this latter most often in the Csángó melodies). But $f + c\sharp$? Indeed with Kodály most often! A typical example is the Székely Lament:

Ex. 13

Székely Lament

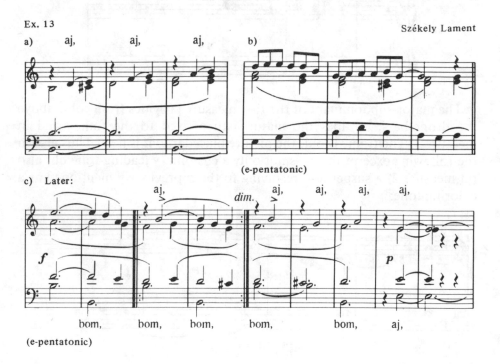

III. *Lydian with augmented-fifth. The line F-G-A-B-C♯(D-E)F* is perhaps the least common among Kodály's works. There is however one example:

Two Songs, Op. 5, I

On the stressed beats

This still sounds very much as if it were in *d*-minor. More copious and more original is the Ballad of Görög Ilona (in the folk opera The Székely Spinning Room):

Ex. 15

The Székely Spinning Room

The *c''* of the principal melody belongs within the *e*-phrygian while the *c-sharps* put forth by the accompaniment over the *F* bass, along with the prominent *b*-tones, brings us into the realm of the second seven-tone order, mode III. (We shall soon see examples of even greater interest.)

IV. The acoustical scale. By now one of the already widely well-known lines among the individual modes of our (new) tonal system, the acoustical scale combines the characteristics of the three major-type diatonic scales: onto an ionian base the lydian augmented-fourth and the mixolydian minor-seventh are added *(Ex. 9 IV)*. We call this scale acoustical since, disregarding the finer but allowable differentiations of tuning, its substance corresponds to the first 13 member-tones of the overtone series. (Some refer to this as the Bartók-line. True, it is a significant element in the works of this composer *also*. But let us not forget Debussy, nor for that matter the Swiss or Roumanian folk-motives of Liszt. That Kodály then used this scale already quite frequently in his early years is borne out by many examples.)

This particular sound-scape shows its link to traditional forms most often in the guise of an augmented $^6_5$-chord completed by means of the "acoustical" fourth. Let us but read *Ex. 16 b* in *b*-minor. It is as if we were hearing the chord in inversion as *G-b-d-e♯*. The melody-tones *a*, running counter to the Western-minor, and *c♯* evoke the acoustical scale:

Ex. 16
a) Serenade, Op. 12   b) (largo)   Two Songs, Op. 5, I

In *Ex. 16 a* and others of this type (which appear most commonly), we have nothing to do with *b*-minor. Here the *G*-acoustical line is heard truly in its own right. An identical case exists when the lydian *c♯* and the mixolydian *f* provide coloration within context of *G*-major with its traditional key-signature:

Ex. 17
Sonata for Violoncello and Piano, Op. 4

The mysteríous inner-"pacing" *(lépkedés)* is heard in the music:

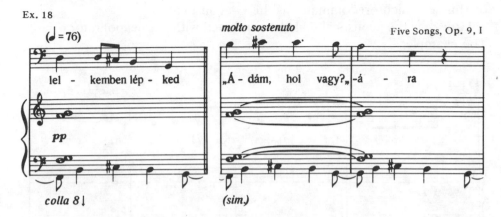

Ex. 18

Five Songs, Op. 9, I

The awakening of Spring, with its overly-sharpened trochees, is much the same as in the luscious motive of the Kálló Dance:

Ex. 19

Seven Songs, Op. 6, IV

Kálló Double Dance

That the modes of this tonal-order are actually at times combined one with another is borne out by examples of this type:

Angels and Shepherds

Ex. 20

(d-dorian)

While, in relation to the principal melody of the middle voice, the *d*-melodic minor provides the set of tones, it is the fourth degree (= mode) of this set which predominates as the *G*-acoustical.

How may the acoustical scale be combined with the neapolitan-dorian? The example:

Ex. 21

Háry János, No. 14

At closer glance the first six measures rest squarely on *G* in regard to both melody and harmony. At the end of the line-pair, however, it becomes clear that we are not in *G* but rather in *E*-pentatonic. The accompaniment is enriched through the "fourth way" of filling in the pentatonic: the *d-b* third is bridged by the *c#*, the *e-g* third by the *f*. For the latter the composer may have been promted by the melody itself: the otherwise pure pentatonic melody is here at the end given a brief phrygian decoration. The overall key of the complete line-pair is thus the "neapolitan-dorian". Within this the *G*-acoustical and the chromaticized *E*-line stand in a similar relation to each other as a major and its relative minor.

After humorous dance-like rhythms once again the melancholy of approaching winter:

98

Two Songs, Op. 5, I

Lassanként koszorúm bimbaja el-virít

quasi b: VI

The asclepiadean rhythms "pulsate like the ever-failing, deeply restful heart-beat" (Dezső Keresztury). How expressive are the *c-sharps* of the wandering $^6_4$-chords above the *G-b* ostinato! And how perfect is the stress of the prosody in the recitative melody announced by the only, therefore more significant, *c♯: elvirít* (= wither)...

In the second piece of the same opus, four octaves higher:

Ex. 23

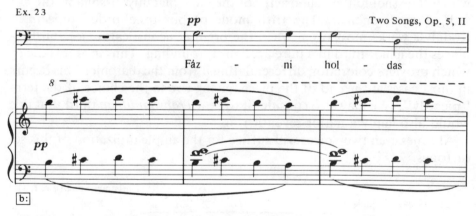

Two Songs, Op. 5, II

Fáz - ni hol - das

b:

But once again the *f* and *c♯* above the *G* affect the silvery-blue coloration of the "moonlit, spellbound night".

The list could be greatly extended. For the time being let us close with one of the most typical examples:

Ex. 24

If the instruments wish to argue very passionately with each other, which tone should they choose if not the most blatanly dissonant, the *c♯*?

V. Picardy aeolian. The fifth mode of our tonal-order appears in Kodály's works most often when the brighter acoustical major-third replaces the minor third in a pure aeolian surrounding. Thus in *A* it is the *c♯* which provides coloration differentiating it from the diatonic. This occurs in most cases at the end of the piece, giving rise to the choice of the term "picardy". (We may also consider it to be a *Transdanubian* third, but this would also imply a major-seventh.)

At times even two voices will suffice for the ample utilization of this set of tones:

Ex. 25   Christmas Song (Bic. I, 1)

The pentachords which begin the Amen also show that this scale is based on *A*, that it is symmetrical with regard to the "imaginary" *d♯/e♭* dividing-point, and then coincides with its own inversion:

100

The second tetrachord, of phrygian character, is the mirror-inversion of the first (major) tetrachord. The lower fifth-run may thus answer completely that of the upper voice in an exact inversion. In other words: the riposta has been able to answer the proposta with a real inversion which is at the same time a tonal answer with this system.

A similar ending may also occur in a dorian melody. The *f♯* of the *a*-dorian need only be modified to an *f:*

Ex. 26   See the Gypsies!

cresc.   *ff*

le - ba!   le - ba!   le - ba!   le - ba!   le - ba!   la!

A three-voice cadence, in the bass the pendulum-motion so characteristic of our composer:

Ex. 27   Hey, Büngözsdi Bandi!

P

haj!

P

Four and five voices resounding in celebration:

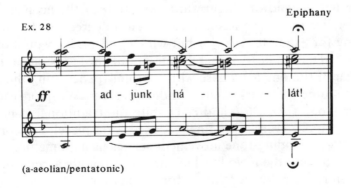

Epiphany

Ex. 28

ff   ad - junk   há -   -   -   lát!

(a-aeolian/pentatonic)

101

A depiction of dancers whirling tempestuously:

Ex. 29

Dancing Song

Szorítsátok, csak járjátok, itt a ja-va, ne hagyjátok! Hej! haj!

A full cadence with three functions *(Ex. 30 a)* in which the diminuendo of the sound level coincides exactly with the lessening of tonal tension. The chords of S–D–T functions in an order of 5-, 4- and 3-voices:

$$F-a-c\#-e-g$$
$$G-b-d\dot{-}f$$
$$A-c\#-e$$

(Symbolically: in the middle-axis of the tonal-ranges once again none other than the *c#*!)

Ex. 30

a)   Epigrams, 3   b)   Epigrams, 4   c)   Evening

It is possible, however, to formulate this particular scale in other ways which do not depend on the upward alteration of the aeolian or dorian third. Were we to lower the sixth and seventh degrees of the major-scale (let us sing for example *A*-major but with *f* and *g*), we would obtain the same result. The similarity is merely one of outward apperance. In actuality we hear in the one a *La*-base with a bright, penetrating third—in the other a *Do*-tonic with dark, dull secondary degrees. We quote cadences of this latter type in *Ex. 30 b* and *c*. Despite the traditional *A*-major key-signature: *f* and *g* even in the final cadences of a piece! The contrasting, "western" *g#-a* leading-tone movement strikes us as something of a later development—and the melody which does not readily accept the leading-tone therefore much more "fitting for Hungarians".

We find exactly the same subtonium (the VII degree altered to the whole-step rather than the half-step below the tonic) cadential turn also in the triumphantly happy finale of The Székely Spinning Room:

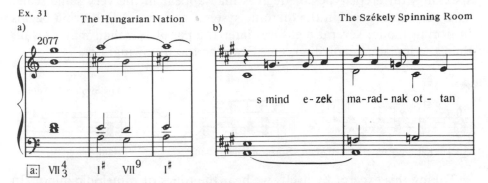

Ex. 31
a) The Hungarian Nation
b) The Székely Spinning Room

2077

s mind e-zek ma-rad-nak ot-tan

[a:] VII$^4_3$ I$^\sharp$ VII^9 I$^\sharp$

While this also falls within the same area as the previously-discussed aeolian with major-third, let us use it for purposes of comparison: The scale will be just the same if in a major setting the composer provides an aeolian-pentatonic character to a particular portion of the melody while leaving the major-third in the accompaniment *(Ex. 31 b)*.

The application of an analytical approach in the particular and the overall: if we view only this portion of the Gypsy melody by itself:

Ex. 32
Hungarian Folk Music, IV, 24

Ros-tát, e-cse- tet csi-ná-lunk, jaj, jaj!
cresc.

8↓ 8↓

(e-phrygian)

we may consider it an *a*-aeolian with major-third. But the more complete tonality of the melody and the piece is *e*-phrygian. Considered from this point of view, the excerpt points to the IV degree. In this case we are then speaking of the phrygian with major-sixth, the *c♯* providing the coloration here. (This is Mode II of our present order.) The same occurs in this folk-song line:

Ex. 33
(Lányok ülnek...)
The Székely Spinning Room

Kert-be men-tek ró-zsát szed-ni, szí-vem sza-kad rá-tok.

103

Let us mention once again that the modes of this particular tonal-system do not always lead separate, independent lives. At times they may appear in several keys each parallel to one another, or more properly speaking, different types of degrees may appear in the very same scale. This also occurs within the diatonic system: a motet of Palestrina begins in dorian mode, several measures later the parallel aeolian may prevail, then the ionian, mixolydian, etc. Examine the following:

Ex. 34

The Swallow's Wooing

A: Két pénzen el-ad-tam, Százszor is meg-bán - tam. C:

Taking this excerpt by itself, we hear the tones of *d*-melodic minor. In its greater context however, the key is *A*-major—with its perfectly appropriate darkening on the words *eladtam* (= I sold) and even more on the word *megbántam* (= I did regret). The first predicate receives its emphasis from the friction of the two "foreign" tones *(f-g),* the second from the minor-subdominant which gives the impression of unexpectedly caving in on itself. (Beside these melodic and harmonic variants, our composer here exploits also the formal element of this tonal-system. The *d*-minor triad within *A*-major is not only a strong means of painting the mood—it is at the same time a link to the returning principle key of *C*-major.)

Here also, in exactly the same way, the common *d*-minor chord leads from the region of three sharps back to the area of the principal tones, but in this case characterized by the two independent descending *b*-tones:

Ex. 35

Hymn of Zrínyi

szab - junk más ren - det dol - ga-ink - nak,

The *d*-melodic minor formula within the *A*-major context is also capable of expressing lamentation, deeply-felt pain—by emphasising the *d-c♯* and the *f-c♯* dissonances:

104

Ex. 36

Ex. 36 Hungarian Folk Music, X, 53

nél - - kül.   Ár - va va-gyok

(f♯-pentatonic)

(At the same time this is also an example of how the melismas of the old Transylvanian folksongs are worked into the composer's instrumental style without becoming merely mechanical copies of the original.)

What rich territory this is! We have already seen from the *A*-mode that it may become aeolian or dorian. But here is the fourth tonality! Let us insert into the mixolydian a minor-sixth in place of the major-sixth, for example an *f* in place of an *f*♯ into the *A*-mixolydian (with key-signature of two sharps), and again we find exactly the same—outwardly—as in the picardy aeolian or in the major-minor. Once again however, with a different character and a different tonal effect. When the melody (in *f*♯ phrygian according to its finalis) of the ballad cadences midway in *A*-mixolydian, Anna's answer of refusal (Nem megyek = I will not go) is heard with its unusual *f-c*♯ dissonance of the minor-sixth mixolydian:

Ex. 37 Molnár Anna

Nem me - gyek én

Ah!

Ruvát   veszek   vasár-nap - ra!

(f♯-phrygian)

Perhaps the "acme of achievement" in this realm occurs when the *entire first strophe* of this choral piece about the three special days (the voice of Jesus is heard three times in a year) receives its special coloration from this mixolydian with minor-sixth:

105

Je-len-ti magát Jé - zus há-romszor esz-ten-dő-ben, Jé-zus magát

(A-mixolydian)

úgy jelen-ge-ti már.

b)

magát úgy jelengeti már.

The stylistic logic dictates that for the final appearance of the refrain the subtonium VII degree be derived from this unique scale, thus bringing forth the *G*-acoustical set of tones *(Ex. 38 b)*.

One of the deeply significant outbursts of the Psalmus:

Ex. 39

Psalmus Hungaricus

a) *largamente*

Hoz - zá fog - ha - tó nin - csen ál - nok - ság - gal.

b)

Te vagy a le - gény, Tyu-ko-di paj - tás,

This solo melody quotes the bitter *kuruc* line (with a much better scansion than the analogous Tyukodi melody: compare the climatic tones of each!)—and the fist-smashing chords which form the frame are built from precisely this scale! (The first is the second inversion of five fourths based on *c♯*, the second is an incomplete form of seven thirds built on the very same *c♯*. Everywhere the *c♯*! ...)

The *kuruc* melody also shows, at the same time, that there is even a *fifth* tonal-order derived from this scale:

Mi–fi–si/la–ti/do–re–Mi

Bence Szabolcsi assembled the rich family of variants for this melody, one of whose members is also the Kecskemét *verbunkos* (recruiting song). The fourth line of this latter completely traverses the scale (we would gladly also call this a *kuruc* scale):

Ex. 40

(Kecskemét is kiállítja...)   *Tura, 1906, Bartók*

Nyolc esz-ten-dő   nem a vi - lág,   le - het pró-bál - ni!

Just as the lines of the Hungarian poet Ady recall those of a former age, in the same way one or another melody of the Psalmus and the Zrínyi piece remind us of Rákóczi's brave fighters—the composer all the while speaking in his most individual, personal language:

Ex. 41

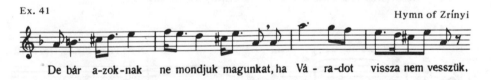

Hymn of Zrínyi

De bár a-zok-nak   ne mondjuk magunkat, ha Vá - ra-dot   vissza nem vesszük,

VI. Aeolian with diminished-fifth. Our sixth mode is one of the most curious of all. (But of course: it is built on the most unstable tone of the melodic minor, the raised sixth degree.) We well know that among the classical alterations the lowering of the dominant tone is precisely the one which does not occur. But if we examine line VI of the table *Ex. 9,* we may observe: the scale appears as if it were a *b*-aeolian with two sharps, except that in place of the pure *f♯* dominant there is an *f*. That Kodály utilizes this tonal-order with such surpassing richness is borne out by this line of beautifully poetic examples, and still in the *B*-mode of the *C♯*-domain:

In this song, which laments the approach of winter, we have just heard: "There is no rose-strewn labyrinth..." And now the instruments echo this thought with great passion. Let us play the accompaniment of the *b*-aeolian motive with *f* ♯, then with the original *f*. No comment is needed to describe the difference.

Neither should we be disturbed if, in this scale, we sometimes see an *e*♯ in place of *f*. In the enharmonic-tempered system of the piano this is often of little matter especially when the composer himself writes the very same tone in two ways. At first as *e*♮, as if he had in mind an augmented-$\frac{4}{3}$ of *b*-minor *(G-b-c♯ -e♯)*. The bass-line taking off from the recitative repeated *B* however provides a clear explanation: in place of the *b*-aeolian penta-chord, the unique, lament-like diminished-fifth mode is heard. (A reveal-ing accent-mark fall exactly on the *f*!) Despite this influence, in the nota-tion of the sustained chord the *e*♯ is changed to an f:

Ex. 43

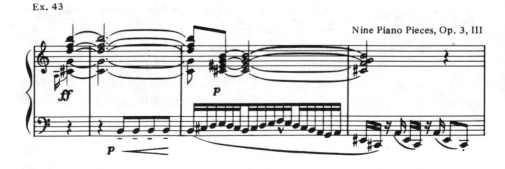

Nine Piano Pieces, Op. 3, III

The diminished-fifth is given even greater prominence in this double organ-point:

Nine Piano Pieces, Op. 3, VII

Moderato triste (♩=88)

A later pattern in the same piece:

Ex. 45

lento   Ibid.

Here something still stronger keeps alternating with the *b-f* dissonances. Our famous *c♯* forms an augmented-fourth with the *g*, a major-seventh with the *d*. This chord built on fourths thus combines two of the greatest dissonances of our tempered system.

If the *f* is so very prevalent above the *B*-bass, we may also turn our thoughts to the coloration of the locrian line. (Locrian with major-second.) Let us think back to our first or fifth example, etc.

Further parallelisms of the modes:

Ex. 46   poco agitato   Two Songs, Op. 5, II

mély   zú - gá - sát.

The acoustical scale appears to take shape about the *g* anchor-tones of the melody—the *d*-ending to the melody could signify *d*-melodic minor (and in this case the *B*-tones of the bass are actually sounding the VI de-

109

gree),—but if we measure the tone-structure taking the *B* as the base-tone, the designation will be the aeolian with diminished-fifth or the locrian with major-second. From all of this one thing is certain: "deep pealing (=mély zúgását) of funereal bells" is artistically painted, an original melodic-harmonic-rhythmic texture in this special seven-tone system.

The *G*-acoustical scale, the *d*-melodic minor and the true *B*-mode of the *C♯*-system are combined in exactly the same way in Op. 7:

Ex. 47

Duo, Op. 7, II

VII. Locrian scale with diminished-fourth. Perhaps the most peculiar of all *(Ex. 9 VII)*. Understandably: both pillar-tones, degrees IV and V, are diminished! (The designation we have chosen presents itself for this reason.) Let us imagine the *c♯-ti*-line of two sharps, but with an *f* in place of *f♯*:

$$C♯/D–E/F–G–A–B–C♯$$

A passage of this type (let there be no misunderstanding: we do not always speak of the entire tonality of a piece; sometimes a part of a melody, a brief succession of chords, even a single harmony may indicate the tonal-order which we are discussing) appears to our surprise in the ballad-chorus:

Ex. 48

Molnár Anna

u-ram   az er-dő   -   be,

Gyere velem!

The first line of the already-mentioned *f♯*-phrygian melody *(Ex. 37)* ends on a *c♯*, its resting-tone is therefore the locrian *ti*. And above it—enchanging the mystery of the ballad—the diminished-fourth, the *f*.

110

Exactly the same type of tone-relations occur when once the lower leading-tone, the *c♯*—with a sforzato!—is introduced into a dorian context:

Ex. 49

Nine Piano Pieces, Op. 3, IV

Lento

Folksong examples. It would not be possible to declare that this "second seven-tone order" does indeed often appear in our folk music. Beside the pentatonic or pentachordal base, as well as the hexachordal and diatonic material extended from them, still other lines of special coloration appear, enriching the overall picture of our folk music with newer and newer strokes of the brush. Let us examine a few pertinent examples.

I. Melodic minor. Beside the examples of the customarily rising *(mi-fi-si/la)* line, those in which the major-sixth *fi* is sufficiently independent so that the melody may even descend from it, are the more interesting. We may consider the following as belonging to the tonal-system under discussion:

Ex. 50
a)

Kórogy (Szerém), Garay

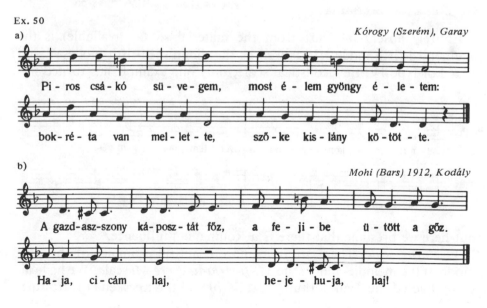

Pi - ros csá - kó sü - ve - gem,   most é - lem gyöngy é - le - tem:

bok - ré - ta van mel - let - te,   sző - ke kis - lány kö - töt - te.

b)

Mohi (Bars) 1912, Kodály

A gazd-asz-szony ká- posz-tát főz, a fe - ji - be ü - tött a gőz.

Ha - ja, ci - cám haj,   he - je - hu-ja, haj!

111

Nagymegyer (Komárom) 1910, Bartók

Hej, ha-lá-szok, ha-lá-szok, mit fo-gott a há-ló-tok?

Nem fo-gott az e-gye-bet: vö-rös szár-nyú ke-sze-get.

II. Neapolitan dorian. A particular fourth way of filling in the pentatonic also occurs, but only very rarely:

Ex. 51

a)

Ploskucén (Moldavia), Jagamas

#fi

Sze-gény le-gény vol-tam, sze-gény le-gény vol-tam,

ßta

gaz-dag lány-kát vet-tem, gaz-dag lány-kát vet-tem

b)

Ördöngősfüzes (Szolnok-Doboka) 1940, Lajtha

etc.
final line:

É-desanyám sok szép szava,

mer el-tellett a jó i-dő.

Entirely absent (at least from the material so far available) is the augmented-fifth mode III, as well as the diminished-fifth modes V and VII. For type IV, the acoustical scale, only one example has turned up:

Ex. 52

Klézse (Moldavia) 1940, Jagamas

Csü-tör-tö-kön es-te vet-tem ma-gam ész-re,

hogy az én é-de-sem vas-ba van ve-ret-ve.

but here we presume that there is a Roumanian influence.

V. Kuruc scale. There are even more beautiful examples of the fifth mode of the melodic-minor, the *Mi-fi-si/la-ti/do-re-Mi* scale. We have already quoted the Tyukodi tune *(Ex. 39 b)* and the Kecskemét recruiting-song *(Ex. 40)*. Kodály collected and readily arranged further well-known examples. Three from the series Hungarian Folk Music (for voice and piano) and three rather less-known melodies:

Ex. 53

a)   *Ghymes (Nyitra) 1906, Kodály*

Zöld er - dő - ben,   sík me - ző - ben,

zöld er - dő - ben,   sík me - ző - ben   la - kik egy ma - dár.

b)   *Ghymes (Nyitra) 1906, Kodály*

El - ki - ál - tom   ma - ga - mat   fel - ső fa - lu - vé - gen,

hagy hallja meg   a galambom   al - só fa - lu - vé - gen.

c)   *Ghymes (Nyitra) 1906, Kodály*

Kör - té - fa,   kör - té - fa,   sok gyalog ka - to - na   meg-pi-hent   a - lat-ta.
gyöngyösi   kör - té - fa,

d)   *Tinnye (Pest) 1922, Kodály*

Ha - rag-szik a   gaz - da,   hogy mink   itt   mu - la - tunk,

vi - gye el a   há - zát,   majd mink   itt   ma - ra - dunk.

e)   *Ács (Komárom), Kodály*

Ó, huszárom, mért likas a   csá - kó?   ezt a hitvány rongyot mi-nek tartod?

113

Körösfő (Kolozs) 1908, Bartók

Kö - rös - fő - i   uc - ca   vé - gig tisz - ta   bú - za,

ar - ra jár el   a ga - lam - bom, majd le - a - rat - gat - ja.

The number of our folk music examples coincides in direct proportion to those found in Kodály's works: independent of direct folksong quotations, *this mode is the most frequently found* among the seven which belong to the "heptatonia secunda". The proportion further coincides with the previously-mentioned varieties: the picardy aeolian, the similarly-colored dorian, the "major-minor", the mixolydian with minor-sixth and the *Mi*-ending *kuruc*-type scale.

Some further observations. If, in comparison to the entirety of our folk music, there is but a small number of melodies belonging to this second tonal-order, still they do occur. Thus our composer was able to draw, perhaps from this source, the incentive to open his art music to its influence. But it is easily possible that the new French music of the time supplied the rest. (In what manner and to what extent this tonal-order appears in the music of Debussy would have to be explored in a separate study.)

What do these fifty-odd examples tell us?

In short, that it is sufficient to alter one tone, let us say *c* to *c♯*—and from the most pedestrian, from the diatony of the white keys, some unusual, special, new type of richness is born. We need only wait for the material to find a master.

It tells us about other things as well. Why precisely the *c♯* instead of the *c*?[2] It is as if it were a symbol of the stance against the "eternal *C*-major"

---

2 All of these scales may appear in the works of our composer in any transposition. We have but chosen the "*c♯*-only" examples for two reasons. In the first place, reducing to a common denominator, it is thus easier to survey this new type of material and easier to come to know its relationships. Secondly, however—as borne out by the examples—from the piece Evening of 1904 to the Hymn of Zrínyi of 1955, and perhaps since then as well, there would appear in Kodály's works a tonal order quite usual with respect to its other member tones, but bound to just this *c♯* with a conspicuous prediliction. The strength of such an identification is familiar in the fundamental sound-phenomena of other composers as well. Let us consider the splendor of *D*-major for Bach or Händel, the brooding *g*-minor compositions of Mozart, the *c*-minor works of Beethoven, Chopin's use of the five-flat key-signature, etc.

to which our great ones more than once gave voice in their writings. My poor Hungarian child, was the ditty about the spotted dog your first music until now? We do have other music. What is more, there is music which is truly yours. Try to play it on the black keys! Or, if you are already using the white keys, at least your first finger need not forever remain where it has been placed. You will not be any the poorer for it!

It tells us, through its rich store of examples, that in the hands of a great creator a change of but one tone is sufficient to enable him to speak freshly of the most varied ideas in a personal, poetic manner. The approaching winter and the awakening spring—a simple children's melody and a vision of the night—a sparkling dance tune and a bitter lament... How may things, how great the variety which has marched before us in the little (yet far from complete) assemblage!

The excerpts tell us also to what extent this tonal-order—among so many other things—came so opportunely to a Hungarian composer who, standing on the ancestral soil of his people, wished to build a higher cultural level of which the entire world would take note. Let us but look:

Ex. 54

pentatony

whole-tone scale

A truly magical display! This second seven-tone order on the one hand embraces the entire pentatonic system, on the other—with but one tone missing—the whole-tone scale as well. An exclusive order of perfect-fifths and an order totally devoid of perfect-fifths. A thousand-year Transylvanian tradition—and the newest Parisian achievements. The East and the West, the ancestral past and the indication of a future direction, "the alpha and the omega".

But was this not perhaps the life-work of all the great ones of our nation: to remain Hungarian and at the same time to be European!...

TRANSLOCATED ORDERS

In the foregoing approximately fifty Kodály-examples we have quoted from that tonal order which maintains the member-tones as they are normally found except that in each case a *c* has been replaced by a *c♯*. Beside the illustration according to scale-types *(Ex. 9)*, let us now place the projected picture of the molecular structure according to the line of fifths:

Ex. 55

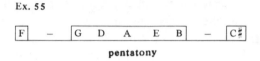

pentatony

In contrast to the closed diatonic chain of fifths, the two outer members of this "second type of seven-tone order" are characteristically removed from the closed central portion by a distance of one missing fifth each. In this way the pentatonic body remains in its entirety while at the same time, by removing every second tone, we arrive at the whole-tone scale as well:

Ex. 56

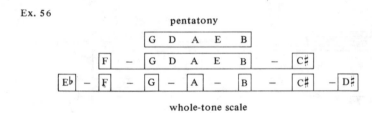

whole-tone scale

In Kodály's hands this tonal-order was thus able to become, among other things, an excellent means with which to create arrangements of ancestral folksongs in a new manner.

We have also seen that among the seven modes of this system, any one, merely as a set of tones, may be interpreted as being in diverse keys according to the content of the actual music. For example, the *c♯*-type line on an *A*-base (see *Ex. 57*):

a) the *Mi*-line with major-second and major-third produced the scale of the Tyukodi-tune *(kuruc* scale, see *Exs. 28, 39, 40, 41* and *53 a-f)*;

b) the *La*-line with picardy third (one of the most characteristic closing formulas used by Kodály: *Exs. 25, 26, 27, 29, 30 a, 31 a)*;

c) the *Re*-line may assume a coloration of similar character: with aeolian sixth and picardy—or, if you like, Transdanubian—major-third, as at the end of See the Gypsies... *(Ex. 26)*;

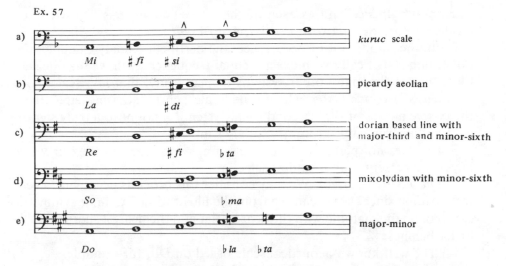

a) kuruc scale

b) picardy aeolian

c) dorian based line with major-third and minor-sixth

d) mixolydian with minor-sixth

e) major-minor

d) the *So*-base with minor-sixth once again gives an entirely different character to the line *(Exs. 8, 37, 38)*; and finally

e) within the context of the major, the lowering of the sixth and seventh degrees provides uniquely dark colors ("major-minor", see *Exs. 30 b, 30 c, 31 b, 34, 35, 36)*.

Let us avail ourselves of that truly useful spotlight, the relative solmization, and with it illuminate what we have stated, illustrating the tonal-system of the previously-listed five *A*-scale types on the grid of fifths:

Ex. 58

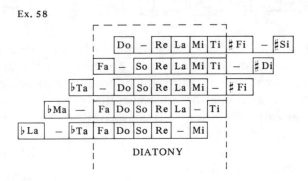

DIATONY

We have thus declared ourselves independent of the *"principal tones but with c♯"* order, which we had established on the one hand because of its frequency of occurrence, and on the other hand for the sake of more easily surveying the material. Now, in whatever transposition we choose to think, we may determine, based on the diagram of *Ex. 58*, that the *five systems* occur *with equal importance and with characteristic frequency in Kodály's music*. And as each of these five systems has its own seven modes, we are dealing with *thirty-five different keys!*

From the standpoint of occurrence, the pertinent Kodály-examples are not found statistically with exactly equal frequency. Still we may declare that—beside the many other systems of pentatony, diatony, scales with augmented-seconds,[3] the whole-tone scale, chromaticism, etc.—these thirty-five modes of the "second tonal-system" amount to a truly significant and unique color-group in Kodály's music.

Space does not permit us to quote examples for each of the thirty-five keys—we present only a modest selection.

I. The TA + FI-system. We may consider this order as occupying a central position since, as we can see from the illustration *Ex. 58*, it symmetrically colors the diatonic with the nearest flat and the nearest sharp. To this order belongs:

A) The well-known acoustical scale based on *Do*, for example:
$$C–D–E–F\sharp(G–A)B\flat–C$$
A lovely example from the violin-cello sonata:

Ex. 59

This line may then be described as being of major-type but with lydian fourth and mixolydian seventh. It even appears that the quoted excerpt fulfills an analysis of the spectrum: the odd-number measures present the mixolydian *ta*, the even-number measures the lydian *fi*.

With greater emphasis, these two characteristic tones appear one next to the other in the following imploring motive. This expressive melody has practically no other material beside the characteristic element of our system, the *ta-fi* diminished-fourth.

---

3 There are twenty types of seven-tone systems with augmented-second, with altogether one hundred forty modes! The treatment of these modes in the music of various peoples and of the more modern composers would necessitate and warrant a separate study.

118

Ex. 60   Three Songs, Op. 14, III

fe - lelj   e - zek - nek

Also pertinent here are the (folksong) examples *16 a, 17, 21, 23, 24* and *53*.

B) After a preceding dorian segment, *fi* and *ta* in the harmony:

Ex. 61   Seven Piano Pieces, Op. 11, 7

d-dorian:

(See also *Ex. 26.*)

C) In the case of a melody ending on *Mi*, the effect is more unusual since the perfect-fifth (*ti*), one of the phrygian pillar-tones, has its coloration altered to that of the lamenting diminished-fifth (*ta*)—while the *fi* does away with the very tone which characterizes the diatonic mode, the *fa*:

Ex. 62

a)   Two Folksongs from Zobor, I

nyugodni a-ka - rok.

f#:

119

In this case the effect is intensified if the melody follows, not the natural phrygian, but instead the more striking phrygian with major-third (the *vachula-bharna* scala of Hindustani music). Let us illustrate what Kodály has done, transposing to our common tonality (*do = c*):

Ex. 62
b)

Melody:

Altos:

After the picardy (or here rather: Eastern) phrygian melody, the alto voices answer in the *Mi*-mode of the *TA + FI*-system. The apposition cuts deep into the heart of the matter. In place of the *fa-ti* augmented-fourth, which is characteristic of the phrygian, we hear the *fi-ta* diminished-fourth, and in place of the major-third of the enchanting melody, we hear the minor-third in the sighing, lamenting lower lines. In other words, the answer has changed exactly the three most characteristic tones of the melody so that, in place of a simple imitation, an original thought heightens the intent of what was heard just before.

The very same combination also appears at the end of the second stanza, yet more richly varied and at a greater dynamic level.

Then later the waves of pain sweep from the depths to on high:

Ex. 63   Two Folksongs from Zobor, I

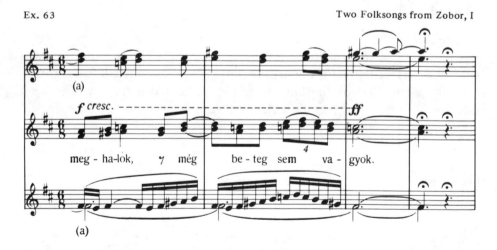

meg - ha-lok, ๆ még be - teg sem va - gyok.

In the middle of the recurring first stanza—here, at the climax of the movement—again the *c* and *g♯* are heard wailing above the finalis of the *f♯*-phrygian melody. And how characteristic this is of the composer's work as he builds: in place of the previous *fi-ta* diminished-fourth, the relation of the two characteristic tones, the *ta* and the *fi*, has been expanded to an augmented-fifth.[4]

D) The *La*-line may also receive *ta* and *fi* as guests:

Ex. 64

National Song

Ra-bok vol-tunk mos-ta-ná-ig, kár-ho-zot-tak ős - a-pá-ink
(kár - ho-zot-tak)

Each of these two tones has its own role to fulfill. The *f-sharps* of the first measure lead naturally to the primary prose-stress of the word *mostanáig* (= until now)—the *B♭* bass serves to paint the underlying mood of the word *kárhozottak* (= damned). This occurs moreover in two dimensions. Horizontally (sing the lowest voice by itself!)—as well as vertically. By virtue of the latter, the melody tone *a* becomes a major-seventh dissonance. To the third dimension we might add the color-spectrum of this set of tones: the lowering-alteration effectively aids the dynamic elevation. (There is an accent mark on the most important syllable!)

The very same intention of tonal-effect in a considerably expanded development:

Ex. 65

cresc. poco a poco

The Aged

É - let-katlan-ban ré - gi é - tek, É - let-szeké-ren ré - gi szal - ma,

ré - gi é - tek

4 We shall again meet with this splendid work in the course of our analyses. Why is it so rarely found on the programs of our choirs?

With the inexorability of fate, below the drumming-knocking *e* dominant, the darkly threatening *b-flats*, then the surprise of the *f♯*. (This latter tone as if it were also preparing in a small way the *A*-major tonality of the following verse.)

To this realm belong *Exs. 13* and *51* as well.

II. The DI-order (see line *b* of the illustration *Ex. 57*).

A more intense quality may be given to any of the diatonic modes if the characteristic new tone of a key signature raised the distance of two fifths, the *di*, appears in place of the *do*.

A) The *Re*-dorian becomes similar to the melodic minor. We may speak of a true second tonal-order however only when the raised seventh degree (*c♯* in *d*, for example) is not a customary leading-tone but rather, in an independent role, provides the possibility for new types of motion differing from the traditional melodic configurations or harmonic treatment. The bass of the following example shows just such a standard handling of the functional leading-tone:

Ex. 66   Ode to Liszt

but the featuring of the characteristically dorian *e*, in place of the *e♭* as we would except in the context of *g*-minor, gives an entirely new color to the progression. A perfect union of text and music! The two outer voices approach the word *súlya* (= burden) in crescendo and by their movement emphasize this word. The upper with a high, long and stressed tone—the bass with a lower changing-note so to speak bent down by the weight (as in Schubert's *Der Atlas*). The two together bring about the effective widening of the harmonic ambitus. Let us add to this the dissonances of the changing-chord (*f♯-e, f♮-c, d-d, d-c*) and the effect of this single chord stopping "exhaustedly" (= elbágyasztó) among the others—and we have appraised each element which produces the effect of this remarkable motive. (We have no measure for the inner, poetic inspiration.)

B) *So*-line with *di*.

We find exactly the reverse in one of the sighing-chords of the Vidróczki. Ballad:

Ex. 67   Mátra Pictures

Hat vármegye vár i - de - ki!

a-dorian:

the *di* (*g♯*) of the dorian is not a leading-tone but rather an upper changing-tone. (The mezzo-soprano voice should realize how important, expressive a role it has here!)

The *D* bass within the frame of *a*-dorian thus supports the construction of an acoustical scale. Let us count up; all seven tones are present:

$$D–e–f♯–g♯/a–b/c.$$

To be sure, if we wish to become immersed in the interconnections of this second seven-tone system, we must set forth statements of this type: "The acoustical *So*-scale may be found on the fourth degree of the *re*-mode of the *Di*-system." Complicated? I know of nothing simpler. I can best help clarify the above with this illustration transposed to the common-tonality:

Ex. 68

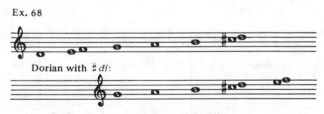

Dorian with ♮ *di*:

on the fourth degree: the G-acoustical line

123

This connection is not rare in the works of our composer. Thus for example, between the two stanzas of the *Piros alma...* this acoustical fourth degree appears in a fleeting figuration:

Ex. 69

Háry János, No. 7

In the singing *d*-dorian coda of the violin-cello sonata, the *G*-based subdominant reigns throughout a significant portion:

Ex. 70

Duo, Op. 7

This corresponds to the often readily-stressed subdominant function in the codas of classical works. (See *Ex. 4.*)

C) In the phrygian atmosphere of the *Mi*-mode, the *di* implies a special dorian-like sixth, which we have already introduced in the folksong line *Kertbe mentek...* (*Ex. 33*, see also *Ex. 13*).

Let us offer yet another example from this most lovely women's chorus:

Ex. 71

Two Folksongs from Zobor, I

Meg-ha - lok, meg-ha - lok,   még be - teg sem va -   gyok,

Meg - ha - lok, meg-ha - lok, még be -teg sem va - gyok,

(Let us compare this excerpt with its lower fifth-change as found in *Ex. 62 a*.) The melody enriches the *Mi*-ending line not only with *si*, but also with *fi*. The scale containing *di* connects to this by means of the principal-tones *la-mi*. Illustrated once again in the common tonality:

Ex. 72

D) *La*-line with *di* (picardy, or "half-Transdanubian" aeolian).

As we have already suggested earlier (following *Ex. 53*): at times the folk melody itself may have provided our composer incentive to use the second seven-tone system. Indeed the first half of *Meghalok... (Ex. 71)* is a case in point. After the slow melody comes a lively one with its own Transdanubian-third (in *f♯*-aeolian-pentatonic with *a♯*). This also is pertinent to our discussion as is borne out by the accompanying voices:

Ex. 73
a)

Two Folksongs from Zobor, II

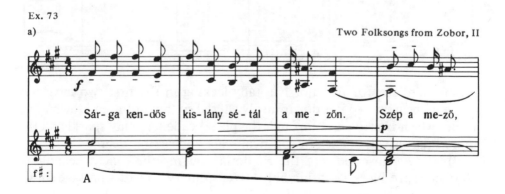

Sár- ga ken- dős kis-lány sé - tál a me - zőn. Szép a me-ző,

125

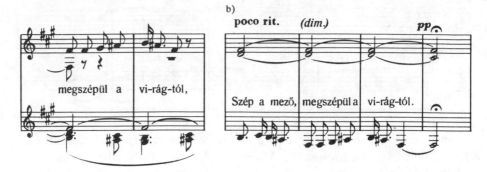

We have already presented a good number of examples showing this type of major-third aeolian *(Exs. 5, 27, 28, 29, 30 a and 31 a).*

E) The *di* above a *ti* creates one of the most interesting lines and one which is most Kodály-like: the locrian with major-second. A typical and lovely example of this is the first piece of the Mountain Nights series (see *Exs. 1* and *2*).

III. The MA-order. A reversal of the preceding. In place of the characteristic tone *(di)* found by the increase of two fifths in the acute direction, the tone which deviates from the diatonic is found by decreasing two fifths in the obtuse direction *(Ex. 58, line 4).* Its seven modes taken altogether provide one of the richest areas in the realm of Kodály's music.

A) In major, this *ma* generally has an indirect role: the *mi* sounding after it sparkles with new light. Older composers also used this *minoremaggiore* effect. Here we quote one example of the newer type only:

Ex. 74

The third step of *E*-major is totally lacking in the first two measures while in the next two it is downwardly altered so that at the end the major-tonic, which is arrived at through the plagal cadence, may sparkle all the more impressively. (The *A*-acoustical scale appears on degree IV.)

B) The *ma* inserted into the *Re*-dorian (giving the tone a neapolitan character) produces a considerably less customary effect. A passage showing this type of "neapolitan dorian":

Ex. 75

22 (and 25)

Székely Lament (for piano), Op. 11, 2

The original key of both the melody and the composition as a whole is *g*-pentatonic. Here, in the second verse, the melody itself undergoes a strong transformation: the pentatony is placed within the frame of the *g*♯-locrian (*g*♯–*b*–*c*♯–*d*!–*f*♯–*g*♯). The second line of the melody—quoted above—moves within the relative key, its coloration altered to the *b*–*c*♯–*d*–*f*♯–*g*♯ pentatony (the Japanese *akebono* scale). The tonality thus temporarily has a *b*-dorian character. As long as the *c*♯ does not appear in the quoted folksong line, our composer builds into the chords of the right hand the *ma* of the system, the *c*, which is thrown into prominence by its complaining character. (Try replacing the *c* with the seemingly more natural *c*♯: the original flavor is lost!) The accent marks also betray the composer's intention.

A noteworthy example of the *Ma*-system is the beginning of the profoundly effecting newer chorus for women's voices:

Orphan Am I

Ex. 76

If we consider only the particular elements in question, we hear the very same *c*♯-aeolian with diminished-fifth in the introductory figurations. But the overall key of the melody and of the piece is *f*♯-dorian. In this regard the lamenting *g(= ma)*-tone would seem to be a borrowing, from the Csángó (Transylvanian) melodies, of the rather frequent lowered second degree.

C) *Ma* in a *Mi*-ending phrygian? Indeed more than once! That the five main types of the second seven-tone order along with their 35 modes really signifies an entire system is precisely verified by such extreme examples. Sometimes the *ma* appears under a phrygian melody, even if only as a passing alteration, as in the following example *a)*:

Ex. 77

(*E* is heard prior to the *E♭* bass.) Elsewhere it is more abundant, as in measures 744–746 (not quoted here) which soon follow the above excerpt—then even more significantly eight measures later as in *Ex. 77 b.* These ever more thickly appearing, strangely dark *ma*-tones insure the unity of the folksong setting as well as the intensifying effect of its individual sections.

A more extended *ma* occurs in the phrygian with major-third:

Ex. 78

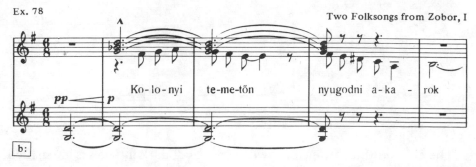

Ko- lo- nyi   te-me-tőn   nyugodni a- ka - rok

The *b♭* preceding the *b* finalis, the restful *g*-minor triad... serves the text in a poetic manner: *temetőn* (= in the cemetery), *nyugodni akarok* (= I wish to rest).

D) In *So*-mixolydian, the *ma* is sometimes only a quotation of the classical minor-subdominant and transfers the material to a modal environment:

Ex. 79   Praeludium

Elsewhere in a more original and more substantial manner:

Ex. 80   Mountain Nights, III

In the heptachordal-lines of the two lower voices we can discover two relative scales. The mezzo sings along the *F = do* with minor-third scale, the alto along the *d = la* aeolian with diminished-fifth. Further examples: *8, 10 b, 37* and the more extended *Ex. 38*.

F) The *La*-line with *ma* has already been mentioned several times *(Exs. 22, 42, 43, 44, 45)*. But since it is a line so typical of Kodály's work, a few examples would seem to be in order here.

Ex. 81

Jesus and the Traders

Ex. 82

Háry János, No. 9

The effect of the low melody which speaks of dark intigues is intensified by the blunt *e-flat* tones of the upper textual ostinato.

The effect is again different when this characteristic tone appears in the bass. The extremely lovely melody (*Tiszán innen...*) reaches its final tone, its most static point. At the same time the bass sees to the necessity of the continuation by picking up the polar-tone (of the *d*), which is the radically foreign, very dynamic lowered fifth degree:

The unexpected chord at the same time also serves to paint the mood of the dreamy, longing quality of the song ("there is where my heart longs to be..."). (We should not fail to mention that the *A♭* serves to further the harmonic construction. It pulls strongly downward to the *G* which may then lead to the *D* closing-chord by means of a plagal cadence. The final tones of the shepherd-pipe figurations once again show how perfectly the second seven-tone system may be combined with pentatony.)

But livelier sounds may also be heard in this scale:

And still more dance-like in the other string quartet:

Ex. 84

a)

b)

If we consider the set of tones in our last example not in relation to the $f\sharp$ of the melody but rather—in its immediate context—in relation to the $g\sharp$ bass, we have reached the seventh mode of the *Ma*-order:

G) A *Ti*-line with *ma* merely signifies that the *ma* may also provide a new coloration, the diminished-fourth, to the locrian set of tones. In our latest example the following line is built upward from the bass:

$$G\sharp/a–b/c!–d–e–f\sharp.$$

Here in a scherzo character–elsewhere in the most extremely opposite mood. *Állni gyászban, súlyos ezüstben, fuldokolni a fáklyafüstben* (= to stand in grief, in weighty silver, choking in the smoke of torches):

131

Ex. 85

a)

Two Songs, Op. 5, II

ful - do - kol - ni a   fák - lya - füst - ben

The classical unity of form and content. Is there a more mournful mode than the locrian? It is thus even as a diatonic mode, and yet made even darker by the diminished-fourth (*b♭♭*). And moreover under the "dark veil" of the many flats. (Kodály likewise set another verse of this same poet Ady, a verse similarly expressing an utter lack of hope, *Those Who Are Always Late*, in the locrian key with seven flats.) — The reader will kindly not be offended—we call into question neither his ability to transpose nor his inner hearing—if we show the motive in the (nevertheless more lucid) common-tonality:

b)

It is difficult for us to stop and not quote further examples of this *Ma*-order which are so very abundant in Kodály's works. But we must set a limit somewhere—let us go further.

IV. The FI + SI-order. These two incisive tones are well known from the melodic-minor. In Kodály's works however we are dealing with something much more than that. The original, independent and innovative handling of these thus altered tones of fixed direction. And not only in the minor, but in all modes.

A) In *Do*-major the *fi* and *si* imply that the principle fourth and fifth degrees are "out of tune". In one instance with a lofty, ceremonious effect:

132

Whitsuntide

mennyor - szág - ba,   min - den - ki   lát - tára

painting the height, the light and the unfolding of heaven—elsewhere
giving a unique, original character to a commonplace children's song:

Ex. 87

The Swallow's Wooing

Jaj!   Jaj!

Tö-rök gye-rek el - vág - ta,   ma-gyar gye-rek gyó - gyit - ja,

dim.

ná - di   he - ge - dű   vel.

síp - pal,   dob - bal,   ná - di he-ge - dű - vel,   dob - bal.

The first measures of the excerpt do not yet hint at the melodic-minor,
but allude only to the augmented-second harmonic-minor above the mel-
ody. The painful utterance of the $g\sharp$ however, leads to the $f\sharp+g\sharp$ area—
and with similar purposefulness to the soon-to-appear A-major section to
which a third sharped tone, the $c\sharp$, is also organically added.

The same first measures are also worthy of our attention from another
point of view. From the beginning of the piece to this point, we have
heard only the melody sung by the altos in unison. The very first sound
from the sopranos (as it appears above) is the penetratingly painful *ti*, the
unresolved leading-tone. The second "jaj" (=alas) intensifies the effect,
as it makes its appearance not in the basic key but on the leading-tone of
the relative minor, the *si*, a tone removed by a distance of three fifths upward. At the same time both the *ti* as well as the *si* are incised into the rests

133

above the *fa*, the deepest, least brilliant tone of the diatonic. In the first instance we hear the augmented-fourth, giving definition to the diatonic—in the second the augmented-second, the characteristic interval of the minor. The two dissonances here fulfill a mood-painting role (poor stork!)—besides intensifying the effect as well. Finally: within the plan of the *C-major–a-minor–A-major* form, they facilitate the modulation and the compact construction.

The quoted sections of both the Whitsuntide and The Swallow's Wooing are based on the fact that the *do-re-mi* core belongs in both the major and the relative minor as well:

Ex. 88

For the sake of reference, let us mention that this
Do–re–mi–fi–si/la–ti
line belongs to the rarely-occurring type III in the first section (see *Exs. 9–III, 14* and *15*).

B) The *fi* and *si* occurring above *Re* form the acoustical scale. We have already seen such examples *(19 a* and *20)*, and newer examples will occur later in our discussion of harmony. Let us simply go on for now.

C) *Mi*-line with *fi* and *si*. A rich area. We have already more than once referred to the *kuruc* scale (*Exs. 9–V, 39, 40, 41* and the six folksong examples under *Ex. 53*). This sound is also suitable for the poor Tyukodi comrade's wealthy, illustrious spiritual relative, Zrínyi. Surely he also raised his voice against his enemy, the "dragon" (i. e. the Turks):

Ex. 89
a)

Hymn of Zrínyi

lát-ván veszedelmét   aty-já-nak,   meg-szó - la-la,   mondván:

Ne bántsd a ki-rályt!

Lá - tok egy ret-tene-tes sár-kányt, mely

mé- reggel, dühösséggel te-li,

Ez a rettenetes sár-kány a török

Ex. 41 completes the motivic relation in this grandiose work for mixed choir.

D) *La*-line with the two sharped tones. We have already seen instances of deviation from the traditional treatment of the (Western) melodic minor in the three interesting folksongs of *Ex. 50*, in *Exs. 10, 11, 12* and *19*, as well as in the immediately foregoing illustrations of *Exs. 86–88*. Let us consider but one more daring example:

Ex. 90   Lament

1. Kér - lel - he - tet - len vég!
2. Jaj, mer - re tűnt a társ?

The statement beginning with the lone *f*♯, the painful cry, rising abruptly, at the climax the piercing, almost screaming *g*♯... The entrance, freely imitating this cry, of the men's voices, with precisely the most acutely tuned minor seventh-chord (*a-c-e-g*♯), intensifies the effect of the climax.

A rich source for examining Kodály's original manner of treating the melodic-minor is the women's chorus with piano accompaniment: Vejnemöjnen Makes Music. This piece will be discussed in the later chapter on Harmony. Until then we recommend that those who are interested analyze it.

V. The ♭*TA* + ♭*LA-order* (see *Ex. 58*, bottom line).

A) From the Classical period, we are quite familiar with the lowered seventh and sixth degrees occuring in a major key. The *b♭* of *C*-major, as the seventh of a secondary-dominant often leads toward the third of the minor-subdominant, the *a♭*. One example from Bach's St. Matthew Passion, No. 72:

Ex. 91

Herzlich thut ...

This is quite closely related to *Ex. 92 b*. But the *maître* already accustoms the young music students to the new tonal order in an ascending line:

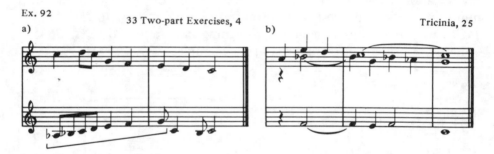

Ex. 92

a)

33 Two-part Exercises, 4

b)

Tricinia, 25

The heptachord in the alto line of the *a)* excerpt displays once again the rare type III (see *Exs. 9–III, 14* and *15*). That is to say: a line of lydian character with augmented-fifth begins from degree VI of the "major-minor".

The slow descent of the alto voice portrays a falling away into sleep:

Ex. 93

Evening Song

pp

ppp

136

A severe, indignant cry:

National Song

És mi mé - gis lán - cot hord - tunk!

Let us examine the prosody: *És mi mégis láncot hordtunk!* (= And still we bore our chains!).

There would seem to be a twin-accent on the middle words (*still* and *chains*). The tenors match both of these with the high *g*. (We have written this excerpt *loco* according to the actual sounding.) But, if we listen even more carefully, the "láncot" (= chains) receives an even greater stress than the "mégis" (= still). A precise, careful piece of craft! The altered tones provide a coloristic underpinning for each *g*. But (just as the words to which they are sung), these are not both of entirely equal weight. The *a♭* is considerably darker ("minus three fifths") than is the *b♭* (the diatonic member found only one fifth lower). And the effect here goes beyond the inherent darkness of this tone: it creates a straining major-seventh dissonance below the second high *g*, the climatic point of the motive. (It is of interest to compare this excerpt with another motive from the same work quoted in *Ex. 64*.)

In the hands of a poet, how many new colors may be granted even such "worn-out" material as the major-minor scale! The kuruc soldiers (of the 18th century) sing bitterly of how the labanc (pro-Habsburg forces) mock them. Unexpectedly, and with a most touching effect, the piano replies to the simple major pentachordal melody with the sighing final motive of the Tyukodi tune:

Ex. 95

Hungarian Folk Music, VII, 40

U- gyan meg is jö- ven- döl - te.

In its rhythm we can hear the "szegény magyar nép!" (= unfortunate Hungarian people!) motive from the Rákóczi tune.

(The accompaniment has already, under the final line of the melody, organically prepared the two altered tones.)

B) The lowered ♭*ta* and ♭*la* above a *Re* bass makes the scale comparable to the aeolian with diminished-fifth:

Ex. 96

Four Songs, 3

cresc.

De jobban sze-re-tem kedves szere - tő - met

cresc.

c-dorian:

An interesting, finely-wrought texture. The rocking, caressing *eb-c* ostinato preserves the *c*-dorian tonality of the melody. The unexpected syncopated *gb* tones seem to point to the axis-related *eb*-melodic minor. This feeling of ours is considerably strengthened by the low *Eb* bass entering after the rest. (The *bb-c-d* trichord of the vocal line fits into the melodic-minor built on this tone.) Then the *Eb-Ab* motion in the bass. Is there anything more banal than this type of primary cadential motion? And yet, as it is used here, the low *Ab* sounds welcomely fresh and sings richly of bells pealing the emotions at the depths of one's heart. Turning to more prosaic matters: the *eb-c* is not only the main third of the dorian with two flats, it can also be adapted into both the *eb* melodic minor and the *Ab* acoustical scale as well. In just the same way, the melody—swaying within the *c*-based dorian trichord—is also seen in three different lights.

C) *La*-line with ♭*ta* and ♭*la*. Once again an extreme example showing the fullness of Kodály's system: the lowering of the basic-tone may also occur (alongside the neapolitan second degree) even in aeolian (minor) pieces. The student should also become accustomed to this at an early stage in his development:

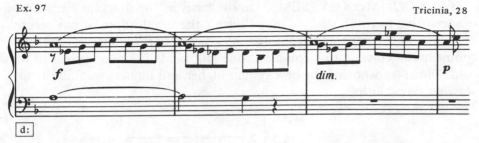

d:

In *d*-aeolian, but more properly, according to the principle material, we are in *d*-pentatonic. A long-held organ-point on the *a* dominant preceding the final return of the theme. This is still in keeping with a classical musical idiom. But this *mi* unexpectedly seems as if it were a member of the *E♭* acoustical scale, or at least of some *E♭*-system. The *a-E♭* polar tension thus, out of the most hackneyed element, the banal dominant, creates a surprising dissonance. From a perfect-fifth has come a diminished-fifth (augmented-fourth). Speaking in the language of physics: the third partial of the overtone series has given over its tiresome role to the eleventh partial.

After an exercise for students, once again an opposite extreme. A song of death:

Ex. 98

Lament

Ím | hozzád vágyom | én, Ha-lál, te | csontos ő-si | rém, a lel-kem | bát-ran vár,

The piece wends its way in a rather loosened tonality: its contours are blurred by tears. Still, the painful, constantly sinking fifths of the first three iambs seem to define the *c*-aeolian tonality. If we thus hear the beginning in this three-flat system, the subsequent harmonies, with the *c♭* lowered *la*, create the mood of a requiem. (Once again: the many flats = being dressed in mourning.) Then in the bass melody we also hear the *ta*, the *d♭*. In the course of remembrance the pain intensifies. The dissonance also intensifies: the *c♭-e♭-a♭* triad now has a more cutting edge to it above the *G* than it had previously above the *F*. (The end of the two paired-motives goes beyond the second tonal-system as we have examined it so far, in order that the *f♭* may render the tones of mourning even darker by one fifth.)

LESS COMMON SYSTEMS. On the basis of the diagram *Ex. 58* it is conceivable to think that we may "push" the tonal-idiom of our second system still further away from diatony. At least, for example, up to the point at which only one common tone still binds the new system to the old. Thus, transposing the new system higher and higher, we find the following possibilities:

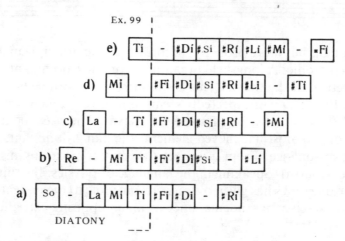

Ex. 99

e) Ti - ♯Di ♯Si ♯Ri ♯Li ♯Mi - ♯Fi

d) Mi - ♯Fi ♯Di ♯Si ♯Ri ♯Li - ♯Ti

c) La - Ti ♯Fi ♯Di ♯Si ♯Ri - ♯Mi

b) Re - Mi Ti ♯Fi ♯Di ♯Si - ♯Li

a) So - La Mi Ti ♯Fi ♯Di - ♯Ri

DIATONY

The number of common tones are fewer and fewer, but we may procede for example from *C*-major as far even as the *C♯*-acoustical line, and still the *b=ti* remains common (see the uppermost line of the above illustration).

On the opposite side, progressing in the direction of more and more flats, we find five newer, even more foreign systems:

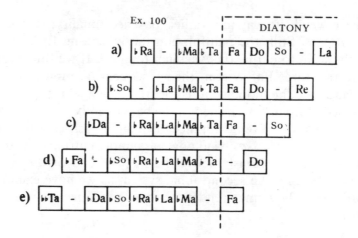

Ex. 100   DIATONY

a) ♭Ra - ♭Ma ♭Ta Fa Do So - La

b) ♭So - ♭La ♭Ma ♭Ta Fa Do - Re

c) ♭Da - ♭Ra ♭La ♭Ma ♭Ta Fa - So

d) ♭Fa - ♭So ♭Ra ♭La ♭Ma ♭Ta - Do

e) ♭♭Ta - ♭Da ♭So ♭Ra ♭La ♭Ma - Fa

140

The mirror-image of the previous grouping: we may procede from *C*-major all the way to the *C♭*-acoustical scale, the *f=fa* remains as the linking element.

That all this is not merely an analytical game for its own sake has already been shown. One of the noted procedures of our composer is that which, to a certain degree we may designate as *bitonal harmonization*: it is sufficient, if there be only a few common tones between the tonal-systems of the melody and of the harmony, for their relation to be all the more colorful and interesting if there are fewer tones of like color and more tones of differing color between them. (Such comparable scale-pairs have already been introduced in *Exs. 62 b, 68, 72* and the diagram of *Ex. 88.*)

The five systems introduced in the grouping of *Ex. 58* (up to two sharped and two flatted foreign tones) we have found as belonging to the inner, basic territory of Kodály's music—those existing beyond these limits are considerably rarer, although they likewise do occur, in one or another of their modes, in the music of our composer. Let us explore this outer territory as well!

VI. The FI + DI + RI-system (see *Ex. 99*, line *a*). Kodály most usually employs this system when, either joined to an aeolian melody, or following an antecedent section in the aeolian, there is heard, built on the very same *la* base, an acoustical line of the same name. This device would seem to develop further the 500-year-old phenomenon of the picardy third—raising the anti-overtone (discordant) minor chord into the family of those (concordant) chords which are brightened by the overtones. One phase of the physical-historical musical logic illustrated schematically:

Ex. 101

minor: acoustical chords:

Thus the following recitative melody with a rich accompaniment:

Ex. 102

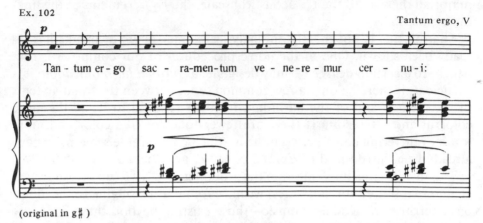

Tantum ergo, V

Tan - tum er - go sac - ra-men-tum ve - ne-re - mur cer - nu - i:

(original in g♯)

In the lines which follow, the melody spans altogether the three tones *do-re-mi*. As long as these appear, "the master is free to do as he pleases" —the harmonies roam with little constraint in distant areas. The relation of melodic and harmonic systems:

Ex. 103

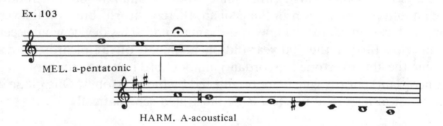

MEL. a-pentatonic

HARM. A-acoustical

The relation of the old minor and its major variant receives new treatment here. If we had heretofore stated that the *maggiore* of *a*-minor is *A*-major—Kodály's musical thought may be thus worded: (one of the) *maggiore* lines of the *la*-pentatonic is the *La*-based acoustical scale.

This very same acoustical *maggiore* appears not in the harmonies but in the melody after an *a*-minor section of the Drinking Song for men's choir. At the same time the three-sharp sound-environment prepares the following four-sharp (*g♯*-phrygian? *c♯*-minor?) section (beginning with the text *Fordulhat a szél…*).

In the adaption for piano of the Székely Tune (*Az hol én elmegyek*) the richly varied second verse arrives at the *b*-pentatonic finalis, which is answered by a *Ti*-major *(C♯)*-chord:

Ex. 105   Seven Piano Pieces, Op. 11, 6

This would indeed correspond to the traditional secondary-dominant of *b*-minor, but there is no question here of its being tied to any functional resolution. Standing quite by itself, a harmony giving a unique extra ingredient to the melody.–At the same time the shepherd-pipe figurations which continue the melody now vary the pentatonic outline with the Transdanubian *d♯* in place of the original *d*. Thus is formed, from the relation of melody and chord, the second tonal order:

Ex. 106

143

Now, as opposed to the three sharped tones, three flatted tones:

VII. The ♭TA + ♭MA + ♭RA-system (Ex. 100 a). The many dark tones are excellently suited to be placed under the word "legelhagyatottabb" (= the most foresaken):

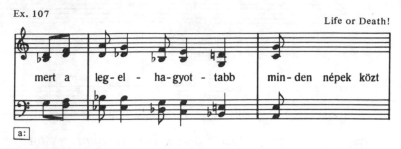

Ex. 107

Life or Death!

mert a | leg-el - ha-gyot - tabb | min-den népek közt

Below the *a*-aeolian melody, the bass sings a line which coincides with mode VII, the *Si*-mode of the *b♭*(!)-melodic minor, the neapolitan minor-scale:

Ex. 108

la

quasi b♭: ♯ fi | mi | re | do | ti | la ♯ si

Later on in the same piece:

Ex. 109

Life or Death!

f Föl nemzetem! | ‖ | ‖ | Föl!

Föl! | Föl! | Föl! | Föl! | Föl! | Föl, nemzetem!

How is this possible? The very same tones expressing both forsakenness and encouragement? On the one hand the recurrence of the bass line serves perhaps to link the ideas, as if it were saying: you, my forsaken nation, it is you whom I wish to stir up.–On the other hand: if the high, stirring cries of the tenor can no longer be intensified in an upward direction, then let us use the indirect method: let the harmony descend even more deeply. And the tenor will seem *proportionately* all the higher! The upper voice, thus illuminated by the varied colors of six different spotlights, is ever more intensively affecting—the most brilliant light reserved for the end above the *La*-major triad appearing after the many *b-flats*.

A few shorter passages:

Ex. 110
a) Hungarian Folk Music, I, 3   b) Háry János, 30   c) Songs, Op. 1, 16

a) They have begun to tear the little bird's nest apart... The harmony with its many flats is suited to the sad text. (The acoustical tone-group appears on the $A\flat$, the tritone of the basic *d*-pentatonic key. This is not the first time that we mention this polar relation in connection with Kodály's music!)

b) After the *D*-mixolydian of the Nagyabony Soldiers' Tune, the melody of the orchestra recalls the pentatonic. The darker sounds of the middle voices complete the tonal-picture: our second seven-tone system. A game of *maggiore-minore* appears here: after the *D*-mixolydian, the diminished-fifth aeolian based on the same tone.

c) In this melody, which sounds in $E\flat$-major, the final tones of the vocal line come to rest on $b\flat$. Below this typical *dominant* half-cadence tone however, a rich *subdominant* harmony is heard. At first only the $A\flat$-$d\flat$-$g\flat$-$b\flat$ four-tone chord, then an expressive augmented-fifth fitting in above. With the exception of one missing tone, every member of the IV-degree "major-minor" tone-family is present:

$$A\flat - b\flat - c/d\flat - (E\flat)/f\flat - g\flat$$

And which is the missing tone? Precisely the one which the composer reserves for the soon-to-appear (and with all the greater effect) *E♭*-major tonic triad. And all this in Opus 1!

An even more copious example. The members of the emperor's court enter with a great din. This does not impress Háry, and he makes rather a sarcastic grimace:

Ex. 111   Háry János, No. 24

Under the final tone of the *la* acolian-pentatonic melody, a great surprise: the *Ma*-major lower polar triad, alternating with the neapolitan *ta*-minor. Measuring the acoustical line to the former (*E♭*-base), the tones of the melodic-minor, in comparison to the unstressed *ta*, render the sound intentionally grotesque.

Let us descend to an even lower depth!

VIII. The ♭TA + ♭MA + ♭LA + ♭SA-order (Ex. 100 b). Four foreign tones, but still three tones in common with the diatonic area. The principal theme of the slow movement is in *g♯*-pentatonic. The composer prepares one return of the theme in this manner:

Ex. 112   Symphony, Second Movement

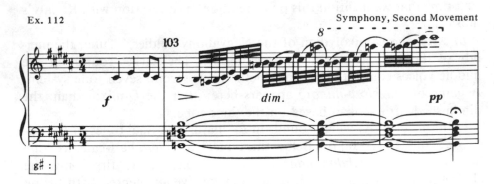

The *b*, the *do* of the *g♯*-line, unexpectedly becomes the third of the *G*-acoustical chord. The tonal structure is thus built on the lowered bass of the principal key (the *G* instead of the *g♯*). In the "vocabulary" of our common-tonality:

146

Ex. 113

MEL. a-pentatonic

HARM. A♭-acoustical

But there is something still lower!

IX. The ♭TA + ♭MA + ♭RA + ♭LA + ♭DA-system (Ex. 100 c) is joined to the diatonic base by only two tones. Nevertheless, in an orchestral piece, a section leading back to earlier-heard material:

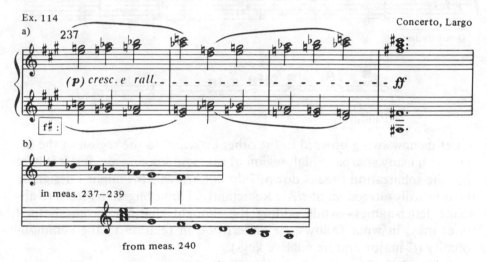

Ex. 114   Concerto, Largo
a)   237

b)

in meas. 237—239

from meas. 240

The procedure is related to several which we have previously discovered. The darker the background, the brighter the principal shape in the foreground. This Rembrandt-like feature of Kodály's music is realized here. The *f♯*-aeolian return, taken from an area lower by seven fifths, *f*-melodic minor, is prepared by the wrenching arsis-like lines of thirds. The functional change of the two linking-tones: the *si (e)* of *f*-minor becomes the *so*—the *fi (d)* becomes *fa*. (A chromatic re-interpretation.)

Although an entirely different type of solution, the underlying thought of the following coda section *(Ex. 115)* makes it a relation to the previous excerpt.

A bass-line seeming to be in *b♭*-minor prepares the closing *D*-mixolydian harmony. When the line arrives at the lower leading-tone, the *A*, this tone becomes the fifth of the closing-chord. The next closest

147

voice to the bass, which is carrying the $\frac{6}{4}$ mixtures, is the line of the actual bass-tones and acts in precisely the same way: it proceeds downward along the 6-flat $e\flat$-minor scale. The end-point of this line, the d leading-tone of $e\flat$-minor, now signifies the basic tone of the principal key, the 1-sharp D-mixolydian. The darker the garden from which we enter into the lighted room, the more blinding will that light seem.

Ex. 115

a)

Organ Mass, Sanctus

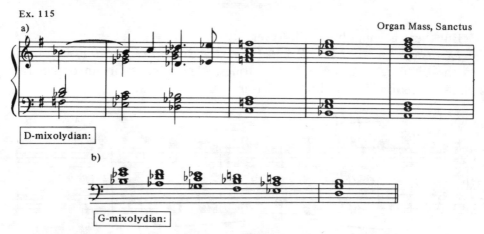

D-mixolydian:

b)

G-mixolydian:

Let us now swing upward to the other extreme, to the region of the orders with many sharps, a high region of rare and bracing air. But it is here that the solmization breaks down: I do not know, how might I designate the upwardly altered *mi* or *ti?*... Reluctantly, I am obliged to return to absolute letter-names—while adding the thought that the given sharped tones may, in what follows, be understood in relation to the common-tonality (*C*-major and its relative keys).

X. The F♯ + C♯ + G♯ + D♯ + A♯ + B♯(!)-system (Ex. 99 d). Now only one single tone joins this system to the basic line. Thus in the final coda of the string trio: the seventh of the *B*-acoustical line, the *a*, with the help of a few major-$\frac{6}{4}$ chords treated in a neo-modal manner, is rendered capable of re-establishing and finalizing the basic key of *F*-major:

Ex. 116

Serenade, Op. 12, III

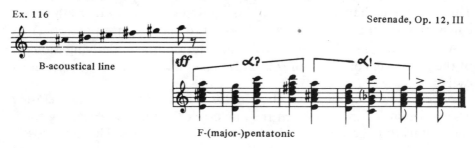

B-acoustical line

F-(major-)pentatonic

148

The upper polar (thus higher by six fifths) *B*-line precedes the *F*-major tonality. The passage attains the seventh-degree peak of the scale on the *a*—sforzatissimo (pay attention, listener, now comes the great feat)—and behold, this very *a* is already "at home" in *F*. Is the jolt perhaps too shocking? Let us tone it down with a few reversely-modulating, less acute tones: with *c*♯, *b* and *f*♯. A small counter-brake; a few passing *b*♭ tones, and smoothly, precisely we sail into our *F*-landing. The balancing element of this very foreign passage is a powerful "native-land" parting word: concise pentatonic motives in a question-answer period relation:

Have we arrived?   *mi-re-so-la?*
We have arrived!   *mi-re-so-do!*

HARMONY

Our essay on the tonal-system of the "second seven-tone order" has so far been treated from the point of view of scale-structure and melodic concerns. The continuation shall now examine questions dealing with the *harmonic-world* of this system. We shall begin with those elements which more readily relate to traditional techniques (although in quite a new manner):

A) unique chords in the new system,
B) cadential motion on the V–I degrees,
C) the semi-cadence,
D) the VII–I authentic progression,
E) the anti-tonic,
F) the V–IV–V pendulum motion,—and finally:
G) plagal progressions.

We shall leave for the final chapter those elements of the newest type, such as, for example, chords of six and seven thirds, color-chords, relation to the whole-tone scale, compilations of seconds and fourths—sequences, mixtures, modulations, etc.

A) *Unique chords*. There are no triads or seventh-chords built on thirds in the tonal system of the acoustical scale (nor thus in any of its six other modes) which should not be familiar from the diatonic system or from the harmonic-minor. However, the moment that decorative tones make their way into traditional chords, the complete tonal-picture will every time then fit into, or will at least be explainable in terms of the new system.

Thus immediately in the very first collection of folksongs which was published jointly with Bartók in 1906:

Ex. 117

a)   20 Hungarian Folksongs, No. 12   b)   The Székely Spinning Room

ha-ján fö-lü   gyöngy, koszorú   ke-ser - ves   nó -   tát

The *a♯* of the melody, accented by virtue of its simultaneous sounding, enriches the *E*-major chord if even for a brief moment, and nearly creates the acoustical eleventh-chord. It is answered by the tenor of the accompaniment (in the next chord) with the more significantly sounding *si*. The two chords together create an *F♯*-line of *kuruc*-type coloration. (See *Exs. 39–41, 55, 57, 89*.)

The *G-b-d-f* seventh-chord of *Ex. 117 b* is given, due to the *a* and *e* suspensions and the *c♯* passing-tone, every color of the acoustical tone-rainbow.

The *g*-minor seventh-chord (the "only-in-the-case" chord of our student days, see footnote 1), due to the *e* changing-tone, fits into an independent melodic minor:

Ex. 118

Duo, Op. 7, III

The secret of the whip(= *korbács*)-chords:

Hungarian Folk Music, IV, 19

Ex. 119

on the one hand the narrowing of the fifth (in *d* an *a♭*!), on the other the sharply-biting changing-tones of the bass. Under the second motive, the same treatment in the subdominant (in *d* a *d♭*!).

A flamboyant "major-minor" effect:

First String Quartet, Op. 2, IV

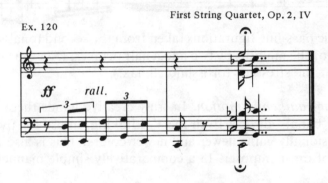

Ex. 120

The heavy ♭*ta* and ♭*la* changing-tones of sharply-rhythmical Hungarian character render the closing-tones of the "good old *C*-major" all the more brilliant.

Exactly the same tonal-material in a full-blooded setting:

Serenade, Op. 12, II

An *f♯-a-c-e* seventh-chord sounding for two measures:

Ex. 122

First String Quartet, Op. 2, IV

with melodic bass-line figurations taken from the second tonal-system and a widening of the ambitus by two and a half octaves. (A steep arsis toward the thesis of the stressed, fortissimo climax.)

B) *Primary authentic motion.* In truly creative hands there is no such thing as a "banal" device. Even the V–I linking, in use for five hundred years, occasionally gains newer and newer colors. This is also the case in the works of our composer. In a comparatively simple manner:

Ex. 123

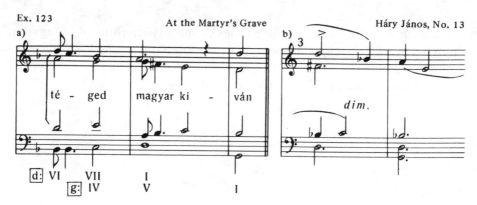

At the Martyr's Grave

Háry János, No. 13

152

The *a)* example moves out in the direction of *g*-minor, but the descending *fi (e)* of the alto tastefully enriches the traditional dominant seventh-chord. (The two upper voices present the entire *D-kuruc* scale.)—The *b)* example is more complex. In the first measure the *b♭* delays the *a* of the dominant in *g*-minor. The resolution to *a* does occur, but by this time it becomes the ninth of the tonic chord which also receives a coloration from the *e*.

Repeated V⁷—I motion in the *G♯-kuruc* scale:

This tonal-system is present for a good number of subsequent measures. The further development of related principal-chords:

The harmony, rich in suspended dissonances, matches the trichords, sloping this way and that, of the melody sometimes with imaginative imitation *(a)*, sometimes with mirror inversions in the bass *(b)*.

Dominant ninth-chords with new colorations:

153

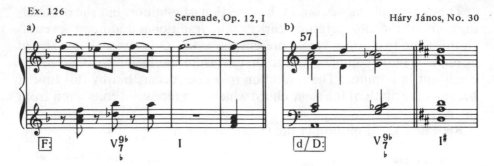

Ex. 126

a) Serenade, Op. 12, I

b) Háry János, No. 30

The dominant in *F*-major is given an Eastern pentatonic quality instead of a Western major-type character (*eb* instead of *e*). The same type of dominant ninth-chord with minor-third lifts the tonality out of the *d*-aeolian and into the *maggiore (b)*.

Repeated cadential motion:

Ex. 127

The Székely Spinning Room

ga -lam - bom-nak! Bár - csak ad- dig le ne ten -nék, míg én

a-dorian: mel.   acoustic   mel.   acoustic   mel.

"The bell is tolling, perhaps for my sweetheart (= *galambomnak*)"... Beneath the *a*-dorian melody the tolling-rhythms present a progression in *g*-minor (darker than the main tonality by two fifths!) which is enhanced by the *g-C* (I–IV) pendulum-motion. The *f♯*-tones of the melody adorn the peculiar *C* subdominant with the character of the acoustical line.

A newer displacement of primary harmonic motion:

Ex. 128

Duo, Op. 7, I

154

The lowered sixth degree *(B♭)* arises in measure 3 beneath the tonic tone of this *d*-dorian (decorated with the Transdanubian *f♯*) melody. This occurrence and the previously reiterated relative secondary-dominant *(F)* together create the sound of the acoustical line.

A similar procedure but more substantially expanded:

Ex. 129   Epigrams, No. 8

The I–IV answers the V–I as if it were the successor of the former chain of secondary-dominants. But the augmented-fourth is heard in every phase, removing the chords from the diatonic to the acoustical system. (The two indicated pien-tones of the melody do not obscure this picture.)

From the many, many additional examples, let us present one of the most daring:

Ex. 130
a)   Four Songs, 4

The *B*, acting as a traditional Dufay-bass, prepares the tonic of an *e*-aeolian. But with what a fantastic "superstructure"! Let us extract the individual tones of the roulade: *B-c-d-e♭-f-g-a-b*. In other words, it is as if we were hearing mode VII of the *c*-melodic minor, understanding the bass now as *Si* rather than as *Mi!* Re-projected in the common-tonality:

155

Ex. 130
b)

a: V   I

It is as if a roulade in *f*-minor—or, speaking in the language of our tonal-system, and *E*-based locrian scale with diminished-fourth—would prepare the *a*-tonic. In other words, instead of our finding the commonplace dominant of the minor mode customarily brightened by four sharps (in *la*-minor, *Mi*-major)—here it is a dominant dampened by four flats which enviously "steals away" the light. (A displacement of eight fifths.)

A less common variant:

Ex. 131

Te Deum of Sándor Sík

Hogy a si-rókkal sír - ni jól - esett

In the second measure the distance between the primary tones *G* and *c* ♯ is not a perfect-fifth, but rather a diminished-fifth. The tones on these two quarter-note beats fit entirely into the *G*-acoustical system. But the first measure is also of interest: it moves within the *e*-melodic minor. A confession. The word *jólesett* (= it was good) receives five types of prosaic stress: accent, height, length, new tonality and beside these the suspended dissonance of the major-seventh (*d-c♯*).

C) *Semi-cadences*. What is better suited to the questioning word than the questioning character of the semi-cadence *(a)*:

Ex. 132

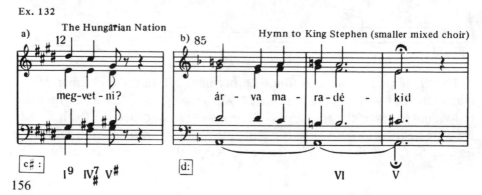

a) The Hungarian Nation
12

meg-vet - ni?

c♯ :   I⁹ IV♯⁷ V♯

b) 85   Hymn to King Stephen (smaller mixed choir)

ár - va ma - ra-dé - kid

d: VI   V

The tones of the first measure fit entirely into the $c\sharp$-melodic minor, —but also worthy of our attention is the relaxation of the chordal-tension parallel to the sloping cadence of the word. On $c\sharp$ a ninth-chord, on $f\sharp$ a seventh-chord, on $g\sharp$ a triad.—Of course, the musical interrogative does have its own place independent of an interrogative text, as we hear in the b) excerpt. The raised sixth degree *(b = fi)*, conspicuously featured in several ways, renders the harmony divergent from the customary *d*-minor.

An answer to a question—how fortunately—in both text and harmony:

Ex. 133

20 Hungarian Folksongs, No. 17

nyár- fát?   hoz-zád.

The harmony follows exactly the main cadences of the folk melody which is of the two-system type, presenting therefore a period effect. The *A* in the middle, and the *D*-based picardy aeolian at the end of the melody rhyme with each other.

D) *The VII–I closing-progression.* A well-known progression in the Classical idiom also. The seventh-chord on the VII degree is fully the negative of the tonic triad: it presents precisely those four tones which do not occur in the resolution. Juxtaposed is the visitor and the host, the dynamic and the static, the arsis and the thesis. Moreover, the seven tones together define the scale:

Ex. 134

a: $VII^7 \longrightarrow I$

What does our second seven-tone system say about this? Let us see:

Ex. 135

VII^7-I progressions:

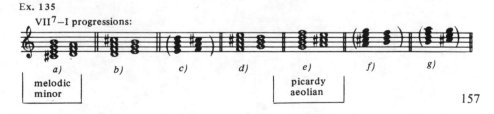

a)   b)   c)   d)   e)   f)   g)

melodic minor   picardy aeolian

157

The *c), f)* and *g)* variants are omitted—at least in Kodály's music—from among the seven modes. These are the three which do not lead to a perfect-fifth. Of the other four, types *b)*, leading to the neapolitan-dorian, and *d)*, moving within the acoustical frame, are rare. The first, that of the melodic-minor, is, however, characteristic. It would seem to proclaim: yes, I will retain the leading-tone, but instead of the deadly-boring diminished seventh, I will place above it something else, the fresher, more original minor-seventh. (For this reason it could be classi-fied as a harmonic-dorian.) And most "Kodály-like" of all is the *e)* chord-pair, in which the VII degree seventh-chord precedes the closing-chord of major-third type.

We have already seen examples of the VII⁷–I progression in minor *(Ex. 10 c)*. Let us once again cite its outline in the following *a)* example:

Ex. 136

In example *b)*, the melody itself, with its emphatic dorian-sixth *(f♯)*, provides incentive for a similar progression. The progression is heard here above the tonic organ-point.—In example *c)*, the *G*-major melody takes a momentary excursion toward *a*-minor. Its proper secondary-dominant would be the *b-d-f-g♯* VII⁶₅. In this case, however, the *f♯* cackles in the melodic-minor. (We may view the *e* melody-tone as a changing-tone ap-proached by leap, or as a root-tone forming a completed V⁹ from the VII⁷.)

A root-position VII–I triadic progression in the major-third aeolian is comparatively rare:

the other measures also containing interesting and pertinent harmonic motion—then, with extraordinary emphasis and brilliance, in the setting of Ady's text for male choir:

Ex. 138   The Peacock

giving staggering power to the "most banal" C-chord, which is later amply enriched in measure 4.—On the other hand, however, the inversions of the triad are much more characteristic of our composer, especially when they develop into chords of more than three tones. The VII_4^6, for example, thus shapes the cadences in two Székely-related pieces:

Ex. 139

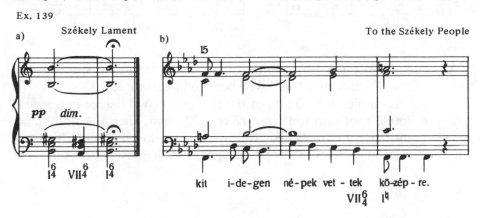

(The same occurs at the end of "Old People" on the *A* and *B* chords.)

Still more frequent than these are the formulas of a higher order. Thus, in the final cadence of a movement, a seventh-chord on the subtonium:

Ex. 140   Communion Anthem (mixed choir)

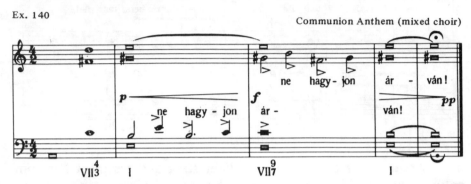

Instead of viewing the *g♯* and *b* of the third measure as simply fulfilling a decorative role, we may hear them as fitting into either the acoustical eleventh-chord, or as the complete thirteenth-chord chain of thirds: *D-f♯-a-c-e-g♯-b.* The imitative motive of the tenor and alto is in perfect accord with the functional order: the tonic *e-b* fourth of the second measure is answered by the dominant *b-f♯* fourth in the third measure. A true acoustical eleventh-chord, equally stressed both melodically and rhythmically, enables the following closing harmony to gleam with a resigned, transfigured light:

Ex. 141   Dirge

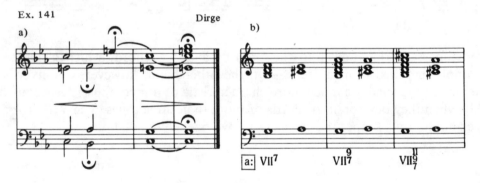

Although devastated "by a bloody curse, by an insane spectre—the song is eternal!" proclaim these wordless coda-harmonies.

We may assemble the variants of the subtonium VII degree in a series: first the simple root-position triad *(Exs. 137, 138)*, then the dominant-based seventh-chord *(Ex. 141 b)*, followed by the ninth-chord *(ibid.* and *Ex. 140)*, and the eleventh-chord *(Ex. 141)* each present the different

160

degrees of effect within the family of non-leading-tone "Eastern dominants".

Our chords may also fulfill a formal role:

Ex. 142

National Song

In the closing movement of this mighty "vocal symphony", the end of the bagpipe-melody, which has been interpolated as a trio, could be jarring to the formal structure if it were to close on the same *g*-tonic directly before the end of the piece. The melody does indeed close in this key—but the harmony sets the matter right! In place of the static *g*-chord, we find the dynamic, open *F*-ninth chord, which may then connect more organically to the final return of the principle theme broadening into the coda.

A uniquely rare variant:

Ex. 143

Mátra Pictures

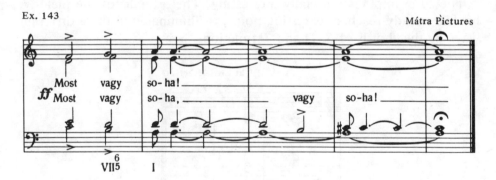

Here the VII$_5^6$ precedes the root-position I. (It is as if the conscience of the composition teacher were speaking: mixed parallel-fifths between the alto and bass? As if suggested by the text itself: now ('most') but never ('soha') again!)

Recommended for analysis, among other items, is The Soldiers' Song (*Katonadal*), measures 41–47, and the last nine measures of the *Justum et tenacem*.

161

Tri-functional full cadences. Much more appealing to our composer than the IV–V–I cliche is the IV–VII–I grouping, functionally identical with the former, and once again with the subtonium (whole-tone) seventh degree:

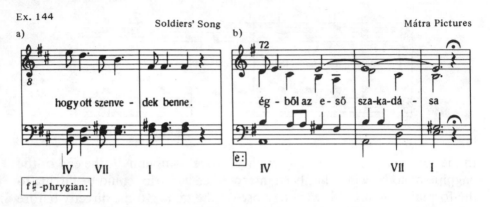

Ex. 144

a) Soldiers' Song

b) Mátra Pictures

Triplex dos libelli! a gift of three-fold virtue:

a) there is no leading-tone, therefore the sound is more like that of a Hungarian folksong,

b) yet the authentic line of force is unbroken,

c) the bass represents the pentatonic scale.

The *b)* example is especially interesting. The *e* finalis of the melody, having already reached its resting point, is illuminated in three different ways by the chords of *S, D* and *T* function.

Ex. 145

Eight Little Duets, 6

This piece also comes to rest, but only in its upper voice. In the changes of coloration wrought by the harmonies it does not. (The penultimate tone of the alto, the unresolved *a* changing-tone replaces the chord-fifth *g*—a procedure which has been common since the "vicariant-sixths" of Schubert's harmonies.)

162

Above an organ-point a complete, tri-functional circle of motion:

Ex. 146

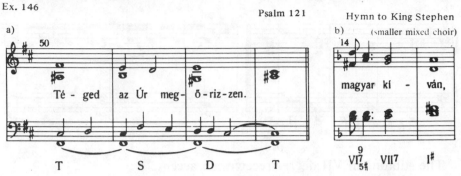

Nor does the third subdominant degree, the VI of the minor, remain outside the circle. (This chord, moreover, much more frequently has an *S* rather than a *T* function, since there is just the same minor-third distance upward from the IV degree (in minor) as there is to the II degree downward. (Ernő Lendvai's axis-principle holds true!) This is borne out by *Ex. 146 b*, once again demonstrating the principle of decreasing tension: ninth-chord, seventh-chord and triad follow one another to the resting point.

The organ-point, moreover, is frequent in Kodály's works:

Ex. 147

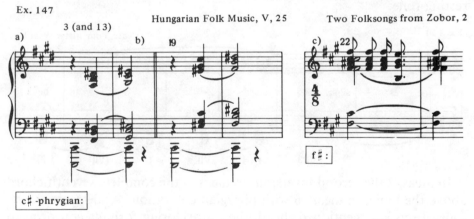

The content of the three brief excerpts: VII–I above the tonic, the I–VII, finally I–VII–I above a double organ-point. A few further examples from among the many:

163

Ex. 148   Organ Mass, Agnus   Concerto, III
a)   b)

The subtonium VII degree receives an accent:

Ex. 149   Serenade, Op. 12, I

The VII degree in several different variants, in part above the tonic resting-tone:

Ex. 150   Cease Your Bitter Weeping

In meas. 2 the second inversion, in meas. 4 the complete seventh-chord above the tonic, in meas. 6 with phrygian coloration. Aside from the $a\flat$ tone of this last-mentioned chord, the entire closing-formula conforms to the dorian mode of the *Ta + Fi*-system. (See *Exs. 26* and *64*.)

A singular combination:

a)

I IV VII I

The voices of the chorus (the upper two line) form the I–IV–I plagal cadence. The organ is still capable of adding the third function: the ninth-
chord on the VII degree. How is this possible? Precisely because this latter
chord also incorporates the triad on the IV degree:

Ex. 151

b)

a: I♯ IV VII⁷₉ I♯

The same occurs here as in *Exs. 144 b* and *145:* the melody, indeed the
bass as well, has already reached its final resting point, but the instrumental inner-voices assume the role of "shock-absorbers", carrying the motion further along and only afterwards do they apply the brakes to ring the
piece to a halt.

Pendulum-motion. In Kodály's works, the pendulum-motion (repeated
progression) on the subtonium VII–I progression, employed with great
variety, is a characteristically frequent occurrence.

In a rather modest manner:

Ex. 152

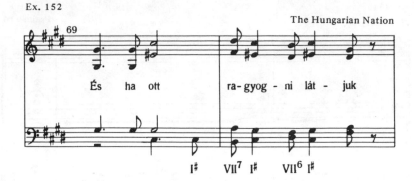

The Hungarian Nation

És ha ott   ra-gyog-ni lát-juk

I♯   VII⁷ I♯   VII⁶ I♯

Thrice the VII–I, each time differently:

Ex. 153

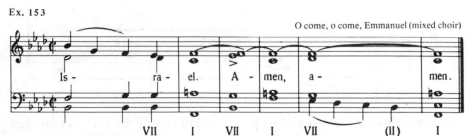

O come, o come, Emmanuel (mixed choir)

Is -   ra - el.   A - men,   a -   men.

VII   I   VII   I   VII   (II)   I

(If we so wish, we may hear the penultimate measure as a subdominant by calling the $b\flat$-$d\flat$-f-g-II_5^6 the prevailing chord, with the $e\flat$ and c being then merely decorative tones.)

Typical "Kodály-like" repeated chord changes:

Ex. 154

Three Songs, Op. 14, III

cresc.

Tán- col - junk   vi - gan,   mint ők   is   haj - dan,

cresc. - - - - -

Both harmonies appear in the most extreme inversion ($_4^6$ and $_2^4$), the upper and lower voice-groups dancing lively (= *táncol vígan*) in contrary motion. The rhythm of the chords renders the *volta*-pattern, a foreign element which has been domesticated in our folk music, more Hungarian—

166

excellently complementing the even-numbered measures of the melody.

The chords of Uncle Marci's drinking-song cackle with good humor:

Ex. 155

Háry János, No. 8

wittily echoing the fourths of the folksong. This occurs, moreover, in two variants above the very same bass: first the $c\sharp$-$g\sharp$ then the $f\sharp$-$c\sharp$ echo of the melody. Yet a different idea at the end of the previous strophe:

Ex. 156

Háry János, No. 8

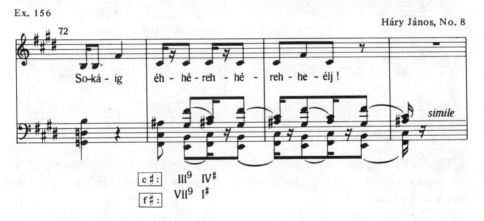

Do and *Re* alternate with each other in place of the *So* and *La* bass-line of *Ex. 155*.

Reiterated VII–I exchanges appear—among many others—in measures 78–81 of the *Honvéd díszinduló* (Military Dress March).

"The closed earth wakes up refreshed" to the breath of spring:

Seven Songs, Op. 6, IV

The lethargy of winter still remains (=prolonged, dull-sounding chords, deep-dark organ-points)—but here and there the buds are already issuing forth (=bright, short, snapping chords).

Our chords are also capable of portraying church bells:

Ex. 158

Seven Songs, Op. 6, VII

The I–VII–I order of massive, metallic harmonies is complemented by the bass on the off-beats: the interplay is removed one third lower to the VI–V–VI plane.

E) *The Anti-tonic*. The $\frac{4}{3}$-inversion of the seventh-chord on the VII degree warrants a separate discussion. The question already arises in the study of traditional harmony when this chord precedes the I: what is the functional quality of this chord? According to its structure, it is of course dominant. The leading-tone motion *(a)* is most certainly present:

Ex. 159

Now no matter how often it is heard, this *ti* is always a leading tone. But is there not perhaps a plagal quality to the *b)*-type cadence? What are we hearing? A brief leading-tone tucked away in some middle voice, or a bass maintaining the subdominant pillar-tone? It is often not possible to decide. If I so wish, I may perceive the *D–T* function from the one pair of voices *(c)*—if I play closer attention to the other two voices *(d)*, the *S–T* quality is clear. In truth, this cadence—most often favored by Brahms in both major and minor—in itself incorporates both of these two colors. It is as if we are dealing with the precursor of certain phenomena of newer music which does not recognize three functions, but only the tonic and the aggregate of tones standing opposite to the tonic, the anti-tonic. (See the illustration *Ex. 134*.)

This simplest type of anti-tonic, the VII$_3^4$, plays a prominent role in Kodály's music. What we have already seen of the IV–VII–I cadence *(Ex. 144)*, is perhaps true here as well: this structure cuts closer to the Hungarian folksong when we have a subtonium VII degree rather than a leading-tone relation—this in regard to both the relation of pentatonic and primary tones as well as the motion of the bass—and because of the anti-tonic quality, the final harmony appears in quite a brilliant light after the entirely foreign sound. With the exception of the lydian and locrian, Kodály readily uses this progression in each of the diatonic modes:

Ex. 160

Let us but consider the end of the great canon *(a)*:

Ex. 161

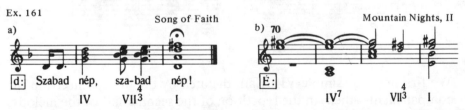

This motive may become our watch-word not simply because of the text (*szabad nép* = a free people), but rather because it characterizes, as a motto, a notable group of elements in Kodály's music. At once Hungarian and European, even though conforming to a Greek model, the ode of the poet Berzsenyi reverberates from a Hungarian heart.

Alongside this well-known aeolian-cadence, let us also quote one example from the other most Kodály-like mode, the phrygian of the Tyukodi-tune coloration *(Ex. 162). Ex. 161 b* is also of the same type, the two third-pairs of the anti-tonic being separated (see *Exs. 159 c* and *d*).

If we are already dealing with the *kuruc* scale, the following excerpt would also seem to belong here:

Ex. 162

Hungarian Folk Music, VII, 40

In one of our composer's undeservedly little-known works, The Adoration, the closing phrygian triad sounds forth with unusual brilliance following the same type of antecedents as in the above excerpt.

The harmonization of the folksong *Öreg vagyok...* exposes the double quality of this anti-tonic:

Ex. 163

Hungarian Folk Music, IX, 51

We first hear the simple VII triad, dictated by the melody itself, in the accompaniment—then, in the repetition of the second half of the melody, under the very same motive, the *a-c-f♯* first-inversion chord on the II degree, that is to say a subdominant. The two together form the anti-tonic seventh-chord, but, broken up in this way, the quality of the bass-motion is at first authentic and later plagal.—The story is complete in the interlude which follows the strophe:

170

Ex. 164

The right hand decorates the folksong motive *(Ex. 164 a)* with the triad of the previously featured VII degree, while the left hand sets beneath it the Rameau-$^6_5$ of pure subdominant quality. The two are of course part of the same element: the *D-f♯-a-c-e* ninth-chord. But separated and yet joined together in this way: the harmonization explains everything about the anti-tonic character of the chord.—In *Ex. 164 b*, even though the *c* is missing, still, in the harmonic sketch of the fiery recruiting-tune quoted here, the *S+D*, that is to say the anti-tonic function of the second-inversion VII chord is clear.

If, however, the root of the chord is missing from the harmony, the chord falls then entirely within the subdominant area. We do not have space to show the final 16 measures of the mole-tune, but we ask the reader to take up the volume of the Children's Choruses (pp. 112–113 in the 1972 edition of Editio Musica, Budapest) and examine the types of variants above the *g-c* alto-ostinato, repeated fourteen times, to determine where we hear the II degree and where the VII degree. The frame of this notable excerpt:

Ex. 165   Mole Marriage

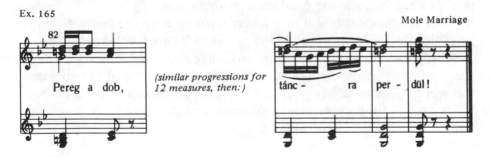

F) *The D–S–D pendulum-motion.* The aternation of degrees IV and V present an exact replica of the subtonium progressions which we have just considered. The difference: the former rest statically on the tonic, the latter float dynamically on the open degrees.

Ex. 166   Organ Mass, Gloria   Ibid.

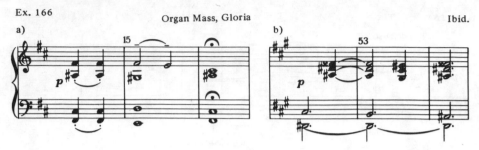

Repeated pendulum-motion:

Ex. 167   20 Hungarian Folksongs, No. 20   Székely Lament

In example *a)*, the folksong itself prompts the repetition of the progression. The accompaniment implements this task with a finely-graded
variant: after the IV_4^6 of the second measure, the II^7 of the third measure
intensifies the stress of the repeated word. The next example, *b)*, is no-
tably beautiful and deeply poetic. The low placement of the voices, the
pealing *bom* syllable, the subdominant (here anti-dominant!) fitting into
the melodic-minor (yet still of a newer type) all echo the text with unforgettable effect: The murmur of the Sea shall be my death-knell.

With great intensity, the swaying arsis-like character achieves its aim in
the harmonies of the tightening crescendo driving toward the climax on
the word *"felemeled"* (= you raise him). This excerpt moreover establishes once again how well the pentatonic and the second seven-tone system fit together (see illustration *Ex. 56*):

Subdominant and dominant alternate five times on the key-word *elő̋re!* (= onward!) which resounds across the entire field of battle:

Ex. 169   Battle Song

a-dorian:

Whoever would like to make a study of a truly substantial *D–S–D–S–D* interchange should analyze thoroughly the accompaniment of Vejnemöj-nen Makes Music.

G) *Plagal cadences.* A subdominant in the penultimate position: a cadence-type favored by the Romantic tradition. That Kodály's inclina-tion and strength stands closer to the Classical tradition is shown, among many other phenomena, by the fact that, alongside the authentic types discussed until now, the plagal closing is considerably less frequent in his works. But such cadences are still to be found within his artistic compass.

Furthermore, the motion of the bass descending by a fourth is well suited to the Hungarian-type of melody line.

The final three measures of this simple little exercise occur within the major-third aeolian mode of the second seven-tone system (who can still suggest a better, more definitive name?):

Ex. 170

44 Two-part Exercises, 22

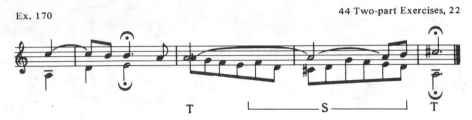

The folksong character of the alto voice is to be found not only in its last interval but in the final five tones. (See the ending tones of the melody *Ex. 144 a*, as well as *Ex. 139 b* and *153*.)

A plagal cadence with minor-subdominant:

Ex. 171

Hungarian Folk Music, VII, 40

(schematically)

The modest *so-fa-mi* melody does not touch upon degrees 6 and 7. Thus the accompaniment has a free hand with which to depict the mood of bitter self-mockery using the lowered *ta* and lowered *la*. If we examine only the piano accompaniment we see the complete I–V–IV–I plagal circle. But together with the melody, the second and third measures present a secondary-dominant ninth-chord on the first degree ($A\flat$-c-$e\flat$-$g\flat$-$b\flat$) as if it were the preparation for the $d\flat$- in the melodic-minor. (We have already met these two altered tones in the lamenting closing-motive of this piece, *Ex. 95*.)

We have also seen a delicate I–IV⁷–I set of chords in the fourth measure of *Ex. 137*. (But please look at this once again!)

A wide-arched cadence brings the variants of the heart-warming, noble Kálló melody to an end in this piece which has become world famous:

Kálló Double Dance

The two high *g♯*-tones have the power to shape the motive: the first is a tense dissonance above the subdominant, making the consonance of the second appear all the brighter. (Anyone who wishes to someday write a textbook entitled "Arsis-thesis in Harmony" should be sure to include this splendid example in his work!)

I recommend for analysis, among many other items, the last eight measures of the *Hegedűszó* (*Violin Melody, Czinka Panna*, eighth movement). This is one of the richest examples of the plagal sounding forth in the *kuruc* scale.

The *augmented-$\frac{6}{5}$* as the basis of the acoustical line. We have already seen in the works of Liszt such instances where the melodic figuration of an augmented-$\frac{6}{5}$ brings about—even if not for its own sake—the acoustical line. Let us bridge the members of the seventh-chord with diatonic passing-tones:

Ex. 173

These passages—appearing so to speak by chance in the Romantic era—are accorded a significant, rich exposition in Kodály's works. We find in them an original plagal progression with a resolution directly to the tonic. We are no longer speaking of a mere figuration! A passionate melody with a sweep of nearly two octaves. (This belongs in a book entitled "Arsis-thesis in Melody" which sooner or later must without fail be written!)

175

In the third movement of the Concerto, measure 442, the logic of the voice-leading demands use of the enharmonic *ma-ri* relation (see diagram, *Ex. 173*). The chord is the *Bb-d-f-g♯* of *d*-minor, extended to a ninth on *c*. Several instruments, however, actually sound the augmented-sixth as an *ab* (in the score!) even though the meaning is clearly *g♯*.

Let us present yet two more of the most Kodály-like excerpts showing this new type of plagal chord relation. The first:

Ex. 175
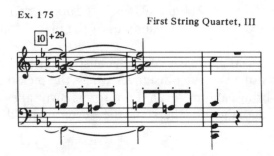
First String Quartet, III

the nearly complete acoustical line is heard above the subdominant. (What did we learn? The *Re*-based natural scale is built on the fourth degree of the melodic-minor.) This stresses the significant recapitulatory role of the *fi* and *si* (*a* and *b*), so that the theme returning in the third measure of the excerpt:

Ex. 176

here contains neither the sixth nor the seventh degree. (See the excerpt of the Labanc Jeering-song in *Ex. 171* and *Exs. 86–88*.)

The beginning of this slow movement sets a crown to the line:

Ex. 177 — Lento assai, tranquillo — First String Quartet, II

The quiet, intimate *A*-major melody begins in the fourth measure. What could stress its warm radiance better than if, in the first three measures, we hear precisely the dark *c* in place of the normally bright third? The effect grows from measure to measure. The first measure hints only at the *minore a*-minor triad. Then one third is built beneath it: a *la-do-ma-so* unique seventh-chord on the VI degree. Then with yet one more third beneath: an acoustical tone-group above the *D* basic-tone on the IV degree. And just when the instruments have drawn the listener's attention toward the depths—above, in the radiance of the blue sky, the melody begins to sing. (Is it not so that everyone hears *A*-major as blue?... I am not able to forget: when almost forty years ago I played second violin in the quartet, what an almost physical pleasure was obtained from gently playing the *c♯* of the fourth measure after the long *c*.)

The second degree may also resolve to the first degree with a plagal motion. Modest chords, but in instructive variants:

Ex. 178

Ex. 178 — Mátra Pictures

The chords of the second tonal-order expand the *e*-dorian of the folksong (just as in the excerpt from the Kálló Double Dance, *Ex. 172*). Among these chords the II–I progression occurs three times. (When the subdominant then appears for the fourth time, it becomes a compact modulating device moving toward the *G*-major theme.)—Before that we also find two variants of the subtonium VII–I progression.

Decorative tones enrich the seventh-chord on the II degree:

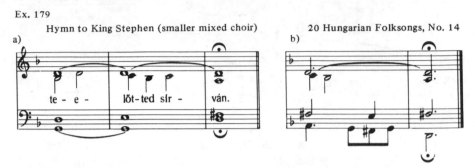

Ex. 179

Hymn to King Stephen (smaller mixed choir)

a)

te - e -   lőt-ted sír -   ván.

20 Hungarian Folksongs, No. 14

b)

The stressed *c* changing-tone of the alto in the *a)* example renders the harmony more concise. (We may also hear this in reverse: the *c* as the chord-tone and the *b♭* as its changing-tone.) In the bass of the *b)* cadence, however, the lower changing-tone *f♯* introduces the special coloration of the second tonal-system.

A most glowing arsis and a very quieting thesis is formed by this type of contrast between degrees II and I:

Ex. 180   Hungarian Folk Music, I, 2

rallent.

II³   I♯

The triplets pulsating in the higher range,—the changing-chords accented by a sforzato (if you prefer: an independent VI degree seventh-chord from the picardy-aeolian),—the reflective fermata,—and then the soft, deep harmony of reconciliation… All of this once again recounts the final verse of the song: The road before me weeps, the path is grieving, and still it says: may God grant his blessing!

Above a dominant organ-point, the *T–S–T–S–T* pendulum gives yet a newer character to the plagal progressions:

178

This three-and-a-half measure excerpt sounds entirely within the *Re*-mode of the *Ta + Fi*-order.

Let us take leave of our circle of themes with the closing measures of one of Kodály's latest works:

Ex. 182   Woe is Me

We find in this the subtonium VII–I cadence, preceded by two interesting plagal progressions. We have seen the same in *Exs. 29, 123 a, 132 a, 143 and 146 b*. Here also the diminuendo of the actual sound level and the slowing down of the motion parallel the quieting of the harmonies: ninth-chords are followed by seventh-chords, so that the final resting point may then be delivered by the triad.

179

EVER ONWARD!

Polyphony. In the foregoing chapters we first discussed elements of melody and tonality as they relate to the tonal-system of the acoustical scale. We next dealt with the pertinent harmonies of Kodály's music in so far as they rested on a traditional base—albeit exhibiting solutions of a new, independent type. Before we examine further, more complex, more daring chordal examples, let us make a brief excursion to the area of polyphony. These examples bear witness to the fact that our composer's contrapuntal art weaves into one texture melodies of Palestrina-like purity "yet still new and Hungarian".

Thus in his two-part work for mixed chorus:

The pentatonic character of the folksong sounding in the lower voice is colored by the *g* *(=fi).* Its counterpart, the *c* *(= ta)* in the upper voices complements the *g♯* and is used to fill in the lower *b-d* third. Thus arises the "fourth way of filling in" the pentatonic, the neapolitan- or phrygian-dorian:

(Worthy of attention here is the order in which motion and rest are perfectly complementary to one another.)

In the following example, however, the answering contrapuntal voices draw from the (*kuruc*-like) scale of the melody itself. The logic of the style is carried through in other respects as well. If the melody line is characterized by conjunct motion, the beautifully arching accompanying voices move in like fashion. Here also, movement and rest complement one another, and what is more, the melodic thesis reaches its lowest point precisely at the moment when the arsis of the lower voices reaches it greatest tension:

180

Ex. 184

'Mid the Oak Trees

This scalar polyphony, in the tonal-system with which we are now concerned, reaches its richest development in the final seven measures of the *Szép könyörgés* (= Beseeching). It is worthwhile to examine this section!

There are also examples of *imitation*. We have already found an octave canon in the middle section of Mountain Nights, I *(Ex. 2)*. Solemn hexachords follow each other at the sixth and at the octave:

Ex. 185

Te Deum

We have met with twofold third-imitations at the end of the Dancing Song *(Ex. 29)*, and with mirror-canons in one bicinia *(Ex. 25)*.

Some unique transformations are heard at the end of this little canon:

Ex. 186

Aurea libertas

The middle voice, in the upper area of the pure ("Peacock") penta-tony, imitates the Transdanubian-pentatonic motive of the lower voice. The upper voice, however, bridges this fifth-distance with the in-between third-stratum, featuring the most characteristic intervals ($b\flat$-$f\sharp$-e) of the second seven-tone system.

The music of the rising moon:

Ex. 187

Evening

The ascending tetrachords depict the sky turning from darkness to the light of the full moon. (Unless we have sung this in a choir, we cannot conceive of the heart-swelling experience accorded by this section.)

There is even an example of a *quodlibet*. The young girl longs "to see the wondrous mill". The mill-tune in the women's choir projects this thought before us. But the mother fearfully warns: "Ne menj!" (= Don't go!) The two melodies are woven together to produce a special effect in the second seven-tone system:

Ex. 188

a) 788

Mother:

The Székely Spinning Room

The key to this ·structural device: the *g* and *a* tones of the principal *b*-phrygian melody, as well as the *c♯-d♯-e* trichord of the *F♯*-mixolydian mill-tune, all fit into a third tonality: the *e*-melodic minor of the accompaniment. The same as compared to the mixolydian in the common-tonality:

showing that the *re, mi, fa* tones of the mixolydian may be re-interpreted as the *fi, si, la* degrees of the *f*-melodic minor (darker by four fifths). The overall effect in context is one of bi-tonality—it is based on an implied major-third relation.

Harmonies of a more complex nature. Let us return to the world of Kodály's chords.

Eleventh-chords. Although such chords arise sporadically in the Romantic era, they generally appear as unresolved suspensions or as formulas tied to changing-tones or organpoints, etc. They have become independent chords of new music only since the time of Debussy. These chords give rise to a significant area in the vocabulary of our own composer's musical language. In the following excerpt we hear an eleventh-chord found on the III degree of *a*-melodic minor:

The chord becomes complete with the entrance of the *e*. At this point the chord sounds in the first inversion, then, over the *g♯* bass, in second inversion.

Twenty-one types of six-member chords may be constructed from major- and minor-thirds. Of these, seven belong to our new order (on each of whose degrees they will sound differently). Among these seven the most frequent in Kodály's works is the acoustical eleventh-chord.

Of this chord used with exceptional variety, we quote but one example:

Ex. 190

Duo, Op. 7, III

In this case it is precisely the youngest member of the harmony, the $f\sharp$ above the c, which is accorded great prominence. And again, in the answer, this $f\sharp$ appears through the same means in the lowest position. In other words, the harmony appears in the most extreme inversion.

In this ever-darkening line of chords, the acoustical eleventh-chord built on $G\flat$ bridges other five- and seven-member chords:

Ex. 191

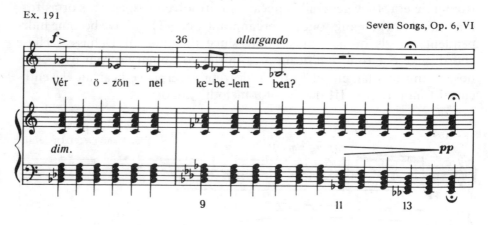

Seven Songs, Op. 6, VI

Of the ($b\flat$-based) ninth-chord which begins the second measure, it is to be noted that, among the twelve various chords which can be built from minor- and major-thirds, this is the only one which exactly typifies the tonal-order under discussion. Neither in major nor in the harmonic-minor is there any scalar chord whose construction includes an augmented-triad above a diminished-triad. It is this very ninth-chord which belongs among those which are the most Kodály-like.

The final chord of *Ex. 191* permits a glance into the third possible (without augmented-second) seven-tone system (heptatonia tertia). In this line, all five major-seconds are contiguous and the two half-steps are joined one next to the other:

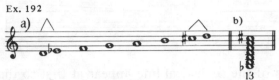

The final chord of *Ex. 191* contains all seven members of this third tonal-order. It is represented one chromatic half-step higher in *Ex. 192 b.*

This chord can now lead us to the group of

Thirteenth-chords.[5] Here also it is comprised of a natural (acoustical) agglomeration:

Although the ninth-tone *c* is missing, we do not really feel its absence alongside the repeated eleventh *(e)* and the climatic tone *(g)* made prominent by its accent.

The entire seven-tone chord is brought about in an original manner:

5 The thirteenth-chord is quite exceptional in the Romantic style. The locrian-thirteenth of the *Ossa arida*, one of Liszt's late works, is famous; according to István Szelényi's findings, another such chord occurs in Ferenc Erkel's opera *Dózsa*. Otherwise we are not likely to find many other true thirteenth-chords prior to Debussy.

Ex. 194

Second String Quartet, II

Only five tones of the acoustical line appear at first so that the two primary tones, the reiterated *D-a*, may serve to provide a background. With this cello motive, the thirteenth-chord, in its fifth inversion, becomes complete.

The seven-member chord of the Epitaph *(a)* builds further on the recently mentioned most typical five-member chord (see *Ex. 191* and the pertinent remarks preceding it):

Ex. 195

Seven Piano Pieces, Op. 11, IV

Symphony, II

Its structure: diminished + augmented + diminished triads.

In the second movement of the symphony, two neighboring thirteenth-chords prepare the recapitulation, the upper *(A)* and the enharmonically adjusted *(G)* leading-tones preceding the g♯ tonic *(Ex. 195 b)*.

Let us listen to one more example from one of Kodály's larger works:

Ex. 196

Honvéd Parad March

The *A-kuruc* scale has taken shape around the dominant of *d*-melodic minor. (We even hear the Rákóczi-motive in meas. 19.) The *G*-based eleventh- and thirteenth-chords precede the central-tone *A*. Of interest is the chordal intensification beginning in the second measure: after the triad, seventh-, ninth- and eleventh-chords, the thirteenth-chord appears once again, so that it may provide a new light for the *A*-triad of the fourth measure.

Changing-chords. Several simultaneous changing-tones may generally bring about changing-chords in two ways:

a) the changing-chord may be used as an independent element within a given style (*e.g.* the I–VII⁷–I chord-pair);

b) the changing-chord is essentially of a more dissonant type, and arises in a particular piece as the total sum of several changing-tones (for example, in the first movement of Mozart's g-minor Symphony, development section, measures 48, 50 and 52).

In the first type (which we may call "concordant" changing-chords), the chord builds on the vertical, harmonic principle; in the second type (the "discordant" formula), on the horizontal, melodic principle of the voice-leading.

An example of the first type, within our new tonal-system:

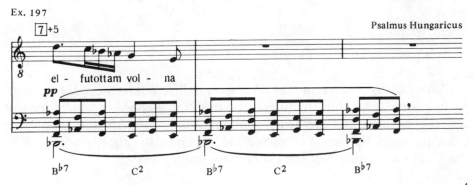

Ex. 197

Psalmus Hungaricus

el - futottam vol - na

pp

B♭7   C²   B♭7   C²   B♭7

in which the figurations of every half-measure alternate the B♭⁷ and C⁴₂ chords in the acoustical scale of the previous key.

In the following excerpt, however, we find several different types. In the second measure, a neighboring-triad alternates with the primary chord. The third measure places a triad of fourths opposite the traditionally constructed triad of thirds—the new chord, in relation to this latter primary chord, may already be understood as a discordant changing-chord. The fourth measure goes even further. In a most succinct manner, the path of the historical development of music opens before us: we be-

187

come accustomed to tones which have previously been foreign dissonances and eventually accept them as consonances. Indeed, the *d-g♯-c♯* fourth-formula was previously a dissonant changing-chord—it now becomes the principal chord which alternates with the even harsher triad of seconds! (These four measures are, from yet another point of view, a splendid example of organic growth: the short tones of the melody appear in the order of a prime, second, third and a fourth distance from the longer main tones.)

Ex. 198

Peacock Variations, XIII

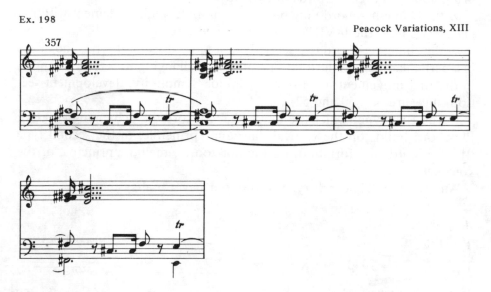

Color-chords. This term may have several different meanings. For now, let us reserve it for that treatment of a traditional chord in which one (or more) changing-tones are heard sounding *simultaneously* along with the principal tone. By means of such added seconds, the chords which paint the "sad murmuring" of the boughs are more expressive:

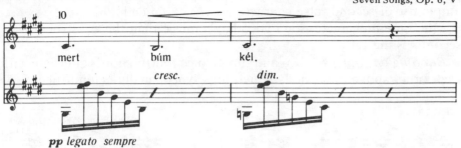

The lowering of the $g\sharp$ to g, that is to say Kodály's diminished-fifth aeolian (to which we have referred several times), helps to intensify the melancholy atmosphere.

The sound is more penetrating when the changing-tone appears in the proximity of a half-step instead of a major-second, as does this f below the $g\flat$:

Ex. 200   Violoncello Sonata movement (1909).

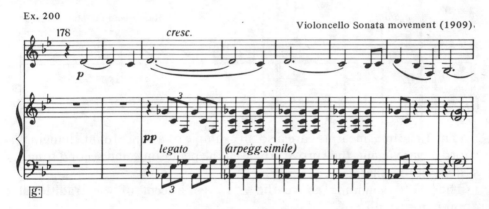

The example is also worthy of our consideration for other reasons. Before the melody arrives at the g finalis, it traverses the tones $d, c, b\flat$ and f. To this the accompaniment adds the $e\flat$ and the $g\flat$ as well as the $A\flat$ root, and behold: in place of the g-pentatonic, the $A\flat$-acoustical scale now prevails.

We have already met with an f attaching itself to the e of the A-major triad in the Gypsy Tune *(Ex. 32)*.

These harmonies, colored by added seconds, may now lead us to the next area, the group of

Agglomerations (clusters) of seconds. Our very first example quoted the Mountain Nights, in which the opening *f-g-a-b* diatonic cluster was ex-

189

panded to the *f-g-a-b-c♯* five-tone cluster at the end of the piece. An ample use of seconds also characterizes *Exs. 206* and *207*.

Much more characteristic of Kodály's music than the construction by seconds is the

Building on fourths. Two- and three-voice fourth-chords alternate with each other above the melody which jogs syncopatedly behind them:

Ex. 201

Nine Piano Pieces, Op. 3, VI

A four-voice fourth-chord is the resting point of the *agitato* measures:

Ex. 202

agitato

Hungarian Folk Music, VII, 37

(The first three measures are also an example of a concordant changing-chord.) Once again, they prove how well the pentatonic and second tonal-system fit together.

The chord sounding above the *B* is reminiscent of the traditional dominant-seventh:

Ex. 203

Te Deum of
Sándor Sík

Hungarian Folk Music, VIII, 45

a)

b)

Há - la lé - gyen!

Egy - gyik teszen,

e: VII   V   I

f♯ :

a: IV   II   V

190

but the penetrating *e* which remains in place of the *d#*-third creates the pentatonic *f#-b-e-a* chord in the first inversion.

Ex. 203 b shows an example of a five-member fourth-chord. Uniquely, the augmented- and diminished-fourths present a profile of the second tonal system.

Composed music arising from a folksong—how much do these few measures from Opus 1 (!) tell us about these oft used words:

Ex. 204

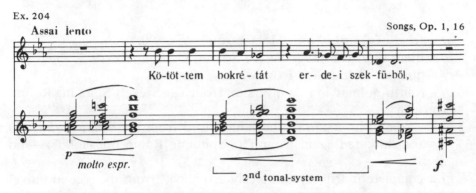

The text is folk poetry, the melody is the composer's own, but folk-like. But being folk-like, it also relates to the pentatonic. Even though the melody itself only in its later lines becomes purely pentatonic—the harmonies here at the beginning of the movement already point to it. And in two ways: the descant of the accompaniment surrounds the motives of the melody with the *g-c-f*, then the *f-bb-eb* and finally the *eb-ab-db(=c#)* fourth-leaps—at the same time, at the point of separation between the pair of motives, under the "nothing" of the brief rest in the melody, stand the "everything" of the complete pentatonic five-member chord of fourths. The third and fourth measures belong in their entirety to the *Ma* tonal-order (see *Exs. 68* and *74–85*). The other chords of this excerpt belong to one or another acoustical scale.

The pentatonic agglomeration of perfect fourths may only be quoted in relation to our discussion when *their surrounding* implants them into the second tonal-system (as we have seen in *Exs. 201–204*.) There are, however, fourth-chords which *in themselves* already point to this. In order for this to occur, the characteristic intervals of the system are necessary: the diminished- and augmented-fourths. A small collection of such intervals:

Ex. 205

a)   b)   c)   d)   e)   f)   g)

a) a triad of fourths from Molnár Anna *(Ex. 48)*

b) a quatrad of fourths from the Second Quartet *(Ex. 4)*

c) a quintad of fourths—from which is formed

d) a fourth-quintad in first inversion from The Székely Spinning Room, measure 985

e) the second inversion of the same chord from the Psalmus *(Ex. 39)*

f) a fourth-sextad again from The Spinning Room (meas. 987)—and finally:

g) a complete fourth-septad, freely arranged,[6] from the second movement of the Second Quartet (two measures before rehearsal-number 3).

To close this series we have a lovely summarizing example in which the melody sings its lament below chords built on thirds, seconds and fourths, as well as color-chords of mixed intervals:

Ex. 206

Woe is Me (women's choir)

g: (original in g♯)

Meg - ha - lok, megha - lok,   még be -teg

6 If we should need to know how to arrange classical triads and seventh-chords in three closed and three open positions, that is in six different ways—the six upper voices of one thirteenth-chord may be permutated in 720 ways. Together with its inversions, one single such chord presents 5040 variants! (We may be thankful that nowhere is this required study material...)

192

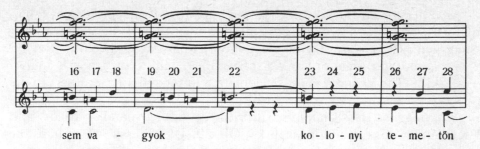

sem va - gyok   ko - lo - nyi   te - me - tõn

(The profound effect made on the composer by his first folksong collecting excursion to the Zobor area is revealing in that he arranged this melody in one of the most poetic works of his early years, the Two Folksongs from Zobor—and also in one of his latest works, the more recent chorus for women's voices quoted above.)

Nineteen different types of chords, and common to each one is the *g-a-f* ternion. Arranged in order according to the number of voices:

Ex. 207

Their importance of course varies according to the type of accent they receive. On the primary accents at the beginning of a measure we hear the

h) quatrad of seconds,—the

m) and *n)* quintad of thirds,—the

p) pentatonic quintad (a quatrad with an additional fourth for coloration),—and finally the

s) and *t)* quintad of seconds.

On the secondary accents of the first several four-quarter measures we hear the

l) color-chord,—the

r) pentatonic quintad,—and the

t) five-voice agglomeration of seconds.

The others, even though they are only unstressed passing- or changing-chords, are deserving of analytic attention because of the slow tempo—but then again also for the sake of a more exhaustive study of the Kodály-style and of our tonal-order. We entrust the details to the reader's analytical skill. (The *k)* and *l)* chords belong to a lower system, the others to the *G-kuruc* scale.)

Mixtures. After Chopin's surprisingly daring parallel triads and seventh-chords (c♯-minor Mazurka, Op. 30, 4), Debussy was perhaps the first to establish the system of mixtures, the parallelism of all voices, hitherto appearing only occasionally. Since that time virtually all composers have availed themselves of this device.

In relation to our subject and to Kodály's music, let us first examine the seventh-chords of our tonal-system:

Ex. 208

The uniqueness of the acoustical line (and of its other six modes, of course) is striking in that there are two dominant-sounding (but only very rarely having a dominant function) seventh-chords on two neighboring degrees. In the above series, the exact same type of chord is built on both the *C* and the *D*. The chords on the *E*- and *F*♯-degrees are likewise both of the same type. (From this point on, we may refer to the latter as *ti*-seventh- and to the former as *So*-seventh-chords. These designations do not describe their functions within a scale, but merely the quality of their sonority.)

These chord-pairs often appear in Kodály's works in a mixture-type relation.

Root-position *So*-seventh-chords:

Ex. 209   Four Songs, 4   Hungarian Folk Music, X, 55

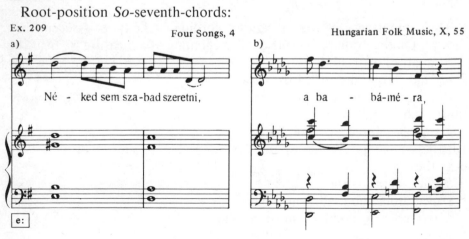

The dark *F-* and *E♭*-seventh-chords, set beneath the melody, sing of death:

Ex. 210

Media Vita

ne | tra- das nos, | a- ma - rae |mor- tis ne | tra- das nos

A:

The line of mixtures is also enlarged through the use of a chord of another type, the yet darker and more penetrating *D♭*-seventh-chord. Is this mere chance? No. We find it set most purposefully under the main word of the sentence: do not deliver us unto bitter *death.* – Chords of *b♭*-minor below an *a*-minor melody... We have already referred to the tone-painting effect. Technically speaking, what makes this combined structure possible? The fact that the four tones of the melody, the *f-g-a-c* tetratonic formula is commonly shared by both *a*-minor and *b♭*-melodic minor:

Ex. 211

The chords of the *D* tonic and the subtonium *C* degree alternate in a sometimes tighter, sometimes looser mixture:

Ex. 212

Organ Mass, Ite missa est

195

The same two chords, their roles reversed:

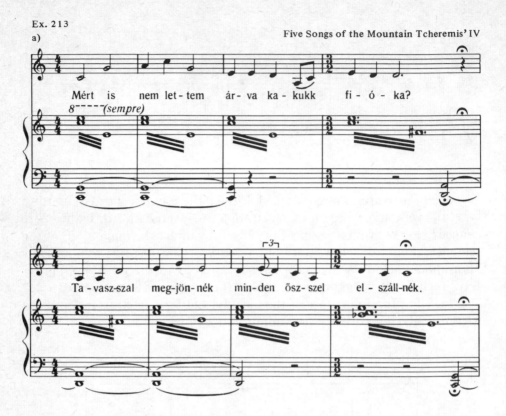

Ex. 213
a)
Five Songs of the Mountain Tcheremis' IV

Mért is nem let-tem ár-va ka-kukk fi-ó-ka?

Ta-vasz-szal meg-jön-nék min-den ősz-szel el-száll-nék.

Now the *C* is the tonic and the *D* the neighboring-degree. The bourdon-fifths of the bass alone represent the mixtures. This partial mixture is combined with the high, tremolo *(c-e)* resting-tones of the piano. In this way the chord on the II degree expands to become the *D-f♯-a-c-e* ninth-chord. — The example is instructive from another point of view. If we established (with *Ex. 54*) that our second tonal-system makes possible the fourth (new-type, not characteristic of our folk music) means of filling in the pentatonic gaps:

La – Do Re Mi – So
La ta Do Re Mi fi So

(we called it a neapolitan dorian)—then it is clear that the other pentatonic modes may also be accorded such individual, most uncustomary types of coloration. Kodály's procedure *(Ex. 213)* attests to this. Let us place this *fi* and *ta* into the *Do*-pentatonic line:

b)

and we have attained the acoustical line which builds on the major-pentatonic. (We may formulate this relation as it exists within the system: just as the upper relative tonality of the natural minor is the major-scale, within the second seven-tone system the upper relative of the neapolitan dorian is the acoustical-scale.)

The two neighboring *So*-seventh-chords need not of course always follow each other exclusively in root-positions. Mixtures in first-inversion:

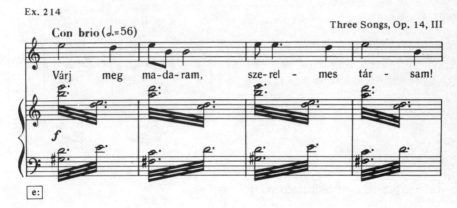

Ex. 214

Con brio (♩.=56)

Three Songs, Op. 14, III

Várj meg ma-da-ram, sze-rel - mes tár - sam!

f

e:

Neighboring $\frac{4}{3}$-chords:

Ex. 215   Czinka Panna (unpublished opera), No. 8

appassionato, con moto

8

ff

Of the many additional examples, let us select but one more. In the orchestral setting of the ballad Kádár Kata (see also H. F. M., Vol. IV, 18) we arrive at a folksong line with the text "Talála egy olá ficsurt" (meas. 37–38). This motive moves along the dorian pentatonic common among the melodies of the Székely people, but the orchestra, following immediately with the sound of a shepherd-pipe—how appropriate!—in the acoustical tonality, graphically depicts the "olá ficsur" (= Roumanian dandy).[7] The order of key-structure and chords: the folksong line is heard in $d\flat$-dorian—the melody of the shepherd-pipe sounds in the $D\flat$-acoustical. This is supported first by the $E\flat$-g-$b\flat$-$d\flat$ seventh-chord and then, by means of a mixture-type slide, the $D\flat$-f-$a\flat$-$c\flat$ seventh-chord. (The piano version of the piece is more modest as it lacks the mixture-type chord-motion.)

Mixtures of ti-seventh-chords. We have seen in *Ex. 208* that the second seven-tone system also defines two neighboring *ti*-seventh-chords one whole-step distant from each other. Let us examine a few examples of these chords in a mixture-type relation:

Ex. 216

Háry János, No. 14   Hungarian Folk Music, IV, 17

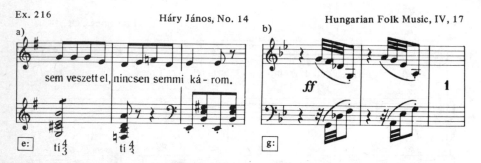

Showing an ingenious relation of keys:

Ex. 217

The Székely Spinning Room

In a section leaning toward *e*-melodic minor, the *d♯*-based chord alternates with the *c♯*-*e*-*g*-*b* seventh-chord. The very same *c♯*-seventh chord may, however, also be used (at the end of the excerpt) to lead back to the principal key of *G*-major as the subdominant raised IV degree of this latter tonality.

We may profitably turn the *pair of designations real-tonal* toward a fuller description of the mixtures. With the term *real* we designate the

7 It is commonly held that Bartók also may have become partial to this scale through Roumanian instrumental folk music.

exact (maintaining the same coloration also) transfer of the formula to another degree as we have done in our examples until now *(209–217)*. By *tonal* we mean those mixtures which remain within the tonality and which therefore change their coloration.[8]

With tonal fidelity, the $\frac{6}{3}$-chords of *a*-melodic minor line up above the organ point:

Ex. 218

Vejnemöjnen Makes Music

Légben szárnyon kik röpültek, lá-bok ujjá-ra le-ül-nek.

Even the high *e*, soaring in the air (= "légben szárnyaló"), trills with the *f*♯ of the scale rather than with the *f*. Tonal $\frac{6}{4}$-mixtures in the major-third *e*-aeolian:

Ex. 219

Minuetto serio

(trumpet)

e:

8 There are borderline cases in which both designations may be applied to the mixtures. For example, the *So⁷-So⁷* and *Ti⁷-Ti⁷* chord-pair types remain within the second seven-tone system and are therefore *tonal*. But, since the chords of each pair are faithful copies of each other, they are also *real*. This also holds true in the diatonic system for the *Fa* and *So* triads and for the mixture of the *re* and *mi* seventh-chords. However, these are the rarer exceptions and are confined to a narrow area.

199

A newer group is presented by those examples in which it is not the two neighboring-chords that *jointly* define the tonality, but rather it is the pattern-type of the mixture line which belongs to our tonal-system. Thus, for example:

Ex. 220   Hungarian Folk Music, VII, 38

Acoustical chords in first inversion, the character of lamentation stressed by precisely the most characteristic chord-tone, the augmented-eleventh.

A similar structure, but with a lively rhythmic character:

Ex. 221   Hungarian Folk Music, V, 30

The stationary tones of the melody are still somehow in motion: they assume a different role in each succeeding chord. (The fourth measure already transforms the figuration: the brief *d♯* changing-tone does not belong to the *C* acoustical scale.)

Fully the same mixtures of acoustical chords, but now in an ascending order:

Dö-göl-tesd meg a ser-té-sit, jaj,   jajjaj,   jajjaj,   jaj!

The *C*- and *D*b-based chords here concisely complement the complaining repeated *g*-tones.

Sequences. A discussion of sequences could follow that of the mixtures. Indeed, it is not at all certain that we could draw an entirely exact dividing-line between the two. There may be some who might place the last two examples under this latest heading because of the figuration making the chords appear more active. Others would say: in these examples we are only dealing with one or another displacement of a single chord. However, we will certainly agree that the following excerpt, because of the pentatonic motive in the lower voice, already belongs within the area of sequences:

Minden ma-dár   tár-sat   vá - laszt.

To this line (seemingly in *A*-lydian) of the *f*♯-dorian melody are added tiny bird-motives built first on *e*-melodic minor and then on *d*-melodic minor. In both cases the diatony of the melody and the pentatony of the accom-

paniment are woven into an organic unity, and their total sum: the heptatonia secunda.

A multiple sequence of a repeated progression:

Ex. 224   First String Quartet, III

In the first measures, two seventh-chords of the diminished-fifth aeolian
on *f*♯ are set beneath the fourths of the pentatonic melody. The arsis-like
swing of the *f*♯-*g*♯ steps in the lower voice carries through to the *a*. The
minor-third sequences are brought about in this way. The end of the series
fulfills the "axis"-principle: it leads to an acoustical theme of
E♭-tonality.

A more complex interweaving:

Ex. 225   Dances of Galánta

In the second and fourth measures of the melody we find a descending
sequence of thirds. The accompaniment, however, does not follow this order rigidly. In contrast to the downward minor-third shift of the melodic
pattern, the harmonies are raised a minor-third upward.

An even newer manner of creating sequences:

202

The harmony remains constant (only in its construction does it expand upwardly)—but above it the melody is sequenced. Our tonal-system creates the possibility for the $B\flat$-harmony to accommodate the *a -g-f* trichord of the first measure in the same manner as the *f-e-d* trichord of the third (actually already of the second) measure. The two trichords shown as part of the acoustical line:

Ex. 227

Let us take leave of this discussion of sequences with two truly rich examples.

The first describes vividly the song of wandering with a motive of sadly trudging steps:

Ex. 228   Hungarian Folk Music, VIII, 46

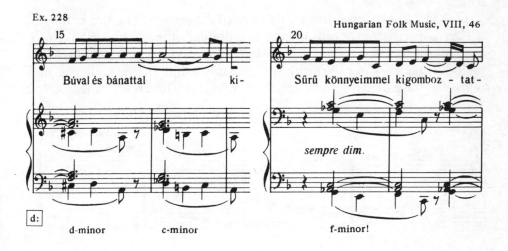

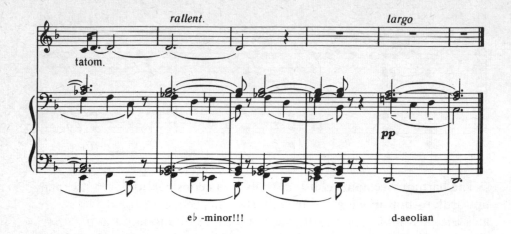

eb -minor!!!   *d-aeolian*

It is wortwhile to analyze how the accompanying motive of *d*-minor, *c*-minor, then *f*-minor and *eb*-minor character fits throughout beneath the melody built around a pentatonic core and always under a complete "tonal roof." The darkening order of the descending sequences expresses with ever increasing intensity the mood of the melody, a mood laden with grief and contrition (= *búval és bánattal*). And the closing! If formerly it was expected that the accompaniment provide the leading-tone motion (this is also the case here, but in the descending relation of *eb*-minor and *d*-minor)—now the *harmonic role* of the final melodic tone assumes responsibility for this connection: at first it is the leading tone (the *d* above the *eb*) and then, without its having moved anywhere, it becomes the tonic.

In the Peacock Variations we find one of the greatest bravura examples. We have space here for only a schematic presentation. If, beneath the melody of the previous excerpt, we were able to observe four different melodic-minors—now, beneath the pentatonic line of the flute, we may marvel at the collection of no less than eight (!) different acoustical scales:

Ex. 229   Peacock Variations, XIV

2meas. 380   384.   388.   392.

(a szegény raboknak...)

394.   396.   398.   400.

In the upper line we have sketched the pillar-tones of the decorative flute lines—beneath are the harmonizing scales. (The harp glissandos do actually fill out the ninth- and eleventh-chords with the complete seven-tone lines.) The harmonizing scales are in general built on the acoustical base. The exceptions are measures 392 and 396 in which the fourth mode (or inversion) of the *C*- and *B♭*-based lines respectively are built into the series. The bass tones indicated by the whole notes in the lower line cast light on Kodály's characteristic method of harmonization: he readily employs equally both the older authentic fourth-fifth relation and the logic of the descending scale: the cadential steps (*B♭-E♭-A♭*) join together the first three harmonies of the excerpt—the chromatic scale then takes over, leading with unmistakable determination from the *f♯* down to the final goal, the *d*-tonic.

Modulation. Just as Kodály shows great artistry in his harmonic procedures, he is likewise a great master of extraordinarily varied modulations. While we could cite many pertinent examples in our second tonal-system, we must be content with only a few:

Ex. 230   Háry János, No. 22

A kvár - té - lyon   mu - la-to-zik,   nyer a menyecs - kék - től!

e: C-acoustical   E-"kuruc"

Here, a simple common chord leads from *C* to *E*. The *D-f♯-a-c* seventh-chord on the second degree of the *C*-acoustical line is at the same time the VII degree of the *E-kuruc*-type key to which we are aiming.

The same type of overlapping structures:

Ex. 231

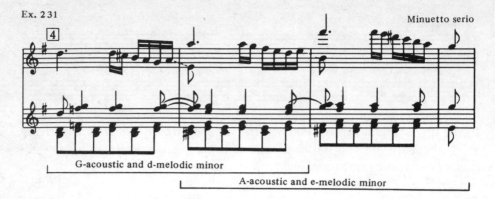

G-acoustic and d-melodic minor

A-acoustic and e-melodic minor

We arrive here at *e*-melodic minor by way of the *G*- and *A*-based acoustical areas.

A five-tone formula binds together the major-third *G*-aeolian of Var. VIII to the *d*-dorian of Var. IX:

Ex. 232   Peacock Variations (VIII–IX)

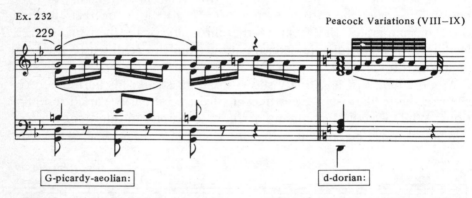

G-picardy-aeolian: d-dorian:

The ingenuity of this procedure: the clarinet figuration of *d-f-a-b-c* becomes *one single* chord in the new key—in the previous key, the very same five tones decorated the alternation of *two* chords, one on *F* and one on *G*. In other words, while the sixteenth-note figure was reinforcing the *G*-tonality for the past eight measures—at the same time, due to the stubborn repetition we slowly perceive: the principal key is after all still *D*!

By means of an enharmonic modulation, a single acoustical chord bridges the eight-fifth distance between *F*-major and *C♯*-major. After a preceding section in *F*-major, the voices lean over toward *D:*

206

Ex. 233

The stationary chord describing the evening quietude slowly accumulates all the tone of the *D-f♯-a-c-e-g♯-b* thirteenth-chord. The *g♯* of the melody —as does the sun sinking beneath the horizon—dips into the bass, so that from the *D*-eleventh it becomes the dominant of *C♯*-major. We seem to hear the enharmonic relation even across the rest: the long-sustained *c* (the dominant of the preceding *F*-major) finally takes on the meaning of *b♯*, as the leading-tone of *C♯*. The external world darkens, and now unexpectedly the brightness of seven sharps? Oh, but this is now the inner light "heard by the soul."

This type of relation (descending *D* leading-tone to *C♯*) is quite common among Kodály's modulations arising from the tonal-order which we are discussing. In the third movement of the Concerto, a long-sustained *G*-thirteenth chord leads back to the *f♯* tonality of the principal theme (measures 256–259). In the third movement of the First Quartet (before rehearsal number 4), a *B*-acoustical chord, sounding across four measures, resolves to a *B♭*-mixolydian. Of further examples from the larger works, we present yet one more:

Ex. 234

Duo, Op. 7, III

Quite unique! If we do not add a sixth member, the *c♯*, to the *G-b-d-f-a* ninth-chord—the more we repeat this chord, the more we wish to hear the *C*-harmony as its natural resolution. However, the moment we add the eleventh partial, the penetrating $c\#$—please play this chord repeatedly on the piano—the resolution to $F\#$ (whether to the major, or to the somewhat paler minor) becomes all the more natural. It is as if this glaring $c\#$ would take over the role of the dominant: it attracts the $F\#$ as the G attracts the C. (Among other things, we also have here a unification of the functional equivalency of tones a tritone distant from one another.) In such a case there is always a role played by the enharmonic relation, as in the c-$b\#$ voice of *Ex. 233*. In *Ex. 234*, the f above the G takes on the meaning of $e\#$—the dominant form of the lower four tones *(G-b-d-f)* then assumes the meaning of an augmented-$\frac{6}{5}$ chord. (See *Exs. 173* and *174*).

This acoustical chord, resolving downward by half-step, is moreover a direct descendant of the Romantic "neapolitan" (or "phrygian") dominants. Let us but think of the downward-straining C-basses in the b-minor of Schubert's *Doppelgänger*. Illustrated in the common-tonality:

Ex. 235

The $\frac{6}{5}$-chord on the VII degree, a characteristic Schubertian coloration, "activates" the bass inasmuch as it intensifies the functional relation with the $b\flat$-a leading-tone motion in place of the neutral b-a motion *(Ex. 235 a)*. The augmented-$\frac{6}{5}$ in our illustration always assumes the form of a dominant-seventh *(Ex. 235 b)*. On occasion, Liszt already extends this chord to the ninth *(Ex. 235 c)*. In the modulations which we have quoted from Kodály's works, this chord is logically then further enriched with a sixth *(Ex. 235 d)* and sometimes even a seventh member.

In place of a common chord, sometimes even a *common* interval is sufficient:

Ex. 236

208

The end of the trio section dies away in *c*-melodic minor. The two *most distant* tones of this scale, the repeatedly proffered *a* and *b (fi* and *si)*—become re-illuminated as the two *nearest* members of the returning *A*-major. After the muted light of the three-flat area, the three sharps sparkle brilliantly.

In the same manner, two tones, the *e-d* minor-seventh, join together three different acoustical keys:

Ex. 237   First String Quartet, Op. 2, II

the *f♯* is common to both the *C* and *E* tonalities (it has a featured role in measures 2-3!)—beside the *f♯*, the *g♯* and *b* are common to the *E* and *D* tonalities and also strengthen the static solidity of the *e-d* double weight-bearing axes:

Ex. 238

This last example may also serve as a "modulating common chord" leading to the last section of our discussion. Let us re-examine *Ex. 137.* Each of its measures all but fits into the whole-tone scale well. (That the entire excerpt does not in the overall belong to this area but rather to our second tonal-system is decided by the *a-g-d* and *f♯-e-b* ternions of measures 2 and 4 respectively.)

The whole-tone scale and its relation to the second seven-tone system. We have already indicated in the diagram of *Ex. 54* how closely our unique tonal-system stands in comparison to the scale built exclusively of major-seconds. Kodály stressed this fact many times in his music. Beside *Ex. 237,* let us also present a few excerpts from this rich source of material. Immediately, in a piano piece of his early period:

Ex. 239   Nine Piano Pieces, Op. 3, I

The melody expressively features a whole-tone section of *a*-melodic minor, and it is only the subsequent fifths which confirm the presence of a seven-tone system. The whole-tone character is stressed even more emphatically in the recapitulation *(b).* Three thirds of the *E*-acoustical scale appearing within an *e*-dorian frame paint the night descending upon the Mátra forests:

Ex. 240   Mátra Pictures

These lines, which cast shadows upon the light of the diatonic, excellently prepare the following stanza: The time is turning to evening (*Esteledik…*).

If we have just seen, in a modest way, the day turning to twilight—similar major-thirds can also describe, with a broader sweep, the decline of the year from autumn to winter:

210

The lonely flute solo, poetically fitting for this verse inspired by an ancient Greek vocabulary and rhythm (Asclepiadean), immediately creates, at the opening of the piece, the appropriate atmosphere.

Major-seconds derived from the pentatonic melody (the quarter-notes with tenuto) and segments of the whole-tone scale repeated over and over:

Ex. 242   Seven Piano Pieces, Op. 11, 4

while finally, all of this comes down to rest on the $c\sharp$ root-tone of the "neapolitan dorian" scale. (This is a grouping of the three elements which we observed in the diagram of *Ex. 54*.)

And should this group of tones not also be a fitting hommage to the memory of Debussy? At the end of the piece dedicated to the French master, our own composer stresses the two whole-tone ternions which change the coloration of the C-scale to that of the major-minor:

Ex. 243   Meditation

in order to reconcile, with reiterated mixtures, the six- and seven-tone systems.

An opposition and a fusion into unity:

211

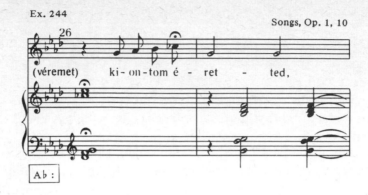

Ex. 244

Songs, Op. 1, 10

(véremet) ki- on -tom é - ret - ted,

Ab :

The piano sounds a whole-tone five-member chord—the voice on the other hand sings along the most typical diminished-fourth of the minor mode. The two together present the *ab*-melodic minor, as if it were the *minore* of the principal key. (The continuing syncopated chords belong to both *ab*-minor and *Ab*-major.)

The displacement, as a changing-note, of one single tone is capable of leading us from pure diatony to a pure whole-tone system. This may be observed in the following example:

Ex. 245

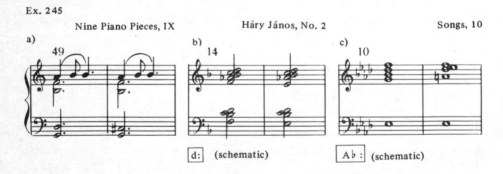

Nine Piano Pieces, IX   Háry János, No. 2   Songs, 10

a)

b)

d: (schematic)

c)

Ab : (schematic)

If but one voice should move, the *d* of the diatonic ninth-chord to the *c♯*: immediately the quality is changed completely, and all within the very same *G*-acoustical frame *(Ex. 245 a)*. The displacement may also occur in the bass *(b)*, or may be combined with a somewhat free regrouping of voices *(c)*.

Diatony and the Debussy-scale may be combined in yet another way:

212

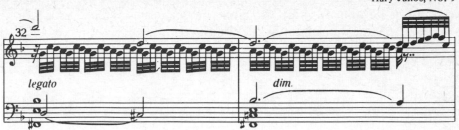

Háry János, No. 9

The Transdanubian third of *d*-aeolian: the *f*♯ bass supports—availing ourselves of Ernő Lendvai's term—omega-formulas in the first half of both measures.

This type of hexatonic grouping may also be heard within a heptatonic frame (here marking the end of a section):

Ex. 247

Two Folksongs from Zobor, I

In this instance, the *f*♯-phrygian becomes a diminished-fifth aeolian—out of this comes the four member *g*♯-*c*-*e*-*f*♯ omega-chord.

The last piece of the Mountain Nights makes ample use of such combinations:

Ex. 248

b)

Mountain Nights, V

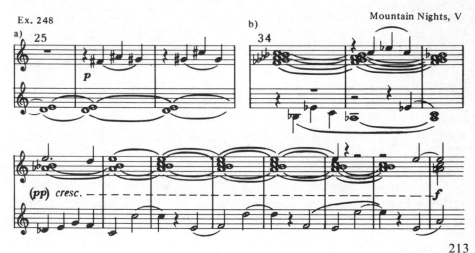

The perfect-fourths and half-step movements indicate the prevailingly whole-step formulas whithin the circle of our tonal-system.

One of the most substantial examples:

Ex. 249

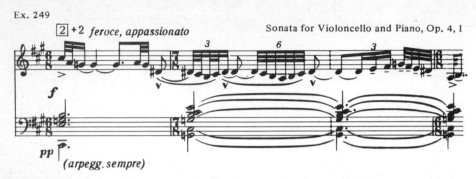

Sonata for Violoncello and Piano, Op. 4, I

Here it is the *e*, concealed in the harmonies and the passionate melody, which provides a seven-tone brace to the otherwise purely whole-tone section.

By way of farewell, let us present one last relevant and symbolically appropriate example:

Ex. 250

Seven Piano Pieces, Op. 11, 6

The theme of the piece is the Transylvanian pentatonic melody: *Az hol én elmegyek* (= There to where I go). The *forte* diminished-fifth renders plaintive the chords of the coda. (Here the characteristic ninth-chord is an augmented-triad above a diminished triad. See *Ex. 192* and the comments about this illustration.) Leaving aside the third of the chord, the *d*, the tones *B-f-a-c♯* provide a motivation for the upper voice to complete the whole-tone line with *d♯* and *g*. D and *d♯* at the same time? The song tells us: "Even the trees are weeping..." (Or perhaps the eastern Transylvania and the western Transdanubia join hands with these two types of thirds?...) A Hungarian musician of Western culture meditates—but about what? He meditates on an Eastern melody. Then let the folksong have the final

214

word, that it may proclaim, as did the composer in his speech and in his writing: "Hold the virtues of the people in high esteem, for if you wish to go further, it is only upon this that you may build."

A closing word. In the course of our discussion, two questions may perhaps have occurred to the reader:

1. Has this study not exaggerated the significance of the generally, and in truth lesser excerpts we have cited by having drawn them into the circle of examination dealing with tonal-orders? Well, in the vast ocean which is Bach's music, we find only a few dozen subdominants of augmented-sixth type. Do we therefore have the right, in an exposition of his style, not to speak of them? With Kodály's music, we may safely declare that the tonalities, melodies and chords which we have discussed are a hundredfold more significant. (It was rather painful to leave off citing from the multitude of additional examples!)—Furthermore: we have stressed repeatedly that "*beside* the many other elements: pentatony, diatony, chromaticism, whole-tone system, etc., the colorations of this second seven-tone system also belong to Kodály's musical language." The examples have sufficiently verified that we have truly been speaking of "Kodályian" melodies and harmonies. Moreover: in the case of pentatony etc., every musician in general knows, and can read enough material, about it. But we must own that the tonal-system which we have discussed, along with its modes and harmonies, has until now been accorded a truly harsh fate. And this is the case in regard to our educational curricula, our professional literature, and the general knowledge of our musicians.

2. Did the composer *consciously* use this tonal-system with its seven modes and with the many different tonalities of each of these latter?

We think not. To great creative minds, it is granted that their thoughts "just simply come" without any premeditation. It is certain, however, that, in most creative work, awareness carries inspiration through to completion. But if we may know only the least amount or—primarily in the case of the old composers—not even anything at all regarding the secrets of their creative work habits, ought we to foresake the study of their works? It would be easy to do so, but it would leave us then barren as well. Let us rather follow the old admonition:

Do not ever tire of further study!

(Magyar Zene, VI [1962], I–III [1963]
Budapest)

KODÁLY: THE 333 READING EXERCISES

For the teaching of rhythm and melody—the two most fundamental elements of music—Kodály's 333 Reading Exercises are an unequalled treasure placed into the hands of the teacher. (If only more pedagogues would avail themselves to a greater extent of this opportunity!) But this little book has great value and richness in another less conspicuous regard as well. György Tegzes has called to my attention that in the area of form as well these are excellent preparatory exercises for understanding folk music. And truly they are! We find here approximately twenty (!) form-types—and each one relates to the structure of Hungarian folksong.

I FORMS

We may consider these small forms as falling into four principal groups: *a)* children's songs, *b)* the old style, *c)* the new style, *d)* other constructions.*

TYPES OF CHILDREN'S SONGS
Three types of order are observable in the compiling of two-measured motives: note-for-note repetition, variation, new elements. Nor is it rare that in the second half of a melody two motives are built together into a four-measure melodic line by virtue of the open-closed line-end order. Immediately among the very first bi-chord melodies we find for example:

---

* The currently-used edition, half in solfa- and half in staff-notation (Zeneműkiadó, Budapest, 1974), serves as the basis for this discussion. Tegzes also indicates the following printing errors: the first note of no. 117 is not *d* but *e*; the rhythm of no. 149, meas. 2 is not ti-ti ta but ta ti-ti; the final quarter-note of no. 261 is not *d* but *e*; the time-signature of no. 324 is not 2/2 but 4/4; lastly the numeral 3 indicating tripodic phrasing is missing in places over nos. 15, 196, 249 and 295.

Ex. 1

closed   *closed*   *open*   *closed*

For more detailed study we further suggest nos. 5, 7, 16, 17, 19, 39, 85, 161, 233, 237, 238, 256 and 268. No. 214 (Itthon-e a gazda?) has a unique dialogue structure and is the volume's only piece with text.

ANCIENT HUNGARIAN FOLKSONG PROTOTYPES
In this realm belong two principal types of our folksongs: the recitativo and the under-set descending line.

Recitativo (do-re-mi) melodies: In itself the *d-r-m* is not purely Hungarian nor is it a feature of the old style only—it is rather an international element for beginning a melody. It is characteristically ours when, despite the initial feeling of major tonality, its final tone is *la*. Of such a type are nos. 51, 144, 152, 159, 176 and 202.

Descending melody. Characteristic of this pure, ancient form is the lower fifth-change. With extraordinary bravura our composer was able to create this kind of tiny melody from a mere tetratonic formula:

Ex. 2

333/75

Examples of richer formulas: 266, 291, 310, 319, 314, 332 and 333.

The under-set line sometimes occurs not at the fifth but at the fourth. (See for example Kodály–Vargyas: A magyar népzene, nos. 5, 179, 302, 329 and 348.) This less frequent type is represented by exercise 52, 201, 304 and 321.

There is a characteristic Tcheremis-type melody in which the second line already descends to the level of the final tone—the second half of the song then remains in the lower half of the octave. (See Kodály op. cit., p. 26 in the 1971 edition, p. 15 in earlier editions.) Of such a type are nos. 86, 290 and 313 ("lesser fifth-change").

The exact under-set line is sometimes loosened by a variant thereby creating a *freely falling* octave line. Relevant examples: nos. 283, 288, 289, 294, 312, 324 and 329.

The melody descends altogether within one pentachord—in no. 149— reminiscent of our funeral laments. (In a humorous guise: Kodály: Gypsy Lament.)

217

THE NEW HUNGARIAN FOLKSONG STYLE

In these exercises Kodály thought of all four variants of the recurring structures.

AA^5A^5A—the simplest, single-element folksong form. In our little collection: nos. 189, 277, 280, 299, 315, 316 and 320. Variants of the line may occur here as they may in each of our categories. The variation may be so strong that it may not even be possible to determine whether the given line is the variant of a former or is to be considered as new material. Such for example is no. 331.

AA^5BA—Here it is as if the third line, after much variation, had arrived at the point where we must perceive it as a new element. Examples from the volume: 285, 317 and 330.—In nos. 90 and 282 the second line is only a fourth higher and the final line strongly varied.

$ABBA$—According to Bartók's findings the most purely Hungarian conformation having no equivalent among the melodies of either related or neighboring peoples nor within the realm of art music. (This form, due to its perfect bridge-symmetry, was obviously close to Bartók's heart. See Mikrokosmos, Vol. V, 127.) In the "333" nos. 73, 120, 186, 267 and 328 are examples of this type.

$AABA$—Perhaps the most frequently-found type among our living folk music of today. The value of this construction: the reinforcement of the opening idea, then something new (occurring in the area of the golden section), finally a rounding-off with the recapitulation. The main object of an analysis is perhaps the third line: in what way different, in what way new, how does it relate to the outer lines? In our exercise book a rather significant group: nos. 4 (bravura on two tones!), 30, 41, 59, 63, 65, 69, 70, 88, 103, 110, 112, 125, 128, 129, 155, 200, 235, 292, 295 and 296.

The bisected third line. It is not a rare occurrence in our folk music for the third line, in contrast to the larger arcs of the outer lines, to be divided into two smaller units. In schematic form: AAbbA or AAbbC. In our little collection: nos. 34, 81, 127, 150, 193-197 and 200. If the two elements of the third line are each equal in length to the outer lines, we may perhaps consider the song to have five lines. But even in this case the third and fourth lines are obviously quite closely related to one another. The content is more important than the dimension. Kodály used this melody as his pattern in the "333" for no. 109.

OTHER CONSTRUCTIONS

$AABB$—Remarkably many (43!) examples are given for us to practice this doubly repeated form. We may suppose the oldest form to be that in which the repetition does not change a single tone: A = A, B = B. Such are nos. 91, 124 and 217. In the others the A = A, B B$_v$ formula comes into play: the two lines of the second half-melody in a period type open-close relation are welded into a larger unit. The major-pentatonic melody of no. 326 has an old style, freely under-set line.

AABC—An even richer group than the previous: 51 examples which build a third, new element into the end of the little song. It is almost a compositional tour de force to achieve all this from only three different tones. But our great magician also knows how to do this: nos. 29, 40, 43 and 55. We can appreciate the fine art of the variation in those melodies in which the last *(C)* line bears a somewhat veiled relation to the beginning *(A)* line, showing a transition from the AABA to the AABC form. Such are nos. 98, 104 and 300. Elsewhere there lies hidden a certain measure of connection between lines *A* and *B*, as for example in no. 181.—In nos. 84 and 250 the second line does not appear in its expected place but rather at a higher position.

ABBC—No. 275 is characterized by its two identical middle lines. With its octave descent it is reminiscent of the old style folksongs. The others— nos. 66, 67, 184, 203 and 210—are narrow-range melodies with an ambitus of 5–6 tones, reminding us of one sub-group of a mixed class which occurs in our folk music.

Organic melodies—It is only with some difficulty that we may use a let- tered formula to describe that type of melody in which every line springs from the same seed but appears always with slight differences. Such an or- ganic structure unites the $A^1A^2A^3A^4$ formula with the $AB^aC^aD^a$ formula. For this type, which is pedagogically quite useful precisely because of the slight differences, we also have examples: nos. 9 and 10 each having two motives, and nos. 15, 89, 113, 151, 167, 170 and 247 which have four el- ements each. Whoever is fond of analyzing will find published herein examples of the most widely differing devices of organic variation (one or another type of inversion, narrowing or widening of intervals, etc.).

"Libidári" songs—Original and delightful songs in which the playful "libidári"-type nonsense-syllables interrupt the flow of the text. These are actually two-line melodies in which the second line receives an internal ex- tension. The internal extension is sometimes achieved by means of re- peated words rather than by nonsense syllables. No. 276, with its own asymmetrical 2 + 4 measure proportion, is patterned after this type.

Ungaresca—It has its own peculiar formula: ab, ab, aa, b. In this case each letter does not necessarily imply absolute melodic identity, but may also refer to a rhythmic or other connection between those lines indicated by the same letter. We may also consider this seven-motive form as having four lines with a short Sapphic-type final line. But on the basis of the relation of elements *a* and *b* it may be taken as a three-line form: ab, ab, aab—with an extended third line. The functional indications of the form say more than the letter designations: open-closed, open-closed, open-open, closed. The ungaresca melodies of the "333": 106, 115, 119, 131, 158, 205, 230, 234 and 254.

Responsorium form—The formula ABCB describes a well-known group of Gregorian melodies. In these so-called responsoria there is a repeat which pertains not to the first but rather to the second musical thought. (We may call them internal refrains.) Once again another Kodály wonder: he is able to create such a form from a mere two tones:

Ex. 3 333/8

No. 18 is equally modest. We then list in order of increasing sets of tones nos. 26, 35, 82, 96, 105, 111, 116, 139, 156, 164, 192, 215, 216, 245 and 255. It is surprising that in comparison to the richness of our folk music this responsorium form is proportionally rare. Our classical example is the theme of Kodály's Gopher-flooding. (Why do we so seldom hear this lively, colorful little work?)—In no. 313 this form coincides with the already mentioned (descending-octave first half-melody) characteristic Mari melody-type.

Melodies in period form—Although the principle of an open-closed musical unit (eight measures in its basic form) occurs internationally, our own folk music also provides interesting examples of it. It is not necessary that we always think of borrowing from foreign sources, for surely the basic principle (arsis-thesis, inhalation-exhalation, departure-arrival etc.) arises from general human phenomena. But when do we consider that a folksong, otherwise seen as a four-line structure, is in period form? We do so when the two-part division is stronger than the four-line demarcations. In other words: when the second and fourth lines cadence more strongly than do the first and third lines. While it is true that there are such melodies among our ancient fifth-changing songs, let us not draw these "Eastern periodic forms" into this circle. They have their own well-known category. In Kodály's little volume the first little exercise is at once such a miniature masterpiece;

half cadence   full cadence

in which the composer, using only two tones, achieves the periodicity with a mirror inversion of the first half-melody. As there are no less than 71 (!) exercises belonging to this group, we shall not list them. Whoever wishes to do so will easily find them. (The most numerous form-type of the volume.) We mention only one or two special cases. No. 14, 271 and 284 are comprised of six motives instead of four. No. 182 is an asymmetrical period dividing into $4+3$, $2+3$ measures. We sing extended half-melodies in nos. 76, 154, 257 and 259 which each have tripodic motives. Entirely tripodic are nos. 251 and 262. We find an amalgamation of period and responsorium forms in no. 209: the refrain is open at first and closed only at the end.

A type of small period also exists among our examples. Here instead of $4+4$ measures, we find $2+2$ measures in a period relation with each other. Nos. 23, 272 and 273 are extended small periods with three measures each in their antecedent and consequent phrases.

Two-part form—In this type of melody two related periods produce the complete form. Our folk music has few of these. The extent of them in the "333" are the typically "regular" 16-measure exercises: nos. 13, 144, 147, 173, 202, 228, 246, 270, 286, 293, 297, 306 and 327.—A narrowed $6+6$ measure is found in nos. 60, 175, 177 and 249.—No. 174 with its AB'CB'' formula shows a relation with the responsorium form.

Lesser three-part form—This term designates the more intricate form which we know from the Ode to Joy of Beethoven's Ninth Symphony. Its formula is $a^1a^2ba^2$. It differs from the very frequent AABA type of our folksongs in that the first two lines are not exact repeats of each other, but instead create an open-closed period. The opinion of analysts is divided. There are those who say: if there are 16 measures, then it is two-part. Others maintain: yes, but the recapitulation provides a three-part experience. Here again: the content is more important than the dimensions. An exact description: the dimensions are indeed two-part but the content three-part = lesser three-part form.—A rarity among our folksongs. But there are well-known examples of it: in Bartók's For Children series Vol. I, 37. Proportionally there are nevertheless rather many examples in the "333": nos. 146, 176, 239, 287 and 303. An extended form is no. 311 with its $12+12$ measures, a narrowed form no. 101 with $6+6$ measures, an asymmetrical form no. 135 with $6+5$ measures.

If one examines the formal elements of the "333" he will be taken all the way from children's ditties to Beethoven. The same may be done with our folk music. Kodály helps us in this endeavor with his 333 Reading Exercises.

II OTHER ELEMENTS

1 MELODIC RESEMBLANCES

A number of exercises, to a greater or lesser degree, bear a clear resemblance to specific melodies of our folksongs. These exercises listed in order: 60, 156, 164, 169, 275, 280, 287, 306, 328, 329, 330.
(For other examples see section *7, Kodály Elements*.)

The wider range and more unusual handling of the pentatony in nos. 332 and 333 indicate a closer relation of these exercises to Mari melodies. (See Bicinia Hungarica, Vol. IV.)

2 ACUTE PENTATONY

Today, as the result of my struggling for many years, the recognition of two other types of pentatony beside the natural *(s-m-r-d-l$_1$)*, one being the "obtuse" with *fa* in place of *mi*, the other the "acute" pentatony with *ti* in place of *do*, has begun to spread:

Ex. 5

obtuse pentatony   acute pentatony

In accordance with the latter, Kodály himself marked the melody of Bic. I, 29 (28 in the newer incomplete edition):

Ex. 6

(The second half of the melody is set exactly at the lower fifth, beginning on *re* and ending on *la*.)

Nowhere in the "333" does this question arise. The given set of tones

222

always remains in the natural pentatony. However, if one has the time, means and courage, he may occasionally attempt to bring to light the acute pentatony in those melodies in which the prime-reiteration (the exposed role of steps 1-5, 8-5, or 1-lower 5) suggests a *la* base, there may still arise within them a second or ninth degree *ti*. Such for example is no. 141:

Ex. 7

333/141

Other such examples are nos. 60, 62, 153, 154, 183, 279, 328, 329 and 330. We may begin each of these with *la* with the exception of no. 279 in which the first measure is *mi-mi-la-la*.

3 UNPREPARED FINALIS

Among our folksongs and other ancient melodies, instances occur in which the melodic closing-tone appears only at the very end of the line without having had any tonal preparation or reinforcement as antecedent. Compositionally a rather enigmatic type: in what way does such a melody make us believe that we have actually reached the end? A well-known folksong example:

Ex. 8

Such are the following "333" exercises: nos. 72, 151, 152, 159, 167, 174, 275, 278, 281, 288, 289 and 329. In these the *la* is the finalis. With *do*-ending: 252, 264 and 265. Finally *so*-endings also occur in nos. 307 and 312.

4 THE CONFINALIS

In old melodies—in Gregorian, folksongs and others as well—it sometimes occurs that the final tone is not the one which the course of the melody would lead us to except, but rather the fifth above that tone. This tone has been designated by older theoreticians as the confinalis. An example from our own country:

Por- ka ha - vak   e – se –dez-nek, de hó ré - me,   ró – ma

There are a considerably large number of such melodies among our children's songs occurring as rudimentary formulas yet with no tonal close.

Kodály has this very type in mind in exercise no. 227. The melody is a major-pentaton on *D,* but still does not end on the expected *d* tone but rather at the fifth above on the *a.*

5 HARMONIC ANSWER

In addition to many other devices, our folk music—and along with it the music of our composer—shows its richness in that, beside the commonly-known traditional real and tonal answers, it is also capable of yet several different ways of giving an answer at the lower or upper fifth or fourth respectively (i. e. at approximately a half-octave distance). Into this area falls the type which we may call the "harmonic" answer. Here the principal tones of the answer are altered in such a way that together with the opposite part of the theme they may merge into an imagined major or minor-triad. Using exercise no. 286 as an illustration:

Ex. 10

a)   b)   c)

real answer   a tonal answer   Kodály's harmonic answer

The first measures of Kodály's solution *c)* form a *d*-minor triad.

6 TONAL KEY-SIGNATURES

There are four main types of key-signatures:

a) No key-signature, the composers writing in the necessary accidental separately in each instance. This practice is found in those pieces of the newer music in which the tonality has been greatly extended or entirely done away with. (Liszt however already employed this technique!)

b) We may refer to a key-signature as being "real" when only those sharps or flats appear which are strictly necessary without regard to traditional key designations. (Such a key-signature does not indicate the solmization—for this we assume rather a knowledge of the specific tones involved.)

c) A third way: other accidentals—sometimes more, sometimes fewer—appear in the key-signature than are necessary and by means of inner accidentals indicate those tones of the melody which do not conform to the original indication. There are two sub-varieties of this procedure:

A proper use occurs when such a key-signature simplifies the (solmization-based) tonal orientation. For example the method initiated by Pál Járdányi which recommends solmization of our dorian melodies on a *la* base with *fi* as the sixth degree. In this case we write for example a signature of one b-flat for a melody in *d*-dorian and indicate with a natural sign that the sixth scale-tone is not *fa* but rather *fi*. It is a useful, logical solution:

Ex. 11

This method is improper when it has no value. We see here and there for example *c*-aeolian melodies with a key signature of two flats and an *a♭* accidental written each time before every sixth degree tone. Or a *b*-phrygian with a signature of two sharps and a natural sign before every *c* tone. A thoughtless, useless procedure.

d) A fourth way: the tonal key-signature. This term is used to describe that type which indicates the frame of the key with the traditional signature—even if one or another of the tones indicated in that signature is missing from the melody. For instance the Ode to Joy of Beethoven's Ninth Symphony is written in *D*-major with a signature of two sharps, even though the tone *c♯* does not occur in the melody. But the two sharps—besides conforming to the composer's style of notation—clearly establish the *D* = *do* base, and include the *c♯* which may be necessary for the further possible development of the melody or which is hidden or implied in the harmonies.

In present day editions it is common practice for example that a *d*-based minor-pentatonic melody be printed with no key-signature, "since the *b♭* tone obviously does not occur." True. But then how does the student just beginning to read staff notation know where the *do* is? Well then, let us write it in. But when the student's repertory of melodies is later extended

225

and he meets with a *d*-based minor hexachord in singing, must we not then write a *b*♭ in the key-signature? Why do we not accustom the student to this earlier? Why should he not learn the "one flat = *F-do*" notation, which he will later put to use, at the time when he makes his general acquaintance with music?

Kodály saw further than many editors of today. In the "333"—especially in the first half of the volume—he employs the useful tonal key-signature with surprising frequency:

One sharp appears at the beginning of the *G* = *do* pentatonic melodies nos. 303. 305 and 317—for the *D* = *so* (mixolydian character) exercises nos. 300, 301, 304, 306, 307, 309, 312, 315, 316 and 322—and for the *e* = *la* minor-pentatonic examples nos. 282, 285, 291, 299 and 302. And yet in none of these does an *f*♯ occur!

Exercises 326 and 327 in major-pentatonic on a *D* = *do* base have a key-signature of two sharps, as do the *b* = *la* minor-pentatonic examples nos 278, 281, 290, 296, 331, 332 and 333. And yet there is no *c*♯ to be found in them!

Exercise no. 231 in *C* = *so* pentatonic has one flat as a key-signature—as do a significant list of *d*-based minor-pentatonic exercises: nos. 275, 276, 277, 280, 283, 284, 286, 287, 288, 289, 292, 293, 294, 297, 310, 311, 313, 314, 318, 319, 320, 323, 324 and finally 328. And yet in none of these is there a *b*♭!

A key-signature of three flats gives a *c*-minor appearance to no. 298, and is also found in the *E*♭-major-pentatonic exercises nos. 271, 272, 273 and 274. In none of these does the tone *a*♭ occur!

This detailed listing should serve to induce *the authors of our textbooks to use tonal key-signatures in the future as often as possible!* Reiterating our point of view: *a)* it renders the *do* placement clearer and unambiguous, and *b)* it nurtures a connection with general musical knowledge. If the student is soon to meet with a key-signature of one flat in a melody of Bach or Mozart, why should it not be long previously known to him that in such a case *F* is the *do*?

7 ELEMENTS OF KODÁLY'S WORKS

We may unmistakably recognize in one or another exercise a link (whether unintentional or purposeful—at this point who knows?) with the composer's other works. Thus for example:

the beginning rhythm of nos. 87, 122 and 123 is identical with the characteristically small-unit rhythms of the choral works God's Blacksmith, Hippity, Hoppity and the trio in The Straw Guy;

the melodic turns of the main motive of no. 221 call to mind measures

226

42–45 of Mole's Marriage and also the beginning of the main theme of the Psalmus Hungaricus;

no. 43 is almost a quotation of the Viennese Musical Clock from the stagework Háry János;

no. 79 is reminiscent of the beginning of the Song of Peace. In rhythm diminution the line of no. 80 is also the same;

no. 276 is, as it were, a preparation for the children's chorus Jó gazd'asszony;

the beginning of no. 235 is reminiscent of the lovely second theme of the Whitsuntide;

the play of dynamics in nos. 23 and 229 (forte measures interrupting quieter motives) repeats the effect used in Bicinia Hungarica I, 13;

nos. 318 and 319 are variants of the "Peacock" melody which was so close to Kodály's heart.

And finally a more significant group. In the final movement of our composer's Second String Quartet this melody, with an engaging trio-effect, sounds forth:

Ex. 12

Variants of this melody may be found in the Corpus Musicae Popularis Hungaricae Vol. III, nos 223–226. From this it appears that Kodály already met with these tunes in the years 1906–1907 during his first folksong collecting excursions. That this melody affected him deeply is shown by the fact that eleven years later he incorporated it into the above-mentioned chamber work. (Furthermore, the theme of Bartók's children's chorus "Only Tell Me!" is also a relative of this melody!) Finally, to our surprise, we may see in the following pieces of the "333" the depth at which this melody remained with Kodály: nos. 59, 63, 146, 172, 192, 203—and more modestly still in nos. 145, 165, 166, 210 and 211 as well.

8 PERIOD FORM

Immediately, during one of the first classes of our first year of study (1921–1922), our *maître* explained to us that for the motive period there are fifteen variants possible from the $a_1a_2a_3a_4$ structure to the richest *abcd* type in which each motive presents new material. He did not give a detailed illustration—he thrusted us to discover the variants for ourselves. (Finishing the lesson, he began to leave, and from the half-opened door turned and said: "Then write down innumerable such instances—or at least a good number of them!") We do not give a detailed list here of the surprisingly many structures of period-melodies of our little volume, rather—following the Professor's example—we entrust this to those who are interested. But at the time of compiling these I had the distinct feeling that with these many types of periods—even after 20 years—he himself giving the solution to his assignment of long ago: the greatest possible richness attainable within the modest eight measures.

"The sixth measure." During one of our composition classes, our professor made a remark to the effect that among certain eight-measure periods of Beethoven the climax appears in the sixth measure. (At that time the concept of the golden section was not current in musical circles. Today, however we know that such a construction bisects the period in a unique way into 5 + 3 measures, that is according to the measure of the golden section.) Well, the "333" also offers examples of such periods: nos. 89, 114, 125 and 240.

9 AMBITUS

In closing, let us examine the range of these exercises. The following illustration clearly shows with what pedagogic consciousness the composer put together his book. He follows the old, well-tried methodological principle: let us progress from the simplest to the more complex. He begins with sing-song-like exercises of two tones. Then step-by-step he extends the set of tones, arriving at one and one-half octaves: the undezime, the duodezime. But he remains always within the pure anhemitonic pentatonic system, the basic system of the traditional Hungarian folksong.

The individual types in order with the number of exercises in each group, and with the appropriate tonal key-signatures:

Ex. 13

228

Conspicuous is the group comprising the melodies nos. 56–139: 84 pieces, full one-quarter of the volume belongs to this section! The reason: this tetratonic formula is outstandingly characteristic of our old folk melodies. Such for example is Kodály's musical motto known throughout the world:

Ex. 14

Föl- szál-lott a   pá- va

(Ének-zene tanítás V–VI [1974]
Budapest)

THE MODUS LOCRICUS
IN THE WORKS OF ZOLTÁN KODÁLY

A "SORROWFUL" TONALITY

I — Introduction. The music of ancient Greece furnishes the earliest information about our own diatonic tonalities. The conception of that era, as we know, was not one of octave-scales, but rather of tetrachords. An octave-line was achieved only by placing one tetrachord either above or below another.

In ancient Greek music, it was possible to create the scale which we now call the locrian (*ti*-ending) in two different ways. Either as the plagal form of the dorian mode (building upon the tone which today we call *e*), as is shown in the second scale of the following illustration:

Ex. 1

basic scale (ancient dorian)   hypodorian   (Terpandrosian)

or by making use of the later-appearing *b♭*, as may be seen in the last example of our illustration. (This arrangement of tones has been attributed to Terpandros.) The first and then the two latter examples of the illustration make clear the two different means by which the tetrachords may be joined. There is either a whole-tone distance between them (*diazeugmenon* = "disjunct" or separated), or they meet on a common tone (*synemmenon* = "hooked" or joined together).

This scale continues to exist in Gregorian music and is found in some folk music. But the burgeoning European polyphony did not know how to deal with it. The basic element of this later style is without doubt the perfect-fifth. In the locrian scale, however, the primary interval of response, the distance between the first and fifth degrees, is "out of tune."

The Romantic era—primarily the music of Liszt—in rare instances makes use of a musical element which may be called locrian. We find such practice somewhat more frequently in the works of Debussy. But the truly great master of this (until then) nearly unknown scale—is Kodály. It is with surprising frequency and variety that he makes use of those unique elements which the locrian makes possible.

230

I must first ask forgiveness if the title of this essay appears to be misleading: we will not always be speaking of the *entire* locrian scale. Under consideration rather will be those passages of Kodály's music which, characteristic of the locrian mode, will be granted such an identity by the diminished-fifth. The degrees of this phenomenon:

a) one or another single tone,
b) one or another characteristic interval,
c) one or another pertinent chord,
d) a longer melodic section or chordal motion based on the above three,
e) an appearance of the entire scale—and finally
f) an entire composition in locrian tonality.

The relation of each tone to its surrounding—merely with regard to its position only—may be judged in two ways. We may examine it "horizontally," that is in a succession of tones (melody), and we may examine it "vertically," within a simultaneity (harmonic):

Ex. 2

mel.   harm.

These co-ordinates of time and place are already present in the early polyphony of European music, as when harmonic *ta-fa* fifth or fourth appears beside the ancient *ta-la* melodic motion.

These two aspects are both found rather abundantly in Kodály's music.

The frequency with which Kodály employs the lowered fifth degree is especially interesting—at least to those of us who studied under him—in that at the time (in 1921) he emphatically stated over and over again: the fifth degree of the classical scale does not descend with a downward chromatic motion! Instead, it is always found as a raised fourth degree. The proper notation in major is thus:

Ex. 3

The situation is even more interesting in minor where the *ti-ta* motion alone corresponds to the direction of the alterations:

Ex. 4

231

Kodály turns the unique qualities of the locrian line to advantage in two ways:

a) as a structural device,

b) to depict and/or express a mood.

(In some examples these two phenomena appear together.) This duality corresponds to external and internal, form and content, technique and thought, physical and spiritual, or to other similar pairs of concepts.

STRUCTURE

Let us begin our series of examples with those excerpts in which Kodály's structural-compositional strength is revealed—through the utilization of some locrian element.

II — The relation of the scale to the principal key. The occasional appearances of the locrian scale may be organically built into the principal key in three ways. The characteristic lowered fifth degree may appear as:

a) the upper minor-third of the upper minor-third (= RR, the upper relative of the upper relative),

b) the neapolitan tone of the primary subdominant degree (= NS, melodic relation),

c) the subdominant of the neapolitan tone (= SN, harmonic relation). As a formula:

Ex. 5

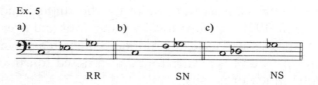

The minor-third of the minor-third (RR). It is relatively rare among the Kodály examples that the characteristic locrian tone is built into the basic key as the upper relative tone of the upper relative scale. This type of axis-principle structure may be observed in the song which begins:

Ex. 6   Three Songs, Op. 14, II

Jaj,   csak ha-lál - ra kè -szül-tém   Ér   ted, óh én   ár -va fe - jem.

We are in *d*-aeolian. Based on a pattern established by certain of our folk-songs, the mid-point cadence comes to rest on the *do* (here the *F*) of the relative major. In the above example, however, the quality of the second melodic line is not *F*-major, but rather *f*-minor. The organic relation may thus be described by the following letter-names: *d-F-f-a♭*. In other words, this striking *a♭* is the minor-third in the *minore* of the major relative-key of the principal tonality:

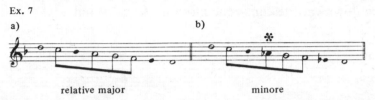

Ex. 7
a)   b)

relative major   minore

We have been speaking here of a single locrian melody-tone only. The following excerpt from a large orchestral work already shows the tonal terraces more completely:

Ex. 8   Summer Evening

pp

D   (schematic)

The variant of *D*-major is *d*-minor, whose relative key is *F*-major. The horns play their line—even though with mixolydian coloration—in this latter key. As their motive, however, does not reach to the *a*, we may therefore also perceive the first two measures as having an *f*-minor quality. Thus may appear, without the slightest awkwardness, after the conceivable *f*-minor, its relative *A♭* tonality. At this point, the English horn and the violas take up the play of the motive. A schematic illustration of the key relations showing the principal pentachords:

Ex. 9

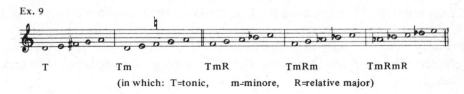

T   Tm   TmR   TmRm   TmRmR
(in which: T=tonic,   m=minore,   R=relative major)

233

The neapolitan tone of the subdominant (NS). The composer much more frequently uses the locrian fifth as the upper changing-tone of the fourth degree. This signifies, at the same time, a truly strong, active leading-tone motion: the lowered fifth degree is drawn to the fourth degree. Let us here touch on the question of "links." In our traditional tonal-system, the three strongest ways in which neighbor tones or chords may be joined are:

   a) the leading-tone motion (upwards),
   b) the cadential fifth (fourth) relation of the primary tones,
   c) the downward leading-tone motion. As a formula:

Ex. 10

melodic attraction   harmonic attraction   the "third link"

The first already occurs within the old monody. The second, the bass line of the V–I degrees, comes into general use beginning in the fifteenth century (Dufay bass). The "third link," the half-tone flexa, is proportionately the least common. Although the *fa-mi* and later the *ta-la* melodic motion is present in old single-voice music—, the others (*e. g.* the ♭*ma-re,* ♭*la-so,* ♭*ra-do* within the major) are, however, in use only from the time of the Baroque. The relation of the lowered fifth and the fourth degree, which is characteristic of the locrian line—as a permanent stylistic trait—is entirely missing from the great styles of the past (see illustrations 3 and 4).

And then comes Kodály!... Even the little first-year violin student is given a taste of this "strange" sound:

Ex. 11   Chamber-music Study

The brilliance of the composer-pedagogue! The child need only practice placing his first finger on the open string, and immediately he may become accustomed to the phrygian, or, indeed, to the locrian sound. (This small etude was prepared for the Gábriel–Vásárhelyi violin method-book.)

In an inner voice. It is not exclusively necessary for the locrian half-step to appear in the bass in order to insure that two chords hold together solidly. The $g_♭$-*f* motion in the right-hand voice accomplishes this task nicely:

234

Ex. 12

(Az alföldi csárdában)

Hungarian Folk Music, XI, 61

c)

At times, with only the mere inclusion of a passing eighth-note, the diminished-fifth may give the required coloration to the passage in question:

Ex. 13

The Forgotten Song of Balassi

g-phrygian

Féreg rág (= The worm eats away)... Try only replacing each *d♭* of the second measure with a *d:* the effect is gone.

Similarly, above another *g-phrygian* melody (sounding in the bass), we perceive a mood of bitterness because of the *d-flats* which surround the bar-line:

Ex. 14

Czinka Panna (unpublished opera), No. 14

g-phrygian

Even sixteenth-notes may provide this effect:

Ex. 15

Czinka Panna (unpublished opera), No. 8

a-phrygian

How commonplace this excerpt would be with an *e* replacing each of the *e-flats!*

In the following example, the alto voice of the accompaniment contains this locrian link ($a\flat$-*g*) within a line of "wandering $^6_4$-chords" which our composer favored so greatly:

Ex. 16

Epigrams, 7

From the upper voices, we are able to pick out the entire locrian line: *d-c-b♭-a♭-g-f-e♭-D.*

A similar excerpt in a setting for women's voices, a song filled with profound lamentation:

Ex. 17

Orphan am I

f♯-dorian Szi-vem ket - tė ha-sadt vol - na

236

Here also it is an inner voice which signs the lowered fifth step *(c')*, progressing toward the IV degree with both functional and kinetic energy.

One of the most surprising effects occurs when the very first harmony of the Lament *(Siratóének)* begins with the locrian coloration. In context of *c*-minor, the tenor enters with the darkened *g♭* in place of the primary-tone *g:*

Ex. 18   Dirge

The inner voices mourn the dead with all the intervals of pain, the descending half-steps: *g♭-f, d♭-c, e♭-d.* The same occurs likewise in the subsequent motive.

In the bass. The strength of the locrian relation intensifies when the leading-tone motion appears in the lowest voice.

We find such tonal links even among the earliest of the folksong settings:

Ex. 19   Bartók—Kodály: 20 Hungarian Folksongs, 11

(In this chapter, the roman numerals written beneath the bass do not indicate the true root-tones of the chords; they merely show the scale-degrees of the bass voice.) The composer perceived the locrian as standing in a close relation to the phrygian. We may, incidentally, in this brief excerpt also marvel at the extraordinarily creative (anti-Romantic) nature of our composer's method of harmonization. Taking the bass-line movements of *Ex. 19* in order: *F♯-G* melodic attraction, *G-C* harmonic link, *C-B* leading-tone motion, *B-E* again a cadential fifth. Only at the end is there the subtonal (attaining the finalis from the lower major-second) *E-F♯* progression which derives from the phrygian. (The "third link" occurs here in the melody: *f♯-g.*)

237

The first stanza of the melody has been heard. The accompaniment continues the further weaving of the harmonies:

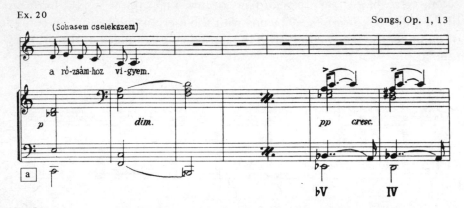

Ex. 20

(Sohasem cselekszem)

Songs, Op. 1, 13

The impetus of the fourth-fifth connections continues on to the root-position neapolitan chord *(Bb)* and then from there to the locrian *Eb*. This latter is in turn, with the force of a leading-tone, drawn to the subdominant *D* bass. (The links here are quite strong!)

The same type of harmonic construction, seemingly solidified by reinforced concrete, also characterizes this excerpt:

Ex. 21

5 Tantum ergo, No. 1

Praestet fi-des supple - mentum Sensu - um de -fe-ctu - i,   Sensu - um de -fe-ctu - i.

In the bass: at first fifths and fourths, then leading-tone motion. Also present among these is the relevant *Gb-F* locrian progression.

Emphasis is given the lowered fifth degree by a special stress when it occurs as the peak-tone of an arc-shaped voice (here the alto):

Ex. 22

A   bV   IV

How fresh and vivid the otherwise indifferent *a* melody-tone has become!

The diminished-fifth may likewise also be heard as a peak-tone and indeed with a truly eloquent, dynamic character. From quiet surroundings a sudden burst of energy, with a *sforzatissimo* the seventh-ninth chord on the V degree of the locrian scale emerges in such a way that the music may then once again quiet down. The bass-line, depicted schematically:

Ex. 23   Hungarian Folk Music, V, 25

c♯-phrygian   bV   IV

This is from the setting of the song *Magos kősziklának* (= Amid the High Rocky Peaks).

In the following example, a significantly prolonged locrian lowered V degree prepares the *A-E* plagal cadence which closes the piece:

Ex. 24   Communion anthem

e   bV   IV

The fourth stanza of the *Magos kősziklának...* begins with a curse (*Verje meg az Isten* = May God strike him):

Ex. 25

Hungarian Folk Music, V, 25

Here also, the diminished-fifth, the *g* in *c♯*, accompanies the harsh text.

The downward leaning bass is suitably set under the *diminuendo* at the close of the piece:

Ex. 26

Nine Piano Pieces, Op. 3, IV

Also related to the previous example is the following section of the Kölcsey-melody (*Búsan csörög a lomb* = Sadly Murmurs the Bough). Paralleling the words of the poem (languishing from the heat, which passes through = "mely átfut"), the bass also "languishes." In an exceptional manner, the locrian *G* here sounds more important that its resolution, the brief and unstressed *F♯*. (The *b♯* changing-tone of the melody comes into a special relation with the *G* bass—in no way do we perceive a *G-c* perfect fourth.)

240

Seven Songs, Op. 6, V

The locrian motion allies itself with surprising frequency to those of Kodály's pieces which are in the *D* tonality. We have already heard the *ab-g* step-wise movement in *Exs. 11* and *16*. Further examples:

Ex. 28

Duo, Op. 7, III

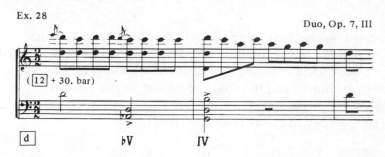

In the version of the Hymn to St. Stephen written for smaller mixed choir, the *Ab* harmony plays a structural role as well. One after the other, the two lines of the melody come down to rest on the same *d* finalis:

Ex. 29

Hymn to St. Stephen

A hidden danger: the twice-occurring close on the *la* could easily rigidify and tear the musical continuity to shreds. But Kodály is "on the alert": beneath the first tonic (in the third measure of our excerpt) he places the most dynamic chord of the section, the chord built on the lowered V degree, so that not for a moment do we feel that the melody has come to an end.

A well-known section is the harmonic progression evoking the image of the immense area of the great Temple depicted by the half-notes, in themselves more restful:

Ex. 30

Jesus and the Traders

(True enough, at that time there was still no organ in the temples. But perhaps, for the sake of the listener of today, the composer was thinking of some type of association which is achieved when the mixtures, the opulently ringing chords, call to mind the sound of the organ.)

In place of a single chord, a tonal area four measures long represents the locrian polarity of the *G* tonality, the *D♭*:

Ex. 31

Organ Mass, Credo

The principal *G*-major tonality is finally achieved by means of the *C*, and with the motion of the "Hungarian fourth".

Let us continue with some more modest examples. In one of the later folksong arrangements of our composer, the very first measures of the -piano accompaniment already sound the *A♭-G* connection within the *d* tonality:

242

Ex. 32

Is it only that Kodály wished to render the *D*-based tonality—already so prevalent in many of his pieces—more colorful? Or is he immediately, here at the beginning of the song, anticipating the later mood: "the leaves fall into the sea"?

Varied types of triads appear above the pure locrian bass-line:

Ex. 33   Organ Mass, Ite ...

And finally yet one more example in our *D* tonality:

Ex. 34   Peacock Variations

A clear example of an "aiming-harmonization": the accompanying chord is glancing *not upward* to the *d-f-g-c* pentatonic figuration, but instead *ahead* to the arriving *G*-based five-member pentatonic chord. In the meanwhile a great deal is happening with the clashing of the *gb-g* and the other dissonances. The drive toward the target is more important than the link to one or another tone of the melody.

The subdominant of the neapolitan tone (SN). With regard to the locrian lowered fifth degree, this section calls to mind the earliest centuries of our European polyphony:

Ex. 35   Bicinia Hungarica, 120

We are dealing with an *e*-phrygian melody. The *bb* occurs four times in the final measures of the piece—each time as the consonant subdominant of the *f*-tones in the cantus firmus. This is exactly the way in which, during the era of organum, composers had to step outside the bounds of diatony—also characteristic of Gregorian music—and write in the *Ta* of the eight-tone system beneath the *Fa*:

Ex. 36

These chords, from the great chorus on the text of Petőfi, call to mind Liszt's neo-modal triadic chords:

Ex. 37   God's Miracle

The *Cb* appears here as the subdominant of the preceding neapolitan triad *(Gb)*.

244

A-major is the basic tonality of this early, poetically beautiful setting for mixed choir of a poem by Pál Gyulai. The final cadence arrives at the tonic by way of a *B*♭-based neapolitan area:

Ex. 38

Evening

The *e*♭ of the flickering upper voices is thus—in context of the surroundings—a subdominant. The final harmony of the to-the-end ever fainter murmuring (the moment of falling into sleep?) also contains this tone. Then we are left with but the truly final rest: "the arms of a sweet dream (= *álom karjai*) has rocked the soul to sleep".

At the end of the regrettably seldom heard great "Finnish" chorus for women's voices we hear the *B*♭-based neapolitan chord no less than five times. Wedged in between these chords in three places is the respective subdominant, the locrian ninth-chord built one the *E*♭-bass:

Ex. 39

Vejnemöjnen Makes Music

At the end of the movement which satirizes the entrance of Napoleon, the *D*♭ neapolitan bass is preceded by its own subdominant on *G*♭:

Ex. 40   Háry János, No. 17

The same occurs at the end of a movement in the key of *D:*

Ex. 41   Second String Quartet, I

In these last two examples, a plagal progression joins together the lowered V and the IV degrees.

III — Polar cadences. The five hundred year old V–I closing relation is granted a surprising new coloration already in one or two Liszt-cadences where the lowered fifth precedes the tonic. This occurs at the end of the Sonata *(F-B)* and in the *Étude de Concert "Un Sospiro"* *(A♭♭-D♭)*. We find later among Kodály's works examples of this locrian closing-formula used both with greater frequency and more variety. Appearing as concise and simply formed triads:

Ex. 42   Eight Little Duets, 7

Similarly, but with minor chords in the accompaniment of this folk-song:

Ex. 43   Hungarian Folk Music, V, 29

(In both instances, the harmony on the lowered fifth degree appears as a first inversion chord.)

The song *Nausikaa* comes to an end with a *B♭-E* locrian tone-pair:

Ex. 44   Four Songs, 2

Here, the final motive of the song descends from the terpandrosian *b♭* to the *e* finalis.

The Liszt-type pairing of the *F*-major and *B*-major chords closes the tenth stanza of the ballad *Görög Ilona:*

Ex. 45

The Székely Spinning Room

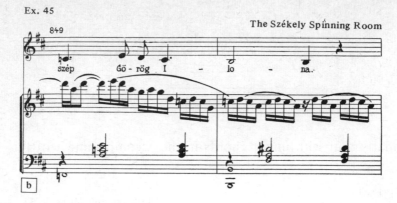

This last excerpt is related to *Ex. 35* inasmuch as here also the *Ta* in the bass forms a perfect-fifth with the *Fa* of the phrygian melody. (Despite the key-signature, this stanza sounds in the one-sharp b-phrygian.)

In the *Ballad of the Ravens*, this relation is more than a unique cadence appearing only once. The introduction to the movement begins in *d*, then slowly slips downward to the *ab*-minor tonal area (shown in our illustration)—and this prepares the *d*-tonality which re-appears in the voice parts:

Ex. 46   Czinka Panna (unpublished opera), No. 21

The pillar chords of the structural frame are thus: *d-ab-d*.
Nor is the locrian line very far from the whole-tone scale:

248

Ex. 47

omega-scale:

locrian scale:

The two scales share a common upper tetrachord in each of which is found the characteristic diminished-fifth (counting from above, the lower tri-tone). We find this type of relation in the beginning of one of Kodály's piano pieces:

Seven Piano Pieces, Op. 11, 5

Ex. 48

The origin of this piece dates from a time (Paris, 1907) close to that of the composer's involvement with Debussy's music. Its opening moves within a pure omega-line, but before these measures may come to rest on the principal *C* harmony, we unexpectedly hear the *g♭-d♭* locrian fourth. This is preceded by the *b♭*—these tones thus together form the *G♭*-major triad which is the polar harmony of *C*.

On the other hand, it is difficult to explain the final accompaniment measures of the folksong *Nekem olyan emberecske kéne... :*

Ex. 49

The Székely Spinning Room

249

The instruments accompany the final line of this Bukovinian melody with some special type of heterophony. In the upper parts are circularly decorative octave parallels, in the bass the lower octaves of the vocal line. But! Why is there a *B♭* instead of an *A* in measure 208? Not necessarily as a definitive explanation, but merely a personal opinion: do we not have in this instance also a verification of the strong structural tendency found in Kodály's bass-lines? The first bass-note of our excerpt, the *F*, attracts cadentially the locrian tone *B♭*. This tone then, by means of the "third link," pulls toward the following *A* of the bass. If the second measure of the quoted excerpt were to continue immediately to the *A* bass, then together with its antecedent it would form the *F-A* plagal-third relation, one of the very weakest progressions. Kodály's solution, on the other hand, creates a doubly reinforced line:

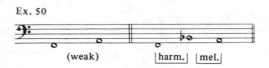

Ex. 50

(weak) |harm.| |mel.|

To conclude this chapter, let us present here one of the most dramatic locrian cadences:

Ex. 51

(Barcsai)   Hungarian Folk Music, IV, 17

Meg-öl - tem Bar - csa- it   's kedves fe - le - sé - gem.

Above the muted, deep *G♭*-chord, the actual subdominant *(g³)* of the principal key trills with its lower changing-tone *f♯³*. Thus both *G♭* and *f♯* sound simultaneously—and not through any error of notation, but quite logically according to the inner integrity of the voice-leading and the chords. Only then is the tonality stabilized by the lone *C* octave. After the *ppp*, a *forte*—the after-throb of horror (the text has just described a husband's murder of his wife).

250

IV — The principle of contrast. Kodály often uses the locrian lowered-fifth degree in such a way that after its darker sonority he may then emphasize all the more the brightness of a subsequent chord. (Indirect emphasis—Rembrandt's dark and light.)

"Days of the past *(Vén idők)* … ," dark *ta* tones, "arise *(ébredj)*:" six fifths higher, the brighter *Mi*-major chord. An effective contrast adequately mirroring the text:

At the time that the Psalmus was premiered, we did not understand why the ordinary subdominant *(E)* of measure 9 sounded with such—almost never-before-heard—brightness:

Of course, the orchestration and the dynamic indications are also a help to this end. But we may not neglect the fact that, immediately before this chord, we hear the locrian ♭V degree, which is seven fifths lower, therefore darker, than the *E*.

The theme of the Violoncello Sonata's second movement begins on *f♯*, the fifth of the *b*-minor-pentatonic (meas. 7.). What could serve better to emphasize this than if, in the introductory measures, the *f♯* is carefully avoided and the *f* is even twice sounded? The beginning of the movement:

251

Adagio

(The second measure demonstrates the SN relation, the fourth measure places the *F-B* polar interval into the melody.)

The *c♭* within an *F* tonality serves to heighten the inner contrast of a small period-type construction:

Ex. 55

Serenade, Op. 12, I

More properly speaking, it is not only this one tone which achieves the effect, but rather the entire *a♭* minor-pentatonic (meas. 3–4) which it represents. A textbook illustration—even if only within four measures—showing the essential character of a period: a questioning, straining, arsis-type first section (*F*-mixolydian), and an answering, relaxing thesis-type second part (a contrasting key with many flats). The last measure of the illustration re-inforces the *F* tonality.

Let us now follow this with three of the most effective examples showing how the locrian serves to provide emphasis through contrast.

In Kodály's great cantata, after figurations in the *G♭* major-pentatonic, the words of the prophet Isaiah's vision burst forth with the power of the cosmos: Sanctus, sanctus... This is sung by the everlasting, eternally-gleaming *C*-major chord:

Ex. 56

Te Deum of Budavár

(schematic)

(The *G♭* group of tones is notated in the score as being in *F♯*, but, because of the preceeding *B♭*-major area, we hear it as *G♭*.)

And finally two excerpts from the variations for large orchestra. The basso ostinato ambles along on darkened tones:

Ex. 57   Peacock Variations

Here, the locrian character is represented by the *a♭* tones. This *b♭-c-b♭-a♭* bass is heard for altogether 30 (!) measures, while the motive above it climbs ever higher. And finally the theme sounds all the more brilliantly and triumphantly in *D*-major:

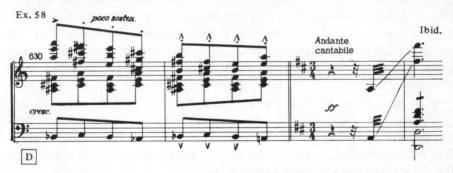

Ex. 58   Ibid.

Furthermore, this entrance of the theme does not begin on the principal *D* tone, but on the third of the *Maggiore*, the *f♯*—thus brighter by four fifths than if it were to have begun on the *D*, as we might have expected.

The other similar occurrence is heard in the very last measures of the piece:

Peacock Variations

Ex. 59

While the locrian area is shorter here than in the previous excerpt, we do find now, in place of the former unstressed eighth-notes, a complete $A\flat$ -major triad sounding in the bright, penetrating tones of the trumpets and trombones. The $a\flat$ tones also occur in the upper figurations. In the fourth-chord passage of the penultimate measure, this locrian lowered-fifth tone occurs likewise in all five voices. The D tonic harmony then breaks forth, and although briefly, still with an effect suitable for ending the piece. Let us examine the complete set of tones belonging to the first six measures of this last example:

Ex. 60

We may clearly see that the tones of the entire neapolitan-major scale assume the role of the pre-finalis. These tones then, supported by the D closing-tone, sketch out the complete locrian scale. Once again, a lesson in the axis principle: if the lowered second degree (the neapolitan tone, chord, scale) pulls toward the tonic, then it clearly has a dominant function.

V — Bitonality. There are examples of Kodály's music in which, for a given tonic, the two types of fifths, the perfect and the diminished, sound not one after another, but simultaneously. These passages have thus a certain bitonal character. This phenomenon occurs for example at the end of the *Trio-Serenade*'s second movement:

Ex. 61   Serenade, Op. 12, II

The two lower instruments have already arrived at the restful, pure C-major triad, but the first violin adds a few gentle sighs with the tones of the parallel locrian scale.

Elsewhere, at the beginning of a movement, we meet with the same g-$g\flat$ tone-pair within C:

These chromatic dissonances have a playful, teasing effect.

The bitonal effect is even more pronounced in the introductory music for this song from the *kuruc* theatre-piece. Following this introduction, the men's voices sing the sorrowful *Őszi harmat után* (After the autumn dew). The beginning of the movement:

Ex. 63

Czinka Panna (unpublished opera),No. 21

The *A♭-do* tone of the upper voice clashes with the fifth of the *D*-based harmony. (We also hear a diminished-octave sounding between the *f♯* and *f*.)

VI — Open strophe-endings. The importance of the locrian passage increases when it appears in a place as important as, for instance, the end of a stanza (or some similarly closed unit). In such places we generally expect to find a static consonance, as the close of an idea would suggest.

In some multiple-stanza forms, Kodály leans toward the idea that, in the interest of the even larger unit, of the entire work, he ought not bring every single verse to a close, but rather, see to the greater continuity. The device which he more than once uses to this end is the relatively dissonant, dynamic locrian sound—for this in turn demands a resolution, and therefore a continuation.

Of this type, for example, is the ending to the first verse of the Kölcsey-song: *Búsan csörög a lomb* (= Sadly Murmurs the Bough):

Ex. 64

Seven Songs, Op. 6, V

Mert   bùm   kèl

This *g* (within context of *c♯*-minor), under the last word of the stanza, affects the listener all the more profoundly since the accompaniment has remained up to this point entirely in the diatonic. Until now, the monotone figurations painting the constant whirling of the autumn boughs has begun each time on the *g♯* (as in the first measure of our example). After this formula is heard for no less than 29 times, the bass bends downward to the "sad" locrian *g*. (If the original meaning of a cadence is a falling away, a bending downward—then this too is a type of cadence!)

At the end of the first stanza of the ballad *Szabó Erzsi*, we do hear a first-degree chord in the accompaniment, but of what type? A diminished-fifth, locrian tonic:

Ex. 65

Hungarian Folk Music, VIII, 44

The *d♭* diminished-fifth has already, two measures earlier, anticipated this color. From a technical point of view, we meet here also with that device —not rare among Kodály's works—which, by means of a special coloration, gives a new type of quality to some traditional construction (here the relation of the V–I degrees).

In the Csokonai-song *A farsang búcsúszavai* (= Farewell to the Carni-

256

val), the first stanza arrives at the—now with phrygian coloration—basic key of *b*. But what does the accompaniment see fit to do? It traverses the entire third-ladder of the locrian scale:

Ex. 66   Seven Songs, Op. 6, VII

Kon-gat-ják a haran-got,   ü-zik már a far - san - got!

The piano anticipates this tonal-environment three measures earlier: the "dominant" ninth-chord *(f-a-c-e♭-g)* on the V degree of the *b*-locrian scale "tolls the bell" (= *kongatják a harangot*). This is followed by a dynamic tonic, and then an "anti-tonic" created by a subdominant *(e-g-b)* inter-weaving with a dominant *(a♯-c♯-e)*—after all of which comes finally the thirteenth-chord set beneath the ending of the stanza.

The most complete example of this chapter may be heard in the Opera House:

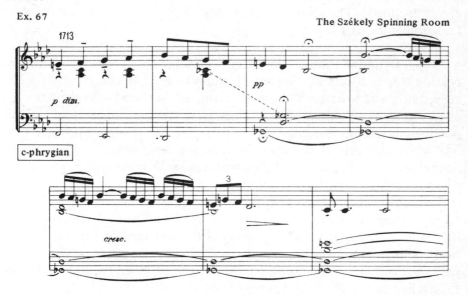

Ex. 67   The Székely Spinning Room

c-phrygian

257

The song of parting sounds through the orchestra in painful-passionate tones. While the fourth line of the melody—extended considerably— reaches the *c'* finalis, the chord in the meanwhile has not changed. The harmony has remained resting of the dark, deep locrian V degree under the entire line. Thus the melodic closing-tone *c'* has been turned into an eleventh of the chord, and is thus accorded great tension. (An insolvable dramatic situation—an unresolvable closing harmony.) In certain instances we will find useful the measurement which tells us: *how many thirds* above the bass is the melody tone? The greater its number, the greater is the tension of the tone:

Ex. 68

When in root-position, with the melody and bass in octaves, the harmony hardly enhances the melody at all. If the melody-tone then becomes a third or fifth above the bass: this is already more interesting. As a seventh? ninth? But indeed! And if it should become the fifth third in an eleventh-chord! (The above formula may of course be read with the most varied alterations.)

VII — Dynamic (non-static) strophe-endings. At this point in our discussion, the subjects of chapters II and VI meet. In the former we discussed how the lowered V degree is attracted to the IV—in the latter we cited examples of the strophe-endings which remain open. If these two phenomena should join together we then find the strongest possible relation which may exist in the setting of multiple-verse melodies. The strophic song does not fall apart into individual stanzas, but instead creates a continuous, organic, wide-arched unity.

In the *Dances of Marosszék*, the second quasistrophe of the *Con moto* section comes to an end in measure 52. At this point in the composition, the theme is brought back (beginning in the last measure of our illustration). This juncture is not characterized by some traditional "dead interval", but rather by the strong relation of the *C*-chord (within the key of *f♯*) leading to the *B* of the continuation.

258

Similarly, serving to join the first two stanzas, the $G\flat$ bass placed beneath the c finalis, and above this bass an augmented-$\frac{4}{3}$ chord:

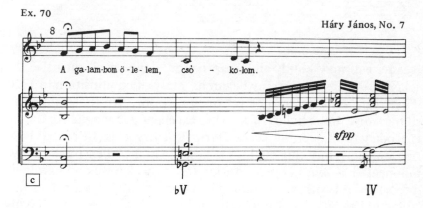

This in turn attracts the F bass which stands at the beginning of the transition section.

The same relation of one sung verse and the next heard in the violins:

Here, in the key of *c*, the *Gb-F* bass motion serves to carry the music onward.

Comparing the critical verse-ending chords of the last three Kodály examples: we may see that in each instance we are dealing with an augmented-$\frac{4}{3}$ chord. Kodály and the augmented-$\frac{4}{3}$ ... Our composer knows what a great power of tension is contained in this (already appearing occasionally in the works of Bach) altered chord. The augmented-sixth itself, joining with two tritones and the friction of a major-second: the functional activity of the chord is intensified fourfold:

Ex. 72   including:

The reader will now kindly allow a private "glance backward."
Our class at the Liszt Academy began its study of composition in 1920. In this first year, Kodály was not yet our professor. We first studied traditional harmony in the hands of another excellent pedagogue. In the fall of 1921, Kodály took over our class. During the first class he asked: have we learned our harmony thoroughly?—Yes.—Alright, then please show me the augmented-$\frac{4}{3}$—but in open position (about which we had hardly heard at that time) and with all possible inversions as well. Each of us in turn had to go to the piano... Rarely were we in such agony as then. To my lot fell *eb*-minor, and I had to come up with something like the following:

Ex. 73

It did not go as quickly as I have now written it down. In any event, it was significant that *this was the only question* with which our Professor examined our knowledge of the previously studied material. (We were later to say: of course, because this chord also fits into the whole-tone scale...)

In the song *Hogyan tudtál rózsám...* another altered chord provides the transition from the first stanza to the second:

260

The juxtaposition of the lowered V and IV degrees occurs somewhat earlier in this setting of *Kis kece lányom:*

Ex. 75

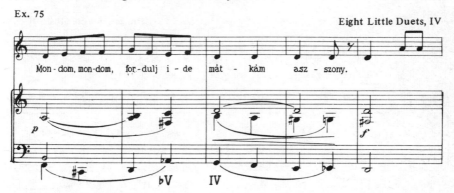

Here, a scale passage starting from the IV degree accompanies the tonic-tone (on the words *mátkám asszony* = my dearly betrothed), so that the second stanza may begin with the *D-maggiore* chord.

The characteristic progression is similarly shifted foreward of the verse-ending in the accompaniment of the rhythmically interesting *Ludaim, ludaim...* The entire final line of the verse (meas. 19) is already accompanied by the IV degree *G*-chord, before which, under the third line of the verse, we hear the *A♭* which Kodály so favored:

Ex. 76

Hungarian Folk Music, VIII, 47

The locrian tone may still have a forward-driving force even when it does not appear in the bass. At the end of a second stanza:

Ex. 77

Hungarian Folk Music, II, 9

Most exceptionally, the *e♭* of the third measure does not resolve to *d*, but, with an unexpected turn, changes to *d♯* so that the continuing material may take up this tone.

In another song, this type of dynamic chord accompanies the ending of the first stanza:

Ex. 78

Hungarian Folk Music, VIII, 45

≈The double suspension intensifies the restlessness of the accompaniment.

In the comical song about "the flea with the big nose," we hear a *G* bass (in the key of *c♯*) under the closing-tone of the third stanza:

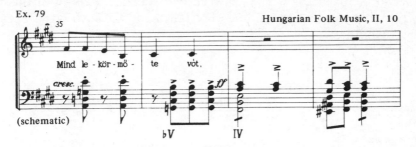

Ex. 79   Hungarian Folk Music, II, 10

Following the locrian fourth-chord is an *F♯*-based five-tone pentatonic chord. This leads on to the fourth stanza.

In the music which roundly satirizes the entrance of the emperor's court, the chord—*A*-major according to the notation, but in actuality *B♭♭*-major—which is heard beneath the *e♭* closing-tone of the melody shows a double profile:

Ex. 80   Háry János, No. 24

In the *prima volta*, on the one hand, the written *E(=F♭)* bass, with leading-tone force, turns back to the *E♭* primary tone of the repetition. In the *seconda volta* continuation, on the other hand, the *A(=B♭♭)* at the beginning of the measure resolves—with just the same type of leading-tone motion—to the IV degree $A\flat$ chord of the subsequent section. A witty Janus-chord!

Instead of providing a link between two stanzas, a chord of this type may also join together the ending of a stanza and the customary repeat of its last two lines:

Ex. 81

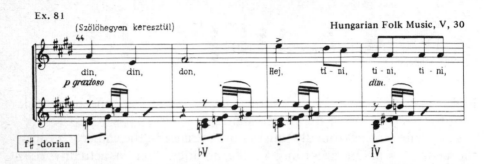

(Szőlőhegyen keresztül)   Hungarian Folk Music, V, 30

A fresh, new idea: the C-harmony of the strophe-ending remains and continues to accompany the beginning of the repetition (measures 2–3 of our excerpt).

The four-line melody, fashioned after a folksong, of the Epigram. No. 3 comes to an end in measure 18. A short coda then follows. The $E\flat$- and D-major chords, set beneath the a finalis of the melody, provide the link which joins this coda to the melody:

Ex. 82   Epigrams, 3

This may also be heard in the last verse of the enchantingly beautiful melody *Tiszán innen, Dunán túl*. Again, now in place of the final, closing D-chord, none other than the locrian (who knows already how many times this has occurred) $A\flat$ bass appears, so that a link may be formed to the coda by way of *G:*

264

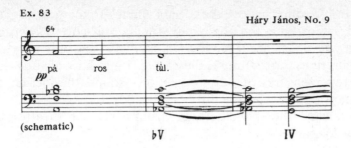

Ex. 83

Háry János, No. 9

(schematic)

Similar also, in the setting of *Meghalok, meghalok...* , is the accompaniment placed beneath the *d♯* closing-tone of the melody:

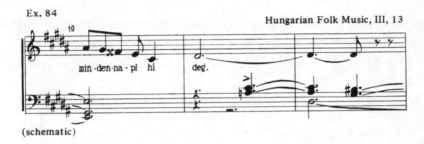

Ex. 84

Hungarian Folk Music, III, 13

(schematic)

A postlude of only a few measures then follows in the piano.

VIII — Movement-endings in the locrian. Even more significant than its appearances in the forms we have introduced so far, is the role of the locrian when it is manifested in the very last sounds of a particular composition.

To the final bitter words of the ballad *Szabó Erzsi*, "Holló lesz a te hóhérod (= A raven shall be your hangman)," a final touch is given by the locrian chord:

Ex. 85

Hungarian Folk Music, VIII, 44

(schematic)

265

in which the *g♭* sounds above the *C* bass. Joined to this is both the picardy third and, intensifying the poignancy, the two seventh *(b♭ and b)*. These three tones do not conceal the locrian character but only provide it with added coloration. Furthermore, the dark *g♭* tones have already—earlier in the first two measures of our illustration—sound the locrian character which is not unrelated to the phrygian melody.

A movement entitled Melodrama (from a musical theatre-piece) also closes in *c*-locrian:

Ex. 86

Czinka Panna (unpublished opera), No. 23

An acoustical perfect-fifth and a locrian diminished-fifth color the final accompaniment measures of the folksong *Magos kősziklának...*:

Ex. 87

Hungarian Folk Music, V, 25

A *C♯*-major and a *G*-major triad together, in the six voices of the closing harmony, heighten the effect of the locrian coloration and the polar interval.

This "strange" tonality is at times used to depict the mockingly grotesque. According to the wild imagination of Háry János, Napoleon laments: I fell into the hole, but only one of my legs is bowed... To this is a "bowed" (crooked) ending:

Ex. 88

Háry János, No. 19

IX — Locrian melodies. After these smaller-or-larger excerpts, let us now follow with several examples of *entire* melodies which move within the diminished-fifth scale.

While it is not generally known in musical circles, there are actually some *Ti*-ending Hungarian folksongs. Of such a type, for example, is the song from the collection of János Berze which belongs to the "half-cadence aeolian" sub-group of locrian melodies:

Ex. 89

The scale for melodies of this type may be illustrated thus:

Ex. 90

Another locrian type is the "mixolydian with third-ending." Its formula:

Ex. 91

This type of "syntono-mixolydian" melody is found in the Collection of Hungarian Folk Music, Vol. II, No. 155:

Ex. 92

Among Kodály's works, we also find arrangements of these *Ti*-ending half-cadence melodies. Such for example is the *Rákóczi kesergője*. Our composer first heard this melody in 1916. The second half of this folksong:

Ex. 93

He used it in his operatic theatre-piece. The end of the melody occurs in the lower voices, thus we are granted a true locrian ending:

Ex. 94

The locrian quality is all the more conspicuous since, in the first measure of our excerpt, we do not hear the *f♯*, as in *Ex. 93*, but rather the *f*—in other words, the characteristic diminished-fifth of the *B*-locrian. Kodály's procedure appears all the more original if we realize that elsewhere—in Serbian folk music always—this closing-tone is customarily the fifth of the accompanying harmony:

Ex. 95

Kodály, however, has more respect for the inherent contours of the melody: if the *Ti* is the closing-tone of the melody, it is worthy of being the root of the closing-chord.

Descending melodic lines. Our composer even knows how to combine the pure locrian scale with the descending octave line of our ancient folksongs:

268

Seven Piano Pieces, Op. 11, 4

True, the critical *c* tone occurs only once in the melody which ends of *f*♯—
but we could not really conceive of replacing it with a *c*♯. The quiet, distant message—who knows what portent it brings?—minor-$^6_4$ mixtures in
the piano. The frame of the form: the piece begins with *e*♭ tones—the first
theme takes an *a* as its principal tone—,and the piece ends in *c*-minor. If
we add to this the *f*♯ tonality of the trio-type melody shown in our example:
the entire functional axis is delineated.

EXPRESSIVE QUALITY

Intermezzo. — My son Andris was five years old when he already began to pick out little
tunes on the piano. Among them was a little song about a spotted calf. I made him try
transposing it to first one and then another "white-key" mode. He played it in *G*-
mixolydian, *d*-dorian, etc. I finally pointed to the *b:* try it from here too! He played:

Ex. 97

Afterwards he looked at me: "The little cow has become so sad!" he said. But what
made him feel this?

X — Mood painting. And what made Lassus feel that this was the way
to describe the painful longing for the homeland of a nation languishing
in Babylonian captivity:

Ex. 98

Super flumina Babylonis

269

And what made Liszt feel that when speaking of tears and death, we must sing:

Ex. 99

And why did Kodály have the same feeling in so very many poetic examples? Certainly, it was not necessary for him to have known the music of Lassus and Liszt in order that he conceive such melodies for melancholy, painful texts:

Ex. 100

These excerpts are from the Seven Songs, Op. 6. But we also meet with such lamenting, downward-leading melodies elsewhere in his works:

Ex. 101

Nor does the enharmonic notation ($e = f\flat$) alter the character:

Ex. 102

Psalmus Hungaricus

Is - ten sza - vá - val ök nem gon - dol - nak,

The repetition of the motive intensifies the effect:

Ex. 103

Poco agitato

Three Songs, Op. 14, I

Va - gyok már szin - te öz - vegy ger - li -ce,

The same minor-second and perfect-fourth downward. When added together, a diminished-fifth. The forms of these locrian ternions in the different modes of the common tonality:

Ex. 104

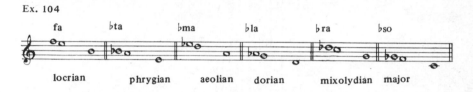

locrian   phrygian   aeolian   dorian   mixolydian   major

There are ample instances of each of these in Kodály's music.

In a unique way, this three-tone melodic germ joins together the two strongest relational elements of traditional musical styles: the leading-tone motion and the perfect-fourth (-fifth) relation. (Is it mere coincidence that with precisely these two types of intervals it is possible to "cover" contiguously the twelve tones of the tempered system? We have so far not been successful in answering this question.)

Furthermore, the thought arises: did Kodály not also feel in this formula the line of the most significantly Hungarian pentatonic closing-ternion:

Ex. 105

pentatonic: locrian:

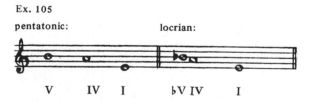

V   IV   I   ♭V IV   I

271

But why is it that among our diatonic modes it is precisely the locrian which is most suitable for expressing resignation, lamentation, sorrow, pain? Perhaps we may find the answer by examining the perfect-fifth structures. We illustrate these in the common tonality *(Ex. 106)*.

If, from the pillar of perfect-fifths, we listen for the spatial difference (in terms of absolute letter-names, scalar position) of the higher and lower tones, we may establish the fact that in the lydian line each member-tone is higher, brighter than the root-tone. It is no wonder that this scale is suitable for vital, joyous melodies (Bartók!). The locrian is just the opposite: each scale-tone is lower, more muted than the finalis. It is suitable for depicting a mood of dejection. And a third observation: exactly in the middle of the series is the dorian scale with its peculiar symmetry and equilibrium. It is no wonder that musical theoreticians of the Middle Ages called this the *tonus primus*.

Ex. 106

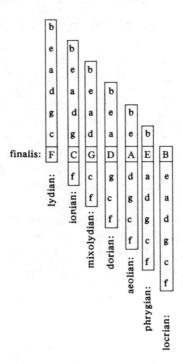

The contrast of the two outer lines is even reflected in their leading-tone motions:

Ex. 107

lydian:

locrian:

The lydian elements strive upward, the locrian pull downward.
It is also instructive to compare the two modes with the phsyical overtone series:

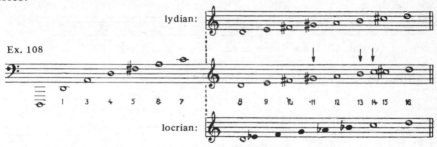

lydian:

Ex. 108

locrian:

Nearly every tone of the lydian coincides with the partials of the root-tone, or at least quite nearly approaches them. This certainly intensifies the brighter sounding. The locrian, on the other hand, clashes everywhere with the natural line, and approaches it only in the vicinity of the seventh degree.

But let us continue with the Kodály examples. The locrian ternion illustrated in *Exs. 100–105* is also heard in extended variants—not at all changing the lamenting character. Thus, for example, in the sixth song of Opus 6, the *g♯* breaks the line:

Ex. 109   Seven Songs, Op. 6, VI

mint   az   e - nyém,   csa-pon-gó

but in the motive of "burning pain (= *lángoló fájdalom*)," the *b-a#-e#* tones prevail. Additional similar, more richly drawn excerpts:

Ex. 110
a)   Songs, Op. 1, 1

So - ha   meg nem   nyug   szik.

b)   Psalmus Hungaricus

Ma - ga -mat at - tól   meg-ó - hat - tam vol - na.

c)   Two Songs, Op. 5, I

nem   len - ge -dez a   ze - phir.

d)   Ibid.

S most min - den   szo-mo-rú   s ki - holt.

A similar idea, even more fully stated:

Ex. 111   The Son of an Enslaved Country

Men - jünk, men - jünk a   föld - be,   be- teg   szi-vem!
└── phrygian ──┘   └──locrian──┘

Five descending intervals: four thirds and one fourth... The first motive paints the poet Petőfi's embittered words with the tones of the *b*-phrygian scale—the second motive adds further the locrian *c-f#* framing-tones.

Let us now follow with two instrumental examples. The first paints a dramatic situation in which a young girl, in advance of the approaching militia, runs into the spinning room and, tugging at the clothes of her suitor, urges him to flee. The mood of the scene, in the following excerpt, is made vivid by those measures which are darkened by the *g♭* tones:

Ex. 112   The Székely Spinning Room

The second may be heard in the piano setting of the *Székely Lament*. Our composer presents one of his most original ideas when the second stanza, instead of remaining in the principal *g*-minor-pentatonic tonality, appears thus:

Ex. 113

Seven Piano Pieces, Op. 11, 2

We have seen previously how the composer lowers the fifth degree of a given scale in order to obtain the locrian effect. Now we find a reverse situation: he raises the entire melody by one chromatic half-tone and leaves only the *d*-fifth-degree tone in its original location:

Ex. 114

There is a double advantage here: the stanza sounds more excitedly, more penetratingly, while the fifth scale-degree changed into the locrian intensifies the "lamenting" character.

275

Let us return to vocal melodies. The locrian effect is especially strong when it appears at some important place in the melody. For example, as the final tone of a piece:

Ex. 115

Songs, Op. 1, 7

I have suffered enough... the slanderous tongues (= *rágalmazó nyelvet*)... The *last* sung tone of this piece in c♯-minor is not c♯, but—*g!*

Sometimes in an upward direction as well! In the course of a passionate outburst, the bitterness of the "most abandoned nation" joins with word of encouragement: "our shadows shall cover the camp of the enemy!" The forceful unison of the men's voices:

Ex. 116

Life or Death!

Harmonies. In this setting of a seventeenth century poem, the diminished-fifth chord written under the *d* tonic tone of the melody has yet a relatively "tame (= *szelíd*)" effect, but this fits well with the text "*nem szelídülsz* (= you will never be tamed)." At the same time it is worthwhile to examine the preceeding measures. The f and a♭ tones, at the beginning of our excerpt, belong to the tonic axis. The tonic attracts the subdominant, and indeed the g appears. This in turn attracts the dominant: the c♯ leading-tone follows. Then with the *d* appearing in both the melody and the harmony, the functional circle is complete.

276

As a formula:

Ex. 118

The phrygian *D-C♯* bass line accompanies the final, pentatonic motive of this touchingly lamenting Transylvanian melody:

Ex. 119   Three Songs, Op. 14, II

but this progression is also prepared by the still darker locrian tone *g*— even if only in an upper voice of the accompaniment. The movement of the bass and the harmonic line is suited both to the descending line of this old melody and to the depiction of the falling leaves (= *levelek lehullnak*) as well.

A similar tonal environment is also appropriate for the text of another song of mourning:

Székely Lament (mixed choir)

Here also, the *b♭* tones in the upper voice of this piece in *e* receive their natural continuation with the *a* in the soprano.

If not quite the same as a bitter lament, there is something similar in the mood of the "ancient forest," devouring all, which swells up from these chords:

Ex. 121

Five Songs, Op. 9, V

In the melody of *B♭*-tonality, the locrian *f♭* is also heard, for which the *d♭*-minor triad is a suitable harmonization. This characteristic coloration is reiterated at the end of the piece:

Ex. 122

Ibid.

278

In another song from Transylvania, Kodály sets this type of accompaniment under a text which proclaims a curse:

Ex. 123

Hungarian Folk Music, VIII, 45

Ott hadd e -gyen, ott hadd rág-jon,

The locrian fifth *(c)* and the friction of two types of thirds *(a♯ + a)* intensify the expressive force.

Before the end of the fourteenth verse in the ballad *Görög Ilona*, a locrian hexachord descends in the accompaniment. The melody is in *g♯-phrygian* but—yet another new idea—the orchestra accompanies it with a line based a fifth lower on *c♯*:

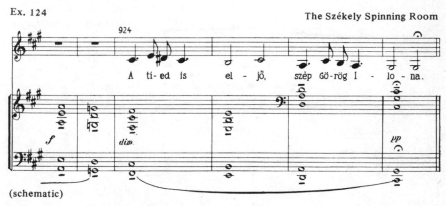

Ex. 124

The Székely Spinning Room

A ti- ed is el - jö, szép Gö-rög I - lo - na.

(schematic)

Adding to the effect of this "sublocrian" line is the line of lifeless, empty fifths, as well as the lessening dynamic from forte to piano. All this together with the dark, lowest registration in the alto part...

The registration itself, quite independent from the content of the verse, may also have its own unique mood. The first three lines of the folksong *Lányok ülnek a toronyba...* occur within the following sets of tones:

Ex. 125

g♯ -phrygian

279

Thus the melody does not even once dip below the *g♯* closing-tone. There is therefore a peculiarly interesting flavor to the fourth line which begins:

Ex. 126

The Székely Spinning Room

Kert - be men - tek ró - zsát szed - ni, szív - vem sza - kad rá - tok.

g♮

The new tone, the locrian *D* bass, is well suited to the new register. The situation is exactly the same in the setting of this Bukovinian melody which is a relation to the preceding song:

Ex. 127

Hungarian Folk Music, X, 57

Úgy be lö - lem friss me - nyecs - ke len - ne,

cresc. poco a poco

f-phrygian

Here also, in the first three lines of the melody, we do not hear the sub-tonal *e♭* tone. It appears only at the beginning of the fourth line *(Ex. 127)* —and likewise with a locrian accompaniment *(C♭).*

The colors of this uncustomary tonality occasionally also describe the grotesque. Such chords accompany the description of the "big nosed, fat bellied flea:"

280

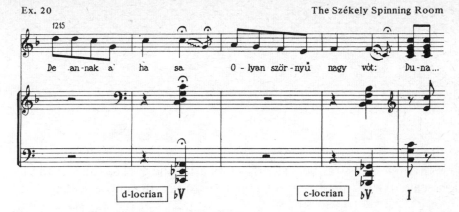

The tonic of the melody is *d*. In relation to this, the fourth-chord built on the *A♭* bass is locrian. The final word of our excerpt is heard on c—and just before it in the accompaniment is the *G♭*-ninth-chord, the locrian of the *c*. A clever double-play.

XI — Entire pieces in the locrian. Beside the locrian elements so far presented: single tones, intervals, chords, smaller-and-larger section of a piece, stand three of Kodály's works in which the basic tonality is locrian. These are:

        a)   Sappho's Love Song
        b)   Mountain Nights, I
        c)   Too Late

Sappho... The world of Ancient Greece, a yearning love, "I die for you"... What could better suit the heated words of the poet Ady than this ancient scale of lamentation! And furthermore, with the dark colors of the six-flat key signature:

Ex. 129   Five Songs, Op. 9, II

281

The first ten measures persistently emphasize the *F* root-tone of the locrian scale. After this, for another ten measures, the entire scale:

Ex. 130

Again, before the third and final verse, another forceful reiteration that indeed the tonality of the work is *F*-locrian. Even though the picardy third *a* brings to it a new color, still the sound of the *f-c♭* primary interval, appropriately "trembling" for seven measures, reflects the words of the poem. Thus:

Ex. 131

Let us also present here two strophe-endings of the melody. The short adonian closing-lines which are typical of sapphic verse dip down to the dominant of the primary tone, both times with the expressive fall of the tritone:

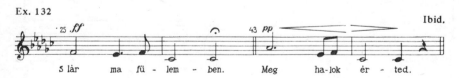

Ex. 132

282

(This shows a surprising agreement with *Ex. 115:* there also, the final sung tone was the locrian lowered fifth!) The piano postlude then closes the composition with the harp-passages which we noted in *Ex. 130.*

Mountain Nights, I... unusual, indistinct images, enigmatic sensations... The melody beginning under the buzzing seconds would seem to emphasize the *A*-tonality—but the end of the line turns upward to the *b*. (Half-cadence type.) Among the six motives of the first main section, we hear four times:

Ex. 133

Mountain Nights, I

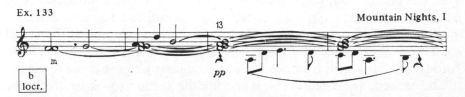

The closing-tones of the six motives in order: *b, b,/ a¹, d¹,/ b, b.* A small three-part section within the larger three-part structure of the entire work. And deciding the issue finally: the very end of the piece closes with a harmony built on the *b*.

It is worth our while to glance at the formal outline of the entire work, because the overall structure is also deeply rooted in the locrian. The pillar-tones of the three-part structure:

Ex. 134

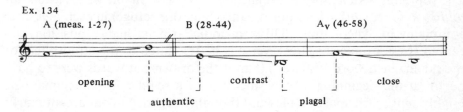

The first section is constructed around the fifth and eighth degrees. The second section reverses this tritone and rests on the terpandrosian *e-b♭* primary tones (see *Ex. 1*). The recapitulation then, with the *fa* and *ti* of the first section, creates—in the broader sense—a traditional V–I cadence. The tritone-frame of the first section moved upward, the diminished-fifth—comprised of the same tones—of the last section then descends. A perfect order: the first opens, the last closes. But let us also examine the intervals connecting each of the sections we have discussed. Between the first and middle sections we hear the *b-e* authentic fifth, and then between the last two sections the *b♭-f* primary plagal motion.

Akik mindig elkésnek (Too Late). After a song and a chorus for women's voices, a piece for mixed choir. Also to a text of Ady, as was the first piece. We have now not the newly-set romantic verse of an ancient Greek poetess, but instead the revolutionary, pessimistic outburst of the early twentieth century.

The work was written in $B\flat$-tonality, with a key signature of six flats. In order to examine the piece more easily, please allow us to present it here one half-step higher, that is instead of $B\flat$, we will examine the piece in the B of the common tonality (with no key signature). See *Ex. 135*.

In the first period, once again, one of Kodály's special devices: the re-painting, with a new type of *coloration*, of a traditional *structure* (here: a modulation to the dominant tonality). In Haydn's B-major, the eighth measure would arrive at $F\sharp$-major—in Kodály's B-locrian at F-major! And this duller sound is so expressive of the text: we have come too late…

The excited, tense sentences of the middle section tower up to the climax, then once again close with an F bass. But as static as the F-chord was in measure 8, it is now, in measure 19, a dynamic, open harmony as is proper for a middle section. (Once again the augmented-$\frac{4}{3}$, Kodály's well-known and favored harmony.)

A locrian return to the principal key of the closing section: the latter F bass is drawn to the E. And indeed, the two measures which introduce the final third of the piece begin on this E tone: *Meghalni se tudunk nyugodtan* (= We cannot even die peacefully). We have arrived at the B tonic. The soprano, with its special displacement of two-syllable words (*késő, álmunk, késő, révünk* = late, our dreams, late, our refuge) in each measure, complains in syncopation. This "melodic" (in its higher position) accented stress of ancient Greek verse is better suited to the atmosphere of the poem (each word "is late") than if the drawn-out words were to have begun at the beginning of each measure in a regular, ordinary manner. Highly sung, principal syllables and thoughtfully written out accent marks make possible the proper choral-declamation.

Still one more traditional element: before the final measures which precede the grand pause (at the end of the work *ölelésünk* = our embrace), we hear a chord in which the leading-tone of the B tonality, the $a\sharp$, is present. Thus the codetta, which brings back the principal motive, is organically linked to the preceding section.

284

TOO LATE

Endre Ady
Zoltan Kodály

As a farewell, let us examine the set of tones for this piece:

Ex. 135

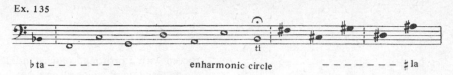

Beneath the diatonic core-formula is the *ta* of the Gregorian- and Palestrina-systems—but, moving upward—we expand into the Renaissance 11-tone system with the *ri* and *li* tones as well. Thus the enharmonic circle of fifths is brought to a complete close: the line progresses from *ta* to *li*. An old tonality speaking in new words.

*

In the musical language of a particular composer or era, one or two elements do not define a stylistic trait. But the number of locrian elements we have enumerated here—not to mention the one we have omitted—is so surprisingly great, that we may unmistakably state: an essential feature of Kodály's music does belong, in varying degrees and manner, to the locrian tonality. Nor is the use of this tonality a rare occurrence.

(Magyar Zene, IV [1976] Budapest)

KODÁLY'S CHILDREN'S CHORUSES

> "Proceed with a profound understanding of the material upon which all else may be built."
>
> (Kodály)

Nineteen hundred and twenty-five, April second. A great day in Hungarian musical history. In universal music history as well. Something new was begun at that time. Something never heard previously which since then has become the personal experience and the joy of a hundred thousand children and their million listeners. On that day The Straw Guy and See the Gypsies were heard for the first time. Thus was opened the treasure-store which we call the children's choruses of Kodály.

But going beyond the enthusiasm, let us not spare the effort to understand as many elements as possible of this musical language.

Let us examine in the following order these subject groups:

      I.   Sets of tones, tonal orders, scales.
      II. Polyphony.
      III. Harmonic vocabulary.

As the roots of Kodály's vocal style are nourished by our folk music, we shall quote his arrangements of folksongs alongside the original works. For surely when a composer accepts an external melody he identifies himself and his style with the arranged melody. (Thus we may at the same time concern ourselves with classifications and folk music study as a "by-product.")

Let us begin constructing our palace with the raw building materials.

I. SETS OF TONES, TONAL ORDERS, SCALES

In taking stock of our "tonal-inventory" we shall examine in turn:

A) questions of *tone-relationships* (fifth-order): bitonic, tritonic, and tetratonic melodies, pentatony, Transdanubian, acute and obtuse pentatony, pien-tones, fifth-change, two-system structures, real, tonal and pentatonic answers (with substitute or replaced intervals), modal answers.

B) Questions of *tone-proximity* (second-order): tri-, tetra-, penta-, and hexachords, diatonicism (with modal scales), the second seven-tone order (including the "kuruc" scale), the major-third aeolian, minor-major, and acoustical scales, minor-sixth mixolydian, Neapolitan-dorian and the melodic minor, systems of eight and more tones, the entire 12-tone system, chromaticism and enharmonic relations (with problems of intonation).

C) Melodies created by *other* tone-groups.

The fifth-chain (tone-relationship) on the one hand and the line-of-seconds (tone-proximity) on the other may be considered as the two main systematizing bases of melodic formulas. Let us begin by examining the details of each.

FIFTH-ORDER

A single fifth—in inversion a fourth—as material hardly serves more significantly than as a motive. Nevertheless such a *bi-tone* folksong line occasionally appears: Elesett a lúd... (in the trio of St. Gregory's Day), and the first melodic line of See the Gypsies.

Tritony

The main possibilities in terms of melodic formula for melodies of three-degrees (tritonic):

Ex. 1

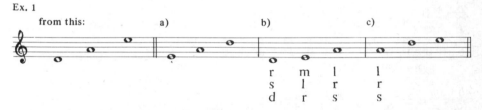

Among these the *a)* type is rare for Kodály (it is used rather by Bartók) but we find an example of it in Bicinia Hungarica II, 74, measures 7–8 of the soprano line. An example of the *b)* form is Hippity, Hoppity, and the two measures which begin the melody of The Bells. See also Bic. II, 65, first half. The *c)* inversion we find in Bic. I, 4, and in the first motive of The Voice of Jesus.

Tetratony

Formulas for a four-member chain of perfect fifths:

Ex. 2

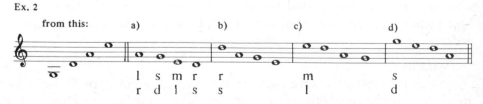

289

The area is suddenly extended. Tetratony based on the chain of perfect fifths is indeed significant in all our folk music as it is in Kodály's world of melody.

In the *a)* formula we recognize the well-known quaternion of Bic. II, 72. From this is derived one half-melody of both Bic. I, 11, and Bic. I, 13, the first four measures of Bic I, 10, and the first half of Bic. I, 18, with its unusual wide-ranging melody (reminiscent of Tcheremis melodies). Compare this last with the melody of Bic. IV, 150.

The *c)* formula appears in the last four measures of Bic. I, 34.

The initial motive of Mountain Nights III derives from formula *d)*.

Other infrapentatonic tone-groups

Into this category we place those formulas which while fitting within the pentatonic system do not use every tone, and which do not show one or another of the (previously introduced) closed fifth-chains. Such "mixed" tone-formulas:

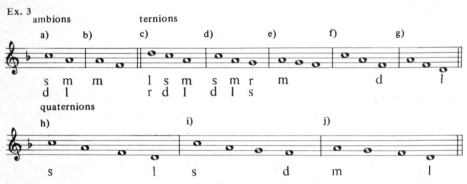

We do not have space to quote an example for each. We mention only the beautiful melody of Bic. I, 57 showing the *i)* form. Let the search for further examples be a useful recreation for those who may be interested. (Either as a voluntary exercise, or as an assignment for students capable of the task: the construction of one's own motives or longer section within the described tone-circles. This may also be done for almost each of our subsequent areas of discussion!)—Let us moreover realize that the tones of the above formulas may also occur in any type of changed order, inversion, repetition of tones, and transposition. For example the tones of a four-member group may appear in $1.2.3.4 = 4! = 24$ types of successive order.

Pentatony

The above examples were each concerned with smaller or larger segments, but pentatony is the entire "ancient homeland" of our Hungarian

290

music. In Kodály's music, pentatony is one of the most significant areas. (We are accustomed to understand the definition of "a set of tones described by a line of perfect fifths" as meaning *D-S-R-L-M*. But we would do well to also bear in mind that no less than 66 differently constructed quinternions may be formed from our 12-degree enharmonic-tempered tonal system. With each of these having five modes, there are thus altogether 330 types of five-tone scales.—Who will construct them?)

In our composer's music the group of la-pentatonic melodies is naturally the most numerous. These may occur either as a folksong quotation—as in Bic. I, 13, 19, Bic. II, 64, 65, 67, 68, 72, 83, and numerous examples in the Fourth Tcheremis Volume, or in his original melodies. To this group belong for example the first statement of Song of Faith, Bent a bárány, Song of Peace, the Bic. I, 7, 8, 10, 12, 14, 16–18, 20–28, 31, Bic. II, 61, 63 and the important 74, along with the theme and many parts of Tricinia 28, etc.

If we then add to this the "333" and the volumes of the Pentatonic Music, the piano pieces on the black keys—we are amazed at the unsurpassed variety with which Kodály uses this relatively modest set of tones.

Do-pentatonic is considerably rarer in Kodály's works. Examples: the first eight measures (open period of The Mole Marriage), Bic. I, 1–6, 30, Bic. II, 71, 73, and examples in Bic. IV.

So-pentatonic has even fewer examples: Bic. I, 23, Bic. II, 62, 69, 76 as well as the examples of Bic. IV. (There are many in the volumes of the Pentatonic Music!)

We find only one *mi-pentatonic* theme in Kodály's works: the melody Bic. II, 66. Among the exercise material we may mention the 69 melodies of Pentatonic Music III, and nos. 221 and 248 from the "333".

We do not actually meet with any *re-pentatonic* melodies in the children's choruses, but among the exercises there are rather many. Such are the melodies nos. 16, 17, 18 and 19 in the "333" (although we may readily hear these as ending on la), Pentatonic Music II, 13, 49, 59, 65, 67, 73, 85, 88, 90 and 100, and finally additional exercises in Pentatonic Music III and IV.

The *Transdanubian third* colors the final thematic motive of the Arany szabadság canon (meas. 7). The footnote for Bic. I, 11, refers to the entire Transdanubian scale (a pentatonic scale with its third and seventh both raised). Here we may read that "in this case the initial tone will not be *la*, but rather *do*." But would it not be better to begin both variants with *la?* To call the raised tone *si* and *di?* To show in this way which degrees have been altered in comparison to the proto-type? Does this not provide a better comparison between the two types of variants?

Acute pentatony. We generally consider it natural that "there is neither *fa* nor *ti* in the pentatonic." And this is indeed true—at least for the most part in our five-degree melodies. But we also meet with another type. Let us first approach the question on analytic ground. Anhemitonic five-degree lines fit into our diatonic system in three places. With each instance relating to *C=do:*

Ex. 4

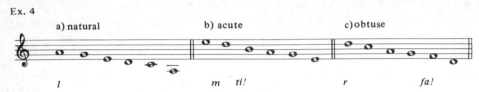

Illustrated on a common base:

Ex. 5

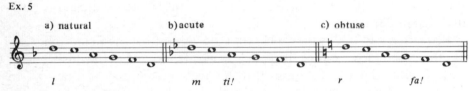

In *b)* there is a *ti* in place of *do*. We may therefore call this the acute type. In the *c)* variant we sing *fa* in place of *mi*, and will call this obtuse pentatony. (We naturally consider each of the three forms to have each 5 modes as well!)

We have two-system melodies which in their first part contain the ninth above the final tone. In such a case it is customary to begin the melody on *re*, so that the higher tone may be called *mi*. But if we begin the second verse—or if we listen to the melody in its entirety, not cut in two parts—it becomes clear that the high beginning tone is not *re* but rather *la!* And then its upper neighbor is certainly *ti!* In this way we may better express the double-system than were we to solmizate the two half-melodies in the same way. Do we close both the open midpoint and final tone on *la?* We deny the essence of the form: the unity in duality of floating and descent. (This is useful as an intermediary step. However *let us not stop here* at the two half-pieces of the bridge, but rather weld them together instead!)

There are cases where Kodály himself specifies:

Ex. 6

292

Let us proceed in like manner even if these syllables are not written above the melodies which move similarly. Thus for example as in the solmization of Bic. I, 41 and in our other similar folksongs. This is the case for the first four measures of Hippity, Hoppity (in *a* acute) and for the melody of King László's Men (in meas. 56–71) as well.

Obtuse pentatony (with *fa* in place of *mi*) is indeed quite rare in our folk music. But several examples do appear. In the volume Children's Games of the Corpus Musicae Popularis Hungaricae (I, 103):

Ex. 7

Hipp, hopp, zenge dob, mint a má-sé, zen-ge dob.

See also melodies number 330, 332 and 919 of this volume. Such a folksong line appears here and there among the songs of adults also. An example is the main motive of Bic. I, 35 (in *C*-obtuse pentatonic). In Kodály's volume of children's choruses:

Ex. 8

Hogy a ka-kas? Há-rom garas. Hát a tyúk? Az is úgy.

Measures 3–4 here present the *d'-l-s-f-r-d* obtuse pentatonic scale. It is a *do*-scale. Although it may seem almost incidental, a small section is nevertheless suitable as an illustration.

Pien-tones

It was Kodály's teaching that three classes of pentatony exist in our folk music. Pure pentatony—here and there (insignificantly) colored by guest tones—in scattered pentatonic figures of our melodies which have been extended to seven tones.

Several examples of pien-tone types:

a) with *ti* only Bic I, 39, Bic. II, 82;

b) with *fa* only the theme of 7 Easy Children's Choruses 4 (lower voice meas. 1–10);

c) with one *ti* and one *fa* each of Bic. II, 97;

d) with one *ti* and one *fi* each Bic. I, 44 and the first six measures of Bic. II, 94.

FIFTH-CHANGE

In this realm belongs the ascending answer (A, A^5...) of the new style, but more characteristically and more originally the descending terraced structure of the old melodies. Here we shall speak of this latter category only.

The question of fifth-change presents an opportunity to examine more thoroughly the tonality of these melodies. It is not sufficient to verify—or to have our students determine—that for instance the Bic. I, 13 is a pure pentatonic melody. It is as if, in analyzing verse, we were to examine each strophe separately by itself without mentioning one word about the syntax. Our musical sentences are the folksong *lines*, independent and complete thoughts as it were. Being worthy of repetition, variation, transposition and recapitulation, they are generally classified as themes. Therefore let us continue to examine in our fifth-changing melodies both the lines and the half-melodies themselves. Thus it appears that the above-mentioned little song consists in truth of not five but of four degrees (4°). This does not detract from the value of the song. On the contrary, we may marvel all the more at what a well-formed little tune arises from altogether only four tones. By means of the fifth-change the two tetratones then produce the pentatonic, but only as the "final sum of the invoice".

As a formula:

Ex. 9

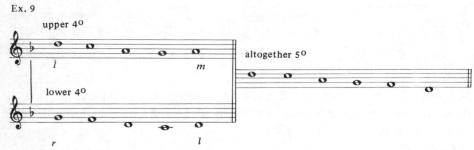

Such is the structure of Bic. I, 11.

We can illustrate what happens in this "arithmetical operation" on descending fifth-lines:

$$
\begin{array}{l}
\ \text{M L R S}\\
\underline{+\ \ \ \ \ \text{L R S D}}\\
=\ \text{M L R S D}
\end{array}
$$

Among Kodály's own melodies that of Bic. I, 23 is pertinent here.

Two-system structures

A consequent development of the preceding examples enriched by one member occurs when the first half-melody is itself also pentatonic. Combining the two rows gives us a hexatonic line. This however does not function as the actual basis for the melody but is derived only as a total calculation. The true phraseology of the melody remains pentatonic. In schematic form:

Ex. 10

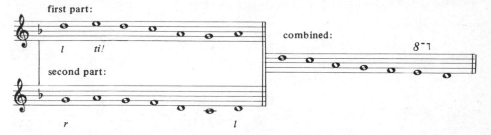

Illustrated as an ascending fifth-line (= descending chain of fourths):

$$\begin{array}{r} \text{S R L M T} \\ + \text{D S R L M} \\ \hline = \text{D S R L M T } (6°) \end{array}$$

We have already spoken of the solmization of such melodies in our discussion of acute pentatony. Putting aside the easily-found folksong examples, let us mention some pertinent Kodály melodies:

a) The first motive of The Bells (meas. 9–10) immediately receives an answer at the lower fifth. A fifth-changing form condensed to a miniature! This play is repeated in the following four measures.

b) Hippity, Hoppity (meas. 1–8). Let us have our students observe how the second part (meas. 5–8) answers the first with such a minute variation! (Why? The descending leap of the third is of a more closed character than the leap of the fifth in meas. 4.)

c) Bic. I, 32 has a beautiful, rich melody, somewhat like a six-line folksong. The *f* -pentatonic of the first part is answered by the second part in *b*.

Other types of answers

In the examples of fifth-change discussed so far, the second part of the melody corresponded exactly to its first half both in structre and coloration. (For example, fourth answered fourth, minor third answered minor third.) Thus we found a *real* answer. (Latin *res:* object, thing—real: faithful to the object.)

But there are also other types of answers!

Tonal answer. From the realm of classical music (and chiefly from the fugues of Bach) we are acquainted with the procedure by which the principal fifth (linking scale degrees 1 and 5) set forth in the theme is not answered by its exact transposition (thereby moving into the dominant key), but rather by the inversion of this interval, the principal fourth (scale degrees 5–1, actually 5–8). Elsewhere it is reversed: the principal fifth answering the principal fourth. Since the answer thus remains in the principal key, we refer to it as a *tonal* answer.

The principal intervals of the tonal answer:

Ex. 11

This structural variant sometimes confines itself only to the principal interval in question. At other times the answering fourth in place of the fifth also takes with it one or more additional tones of the melody. Thus for example:

Ex. 12

Bic. III, 107

After these preliminary remarks let us compare

a) the melody of meas. 10 with that of meas. 13 in the piece To the Singing Youth;

b) the first half-melody (soprano) with the second half-melody (alto) of Bic I, 21;

c) the second melody line with the first of Bic II, 95.

Pentatonic answer. What happens when we must provide a lower fifth-answer to the *do* of a pentatonic first half-melody? The note sung would be *fa*. But if the melody remains in the single-system natural pentatonic we are obliged to sing in place of the *fa* its lower neighbor *mi*. The distance that then occurs between the two melodies is here not a fifth but rather a sixth. The name for this: the *vicariant sixth*. (Cf. vicarious = substitute.) A more fully explained definition: vicariant sixth substituting for a fifth.

296

We meet with it for example here:

The fourth tone of the exact lower answer would be *a♭*, which does not exist in the *c = la* pentatonic. The sung tone "slides down" to the neighboring *g*. This procedure is reversed in the case of an upper answer:

Ex. 14   *mi*   Bic. II, 70

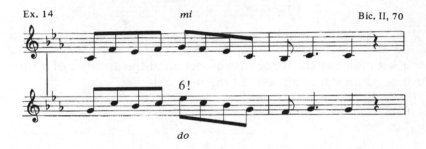

The exact answer to the fifth tone of the theme *(g = mi)* would be the upper *d = ti*. But the melody remains within the confines of its basic system and therefore we sing the high *do* in place of the *ti*. A sixth has substituted here for the fifth.

As a summarizing formula:

Ex. 15

The explanation of this phenomenon can also easily be read from the pentatonic row of fifths: *D-S-R-L-M*. The *do* has no lower fifth *(fa)*, the *mi* has no upper fifth *(ti)*.

Vicariant third. Considerably rarer is the inversion of this sixth, the major third standing in place of the fourth:

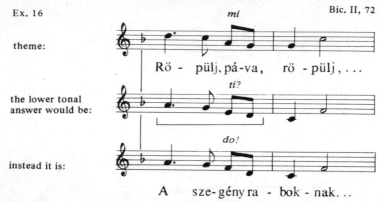

The bracket indicates the tonal answer section at the distance of a fourth. In the case of an upper answer, in the new style:

As a summarizing formula:

From the point of view of the vicariant intervals, let us examine—searching for these thoroughly—Bic I, 12, 14, 17, 18, 25, 26, 27, 44, Bic. II, 94, and compare the first four measures of Song of Peace with the alto answer in measures 9–12. A more independent, more interesting task: "let us hunt" for the vicariant intervals in the fourth volume of the Bicinia! The hunter will not be without his reward.

The heading of this section designates the answer with these vicariant intervals as being a *pentatonic answer*. There may be objection to this since both the real answer and double-system answering are also purely pentatonic—nor does the tonal fifth-fourth exchange step beyond the limits of pentatony. And yet: while these latter bear the traditional, commonly-known real-tonal designation, somehow we must distinguish these from the third type of answering with its fifth-sixth or fourth-third exchanges. Since these occur only in pentatony we offer the section heading: pentatonic answer. But if the term *"vicariant answer"* appears to be better, let us encourage its use.

Vol. IV of the Bicinia, with its—Tcheremis folksongs, serves as a plentiful store of examples for real, tonal and pentatonic answers, as well as the different combinations of these.

Modal answer. We have already seen that it was necessary to devise the terms pentatonic and vicariant answer since these types are not usually included in a discussion of real and tonal answers.

But there is yet a fourth way of giving an answer at the fifth. Hum the following melody:

Ex. 18   Bic. I, 33

E - sik e - ső, á- zik a he-ve-der,

A lá - bo - mat szorít- ja vaskengyel.

What happens here to the theme? In an exact fifth-answer the tone indicated by the asterisk would be *b* and not *b♭*. As in countless other instances this is a case where the answer given to the tonic trichord is real. (See for example Bic. I, 43, II, 88, III, 111 etc.)

In a way this is also a tonal answer since it remains within the tonality of the theme. But then how shall we distinguish this from the true tonal answer with its fifth-fourth exchange? Here there is no question of structural change, only the coloring has been altered.

We have only to examine the previous example. In the fourth measure of the first line we find an aeolian trichord—in the corresponding place the answer is sung in phrygian mode. In such a case the term "modal answer" is therefore desirable.

In Bic I, 37 we find the situation in reverse with the phrygian trichord heard first and then immediately—within the same line!—an aeolian trichord in the fourth measure.

From Kodály's Háry János we quote an exceptionally interesting example of the modal answer. The motives at the end of the third and fourth lines of the well-known recruiting song:

Ex. 19

...en - nél szebb sem le - het,

a - ki ily - lyet sze - ret!

Under the brackets of the third line we sing a phrygian trichord, for the corresponding section of the last line a major-third answer with the augmented second providing an Eastern color.

Let us compare the tetrachords of the theme and its answer from the point of view of modal answer:

Ex. 20   Tric. 9

This Kodály melody has an original construction:

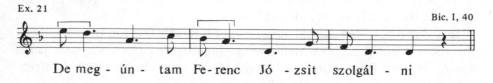

Ex. 21   Bic. I, 40

De meg - ún - tam Fe - renc Jó - zsit szolgál - ni

300

a) The octave descent is achieved in these measures. This ancient line-type is moreover characteristic of the complete range of our old-style melodies. But in our new-style melodies this entire ambitus may be delineated within one melodic line. (See Bic. II, 80 and 86, Shepherds' Christmas Dance, etc.)

b) Kodály compresses these ancient elements even further in his theme based on the new-style folksongs: here—in the second measure—an answer to the first measure is given at the lower fifth.

c) This is a tonal answer: the d^2–a^1 main fourth of the first measure is answered by the a^1–d^1 main fifth of the second measure. (These tones are also marked by their extended length!)

d) For prosodic purposes, a higher tone begins each measure in accordance with the main stresses of the text. In relation to the principal tones mentioned above these are upper-neighbor tones. Nor is the third measure an exception in this respect: its first tone is the pentatonic neighbor to the *la* which ends the line.

e) This accented neighbor-tone is in the first instance a major second and subsequently a minor second above the principal tone. Thus a modal answer is joined together with the tonal answer discussed under *c)*.

f) The basically pentatonic melody line also corresponds to our old-style folk melodies. The two pien tones, the upper *ti* and the *fa* of the second measure, are however more than guests. By virtue of their stressed positions they complete the aeolian scale, illustrating how our folk music arrived at diatony from the pentatonic.

Let us compare the previous example with this pair of motives:

Ex. 22

(Most szép lenni...)

Kossuth La-jos   nem lett vol - na,

ka-to - na sem   let -tem vol - na

Summary

Let us enumerate the characteristics of the four types of answering discussed so far:

a) in a real answer both the structure and the coloring remain the same;

b) in a tonal answer the structure is altered (fifth-fourth exchange);

c) in a pentatonic (vicariant) answer the structure is also changed but in

301

such a way that sixth answers fifth, third answers fourth. *(Do* appears in place of *ti, mi* in place of *fa.)*

d) in a modal answer the structure remains, but its coloration is changed, as if appearing in a different mode.

SECOND ORDER

Tone-proximity generates the various *-chords*. The *bichord*, in our folk music and in Kodály's children's choruses, is generally of major-second type, especially if we consider its more serious role in forming motives or lines. While it is true that this interval fits into the pentatonic system, indeed in three places, the minor third is the more characteristic interval of this order than is the step of a second which may be found in many types of tonal-systems. It is mentioned here only for sake of completeness.

Bichord. In Kodály's music there are altogether few examples of musical ideas comprised of seconds only. In this category belongs the bichord of Grow, Tresses, the beginning melodic line of Mole Marriage in measures 42–43, and, quoting from the children's songs the first two motives of Honey. He handles the two-note exercises with even greater variety: of the 333 Reading Exercises the first to appear are all derived from the *do-re* bichord. (We may also try these with a *so-la* designation. See the Afterword of the volume: "A melody comprised of few tones will also accommodate several different tonal interpretations.") *A Trichord* forms the greater part of the melodies of *Ladybird, The Swallow's Wooing* and *Thieving Bird.* Here we may also mention the first three measures of Versengés (7 Easy Children's Choruses 4), etc. A minor trichord forms the first eight measures of Dancing Song, the first two lines of Gypsy Lament, etc.

A Tetrachord forms the entire melody of The Swallow's Wooing, and the principal motives (the first two measures) of Bic. I, 45–47. But a tetrachord is not only the span of the keytone to the fourth degree. The ambitus may also shift:

Ex. 23

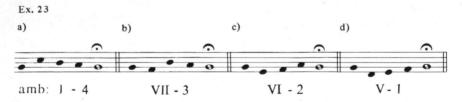

We write no clef-sign or key-signature as these groups of tones may take different colorations. (How many for each possible scale?)

302

Examples of type *b)*: The Deaf Boatman measures 5–6 and 7–8, King László's Men measures 21–24, the first motives of Bic. I, 45, 47, Bic. III, 114, etc.

We meet with type *c)* in the first four-measure melodic line of Whitsuntide.

Type *d)* is heard in measures 110–111 of King László's Men.

We may think of ambitus-shifts for the other chords as well—we shall not list all of them.

Pentachord melodies are abundant among both our children's songs and adult melodies. Of such type is The Leveret, the second (non-fifth-changing) variant of Dancing Song (measures 29–56), and the "Talalaj" trio section of The Straw Guy. There are even four pentachord melodies in Whitsuntide: measures 80–87, 208–215, 223–235 and 286–319.

We find a minor pentachord in pieces nos. 77–79 of Bic. II. A Christmas Carol has a rather unique pentachord: it ends on *mi* but with a *re-la* ambitus and a *fi/fa* alternation. (Or perhaps it ends on *ti* with a *di/do* tone-pair? Who hears it in which way?)

A lydian pentachord emerges in the third melodic line (measures 11–13) of See the Gypsies.

A pentachord set of tones does not always imply of tones may take different colorations. (How many for each possible scale?)

Examples of type *b)*: The Deaf Boatman measures 5-6 and 7-8, King László's Men, measures 21-24, the first motives of Bic. I, 45, 47, Bic. III, 114, etc.

We meet with type *c)* in the first four-measure melodic line of Whitsuntide.

Type *d)* is heard in measures 110-111 of King László's Men.

We may think of ambitus-shifts for the other–chords as well–we shall not list all of them.

Pentachord melodies are abundant among both our children's songs and adult melodies. Of such a type is The Leveret, the second (non-fifth-changing) variant of Dancing Song (measures 29-56), and the "Talalaj" trio section of The Straw Guy. There are even four pentachord melodies in Whitsunstide: measures 80-87, 208-215, 223-235 and 286-319.

We find a minor pentachord in pieces nos. 77-79 of Bic. II. A Christmas Carol) has a rather unique pentachord: it ends on *mi* but with a *re-la* ambitus and a *fi/fa* alternation. (Or perhaps it ends on *ti* with a *di/do* tone-pair? Who hears it in which way?)

A lydian pentachord emerges in the third melodic line (measures 11-13) of See the Gypsies.

A pentachord set of tones does not always imply a five-tone ambitus. The melody may be extended to include the dominant tone at the lower octave:

Ex. 24

This type occurs rather frequently in our folk music. Elsewhere it is reversed: the tonic finalis appears at the upper octave:

Ex. 25

as for example in the trio of Gypsy Lament, measures 18–29.

(If anyone is concerned as to why we consider these to be pentachord melodies, let him remember that the scale of a melody remains major even if it does not remain within the span of one octave but instead expands its ambitus outward in either upward or downward direction.)

Hexachords. An enormous territory! Before the order of octave-scales or the musical thought which gave rise to them took form (c. the Baroque era), the frame of melodic creation was the hexachord. This was true in Gregorian melodies and in the slowly developing polyphony as well. Ever so many themes of Palestrina and even of Bach encompass one hexachord. The same applies to our children's songs and our folk music also. In the latter it is often only the principal line which is hexachordal, but we already demonstrated the pertinence of examining independently one single melodic line.

Hexachord examples from Kodály's works: Versengés, Honey, The Filly (extended to include the lower dominant tone), the coda of St. Gregory's Day (meas. 94 to the end!), and two melodies in Whitsuntide (measures 236–245 and 246–253). See also Bic. I, 42 and the first melodic line of Bic. III, 110.

We find examples of the minor hexachord in Bic. II, 87 and in the melody of Shepherds's Christmas Dance (measures 1–8).

Further hexachord of more than usual interest:

Ex. 26

a) We find a phrygian hexachord for example in Epiphany, third melodic line of the theme;

b) an Eastern phrygian with major third in the theme of King László's Men and in Tricinia 24;

c) the augmented-fourth minor hexachord is derived from Liszt's "gypsy" or more properly "ungar" scale. Of such a type is the Gypsy Lament (measures 1–2, including the accompanying voices);

d) the augmented-fourth dorian hexachord is a close relative of the previous type. The ending of Gypsy Lament is relevant here as the five tones of the final chord fit within this set of tones;

e) the altered major becomes a lydian hexachord as for example in the first four measures of 6 Humorous Canons V;

f) the segment of the melodic minor scale is well known to us in the Song of Faith, measures 6–8.

From among the ambitus-shifts we mention here only the pentachord which is extended to include the lower VII degree:

Ex. 27

An example of type *a)* is the mixolydian theme of The Voice of Jesus, of type *b)* the aeolian melody of St. Gregory's Day.

MODAL SCALES

The most natural seven-tone system is the closed diatonic line of perfect fifths: *F-D-S-R-L-M-T*. Already present in this set of tones are both tone-relations and all the tone-proximities within the octave range. It is understandable that our folk music, as well as the new Hungarian vocal music based upon it, both exist predominantly within the diatonic modes.

a) Dorian examples: 7 Easy Children's Choruses I, V, Garden of

305

Angels II, Gypsy Lament, the melody beginning in measure 55 of St. Gregory's Day, To the Singing Youth, The Bells (in which the final descant tone, just as also at the end of Gypsy Lament is precisely the characteristic major-sixth of the dorian), Dancing Song (the more complete fifth-changing structure, soprano voice measures 5–14), See the Gypsies, Orphan am I, the first of the Six Humorous Canons, the principal melody of Angels and Shepherds (measures 39–54).—We also find good number of dorian melodies in the volumes of the Bicinia: I, 44, II, 83, 95, 99, III, 102, 103 and the more intricate 107 (with a principal melody in a dorian, and a second verse in *a* dorian). Examples of fifth-change in dorian mode: Bic. I, 43, 45, 47, II, 81, 84, 94, 96, III, 111. In these we may observe how both our folk music and our composer utilize that property of the dorian scale which allows the exact duplication of the upper tetrachord at the fifth below.

The entire dorian scale is heard in the second melodic line of Bic. II, 80. We may well use this as an illustration.

We may at this point discuss an argument and a misconception in connection with the dorian. The argument: should we solmizate this mode on a *re* or on a *la* base? It is not a question of either-or but rather both! There is use for both. With the one we may show how, with no altered tone, it fits within the diatonic system, and with the other how closely it is related to the aeolian, natural minor.

The misconception: at one time, understandably, it was believed that "there is no dorian in our folk music. Such a term may only be used in referring to early Western music!" The above quoted melodies—and others numbering in the hundreds—are certainly pure dorian lines. And if this superstition here or there should raise its head, let us help do away with it.

b) Phrygian melodies appear with considerably less frequency both in our folk music and among Kodály's own melodies. There exist however some rather tasteful, characteristic examples: the second theme of Three Songs from Gömör, False Spring, the principal melody of Epiphany (in its pure form in the alto measures 52–67, then later in the soprano measures 101–112). See also Bic. III, 114, 116 and 120.

c) The *lydian* scale is foreign to our folk music. At best we find occasionally one or another raised fourth among melodies of major character. (Among the Hungarian folksongs which have so far appeared in print there are hardly more than a dozen melodies of pure lydian structure.)— Among Kodály's works we may mention one motive in each of the following: the first line of 7 Easy Children's Choruses II, the first half of Bic. I, 42, the well-known *f-s-l-t* agglomeration of simultaneously sounding seconds in the first piece of Mountain Nights. A lydian melody occurs almost by chance in the upper voice of Bic. I, 48 since the first line modulates to the dominant C-major in which there is therefore no b , while the melody of the second half answers in F-major pentatonic in which there is no b♭ either. (There is altogether one b♭ occuring in the accompanying voice.) We may also mention the F-lydian half-melody in the introduction to Angels and Shepherds, measures 18–23.

d) In *mixolydian* mode is Garden of Angels III, Arise my Horse and nos. 110 and 118 of Bic. III.—The small number of these examples is surprising as there is a relatively large portion of *so*-ending melodies in our folk music.

e) In aeolian mode is the theme of Shepherds' Christmas Dance and the third movement of Whitsuntide, measures 179–186. See also the melodies of Bic. I, 33, 36, 37, 40, 53, 56, Bic. II, 75, 90, 95 and Bic. III, 119. The aeolian (natural minor) plays a much greater role in our folk music than is shown by the Kodály examples.

f) Our *ionian* scale is identical with that of the major. In principle let us use former name for the older, non-functional (without tonic-dominant significance or use of broken triads) *Do*-scaled music, and let us designate as major the newer melodies in which the former "missing" elements appear. (It is not always easy to draw a clear dividing line between the two. In such cases we may alternately usè the Greek or Latin word respectively.) Since we find a surprisingly large number in Kodály's works, we shall not cite examples here. We trust the reader with seeking them for himself.

g) Locrian scale. This mode fulfills a singular purpose in the works of our composer. Among his works for adults (whether instrumental, choral or for solo voice) there are surprisingly many examples illustrating how he uses this *ti*-ending line—one of dejected mood because of the diminished fifth—to describe feelings of complaint, resignation, pain, bitterness and grief. However he also knew that these sentiments were not suitable for children. It is obviously for this reason that we are not able to quote any pertinent examples from the children' choruses.

THE SECOND SEVEN-TONE SYSTEM (HEPTATONIA SECUNDA)
Standing closest to diatony is that tonal system which likewise builds its scales on major- and minor-seconds, but with a different distribution. Here the consecutive whole-steps do not appear in groups of two and three members, but rather in a 4 + 1 division. Using the half-step as a measure, we designate the whole-step as 2 and the half-step as 1:
$$... 2\ 1\ 2\ 2\ 2\ 2\ 1\ 2\ 1\ 2\ 2\ 2\ 2\ 1\ 2\ ...$$

is the picture of this tonal system. That this is less natural and therefore less frequent is shown also by the diagram of perfect fifths:

$$B\flat \; — \; C \quad G \quad D \quad A \quad E \; — \; F\sharp$$

The function, the solmization, of these tones may of course be of many types. The absolute note-names have been chosen at random.

A seven-member tonal system has seven modes, as each member may be a base-tone upon which a scale can be constructed. The universality of Kodály's music accounts for the fact that all seven modes are used with surprising richness. In his music for children's choir he is however more restrained and only here and there does he give an example of one or another scale of the heptatonia secunda.

1. The *kuruc-scale* is a *mi*-ending line decorated with *fi* and *si*. (*Kuruc:* Hungarian insurrectionist of the 17th and 18th centuries. The historical songs of this era often use this type of *mi* ending line, therefore the designation *kuruc*-scale.) A beautiful example from Kodály's volume of children's choruses is the well-known 'Mid the Oak Trees. The cadence in the final four measures (30–33) of God's Blacksmith is formed exclusively from this scale as well. Likewise the end of Epiphany: in *a*-phrygian we sing the *b* and *c♯* in place of the diatonic *b♭* and *c*. (See the final five measures!)

2. *Aeolian with major-third.* One of Kodály's favorite cadence-types in which, at the end of a piece in aeolian mode, he sets the picardian major-third in place of the minor-third, and then not only in the final chord, but earlier as well. The scale of these sections: *l-t-di-r-m-f-s-l*. Examples: the last four measures of Bic. I, 1, the last three measures of See the Gypsies, the final eight measures of Dancing Song and the final two measures of Aurea libertas. And in the most prolonged manner the end of Mole Marriage: beginning in measure 82, the "picardy aeolian" extends for 16 measures.

3. *Minor-major.* From a certain point of view this is a reversal of the previous type: the upper tetrachord of the major scale now takes its sixth and seventh degrees from the parallel natural minor. For example: *C-d-e-f-g-a♭-b♭-c'*. We hear this at the end of the middle section of The Swallow's Wooing, measures 45–50. The melody is in *A-major, but the accompanying voices offer coloration to the scale by providing the tones f* and *g*. (The tone-painting under the word "megbántam" [=I am regretful] is outstanding!)

4. *Acoustical scale.* A scale of major-type but with augmented-fourth and minor-seventh, it unites the diatonic major-third scales: the characteristic tones of the ionian, lydian, and mixolydian scales are all present. An

example of this: Angels and Shepherds, measures 95–103, in which the predominant set of tones is *G-a-b-c♯-d-e-f-g*.

5. *Mixolydian with minor sixth* is the line we hear in the first eight measures of The Voice of Jesus. The prolonged *f* in the middle voice here transfers the basic *A*-mixolydian line to the area of heptatonia secunda. *(A-b-c♯-e-f-g-a)*.

6. *Dorian with minor-second* (Neapolitan dorian, phrygian-dorian) gives a special character to the first eight measures of Orphan am I. Here the accompanying ostinato to the *f♯*-dorian melody (in four sharps) builds its figuration with *g* in place of *g♯*. The resulting scale: *f♯-g-a-b-c♯-d♯-e-f* .

7. The *melodic minor* also belongs to this tonal system. In ascending direction it is much easier to sing (with the *mi-fi-si-la* tetrachord) and therefore also more frequent in music literature. The descending melodic minor is much rarer. The *la-si-fi-mi* melodic minor line was almost completely displaced by the *l-s-f-m* tetrachord of the natural minor. (We have even become unaccustomed to recognizing this segment as being part of the "melodic minor"!)

Among Kodály's children's choruses we find one noteworthy place in which we may observe that yes, the line of the melodic minor may indeed occur in a downward direction. We are speaking of Gypsy Lament. In measures 75–83 of this piece one voice of the divided alto part sings the line *d-e-f♯-e-d-c-b♭-a-g* in half notes. This is within the context of *g*-melodic minor. (A practical suggestion: as it is rather difficult to divide the alto into three parts, let the sopranos sing the two upper parts in parallel thirds, while the first altos sing the above-mentioned succession of half-notes, the mezzos sing the *D* of the syncopated ostinato, leaving the low *G* for the second altos. The lower voices are otherwise threatened by a thin sound which cannot carry the entire network of parts built upon them.) Several additional short examples of the descending melodic minor may be found in the Tricinia, No. 2, measure 16, and No. 9, measure 6.

OTHER SEVEN-TONE SYSTEMS

Foremost among those scales differing from diatony and the heptatonia secunda by one or more modified tones is the traditional *harmonic minor*. This *la*-scale, made functional by its *si* leading-tone, is rare in our folk music. This fact obviously explains Kodály's reluctance to use it often. The csárdás-like theme of Bic. I, 55 refers back to the "magyar" music of the past century. Besides the leading tone, the large leaps and obvious tonic-dominant relations reinforce this feeling.—We find to an even greater extent among the pieces of the Tricinia—even though in a form thickly enriched by alterations, tonal excursions, and modulations—examples of constructions built on the Western minor. See nos. 2, 6, 7, 8, 9 and 23.

Dorian with augmented-fourth. This scale likewise belongs to the *si* tonal system, but with a *re* base: *r-m-f-si-l-t-d-r.* (We may of course hear it as being *la*-ending as well. In this case its raised fourth step is *ri* and the sixth step *fi.*) Our best-known folksong in this scale became world-famous due to its inclusion into Kálló Double Dance. This "oriental dorian" exists also in Hindu music. If we put together the melodic and harmonic tones of the last verse of Gypsy Lament (measures 67–70), we find the *g-a-b♭-c♯-d-e-f-g* scale. (This is a reference to the historic connections existing between our gypsies and India.) The closing chord of the piece is also derived from this scale.

Phrygian with major-third. Likewise a scale containing *si*, but on a *mi* base: *M-f-si-l-t-d-r-m.* This scale which came from the East—its origin may similarly be traced back to India—is already closer to our folk music. There are truly beautiful melodies based on it. One of these was arranged by Kodály as the first melody of King László's Men. The melody of Bic. III, 106 also belongs to this scale, even though a *so* passing-tone slips in toward the end of the piece. We may perhaps also refer to this scale as an "Eastern phrygian".

Kalindra. This even more colorful variant of the oriental phrygian has a raised seventh degree: *m-f-si-l-t-d-ri-m.* It is also an important basic scale of Hindu music. As these scales with augmented-seconds, having originated in India, later spread to Persian, Arab and Turkish areas, our composer correctly affixes the indication Modo arabico to Tricinia No. 24. The middle section of the piece, beginning in measure 15, transposes the theme from *b* to *e* tonality. Here, in the middle voice, we find the scale more completely, thus more suitable for purposes of illustration.

Ungar. Similarly, *si* and *ri* provide the coloration for this *la*-line which Liszt, on the basis of gypsy music, considered to be the most characteristic "Hungarian" scale. But he himself also used the term "ungar" which will be more useful for our purposes. We now know, following the work of Kodály and Bartók, that this is not "the" Hungarian scale. Our composer gently replaces it to the area to which it rightly belongs when, in the first two measures of Gypsy Lament, the mournful *g♯* of the middle voice renders gypsy-like the *d*-minor tonality. We have however no other examples of this scale in Kodály's choruses.

EIGHT-TONE SYSTEMS
The most natural further development of diatony links one additional

member to the chain of perfect fifths. Contained within these octaton melodies will be either the *ta* (a fifth below the *fa*) or the *fi* (a fifth above the *ti*). In the first case the *ti-ta* tone-pair is the characteristic of the scale, in the second it is the presence of the *fa-fi*. Such melodies combine the characteristics of two fifth-related modes even if the two modes are not always accorded equal importance. As there is as yet no proper nomenclature for these eight-degree lines, we may describe their construction only in terms of the already-mentioned duality:

a) Major + lydian: Bic. I, 42, Bic. III, 115, the 7 Easy Children's Choruses II, The Deaf Boatman (the upper voice in its entirety), the cantus firmus of Psalm 150.

b) Major + mixolydian: Bic. III, 105.

c) Mixolydian + dorian: Bic. III, 101 and Arise, My Horse (second half).

d) Dorian + aeolian is perhaps the most frequent: Bic. II, 88, Bic. III, 104, 108 and the first of the Three Folksongs from Gömör etc.

e) Aeolian + phrygian: Bic. III, 103 (although with a range of only five tones) and also, in an easily recognizable form, the melody of the previously mentioned Christmas Carol.

f) Phrygian + locrian (for which we have but one brief, fleeting example): towards the end of Bic III, 120 the counter melody of the *e*-phrygian theme sings a *bь* which forms a diminished-fifth.

There are other types of eight-tone systems which are not structured on the closed line of fifths. For example, melodies which alternate natural and harmonic minor (with a *so-si* tone-pair). Or that type of phrygian in which both minor- and major-thirds occur (also with a *so-si* tone-pair). We may also consider the well-known melody from The Székely Spinning Room (with a *do-di* tone-pair).

A NINE-TONE SYSTEM

A set of tones becomes one of nine degrees when the diatonic row of fifths is extended on both ends to include the next nearest fifth. For example: *ta-f-d-s-r-l-m-t-fi*. Of such type is the 7 Easy Children's Choruses I (last two lines), the first and fifth of the Six Humorous Canons, etc.

The search for more colorful sets of 10 and 11 tones is once again entrusted to the reader. Let us close this chapter with a discussion of the maximum possibility to be found in Kodály's works (also the maximum to be found on the keyboard: our complete tonal system).

THE TWELVE-TONE SYSTEM

In Kodály's music—now in respect to tone-sets on the very highest plane—a significant role is played by the entirety of our tempered-enharmonic tonal system. Let us refer to this as dodecatony (distinguishing it thus from the strictly rule-bound dodecaphony of the Schoenberg school).

Our *maître* well knows however that chromaticism and, to an even greater extent, enharmonic relations are not easily dealt with by children. (Nor are chromatic steps, i. e. augmented primes, known in our folk music; at most there are altered tones placed between easier intervals.) On the other hand, Kodály knew that our aspiring choirs must be trained to move into the realm of newer music with its chromatic-enharmonic tone-sets.

Chromatic movement is a great rarity in the children's choruses of our composer. Yet such must be sung in measures 4 and 8 of Gypsy Lament, measures 16–17 of False Spring, in The Swallow's Wooing (measures 36–37), and Evening Song (measures 6–7). There is considerably more chromaticism in the larger works for women's choir (Mountain Nights, Italian Madrigals, Woe is me!, Orphan am I etc.).

We meet with an enharmonically notated chord in this sonorous passage of God's Blacksmith:

Ex. 28

It is obvious here that in measure 14 an $a\sharp$ must be sounded rather than a $b\flat$. For the middle voice it is of course easier to read the line as f-f-a-$b\flat$ than were it to be written as f-g-a-$a\sharp$. Still, it is hardly a simple matter since, in pure (a cappella) intonation, $a\sharp$ is not identical to $b\flat$. However unbelievable it may appear, the $a\sharp$ is lower than the $b\flat$! $A\sharp$ above $f\sharp$: a natural major-third with a frequency ration of 5:4. The $b\flat$ above the $f\flat$ however is 32:25. Converted into decimal fractions:

$$f\sharp : a\sharp = 1.25$$
$$f\sharp : b\flat = 1.28$$

312

In other words the $a\sharp$ is lower than the $b\flat$ in the ratio 125:128. Thus if we wish to obtain the sounding of a pure $F\sharp$-major triad under the fermata, we must have the $b\flat$ (of $a\sharp$ value) sung lower by this enharmonic comma than were we here truly in need of the f-$b\flat$ tetrachord. The downward leap from here to the f should then be adjusted to the d-minor triad.

Kodály wrote numerous pieces of the Tricinia for thorough practice in chromaticism and enharmonic reading. We may marvel at how the composer knew how to bring forth, in these pieces, such rich, varied music with so few voices. We may also suspect that in these pieces he had in mind the tempered system in which the minor-second is equal to the augmented-prime, the minor-third to the augmented-second, and so forth. (This thought is re-inforced in the fifth piece of Mountain Nights, where, in meas. 60, the written $g\sharp$ and $a\flat$ are sounded simultaneously. Also, in the piano accompaniment to Vejnemöjnen Makes Music, measures 30–31, $G\sharp$-major is re-interpreted as $A\flat$-major.)

Since our choruses must from time to time perform pieces with piano accompaniment "there remains nothing left but to get on with it!"—we must on the one hand learn acoustically pure a cappella singing and on the other hand the intonation of the tempered system. The same ability is required for works in the newest style which are conceived in the tempered dodecatonic system. What does this mean? If we take only the whole step, its variants measured in cents (the hundredth part of a semi-tone in equal temperament) differ from each other thus:

wide whole-tone (e. g. *do-re* in major) .... 204 cents
narrow whole-tone (e. g. *re-mi* in major) .... 182 cents
diminished-third (e. g. *ri-fa*) .... 224 cents
each of the above on piano .... 200 cents

Principal variants of the half-steps:

the natural minor-second (e. g. *mi-fa*) .... 112 cents
a wide half-step which may occur in dorian and
mixolydian between steps 6 and 7 .... 134 cents
a wide chromatic step (e. g. *do-di*
in major) .... 92 cents
a narrow chromatic step (e. g. *re-ri*
in major) .... 70 cents
each of the above on piano .... 100 cents

If everyone would thoroughly learn these nuances there would be less out-of-tune choral singing and more and more of the "harmony of heaven".

The result of our taking stock of this material: nothing short of an immense diversity, abundance, wealth.

AMBITUS

One of the most revealing characteristics of the inter-connection between tone-set and melodic line is the range of the melody with specific regard to its final tone. By establishing the range (ambitus) we thus examine the tone-set from a tonal point of view.

Our folksongs, including children's songs, may be classified in six main categories according to range:

Ex. 29

The absence of clef-sign and key-signature in our illustration allows us to set forth a formula alone, without regard to the coloration arising from the alternation of minor-, major- (or even augmented-)seconds. The types illustrated:

- *a)* children's ditties (range of 1, 2, or 3 tones);
- *b)* melodies of narrow range (4, 5, or 6 contiguous tones);
- *c)* authentic melodies (within one octave above the final tone);
- *d)* plagal melodies (within the octave surrounding the final tone);
- *e)* tonus mixtus (unites the upper extent of the authentic with the lower extent of the plagal);
- *f)* Upwardly extended melodies (with range extending 11, 12, or [rarely] 13 tones above the final).

These classifications, with the exception of the very last, also correspond to the range-type of classical European monody (Gregorian, etc.).

A characteristic not to be found within the sensibility of traditional melodies common to a community: melodies extending downward and ending high are missing. This high culmination, aiming more or less at show ("let's shoot for the high *c!*") is foreign to the spirit of both older European composed music and Hungarian folk music.

All these types—with the exception of the first—may be found in Kodály's choruses for children. (He does, however, abundantly provide melodies of only several tones in the 333 Reading Exercises, the volumes of the Pentatonic Music and the 50 Nursery Songs.)

Let us examine each of these range-types.

Melodies of narrow range

The basic type is the pentachord *(b)*. The reduced form is the tetrachord *(a)*, the extended form the hexachord *(c):*

Ex. 30

1–4. There is a tetrachordal melody for example in the chorus entitled Thieving Bird. We may extract the principal melody from measures 5–16 of the piece. Of such type also is the cantus firmus of The Swallow's Wooing as well as the second theme of Vejnemöjnen Makes Music (measures 11–14).

1–5. The pentachord provides the frame for a great number of our children's songs, but we also meet with it among the songs of adults. Of the Kodály choral works belonging to this classification we may cite The Leveret, the "Talalaj" trio of The Straw Guy, three melodies of Whitsuntide (those beginning in measures 80, 208 and 286), as well as Bic. I, 57 and Bic. II, 77–79. This type is however surprisingly rare among his original melodies. Relevant examples are Bic. I, 3 (if the soprano sings the lower *do* in measure 4), and the first principal melody of God's Blacksmith (measures 5–14).

1–6. Hexachordal folksongs arranged by Kodály: Versengés, two melodies of Whitsuntide (measures 236–245 and 246–285), Bic. I, 42, the final melody of St. Gregory's Day (beginning in measure 91) and the theme of the double-chorus Honey. The ostinato of the Modo arabico (Tricinia, No. 24) is a special oriental hexachord *(d)*.

Lower extensions. The above ranges are sometimes extended by the addition of one tone below the finalis. In our folk music this is not a leading-tone but rather the *subtonium* seventh degree which is a whole-step below the key-tone. It is not a leading-tone since it originates on the one hand from pentatony and on the other hand from the modal subtonium of the dorian, aeolian, phrygian, mixolydian scales. The raised seventh degree, the leading-tone, is primarily a characteristic of the Western major-minor system. (We find rather few such leading-tone themes among Kodály's works. Two such are Finnish melodies [Bic. IV, 121 and 179], and one is an old "art" song Don't Despair!)

These are the narrow ranges extended downward:

Ex. 31

VII–4. A unique example of type *a)* is the phrygian melody of A Christmas Carol. Its ambitus reaches only from the seventh-degree subtonium upward to the fourth degree of the scale.

VII–5. A downwardly-extended pentachord *(b)* is for example St. Gregory's Day and the folksong theme of Bic. II, 67. Also pertinent here is the Finnish melody of Bic. IV, 122 as well as the unusual *mi*-ending theme of First Communion (for mixed chorus) which is built on the *ti-la-so-MI-re* acute pentatonic system.—Among Kodály's original melodies of such ambitus is Bic. I, 22, which is constructed in the spirit of our pentatonic melodies beginning on *do-re-mi*.

VII–6. The third of the Six Humorous Canons is a downwardly-extended hexachord. Otherwise among the melodies arranged by Kodály only two old ''art'' songs show such an ambitus: Bic. III, 114 and 119.

Authentic melodies

The finalis and its upper octave tone function as the boundaries limiting the range of those melodies designated as authentic. At times however we meet with some shortening or extension:

Ex. 32

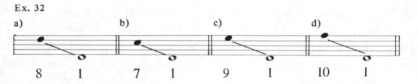

1–8. The basic type is the octave. Since a great number of our folksongs are of this type, the Kodály works also contain such themes in large measure. Several of the best known: Bic. I, 13, 38, III, 111 and the second melody of Gypsy lament (beginning in measure 18). Our composer also gives examples of this ambitus-type in the major-pentatonic melody of Bic. I, 3 as well as in Bic. I, 60 and Bic. II, 63.

If we wish to sing such melodies in unison, let us always choose the tessitura according to the given circumstances. The singers' voices, especially those of the boys, are lower in the morning. We may consider the *b*- or even the *b♭*-octave! Generally speaking the *c* or *c♯* is suitable as the keytone. If it can be easily taken, we may even place the octave range higher.

1–7. In our older songs the role of the octave-tone above the finalis as a re-inforcement of the tonality is not always realized. The 1–7 ambitus leans rather on the first and fifth degrees only. Of such type among Kodály's settings is the melody of Bic. III, 101, Gypsy Lament and the theme of Dancing Song, the pure form of which appears in measures 57–72. In these the arc-motive of scale degrees 5-6-7-6-5 is predominant.

Of much greater frequency is the upper extension, by one tone, of the authentic range. In our folk music this arises mainly from the double-system structure: the thematic line is pentachordal and is heard both on the dominant "upper story" (5–9) and on the tonic "ground floor" (1–5) as well. And this is irrespective of whether in the old, descending or in the new, ascending system of answering.—A few examples from the many: Bic. I, 43, 52 (in its entire fifth-changing form), See the Gypsies and its trio, etc.—It is on this type that Kodály also patterned the Tyúkkergető, Bic. I, 23, II, 98 and the fifth-changing *so*-pentatonic melody of Bic. I, 23.

1–10. Our authentic melodies may at times also arch upward to the tenth degree. (When singing in unison the beginning tone must be chosen with great care.) It is almost as if, in aeolian- (minor-)character melodies of this range, the song would not readily "accept" the *ti* being the upper boundary, but wants rather the support of the acoustically firmer upper *do*. At other times, remaining within the limits of single-system penta-tony, the upper *do* is heard in place of the high *ti*. Bicinia examples: I, 36, 37, II, 82, 90, 97 and 99. There is also a melody of this type in the Tchere-mis volume (No. 124). Kodály readily used this ambitus-type in his orig-inal melodies as well: Bic. I, 40, III, 102 and in the canon entitled Kár! (in the volume of children's choruses). There are yet three more famous Ko-dály themes of this type: those of Hymn to King Stephen, the great canon Song of Faith, and Psalmus Hungaricus.

The major-tenth is somewhat less frequent but does occur. Of such am-bitus are the Bic. I, 35, those melodies of Bic. II in folksong style (nos. 71, 73, 92), and four Tcheremis melodies of Vol. IV (nos. 128, 147, 162, 170). Finally, the original melody of Bic. I, 58 climbs upward along ten tones of the major scale. We may use the first ten measures of the alto as an oppor-tunity to learn the names of the intervals, singing:

Ex. 33

ad Bic. I, 58

prime, second, third, fourth, fifth, sixth,

seventh, octave, ninth, tenth.

A *lower extension* also occurs in authentic melodies. Here, in our the-matic material (folksongs or original melodies of Kodály) this lower neighbor-tone is always a subtonium degree, not a leading-tone. Types of lower extension:

Ex. 34

a)　　　　　　　b)　　　　　　　c)　　　　　　　d)

7　　　　VII　　8　　　VII　　9　　　VII　　10　　　VII

VII–7. Songs of more modest range without the upper octave-tone are 7 Easy Children's Choruses I *(a)* and the *la*-ending melody of Advent song O come, O come Emmanuel (for mixed choir) which also remains within the frame of the lower and upper *so*. Bic. I, 31 refers back to a character-istic ancient folksong type. The first phrase (measures 1–4) is in pure *Do*-major and only the answer (measures 5–8) reaches down to *la* at the end. The game is repeated in the second half of the piece, now with a new start-ing phrase (measures 9–12). The fourth line (measures 13–16) is the same as the second. The set of tones in formula structure:

Ex. 35　　　　　　　　　　　　　　　　　　　　　　　　ad Bic. I, 31

VII–8. We arrive once again at a common type: the group of melodies reaching upward to the octave-tone but also extended downward by one additional tone *(b)*. Our most famous prototypical example is the Peacock melody (Bic. II, 72). The folk-melodies of Bic. I, 11, 46, II, 75, 96 and III, 112 are also of this type.—There are more examples of original Kodály melodies in this category than in any previously-discussed group. In the volumes of the Bicinia: I, 7, 8, 10, 15, 17, 28, 47 and III, 107 (the theme in the first 16 measures). In other of his works: the theme of St. Agnes's Day (measures 1–16) and the second, more lively melody of Mole Marriage (measures 42–49). It is worthwhile to compare this latter with the famous theme of the Psalmus:

Ex. 36

Megkezdődik　　a lak-zi,　　So-se　lá-tott　víg-ság,

Mi - ko - ron　Dá - vid　nagy-bú-sul -　tá -　ban

318

so that we may trace what makes these two melodies so obviously similar in tonal outline, still so different one from the other. (Rhythm, meter, tempo, text, etc.)

VII–9. The octave now expanded both upward and downward means a range of ten tones. For unison singing let us put it somewhat lower rather than ruin the voices of our singers with high tones. But when the melodic construction permits, it is best to divide the singing group in two and have the two sections answer each other. (Ethnomusicologists suggest that fifth-changing construction were originally sung in answering groups.) Kodály does likewise with his pieces of similar construction in Bicinia I: nos. 29, 49, 50–51. The folksong prototype is Bic. I, 41. Of similar construction also is the first of Three Folksongs from Gömör. In place of the former descending line, the fifth-change of the new style brings about such an ambitus in the melodies of Bic. II, 93 and III, 104. Lastly let us mention here the theme of Golden Freedom canon. (A double-system pentatonic with a Transdanubian third in the final motive.)

A special, unique example is the cantus firmus of Epiphany. (In its pure form the alto voice, measures 52–67.) A phrygian melody downwardly extended to the subtonium *re.* However since the ninth degree is *fa,* the melody extends upward to a minor-ninth only.

VII–10. At the outer limit, but still among the authentic melodies, we may include those lines which reach upward to the minor-tenth and extend downward to the VII degree *(d).* This is a range of eleven tones and therefore, when singing, we must choose the absolute pitches with great care. Of such an ambitus are Bic. I, 45, Bic. II, 68, 70, 91, 94 and the Tcheremis melodies of Bic. IV: nos. 126, 137, 151, 152, 171 and 172.—Among Kodály's original melodies showing such a range are Bic. I, 14, 26 and 44 as well as the theme of Song of Peace which is developed into a concert piece from a singing exercise (Pentatonic Music II, 83). Lastly, the Canon for Solmization, not counting the major-tenth of the brief harmonic codetta, also belongs here.

Plagal melodies

With regard to ambitus, another principal type of old monody and of our folk music is that octave-melody which extends not *above* the closing-tone (1–8), but rather *around* it (V–5). (These would seem generally to be calmer melodies, of a lesser emotional sweep than those of the high-reaching arc-shape.) The basic type and its variants:

Ex. 37

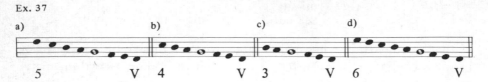

(The whole notes will in future also indicate melodic closing-tones.)

V–5. Among Kodály's choruses both Birthday Greeting and Seven Easy Children's Choruses VI respectively offer one example each of the major and minor plagal melody-types. The Finnish principal theme of Vejne-möjnen Makes Music (measures 5–10) is yet another such example. Among our composer's original melodies, the first eight measures of Mole Marriage are also pertinent here, even though the melody, serving as an introduction to a larger form, remains open on the low *so*, the lower limit of the range. We nevertheless clearly hear the true tonic as the *g = do*.

V–3. The principal theme of Whitsuntide has a range of unusual modesty but nonetheless is a chorale melody of great substance. From the lower dominant tone it reaches upward altogether only to the third degree above the keytone. (It is an example of the economy of classical melodic form: this high tone *mi* radiates forth for the first time only at the end of the third line!)

V–6. Plagal melodies may readily break through the "prison bars" of the upper dominant and sweep upward to the sixth degree *(d)*. We have many such upwardly-extended folksongs; Kodály also wrote numerous melodies of this type. In his children's choruses we find arrangements of folksongs which remain within this ambitus: The Shepherd, Evening Song, 7 Easy Children's Choruses II, The Filly and both melodies of The Lad of Harasztos (the second theme appears in measures 37–53). We may also mention that the Marseillaise has an upwardly-extended plagal melody of this type.—Kodály was especially fond of this melodic frame. Examples: 6 Humorous Canons II, V, one theme of King László's Men (from measure 160 to the end!) and also the melodies of Bic. I, 2, 4, 5, 6, 9 and 48 (this last in hypolydian tonality).

Much rarer is the uppermost tone occurring at the minor-sixth rather than at the major-sixth above the finalis. The folksong of Bic. II, 87 is hypoaeolian, the melody in the first nine measures of False Spring is in $f\sharp$-phrygian (remaining open at the lower V degree).

Tonus mixtus

In some melodies the height of the authentic type is joined to the depth of the plagal. The ambitus of these melodies has an old name: tonus mixtus, or mixed tonality. The types in question:

Ex. 38

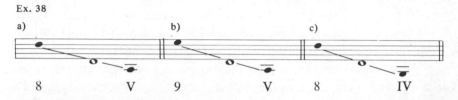

V–8. The melody of Bic. I, 20 is of this type. Our composer naturally divides the wide-arced melody between the alto and soprano.—There are, beside this single example of Kodály's, considerably more melodies of upwardly-extended ambitus.

V–9. Of such range are the melodies of Bic. I, 53–55, as well as the pieces composed to poetic texts: Bic. I, 34, and Bic. II, 74.—A similarly large ambitus occurs among the Tcheremis songs of Bic. IV: nos. 155, 166 and 175.

IV–8. The melodies of Bic. I, 12 and Bic. II, 61 have an ambitus extending downward all the way to the lower fourth degree. In the former piece the alto descends to the low *g* while the soprano reaches upward only to the d^2. For this reason we may sing this exercise, with its interesting melody, transposed to a higher pitch.

Melodies reaching to higher pitch levels

Ex. 39

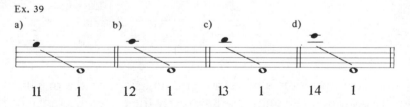

1–11. Of this type ("hyperauthentic"), which rises to the eleventh degree above the key-tone, we find but one folksong among Kodály's children's choruses: Bic. II, 85. It is however surprising that there are five such original Kodály melodies in the volumes of the Bicinia: I, 39 (the melody remains in the soprano part throughout!), II, 69 as well as the melodies created in the new-style form II, 76, 89 and 95.—Among the Tcheremis melodies, Bic. IV, 129, 131, 146, 153 and 154, all are relevant.

1–12. Perhaps the best known example of our melodies with a span of a twelfth is Réten, réten... Bic. II, 86 is Kodály's setting of this folksong. In contrast to this new-style structure, the main themes of Hippity, Hoppity (measures 1–8) and The Bells (measures 9–16), with surprisingly few tonesdespite the wide range, are formed by the lower fifth-answer of the old-style. (It is truly amazing how fresh and timeless these two themes are despite the older type of construction and melodic motion!) The Tcheremis folksongs of Bic. IV, 130, 158 and 160 are also of similar ambitus.

With rare exception we meet with even larger ranges:

1–13. One octave and then a sixth is the span of the Tcheremis folksong of Bic. IV, 165. (The large range is characteristic among the songs of this nation which is related to the Hungarian people.) But we may also find a Hungarian example in Bartók's book "Hungarian Folk Music", no. 132.

1–14. Bic. III, 108 is a puzzling case. The melody written "in folksong style" obviously follows the AA⁵BA structure of the new-style. The ambitus of the line—transposed to *g*—may be thus illustrated:

Ex. 40   ad Bic. III, 108

$$A \qquad\qquad A^5 \qquad\quad B \qquad\qquad A$$

Our composer presents the second line not at the upper fifth but rather, by means of an octave displacement, at the lower fourth. Now illustrated in the original *d*-aeolian of the Bicinium:

Ex. 41

$$A^V(?)$$

This octave transposition is therefore puzzling since on the one hand the previously indicated g-f^2 ambitus fits exactly the two-voice range of children's choirs with which the composer in numerous instances showed his familiarity, and on the other hand Kodály refers disapprovingly to such octave fracturing of wide-range melodies in his footnote to Bic. II, 86.—In the case of a unison performance, let us in any event transpose the

322

basic melody to the tonality and structural form of the first illustration.

A lower extension may also occur in melodies of such wide ambitus. In the Kodály material there are three variations:

Ex. 42

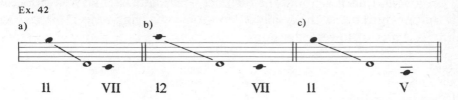

VII–11. Together with the subtonium degree VII and ascending to the eleventh scale step, these melodies have a range of twelve tones. Somewhat surprisingly the composer places such melodies in the first volume of the Bicinia. Quite early on there are five such pieces: nos. 18, 21, 25, 27 and 32. Then only in Vol. II do we meet with another such example in no. 103 composed in folksong style.—In this same category are Nos. 135, 140, 148, 149, 150, 157, 159, 169, 173, 174, 177 and 180 from the Tcheremis volume (Vol. IV).

VII–12. We even find one melody with a range of 13 tones in Bic. IV, 141.

V–11. One of Kodály's original melodies has a range which is one tone short of two octaves. Kodály places it surprisingly early on as Bic. I, 24. This melody unites the low area of the tonus mixtus with its area, the melodic line being carried all the way up to the eleventh scale degree. By "building floor upon floor" the arc-shape of the new-style is extended: the third line is considerably higher than the second, and is in fact exactly an octave higher than the first line. A sketch of the sets of tones and linear structure:

Ex. 43

ad Bic. I, 24

While remaining within the frame of possibility for children's voices, it reconfirms in a broad manner (with regard to ambitus) the structural principle of "the differentiation of the third among four".

A unique Tcheremis type. We have already seen how various types of ambitus are commonly extended downward by one degree to the neighboring tone below the finalis. We have also seen that this tone is a major-

second below the closing-tone *(la* below *so)*. In the melodies of our Tcheremis relations however the *do*-pentatonic is also common. In these melodies the lower-neighbor tone—the nearest tone in the five-tone system—
is the low *la*, thus it is not at the distance of a major-second but rather at
the minor-third below the finalis. (Pentatonic changing-tone.) Comparing
the two types of lower extensions:

Ex. 44

in *la*-pentatonic   in *Do*-pentatonic

The structure is different, but the essence of the matter remains un-
changed.—Our Tcheremis examples at the same time also extend the main
octave in an upward direction. The types which occur in Kodály's volume:

Ex. 45

To the first group belong the melodies of Bic. IV, 123, 127, 132, 138, 167
and 176. The themes of the volume which reach upward to the tenth
degree are nos. 125, 134, 136, 139, 143, 144, 145, 156, 163, 168 and 178.
Lastly with a span of one tone short of two octaves, is the melody of
Bic. IV, 142.

Melodies of six-four structure

If we examine the following Hungarian folksong—perhaps our only peculiar example in *mi*-pentatonic—according to its ambitus only:

Ex. 46   Bic. II, 66

324

we should say that it is authentic since it is placed within the 1–8 degrees of the octave. But is this finding, based on outward appearance, sufficient? Is there not something in this melody entirely different from what generally occurs within the authentic range? What is the main difference? In the authentic—but also in most other ambitus-types as well—next to the first degree (closing-tone, finalis, tonic) it is the fifth step which reveals itself to be the most important. It carries by right a dominant or reigning attribute. (The main 1–5 fifth of such melodies has been called "repercussion", an echoing interval, resounding again and again.)

In the above-quoted Transylvanian folksong however, the fifth step does not play any role (nor does it even once occur). In the reigning position rather is the fourth degree *(la)*, and next to it the sixth degree *(do)*. In sketched-out form *(a)*:

Ex. 47

These tones, together with the *mi* finalis, present a broken six-four chord. For lack of better, we may in the meanwhile designate these as melodies of six-four structure. And if we then establish from the ambitus that the melody falls within the authentic octave, we must further add something to the effect that the internal structure diverges greatly from the typical melodies of this type. Its interval of repercussion is not the 1–5 fifth, but rather the 1–4 fourth.

It is often heard, through a mistaken use of the word, that such melodies are "plagal". What gives rise to this error? The principal tone is *la*, and in this respect the octave is placed about this tone in a truly plagal manner. But still the closing-tone is not the *la!* If this were the case *(b)*, we would truly have to speak of a plagal melody. In this event the demarcation of the outer tones would be V–5. In our Transylvanian melody however it is 1–8.

The *la*, sounding mid-range in the ambitus, has such an important role that it merits a new technical-term. By no means is it the tonic, nor may we call it the closing-tone (finalis) or the dominant. If taken merely as the numerical degree of the scale, we could call it a subdominant since it is the fourth degree to the closing-tone. But since, both melodically and within the scale, it is so utterly different than a fourth degree of a tonal melody, we may not place it in this category. However, since it lies in the mid-range of the ambitus, and since it also has a mid-point significance, the designation *central* tone presents itself. This corresponds to the *mese* (middle) concept of the ancient Greeks who—similarly to our above song—considered the primary central tone of the line *mi-re-do-ti-LA-so-fa-mi* (at the time called dorian) to be the *la*.

Drawn on a characteristically six-four plan is the melody A csitári hegyek alatt, in which the first four tones immediately, as if a text-book illustration, present the steps 1–4–6–8. (Although not included in his children's choruses, Kodály does present a beautifully poetic setting of this folksong in The Székely Spinning Room.)

Since we have become acquainted here with several new concepts, it will not be superfluous to examine thoroughly all the six-four melodies of Kodály's children's choruses.

Among the hexachordal melodies, at a glance, belong the principal themes of King Stephen's Men *(a)*, 'Mid the Oak Trees *(b)* and The Straw Guy *(c)*. A schematic delineation of their sets of tones, ranges and internal structures:

Ex. 48

In these the repercussion tetrachord, between *mi* and *la*, presents the same colorfulness as the upper four tones of the Western minor, in which *fa* and *fi*, *so* and *si* alternate with each other.

A downwardly extended hexachord, but with a six-four structure, is the second melody of Three Folksongs from Gömör *(a)*. The folksong of Bic. III, 106 has the richest set of tones *(b)*. An entire octave, with both *so* and *si*.

Ex. 49

In addition to the above-mentioned six *mi*-ending melodies, Kodály has one original *so*-pentatonic song which similarly is supported by pillar-tone intervals at the fourth and at the sixth: Bic. II, 62. The melody:

326

We have here an ABBA new-style construction. Both the outer and inner lines each use only four tones of the pentatonic scale. The second measure of the third line shows intensified rhythmic activity and is linked to the recapitulation by two returning tones (asterisk). The first and last intervals of the melody, *so-do* and *do-so*, respectively, determine the tonality: So-pentatonic with six-four construction.

The aim of this detailed investigation is not merely a deeper understanding of formal elements. It is much more a demonstration, even in such relatively superficial terms, of the extent to which our folk music and the world of Kodály's children's choruses share a common ground.

II. POLYPHONY

Zoltán Kodály was the creator of Hungarian polyphony.

Once having developed his Hungarian melodic style, rooted in the soil of folk music, yet still individual, rich and of a new type, he recognized that polyphony is the true idiom of choral music. The equal melodic importance of each voice. The singer is neither a piano key nor a fourth horn in a brass band. He does not wish to accompany the melody, but rather to sing. According to our knowledge, Kodály was the first to bring an exhaustive exploration of the Palestrina-style to the teaching of composition. And of course of the Bach-style as well.

It is true that Bartók also created polyphonic choral works, but alas all too painfully few. Moreover his style is often more international than Kodály's in which each vocal work is deeply Hungarian. Of Kodály's contrapuntal works, if we count up only the two-voiced compositions, the 15, 22, 33, 44, 55, 66 and 77 singing exercises, the 180 pieces of the Bicinia and the dozen and a half works for children's chorus belonging to this category (not to mention the two-voiced sections of works for three or more voices), we are speaking of five hundred pieces!

The forms of polyphony which appear may generally be divided into two main groups:
a) free counterpoint,
b) contrapuntal imitation.

FREE COUNTERPOINT

Free counterpoint offers independent melodies, not tied to the theme and as differentiated from it as possible. It is customarily classified by name as either simple or double counterpoint.

Simple counterpoint. We immediately have a contrast to the theme when a different melodic line, even if in an identical rhythm, is set against the cantus firmus:

Ex. 51   77/9

An organic link: the melody in a pentatonic line, the counterpoint in the diatonic both move always from one tone to a neighboring tone only!

The effect is intensified if the rhythm is also different. Our *maître* also gives an example of the difficult syncopated counterpoint, a type of Palestrina-like contrapuntal exercise:

Ex. 52   Seven Easy Children's Choruses, 6

Jó   gazd' asz' szony   va - gyok én, no de   va - gyok   én,

Jó   gazd'   asz - szony   va - gyok

The highest degree of the above-mentioned exercise is the *contrapunctus floridus*, a counterpoint of a florid, or free-rhythm construction. One of Kodály's interesting examples is the devising of a counterpoint against the held tones of a chromatic scale:

Ex. 53   44/37

That Kodály wrote five additional contrapuntal voices to the chromatic scale (44 Two-part Exercises, nos. 38–42) attests to the composer's extraordinarily rich contrapuntal inventiveness. It is worthwhile to study each of them thoroughly! Among the many other examples of free, simple counterpoint, that of The Leveret, with its wealth of contrapuntal ideas is outstanding.

Double counterpoint is the name given to that type which is based on the exchange of voices. Such for example is the lively dance section of Three Folksongs from Gömör:

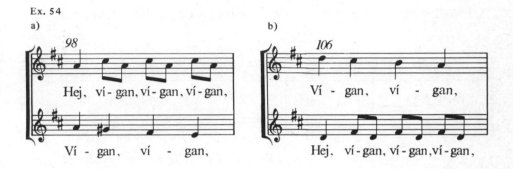

Ex. 54

a)

b)

in which the same ornate counterpoint is sung first by the soprano and then eight measures later by the alto.

IMITATIVE COUNTERPOINT

Imitation has been a device used in polyphonic music for many hundreds of years. Kodály knew how to use it with astounding diversity. Let us attempt to establish an order of the different types.

Imitation at the prime and at the octave. The beginning on an identical tone sometimes follows the theme exactly for only a few notes. But even in such a case an organic connection is established between the two voices. A well-known example:

Ex. 55

The Shepherd

Elsewhere the melody of both voices is identical for a longer section:

Ex. 56   Bic. II, 87

Az ma - ró - ti za-bok-ba'

Az ma - ró - ti za-bok-ba'

A broader choral sound is given by the imitation at the octave:

Ex. 57   Bic. III, 107

A- rany, e - züst - ért, cif - ra ru - há - ért

A- rany, e - züst - ért cif - ra ru - há - ért

A real answer, the exact imitation of the theme in the key of the dominant, is an old, basic form of imitation existing for centuries. Kodály certainly does not ignore it. From among many examples we quote the fourth
verse of Hymn to St. Stephen:

Ex. 58

73

E - lőd - be bo - ru - lunk

E - lőd - be bo - ru - lunk bús ma - gyar fi - a - id,

The lower fourth is also dominant:

Ex. 59   Psalm CL

330

A *tonal answer* alters the structure of the theme: the main fifth (scale degrees 1–5) is answered by its inversion, the main fourth and vice versa. This is the case even if the pillar-tones do not stand immediately next to each other:

Ex. 60

77/9a

The *mi-la* fifth answers the *la-mi* fourth, and thus the bracketed third becomes a fourth in the answer.

A fourth answers an ascending fifth:

Ex. 61

Bic. III, 101

The two principal tones sometimes occur at a distance from each other, but still the tonal unity is maintained:

Ex. 62

33/15

The initial minor-second becomes a minor-third in the answer.

Subdominant answer. When the tone *ti* was heard in the theme, the old masters—especially the composers working in the Palestrina-style—did not answer in the dominant as the *fi* would then have been the corresponding tone to the *ti*. Moreover the *fi* was permitted only as the leading-degree to the *so*. Thus they answered either at the fifth below or at the fourth above, in which case the diatonic *mi* corresponded to the *ti*. Kodály at times also employs this method of imitation:

Ex. 63

The *fi* in the theme is even stronger than the *ti*—the subdominant answer even more warranted:

Ex. 64

The composer also uses such counterpoint in the piece designed for practice of the augmented-fourth:

Ex. 65

Pentatonic counterpoint. The same amazing richness with which Kodály treats the pentatonic scale also prevails in his polyphony. He has many pieces in which both voices remain entirely in the pentatonic scale. And yet the possibilities of sound combination are far fewer than in lines of seven tones! One of his most beautiful and significant pieces is the bicinium written to a poem of Weöres:

332

Ex. 66

Bic. II, 74

Szál - lunk ke-ring - ve a nyá - ri lég - ben,

Szál - lunk ke - ring-ve a nyá - ri

The melodies "circle about" and "dance", transforming the words of the text into poetic musical picture. And throughout all 24 measures, all within a modest set of five tones!

Answer with vicariant intervals. As we have already seen (concerning *Exs. 13–17*), an answer remaining in the same pentatonic system chooses the low *mi* in response to the high *do* (and vice versa), so that we may avoid singing the *fa* (or the upper *ti*). It is not only in melodic progressions that this holds true. Kodály has also carried it over into the imitative style:

Ex. 67

Bic. IV, 123

Cse - veg - ni jöt - tünk, gazd' u - runk,

Cse - veg - ni jöt - tünk, hej,

The high tone of the motive is *do*, its lower fifth would be *fa*. The alto sings the *mi* instead.

In the reverse situation of the tonal answer, *ti* would answer the high *mi* of the upper voice. In true Tcheremis style we remain in this one system and have the alto sing *do:*

Ex. 68

Bic. IV, 128

Be - gyes cin - kénk, az is itt ma - rad

Be - gyes cin - kénk, az is itt ma - rad,

333

Acute and obtuse answers. We also agreed (in our discussion of *Exs. 4–8*) that we must recognize, beside the natural pentatonic, the acute and obtuse pentatonic systems as well. In the former there is a *ti* in place of *do*, and in the latter a *fa* in place of *mi*. Kodály also incorporates these into his polyphonic style:

Ex. 69

The theme beginning on *mi* does not take the tonal or subdominant answer starting on *la* in the imitating voice, but rather the *ti* of the acute pentatony instead. Nor is it very easy to find the ninth degree above the low *b* of the theme. (But perhaps this also is one of the aims of the exercise?)

Even though not in imitative style, but only in simple counterpoint, we nevertheless mention this well-known example of an answer in obtuse pentatony:

Ex. 70

By virtue of the two different key-signatures, the composer already makes clear that the two voices are each moving within different systems. The theme has a scale in which *b♭* is the *do*, while that of the counterpoint has an *e♭* as its *do*. This is the case taking each voice separately. But if we are to listen and hear the piece as a whole, then the *e♭* of the lower voice functions as *fa*. The answer then moves—when compared to the theme—in the obtuse pentatonic scale. (The piece ends surprisingly not in *d* but in *g*, in the relative *la*-key of the lower voice. It is as if the composer had wanted all the more to focus our attention on the obtuse pentatony.)

Modal answer. With Exs. 18–22 we were led to the concept of the modal answer. The intervalic structure of the theme is not varied, as in a tonal answer with a fifth-fourth exchange, only the coloration is altered. The alto answers the diminished-fourth of the theme with a perfect fourth:

Ex. 71   66/51

Further changes of coloration occur as the piece continues. (Where? Look for them!) Thus the "ungar" (Liszt!) scale of the theme is answered by the natural minor which does not use the two altered tones. Further examples of modal answer may be found in the 33 Two-part Exercises, no. 10 and in the 66 Two-part Exercises, no. 48. (Please examine these also!)

Heteromodal answer. From the works of Liszt we are familiar with the procedure by which the pairing of parallel major and minor scales (maggiore-minore, variant scales) is extended to other modes as well. This also occurs among Kodály's singing exercises:

Ex. 72   77/77

The initial minor pentachord is answered by the five-tones of the variant lydian mode. Later, in measure five, the lower voice shows that there is a more hidden common element shared by these two different types of lines; the *a*-minor melodic scale starting from its fourth step is like the lydian starting from *d:*

335

la   Re-lydian

Harmonic answer. Beside the real, tonal, modal and vicariant answers, we must also introduce the concept of the harmonic answer. In our Hungarian folksongs there are numerous examples of, for instance, the *la-mi* descending fourth which is not answered by the *re-la* fourth but rather by the *do-la* third. Thus these intervals of the question and answer nestle together in a hidden *la-mi-do-la* minor triad. An entire folksong example in major:

Ex. 74

In this Transdanubian bagpipe melody, the first and third tones (those more stressed than the others) rest on the *do-mi-so* triad.

In place of an exact imitation, the alto answers while remaining within the hidden harmony of the exercise:

Ex. 75   77/36

Imitation at secondary intervals. The old masters of polyphony also employed, in addition to answers at the fifth or at the fourth, entrances at other intervals. (Among the Renaissance masters perhaps Orlando di Lasso most often.) Kodály also knew of this:

Ex. 76   77/34

In addition to the third, the sixth also easily provides a consonance between two voices:

Ex. 77   66/14a

Although more difficult from the standpoint of compositional technique, imitation at the second and at the seventh probably has a more interesting effect. Kodály uses this even in a simple little children's song:

Ex. 78   Garden of Angels (Five Plays), 5

Én a tyú-kom nem a-dom, inkább körül - sza - la-dom,

Én a tyú-kom nem a-dom, inkább körül - sza- la-dom,

The major-seventh is capable of lending significant tension to an imploring exclamation (exactly at the point of the golden section!):

Ex. 79   Ave Maria

O - ra pro no - bis, pec-ca - to - ri - bus,

O - ra pro no-bis, o - ra pro no -

(We quote a three-voice excerpt here as an exception. The middle voice however does not take part in the imitation, but only fills out the harmony.) The alto should also be forte, indeed!

Free imitation. The melodic contour of the theme is maintained without any restriction on the size of the interval. In this exercise thus:

337

The tones of the answer are lower than the corresponding tones of the theme by a third, fourth, fifth and seventh. And yet the counterpoint has an imitative character which, melodic contour aside, is reinforced by the characteristic syncopated rhythm.

Imitation with augmentation. From Josquin through Bach and on to the later masters, this was one of the devices which increased the richness of polyphonic technique. Our composer did not remove himself from this tradition:

Ex. 81

Dancing Song

The middle voice presents the theme in doubled note values. (This melody unfortunately tends to be lost in performance. Let us see to its appropriate prominence as this voice "struggles" alone against the whirling rhythm of the other two.)

Imitation with diminution. The reverse of the previous device: the counterpoint imitates the theme in lesser note values. Thus for instance in the following song:

Ex. 82

Seven Easy Children's Choruses, 1

Imitation with projection technique. Musical projection, known especially from the works of Bartók = the narrowing or widening of intervals. This does not mean that it is used at only one or two places, as we have already seen for example in the tonal answer, but rather throughout a more significant section, at least the length of one motive, of the melody. A lovely example of this is Kodály's chorus on a poem of Arany:

The pentatonic theme, with prominent intervals of third and fourth, is projected into a diatonic, ideed in certain measure, chromatic answer. We find the most diverse examples of this type of melodic projection throughout the piece. Let us not spare the effort: let us also investigate the entire piece from this viewpoint!

Imitation with mirror inversion. As the old masters were conversant with this technique, so was Kodály:

The mirroring is exact for the first ten tones.
Retrograde imitation. While used much less frequently by Kodály, he does present an example of it (in the first two measures, with a mirror-inversion in the subsequent measures):

Countersubject, ostinato. The former: the same counterpoint joined to each recurring appearance of the theme; the latter: the "stubborn" repetition of a motive. Related to these is this example of Kodály's:

Ex. 86

(Cantio optima)   Bic. III, 119

Si - ral - mas én - né - köm   te - tő - led meg - vál - nom

Si - ra - mas   én - né - köm

ál - dott Ma-gyar - or - szág,   tő - led el - tá - voz - nom.

te - tő - led   tá - voz - nom.

He had a sharp enough eye to see that the lovely falling ternions could be placed exactly under the eight-measure melody in scale order. These ternions apply the suspension in "strict" classical style: unstressed, consonant prepatory tone; accented, dissonant suspended tone; unstressed, consonant resolution.

A rich example once again is Éva, szívem, Éva. *(Ex. 82)*

Still more concentrated is the counterpoint of the "Arabian" melody:

Ex. 87

(Modo Arabico)   Tric. 24

Pál - mák   al - ján   búj - kál   né - hány

Pál - ma - fák   a - latt   száz   a - rab   búj - kál,

Quodlibet = the contrapuntal pairing of two independent given melodies. While it can become merely a matter of unconstrained manipulation, a true artistic creation of stylistic and esthetic consideration may on

340

rare occasion be conceived with this device. How appropriate was his idea to bring the old *kuruc* theme to verbal battle between the Germans and Hungarians! The dialogue of the third stanza is enriched by this stirring sound:

Ex. 88   King László's Men

There is no need to force the sound here as the high voice will be heard clearly in any event. To be sure, it is from the depth of our memory that the sound rings forth. The middle voice then clearly serves to advance the verse, the story itself. (In most performances the importance of the "Magyars" gets lost here.) Let us consider measures 25–28, 34–37, 42–45 and 96–100 in a similar light as well. Unfortunately, the dynamic marking of the score do not give clear enough directions, but we may establish the appropriate order if we know: the carrying forward of the verse-theme is primary.

Counterpoint with consecutive thirds. Also known from the Palestrina-style: an imitative voice strengthened by parallel thirds. While more than a two-voice texture, it is still not true three-part writing. (My students jokingly refer to this as two-and-a-half-voice writing.) One of Kodály's examples:

Ex. 89   Arise, my Horse

In a richer variation of this technique, groups of chords stand against one lone voice:

341

Ex. 90   A Christmas Carol

Hir-de-ti már   a Mes-si-ást

Hir - de-ti már   Mes-si-ást

The anticipatory beginning of the lower voice pertains only to the first
tone: it is actually an imitation, in a rhythmic transformation, of the
theme enriched by the triads.

Double-chorus polyphony. Let us go one step further: the imitative
voice may also sound in triads. Kodály begins this unfortunately rarely-
heard but magnificent piece:

Ex. 91   Honey

Méz, méz,   méz,   ter - mett   méz,   ter-mett méz-nek

ál - dott-sá - ga,   le - hul - lott vi - rá - ga.

The imitation is easily realized under the first motives as the changing
chord can be sung under the rest of the upper voices. But the sound is
greatly enriched in the subsequent section: chords of four and five tones
ring forth in the imitative play of the eighth-note motion.

Imitation with stress-change. This presents an essentially different
degree of contrapuntal technique than we have so far encountered. In
question here is not merely a counterpoint which differs in melody,
rhythm, perhaps also in dynamic, but now in meter as well. That is to say

342

the metrical stress, the place of the accented and unaccented tones. In the "imitatio per arsin et thesin" technique, the polymetric style with changes of stress, Kodály was just as well versed as any of the old masters.

The most modest application, relatively speaking, occurs in a meter of four quarter-notes per measure, the imitative voice answering the theme at a half-measure distance:

Ex. 92   Bic. II, 80

In this case at least the primary and secondary stresses coincide with each other. But this is already polymetric as the first tones of the four-syllable measure stand out—and in correspondingly different places in each voice.

Even more exciting is that metrical play in which the primary stress of the one voice continuously falls under the unstressed beat of the other:

Ex. 93   Bic. III, 112

In three-four meter the answer begins after two beats:

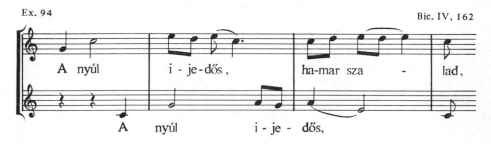

Ex. 94   Bic. IV, 162

343

The metrical tension is further intensified by a syncopated-like displacement of the simple two-beat measures:

Ex. 95 Bic. I, 53

While, in the lower voice, the upwardly drawn stems and cross-beams show the original notation, we and our singers must feel the stresses as indicated by the cross-beams of the downwardly drawn stems.

There are instances where the composer himself also writes in the counter-voice of the stress-changing polymeter in this way:

Ex. 96 77/3

We may also take note of the pure pentatony and mirror-inversion of this excerpt.

It likewise happens in three-beat measures that the voices enter one on the heels of the other:

Ex. 97 Bic. I, 51

Naturally, we must imagine here—as in each similar case—the bar-lines of the alto placed elsewhere, other than as written.

A similar displacement with mirror-inversion:

344

The following section is worthy of our consideration for more than its stress-change: it is an example to show that Kodály employs, although rarely, the whole-tone scale:

Ex. 99   33/33

We must consider the voice to be in the tempered tonal-system. The *e-g♭* diminished-third appears in the imitative upper voice as the *d-e* major-second. This is not meant to be two different intervals! The whole-tone (in Ernő Lendvai's term: omega) order is built relative to the tuning of the tempered piano. Somewhere within the perfect octave we must notate a major-second as a diminished-third (i. e. *b♭-c-d-e-f♯-g♯-b♭*).

The polymeter of changing measure-lengths permits interesting combinations. A crossing of two and three-beat measures:

Ex. 100   Bic. I, 57

Related to this is the meter of the five-beat measure, since it seems to combine units of two and three-beat measures. Kodály's example of stress-change displacement:

Bic. IV, 139

Mit bán-kó - dol, sö - tét er - dő?

Mit bán-kó - dol, sö - tét er - dő?

A special, asymmetrical eight-beat measure presents a combination of 3 + 5 quarters. Our composer finds the polymetrical imitation for such a melody, and with the most traditional consonant treatment (thirds, fifths are heard):

Ex. 102

Bic. III, 120

Ha meg-so - ka-so-dik a bűns meg - ra - ko-dik

Ha meg-so - ka - so - dik a bűn...

Stress-change imitation extends elsewhere to the extreme limit when the voices are displaced by altogether only one half-beat:

Ex. 103

44/3

The same situation pertains in alla breve notation:

Ex. 104

66/62

346

Here the half-step pendulum is given a counterpoint in a syncopated mirror-inversion.

Imitation in three voices. Imitations at the unison and stress-change provide great movement to the beginning of Tricinia, No. 1:

Ex. 105

Voices pledging a vow follow each other at the distance of a fourth and a fifth:

Ex. 106

Once again an example of Kodály's meticulous care. This most intense manner of voice writing appears not just anywhere in the relatively long text of King László's Men, but only in the last stanza, the culmination of the argument. And, appropriately, to the final words of the Hungarians.

In a two-fold, masterful solution, Kodály adds the imitative voices in the third movement of Whitsuntide:

The initial tone is answered first at the lower third, then at the lower seventh. In the second stanza the alto begins the theme which is then answered at the upper octave and subsequently at the upper fourth. At each point the voices are heard to sound in pure consonance.

Canon. The strictest form of the imitative style: the voices follow each other in exact imitation throughout. (At most a brief homophonic codetta is added to the end of the piece.) In order to study canons printed on one staff, in one voice, we must prepare a score, which in any case is useful to us as conductors.

In 1936 Kodály composed the Six Humorous Canons. A few words about each of these:

a) No 1. Rare for Kodály, altogether only two voices. The contrapuntal voice is lively, decidedly different from the theme.

b) No 2. a. The fluttering rhythms of the two-eighth measure are excellently suited to the text. (One measure = one beat!) The "little birds" follow each other in a thick three-voice texture.

c) No 3. A "bravura exercise" in counterpoint: each entrance is a second above the previous one. For this reason especially, the composer printed his miniature work in score.

d) No 4. A witty representation of the hen's "bustling about". (In the fourth measure of older editions a *d* incorrectly is found while an *e* should be sung here!)

e) No 5. Rich four-part writing interrupted by rests. (The entrance cues following the measure-long rests must be memorized!)

f) No 6. An irresistably humourous piece, if the choir is able to successfully imitate the "boo-oo" sounds of the bellowing cattle. The audience always laughed aloud when Endre Borus, who presented the unforgettable premiers of Kodály's children's choruses, had his boys "moo". ("let us not sing sweetly! Bellow like the *other* cattle in the meadow!", he said at the rehearsal.) The entrance-order of this canon is not the customary one.

The second group is brought in after eight measures, then the third group after another four measures, finally the fourth group after yet another eight measures. A well-tried procedural outline: the first group sings the piece two and one-quarter times through, the second group one and three-quarter times, the third group one and one-half times, the final group then exactly once only. A "map" of the cues in which each section represents four measures:

Ex. 108

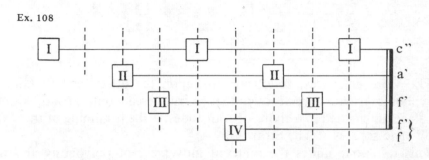

The 1972 jubilee edition of Kodály's Children's Choruses includes three additional canons which were previously not found in the volume. These are:

g) Aurea libertas. It is better for us to sing this piece with the original Latin text as the Hungarian translation, in the third section, has unexpected difficulties of prosody.

h) Kár! This canon was originally published without a title in Kerényi's magazine Éneklő Ifjúság (= Singing Youth). The year in which it was composed, 1944, explains much about the piece, about its text ("Hungarians are injuring Hungarians, great shame!"), and about the motive for setting it to music.

i) Canon of Solmization. Kodály's own text, intended primarily to counter the perennial scale-type approach to teaching music: "the ladder is not needed"!

j) Beside these smaller, rather playful little melodies stands one of Kodály's most imposing vocal works: Song of Faith, written to a text of the poet Berzsenyi. It is sufficiently well-known that we need not speak of it here in detail. But may we simply voice our desire that this piece become, as soon as possible, a part of our common national treasure. Is it not possible that we all learn this piece? And then sooner or later Zoltán Kodály's great gift to the nation, this canon-ode which welds Hungarian melody to a searing polyphony, may become our common song of celebration.

III. HARMONIC VOCABULARY

The following three measures may serve as the link of a chain joining the polyphony discussed in the last section and Kodály's world of harmony:

Ex. 109

Grow, Tresses

Ess, e-ső, ess, e-ső, ess, e-ső, ess!

The voice entrances, following one upon the other, call to mind a polyphonic structure even though they in truth create only a triad. A similar place, intensified to a chord of four tones, is the beginning of the "Talalaj" trio section of The Straw Guy.

This technique unites the inherent movement of polyphony and the clear chordal structures of homophony.

We thus cross over into the realm of traditional chords which even the composers of our own age have not discarded. (The words and structures of modern poets may likewise be traced back to the poets of several previous centuries.)

Neomodal harmonies. Foremost, and most profusely, to renew the use of consonant triads after the Palestrina-style was Franz Liszt. These chords live further in the music of our twentieth-century masters. Among the many types of harmonic movement, one of the most characteristic is the plagal motion by a second, by which we mean the descending-second relation to the primary tones. (This type of chord movement is most often missing from the functional major-minor idiom.) A motion of this type adds emphasis and light to the words "százszor is" (= even a hundred times):

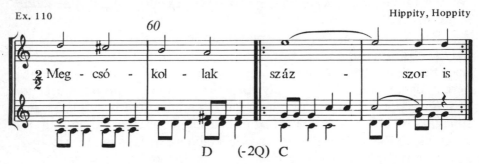

Ex. 110

Hippity, Hoppity

60

Meg - csó - kol - lak száz - szor is

D (-2Q) C

Beside the *D-C* movement of minus two fifths, the upward melodic leap and the opening of the harmonic spacing also move the text ahead to a higher level of prominence.

Especially characteristic is the treatment of modal cadences. As much as the essential element of classical cadences was the leading tone, in the neomodal style it is most usually avoided. Cadences are created rather by means of the whole step below the finalis, the subtonium seventh degree. For example, in mixolydian:

Ex. 111

a)

b)

Arise, my Horse

a há - tá - ra.

Eggy- egy saj - tot ad - nak.

Mix: VII   I V^7

An aeolian cadence, yet one into which the traditional cadential six-four is also built:

Ex. 112

a)

St Gregory's Day

Omne di-gnum le - ve - ren- dum lau- de.

b)   c)

The natural seventh degree, the subtonium, is also available for cadence in dorian:

Ex. 113

St Gregory's Day

Súr- ga sar-kan- tyús csiz - má - ját.

351

The same holds true in phrygian as well. The cadence may be formed the six-five position of a chord built on the V degree:

Ex. 114   'Mid the Oak Trees

Ti-éd le-szek már!

or with the first inversion of the VII chord:

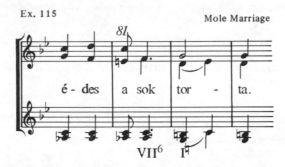

Ex. 115   Mole Marriage

é - des a sok tor - ta.

The construction is traditional, the coloration neomodal. (See also the phrygian cadences of King László's Men and False Spring.)

While in major there is no subtonium degree, the alteration of *ti* to *ta* will provide for it:

Ex. 116

The Swallow's Wooing

Ná-di he -ge - dű - vel.

Our composer was fond of cadences created with the second-inversion chord on the natural VII degree:

Ex. 117

a) Song of Peace

b) Song of Faith

Bé - két vár!   Sza-bad nép, sza-bad   nép!

VII$_4^6$ I$^\sharp$ VII$_3^4$ I$^\sharp$

The end of Canon of Solmization is also of this type. Let us also examine the endings of Hippity, Hoppity, God's Blacksmith, To the Singing Youth and the canon Kár!

Kodály, in his compositions, even extends the new type of modal-character endings to chords of five tones:

Ex. 118

Honey

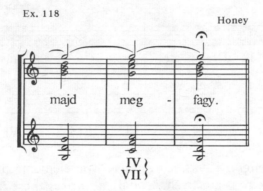

majd   meg - fagy.

IV }
VII }

The upper chorus quotes the opening motive *(d²-e²-d²)* of the children's song with T-S-T functions. The lower chorus supports this on degrees I–VII–I with T-D-T mixolydian chords. Thus in the penultimate measure we find—even though as a resultant—a ninth-chord on the VII degree *(F-a-c-e-g)* which is actually both a dominant and subdominant sounding simultaneously. What name shall we give to this function? Perhaps the best would be the term *antitonic*.

Modal cross-relation. The old masters well understood the difficulties caused by chromatic movement (for example *fa-fi*) in singing a cappella works. Thus, even if they wished to use a direct succession of such tones, the difficulty was avoided by means of a special manoeuver. The scale tone was sung in one voice, while the altered variant-tone was sung in another voice. Thus it was typical that, in a given pair of voices, a major-third was shifted a distance of a minor-third. In the Palestrina-style this occurs at four places:

Similar, in the identical key even, is the great Christmas piece:

Ex. 123

Angels and Shepherds

These excerpts are all forerunners of the chord progression which opens the mighty cantata:

Ex. 124

Te Deum of Budavár

Pedal point, bagpipe music. Characteristic elements of music in general, and of folk music as well. Kodály also uses these in his children's choruses. Typical in its simplicity is this example:

Ex. 125

St Gregory's Day

A fortuitous idea: the *la-mi* alternation of the middle voice above the pedal point gives a bagpipe effect, but in such a way that the a^1 always meets with the *e, c, a* (tonic) tones of the melody and the e^1 with the un-

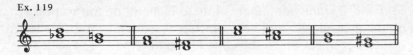

Ex. 119

completing various major and minor triads. This is to be found both at the beginning and end of False Spring:

Ex. 120

a)

nem tavasz,

tél   ez,   nem tavasz,

b)

False Spring

hogy már   o - da van

See also Tricinia No. 18, measure 7. (NB: all references to Tricinia correspond to the 1963 edition containing all 29 pieces.)

Pendulum motion. Leaving the area of neomodal harmonies, and now drawing from the truly varied use of classical chords, there appears singly before our eyes one of Kodály's favorite devices: the pendulum-like alternation of two chords. There is a floating, expectant effect in the repetition of such movement:

Ex. 121

205

Whitsuntide

...fé -   nye.   Mi...

The repetition of the minor VI–III–VI degrees (as primary movement between secondary tones) appears many times in the choral works of our composer. Thus, for example, the trio of Gypsy Lament:

Ex. 122

27

Gypsy Lament

Hej,   ti - raj - lej,   ti - raj - le - je   ti - raj - lej.

d: VI   III   VI

355

stressed *d* and *b* (quasi-dominant) tones. The end of the section remains open on the melodically and harmonically dissonant *ti* in order to form a more organic connection to the coda (Jobb az árpa...) in which we find an even richer bagpipe effect.

We recommend for analysis the following pertinent works: Evening Song (measures 1 and 3), The Bells, Mole Marriage (measures 10–17), Gypsy Lament, See the Gypsies, The Straw Guy (measures 48–93), King László's Men and Whitsuntide (measures 52–61, 75–99, 125–134 and 286–319).

The most characteristic chords of classical music, the dominant-seventh and the diminished-seventh, are neither typical of nor do they often appear in Kodály's choral works. However, among his works which draw upon elements of the Romantic style, he does use, here and there, some of the more unusual structures.

The independent six-four. The masters of older styles (Palestrina, Bach, Mozart) treated the second inversion of the triad in a severely restricted manner, almost always as a dissonance with appropriate preparation and resolution. (From the works of these periods we may find altogether only eleven ways of treating six-four chords.) The Romantic era freed this chord, along with many others, from its restrictions and in this style there often exists a free, independent six-four structure. Naturally, this use prevails in our own century as well. In this lovely section from the trio of King László's Men:

Ex. 126   King László's Men

We entrust to the reader the collecting of further examples.

Third-related chords. The modal cross-relation most often joins together third-related chords. But this connection is more in the spirit of the nineteenth century if the voices no longer refrain from using chromatic steps. An example of voice-leading between a *c♯*-minor and an *a*-minor chord:

False Spring

ko-ra nyi - lá - sát   bú   kö - ve - ti

c♯   a

G-major leading to *B♭*-major is the essence of the following progression, even if the latter is enlarged to become a seventh-chord:

Ex. 128

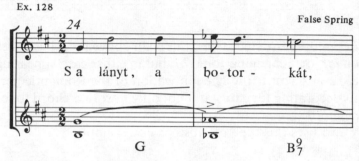

False Spring

S a   lányt ,   a   bo - tor -   kát,

G   B$^9_7$

(Caution: the augmented-prime is narrower than the natural half-step of the minor-second! The proportion of frequency vibration in the latter is 15:16, in the augmented-prime only 24:25.)

But there is another way, beside the modal cross-relation, by which the chromatic step may be avoided. It is truly clever and Kodály's deepest knowledge of a cappella (children's choir!) singing is proven by this procedure of joining together two third-related keys through a long-held single common tone. During the time of the single tone the voice threatened by the chromatic step practically speaking forgets the previous key and shifts over to the new key. Thus, for example, the first section of Whitsuntide ends in *C*-major; then the third of the chord, the *e*, is heard (Zeng...), and the chorus has time during the fermata to reinterpret the former *mi* as the *so* of the new *A*-major tonality. The same occurs also in measures 15–16 of The Swallow's Wooing. Schematically:

Ex. 129

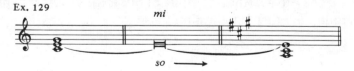

mi

so ⟶

357

Vicariant tones. We have already discussed, in melodic context within the pentatonic system, the occurrence of the neighboring sixth substituted in place of an otherwise expected fifth, or a third in place of an expected fourth. Since the time of Schubert such vicariant tones appear in chords as well. By chance it is exactly the vicariant sixth (replacing the fifth tone) that is the most common in Romantic cadences:

Ex. 130

In the older, more restricted styles, this sixth above the *g* bass was either a suspension *(a)*, or a changing-tone *(b)*, but in either case appearing before or after the consonant fifth. The innovation of the Romantic period permitted this decorating tone to stand not only *next* to a chord tone, but *instead* of a chord tone.

Kodály also uses this type of closing. For example:

Ex. 131   Tric. 16

$$II^{5\#} \quad III^6$$

We also find many other vicariant chord-tones in his works. Perhaps the best known is the *e* of the "leba":

Ex. 132   See the Gypsies

le- ba!

If we wish to take this and return to traditional voice-leading, then we would resolve the *e* to a *d* (the *a* formula of our Ex. 130). As it happens the same e^2 is found in other similar places also:

358

Ex. 133

a)   Hippity, Hoppity   b)

e-gye-tem,   e-gye-tem,begyetem

7 —
6   5

In more complex arrangement:

Ex. 134

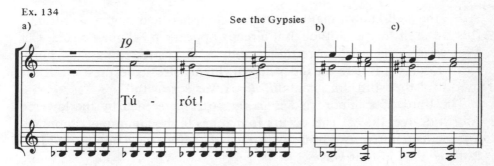

a)   See the Gypsies   b)   c)

19

Tú -   rót!

The e^2 of measure 20 would formerly have been resolved to a d in order to form a complete augmented-six-five *(b)*. However, the $c\sharp$ following the e^2 may be interpreted as the lower vicariant tone of the very same d^2 *(c)*.

The end of The Straw Guy is reminiscent of the older sustained six-four cadence in which the sixth proceeds from a suspended seventh over the bass:

Ex. 135

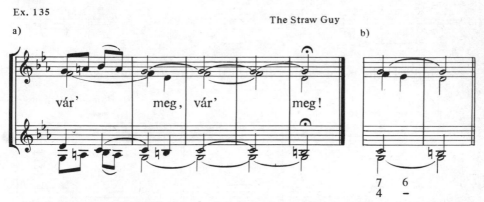

a)   The Straw Guy   b)

vár'   meg, vár'   meg!

7   6
4   —

The omission of the possible $e\sharp$ resolution renders the atmospheric ending of the piece more modern and at the same time more pentatonic.

Each of these examples also shows that the closing consonance is comparatively brighter when preceded by a greater dissonance.

359

Less frequent alterations. The standard harmony textbooks do not really know much about the many interesting altered chords of the Romantic school. But Kodály knew about them.

In The Swallow's Wooing we find a triad with diminished-third:

Ex. 136

The Swallow's Wooing

száz - szor is meg - bán - tam,

After the well-known major, minor, diminished and augmented-triads, this is the fifth type. Although it already appears in Schubert's song Der Wegweiser, it is heard there rather only as an unstressed passing-chord. With Kodály it is here the independent, highly stressed expression of the mood for the word "megbántam" (= I was sorrowful).

The third of a minor-triad is in rare cases preceded by the lowered fourth degree, the *ra*. This occurs four times in the humorous canon Mikor mentem misére. We hear this strange *d*♭ before the *a*-minor triad first in three then in four voices:

Ex. 137

Six Humorous Canons, 6

a)

b)

then similarly the *g*♭ preceding the third of the *d*-minor triad:

Ex. 138

Six Humorous Canons, 6

The volume of the 29 Tricinia is an abundant storehouse of such uncustomary harmonies. We ought not neglect to study and perform these pieces.

Double suspensions, at least the less frequent of such type, are also used by Kodály. In traditional styles these moved only in parallel thirds or sixths. The following excerpt has therefore a more modern effect:

Ex. 139

Tric. 21

There are parallel fourths in measure 49, suspensions in the outer voices (formerly very rare) of measure 50, fourths again in measure 51 with the lower voice also moving into the resolution. (The *c#-f-b* at the beginning of this measure may be heard enharmonically either as a *c#-e#-b* dominant-seventh or as a *db-f-b* augmented-sixth.)

Changing-chords. Three or more simultaneous changing-notes bring about a changing-chord. We may find the greatest number of such examples in the series of Tricinia. We quote several of these:

Ex. 140

Tric. 14

The notes in black show the other harmonies to which the changing-chords are enharmonically equivalent. Hearing the progressions in this way, we may realize the rather large scope of the excursion: the central members of the *g-B-g* and the *f-A-f* chord-ternions are not less than seven fifths (on the circle of fifths) distant from (i. e. above) the base-chord.

The opposite may be seen in the following excerpt:

Ex. 141

Tric. 18

(♭VI)   (♯V)

361

Here, also taken enharmonically, foreign minor-chords resolve to major six-four chords. We may view these as triads built either on the lowered VI degree *(bb-D)* or on the raised V degree *(g#-C)* of the minor. The original notation, however, does not follow this interpretation but more naturally the logic of each individual voice, the chords in question appearing actually as changing dissonances according to the score. These chords belong incidentally to the "diminished-seventh with major-third" type (for example *mi-si-ta-ra*) of the Romantic style.

The following sequential excerpt has resolutions to both major and minor with less customary suspensions in the consonant resolution:

Ex. 142

Tric. 14

A witty game: the first suspension sounds as a disguised minor-triad, the second as a disguised major-triad, thus reversing the order of the resolving consonances.

Mixtures. A chord progression with voices movig exclusively in parallel motion already points beyond Romanticism. It was primarily the era of Debussy–Ravel–Puccini which adopted the use of such mixtures. The objection is often justified: what could be easier—when harmonic invention is wanting—than merely accompanying a melody with parallels? But in the works of the great masters it is never merely a facile device, but rather a means for providing a variety which is integrated into the entire piece (not used too often) and only after careful consideration. It lies halfway between a simple unison and a fully harmonized setting. When used appropriately, parallels have the power of lending emphasis and painting a mood.

A line of open fifths renders the children's words even more sarcastic:

Ex. 143

The Deaf Boatman

Sej,   ki - lu - kadt a,   ki - lu - kadt a   fe - ne - ke!

A succession of root-position triads may be playful or serious. An example of the former is St. Gregory's Day, measures 73–79, of the latter this earnest sentence in the verbal conflict between Germans and Hungarians:

Ex. 144

King László's Men

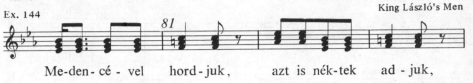

Me-den- cé - vel   hord-juk,   azt is nék-tek   ad - juk,

Notice also the organ-like effect in measures 99–100 of Cease your bitter weeping.

We are already familiar with seventh-chord mixtures from the Talalaj trio (The Straw Guy, measures 46–47) and from the work for double choir:

Ex. 145

Honey

Süss fel,   nap,   Szent György   nap,

(There are also many mixtures of root-position triads in this piece!)

Whole-tone scale. It was likewise the Debussy period which saw the wide-spread use of this six-degree distance-scale (a line of equidistant intervals), although it is only fitting that we acknowledge the bold inventive spirit of Liszt who already used it here and there among his works. Kodály did not consider this weakly-defined tonal order, which is also difficult to sing, suitable for his children's choruses. We find altogether only one omega-chord in each of a very few larger choral works. For instance the rather difficult, but exceedingly poetic cadence of this piece:

Ex. 146

Orphan am I

dim.   -   -   -   -   -   -   -   -   *pp*

Kodály accustoms the children early on to the free sounding interval of the seventh. Already in the first volume of the Bicinia:

Ex. 149

a)

Nekem si - ra - lom - ra, Jaj!

Nekem si - ra - lom - ra.

And more generously prolonged—for the prominently elevated word stress—at the end of the little motet:

b)

Ave Maria

A - ve Ma - ri - - a.

Similar to this is False Spring in which the *e-c♯* melodic turn is heard over the *f♯* of the lower voice.

A characteristic example of Kodály's independent, consonant treatment of seconds occurs at the beginning of one of the later choral works:

Ex. 150

Woe is Me!

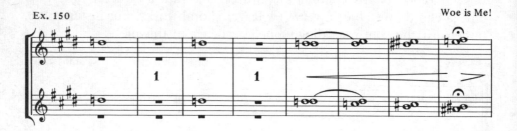

The solitary sigh occurs twice, after which there is a dispersion of the sound, contrary motion with the voices paired in parallel seconds.

A closing harmony may also be formed upon a compilation of seconds:

364

Here the penultimate measure is a five-tone chord taken from the whole-tone scale built on an *F♯* base. It very effectively prepares the resolving consonance. At the same time the tones of the final two chords coincidentally form one of Liszt's Hungarian-like scales, the aeolian with augmented-fourth. How perfectly the cadencing function of the harmonies promotes the duality of arsis-thesis, tension-release, dissonance-consonance. The antitonic of the next to last measure likewise sounds every tone of the scale with the very exception of the *a* and *c♯* which belong to the tonic region:

Ex. 147

If we also include the first-degree seventh-chord of the third to last measure, the internal order of the last three measures is:

44. dynamic tonic,
45. extremely dynamic antitonic,
46. static tonic.

In one of Kodály's late choral works (1957), the entire six-member omega-chord becomes a closing harmony:

Ex. 148

How aptly he paints the fading chime of the bells!

Consonant seconds and sevenths. The previous examples show that, in newer music, intervals of the second and seventh are no longer dissonances requiring resolution, but are consonances capable of use in chords. An old story: to what is at one time surprisingly new, one slowly becomes accustomed. When, after the era of organum, the triad appears (ars nova), those accustomed to the older way of hearing indignantly denounced the others who had the audacity to have a dissonant *mi* sung within the pure *do-so* fifth. "What will become of the beauty of music?"

Gypsy Lament

szusz - ki - ri   Jaj!

The sound-cluster, derived from the gypsy-like (augmented-fourth) scale, magnificently conjures up the wailing of the tent-dwelling nation.

A slowly building quaternion of seconds has an entirely different effect:

Ex. 152

Mountain Nights, I

Night in the mountains... At the end of the piece yet a fifth member is built onto the cluster of seconds *(b)*. Together with the tones *e* and *d*, which immediately precede these final two measures, we may complete the "heptatonia secunda" scale so characteristic of Kodály, the *b-c♯-d-e-f-g-a* locrian scale with major second.

We find consonant seconds and sevenths, and triads built on seconds most abundantly in the volume of the Tricinia. I cannot recommend strongly enough a thorough study of these pieces.

Pentatonic chords. Both Kodály and Bartók stated that chords derived from the pentatonic system are the harmonies which are most naturally suited for the accompaniment of pentatonic melodies. Even among the pieces of the Bicinia we find—in a rare three-voice setting—a pure pentatonic set of chords. See Vol. II, 63 a.

This example of a pentatonic dominant in Whitsuntide is most typical:

Ex. 153

Fe - le - sé - ge   jó tán-cos

In the original edition there was no crossing of the parts *(b)*. Then in the course of performances, the composer found that more than once the conductor did not believe his eyes, and thinking the *e* to be a misprint, had the alto sing the "more suitable" *d* in the lower voice *(c)*. But how much blander and more commonplace it is with the *d!* There is no doubt that the dominant *e* bass must be sung beneath the *D*-major triad of the upper voices. The spurs of the lively dancer clang so much more clearly in this way! (The first alto should sing this *e* with sufficiently strong accent. This is now the tone which bears the chord!) To avoid this incorrect reading, the composer later corrected the score so that the cross-voicing insures the proper reading.

A pentatonic fourth-fifth-chord relieves the tonic *g*-minor triad for four measures:

Ex. 154   Gypsy Lament

Similarly we find pentatonic chords (this time four-note chords) on a *c* bass in *g*-minor in measures 58–61 of Mole Marriage.

Once again an enormous effect through contrast: after the pentatonic triads of measures 27–29, the free-standing *C*-major six-four seems to eminate a radiant light. The fermata is indeed appropriate!

Ex. 155   Hippity, Hoppity

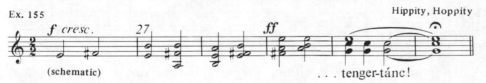

New types of cadences. Beside the already illustrated neomodal and other cadences, Kodály also employs new types of cadential movement. Again most abundantly in the series of Tricinia. We offer a few examples, entrusting the analysis to the reader:

Ex. 156

In this group belongs, among others, the close of Orphan am I. (See *Ex. 146* in the section on whole-tone scales.)

The chromatic intervals. The sharpest dissonances of our tonal system which is based on the Bach-tradition—the tempered 12-tone system— are the chromatic intervals. Let us understand by this the simultaneous sounding of a scale-tone and an accidentalized variant: the augmented-prime, the diminished and augmented-octave. The teaching of Kodály's purposeful educational concept begins with children's songs and the pentatony of our folk music, but then leads the children further along, singing in ever more complex tonal systems, to the outer limits. This, however, is always done with due consideration given to the vocal possibilities.

An augmented-prime may be easily sung if the logic of the voices happens to lead to such a meeting-point:

Ex. 157   Dancing Song

Even after a rest, and without preparation, our singers will find the *a* under the *a♯* (the *so* under the relative *si*):

Ex. 158   The Deaf Boatman

An altered-chord with augmented-prime, and in sequence:

Ex. 159

Tric. 18

If we permutate the upper and lower changing-tones at the distance of both minor- and major-second, then there are 64 changing chords for every triad. The one introduced above is one of the most intense among them. (Please try all of them!)

This series of suspensions superbly illustrates the use of the augmented-prime:

Ex. 160

Woe is Me!

(If we try this on piano, the tied-notes should always be restruck on the strong beat of the suspension!)

A diminished-octave may also be easily sung. For example, as an upper changing-note:

Ex. 161

Gypsy Lament

Gá - re gyo-pár bin-gyász- ku- le, gaj - du - le,

369

An augmented-octave, as a passing-tone:

Ex. 162

Dancing Song

The neighboring measures (appearing schematically) illustrate the logic of the alto.

A rich example of pentatonic- and changing-chords, along with augmented-octaves:

Ex. 163

Mole Marriage

We have already mentioned several times the richness of the Tricinia. We also find many examples of chromatic intervals among them. Let us look through these!

There are augmented-primes in nos. 5, 9, 18, 22, 27 and 28;

diminished-octaves in nos. 5, 6, 8, 13, 15, 17, 22, 24, 27, 28 and 29;

augmented-octaves in nos. 12 and 23. (In several of the pieces listed above, the particular interval in question occurs more than once. Let us also look for the harmonies created by these daring intervals.)

But all this is surpassed by the composer's use of yet two other intervals.

A doubly-diminished-octave is heard above the lowest point of the alto voice:

Ex. 164

Tric. 26

This measure contains its own neat little collection: a diminished-fourth, a doubly-diminished fifth, a doubly-diminished-sixth all are heard within the span of its four beats.

A doubly-augmented-octave occurs in our next example:

Ex. 165   Tric. 21

Here everything develops out of the leading-tone motion of the very first measure. The force of attraction moves the *a* to *b♭*, the *g♯* to *a* (although the middle voice, following the frequent example of the Bach Chorales, renounces the strict leading-tone motion and serves to fill in the missing chord-tone), and the *b♯* to *c♯*.

The exact same tones occur coincidentally in another piece as well:

Ex. 166   Tric. 13

＊8

Twelve-tone system. The ever-increasing use of altered-tones during the Romantic era ("Tristan-style") slowly led to true chromaticism: the complete equality of the 12 tempered tones. Young people can also secure proficiency in this area through the singing of Kodály's exercises. We have already seen pertinent examples, but let us close this section with yet one more typical illustration. Of course, we once again take our excerpt from the Tricinia:

Ex. 167   Tric. 29

371

The central, basic consonance here is the *do-re-mi* chord of seconds. We find this as our resting-point at the beginning, middle and end of the excerpt. Around this chord, the composer has us practice chromatic voice-movement and the uncommon harmonies and linking-tones which arise from it. (The exercise may be sucessful only through the employment of the 100-cent half-step distance; there is then no difference between the written augmented-prime and minor-second. Half-step is half-step!)

By now the reader may have observed that we have placed Kodály's world of children's choruses within the realm of a certain historical view of harmony. Beginning with the elements of the Palestrina-style, we have then viewed our examples in comparison to the elements of the classical, Romantic and Debussy eras. Our aim has been thus to show that in the hands of a great artist any and all devices may be fused, in the forge of a creative mind, into the elements of some new, individual and personal style. And, in addition, perhaps we may have presented, in a very limited manner, some understanding of the harmonies comprising those styles and of elements which are often not dealt with in a traditional study of harmony.

There are yet further areas to investigate in the spacious world of Kodály's children's choruses. Our knowledge might be enriched by formal, aesthetic or atmospheric points of view. We could speak of Kodály's choice of texts or about questions of prosody. Within the limits of this study, however, we must be content with a relatively brief survey of the more modest, fundamental elements. If this article has stimulated the reader to further investigation, then our efforts were perhaps not in vain.

(Az ének-zene tanítása, V–VI [1972],
I–III, V–VI [1973] Budapest)

STYLISTIC ELEMENTS OF BARTÓK'S MUSIC
IN THE 27 CHORUSES FOR EQUAL VOICES
AND IN THE MIKROKOSMOS

(A BASIC INTRODUCTION)

Bartók's 27 Choruses for Women's and Children's Voices were first heard in June, 1937 in a performance on the Margaret Island in Budapest. Since this memorable debut the older generation has happily seen these little masterpieces gain in popularity.

But do we really know these works in all respects? Perhaps it will not be superfluous to examine these choruses from specific viewpoints in the following pages. Of course, space will not permit us to examine every aspect. We will not touch upon Bartók's rhythm, nor the great variety of ways in which he writes for chorus ("vocal instrumentation"), nor will we enter into a long discussion of form or aesthetic appreciation. However, successive analyses of technical elements will perhaps bring us close to a full understanding of Bartók's music.

Our composer also wrote the six volumes of the Mikrokosmos for young people. Although written with the aim of setting forth a pedagogy for piano, its content is both artistic and poetic.

Using these two series of works, we shall discuss the following musical elements:

A) *Melodic Elements*: I. Pentatony — II. Melodies Built on Perfect Fourths — III. Modal Scales — IV. Polymodal Chromaticism — V. Scales with Augmented Seconds — VI. The Acoustical Scale — VII. A Second Seven-tone Order — VIII. Confinalis — IX. The Whole-tone Scale — X. Dwarf Tonality — XI. Scales of Alternating Intervalic Distances;

B) *Harmonic Elements*: XII. Modal Chords — XIII. Melodies with Half-cadence Endings — XIV. Polar Relations — XV. Pentatonic Harmonies — XVI. The Diminished Octave — XVII. Chords Built on Seconds and Fourths — XVIII. Chords Formed from Neighbor Tones — XIX. Bitonality — XX. Ostinato — XXI. Axis Order — XXII. Alpha Chords;

C) *Questions of Form*: XXIII. Variation and Projection Technique — XXIV. Symmetry — XXV. The Golden Section — XXVI. Folksong Forms;

D) XXVII. The Elements in Combination.

When looking through this study, every reader should have at hand a copy of the 27 Choruses and the six volumes of the Mikrokosmos. Only an edition with numbered measure should be used. If such is not available, do not hestitate, at least for those pieces discussed in the study, to number the beginning measure of each line.

Assignments. The study of the material is worthwhile only if practical work is included along with the analysis. Alongside the specific tasks of each chapter, let us take the opportunity to also do the following:

a) learn (also play and sing) the examples from memory,

b) transpose the examples (on an instrument) either from the score or from memory,

c) seek out the elements discussed in each chapter in other pieces not dealt with in the study.

Performance. It is not enough to be content with analyses of the works in grammatical and musical terminology. Let us reach toward a total experience through as many performances as possible: sing through each of the chorus pieces, play each of the piano pieces or listen to them on recordings. Those works which are referred to but for which no examples are given must by all means be examined and listened to as well.

I. PENTATONY

It is only natural that our great composers use pentatonic elements in their works built upon the soil of our folk music. However, the richness with which they have been able to personalize the world of pentatonic melodies is a source of wonder. Bartók achieved this in the 27 Choruses.

Ternions. Let us begin with the tone groups of three members. Among the most characteristic three-tone endings are those of the 5–4–1 type:

Ex. 1

köny-nye - im - mel.　　Szemem-bül a könny ki - csor-dult.

Is it only by chance that at the mention of tears exactly the same phrase is quoted as in Elindultam...? Does it belong to that folksong which appears as the first piece in the first joint publication of Bartók and Kodály, Hungarian Folksongs (Magyar Népdalok) of 1906? (And when this song was heard as a farewell at Bartók's last concert in his homeland, did tears not flow from the eyes of everyone who was present?) Perhaps this is the most

374

common among the pentatonic cadences of the volume, either as the ending of an internal phrase within a piece, or as the final cadence:

Ex. 2   Lover's Farewell   Don't Leave Me

Ná - lad nélkül él - jek?   az é - gig fel - ér -   jen!

The ambitus of the last example is already extended to a sixth, and in the following example to a seventh:

Ex. 3   Pillow Dance   Mocking of Youth

Fe - hér gerli - ce?   Ha - nem csak zab - o - csú.

The end of the melody may also span an octave:

Ex. 4   Enchanting Song   Stamping Feet

Ez az é - let   gyöngy - é - let!   ne fér - jen hoz - zá - ja.

It is characteristic that if the melody is at first constructed differently (4–5–1), it is consequently "corrected":

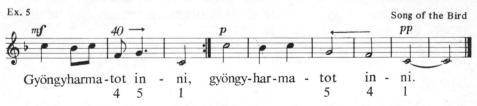

Ex. 5   Song of the Bird

Gyöngyharma - tot in - ni,   gyöngy - har - ma - tot   in - ni.
              4 5   1   5   4   1

Instead of appearing as a closing, the same three tones may also create a floating, open effect, as in the piece ending in C-major:

Ex. 6   The Wooing of a Girl

Another characteristic closing melodic turn is the *do-so-la* figure:

The figure may also serve as an opening, in the major for a festive mood:

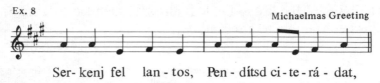

and may float in a central portion of a piece, as here, in both possible positions within the scale:

A similarly well known opening is the *la-so-mi* group of three tones:

The folksong quoted next to Bartók's melody was likewise close to our composer's heart, as he wrote a magnificent accompaniment to it (see Eight Hungarian Folksongs, No. 8).

Quaternions (a group of four tones). Four possibilities exist within our pentatonic system, one of which is the *mi-re-do-la* figure (the *so* is omitted):

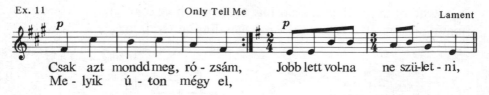

(See the closing of the folksong *Ex. 1!*)

Ending with a leap of a fourth:

Négynek li - kas   lá - ba,   van né - ked, van,

Besides forming an ending, the four tones may also serve to advance the motion:

Vi - lá-gon   míg   é-lek, so-ha nem   fe - lejtlek;

Annyi   jót kí - vá-nok   te-né-ked, annyi jót   kí - vánok, (ked -)

The resigned final tone adds the *so* and fades away on the confinalis (the dominant tone on which the piece ends):

Tu - dom,   töb - bet   nem jő,   so-ha-sem...   nem!

The famous four tones which begin the Peacock motive (without *do*):

Fel - szállott a   pá-va...   Fel - sü-tött a   haj-nal-csil - lag,

But the quaternion may also serve as a closing:

Ex. 16

più f *124* Pillow Dance

Ü - res, pusz-ta   a   ma - lom,

A four-tone group may likewise appear on *la-so-mi-re*, as for example in measures 4–8, upper voice, of Bread-baking (c♯-b-g♯-f♯). This formula has a second position in our scale on the tones *re-do-la-so*.

There exists one set of four tones from which the *la* is missing. The formula is well known from our recitative songs, in which a *so* appears after a *do-re-mi* trichord. This pair of motives moves within that frame:

Ex. 17

f *114* Pillow Dance

Pusz- ta   ma-lom-ba, haj,   Cser-fa   ge -ren-da, haj!

Finally there is a fourth pentatonic quaternion, the *so-mi-do-la* formula from which the *re* is missing. (This is called the harmonic quaternion as it includes both the *Do*-major triad and the *la*-minor triad.) To begin with folksong examples:

Ex. 18

Bé- ve-tet-ték a Ti-szá-ba... Ró-zsa, rózsa, ba-zsa-ró-zsa le-ve - le...

The same tones in different order and a beautifully evocative swaying melody:

Ex. 19

16 Song of Loneliness

Csen- des   fo-lyó - víz - nek csak zú - gá - sát   hal - lom.

With different melodic turns:

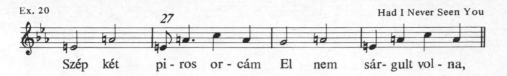

Ex. 20   *27*   Had I Never Seen You

Szép két pi - ros or - cám El nem sár- gult vol - na,

If we are already talking about an unfolding, let us examine one example in order to observe how our composer further develops an opening on three tones to a four-tone phrase, finally achieving the entire pentatonic range with the inclusion of the $f^1 = do$:

Ex. 21   The Fickle Girl

70

Sej,   haj,   haj,   haj!

bun - dám, bundám lesz, i - ca - ri - ca te!

Elsewhere a melody unfolds in a surprisingly personal manner:

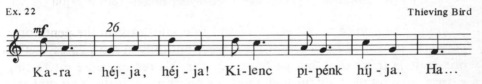

Ex. 22   Thieving Bird

mf   *26*

Ka - ra - héj - ja, héj - ja! Ki - lenc pi- pénk híj - ja. Ha...

This pair of dance motives may serve as a typical example of the frequently used *la-pentatonic:*

Ex. 23   Stamping Feet

f   *62*

Úsd ösz-sze a bo-ká - dat, Úgy ug-rasd a ba-bá - dat,

(We may place the two motives—for practice only of course—in reverse order, thereby obtaining an arsis-thesis unity in a more closed form.)

The *do-pentatonic* rarely appears in our folk music. It may, however, appear occasionally and Bartók in no way avoids using it:

Medve vár-ja, med-ve vár-ja, De nemaz ut-cá - ért,

We may find it in a longer section in the second piece of the collection:

Ex. 25   Hussar

Szé-na lesz meg ab-rak,sej de lesz, lesz, Szé-na lesz meg

ab - rak lesz.   nem hagylak itt, nem nem nem hagy - lak!

The *so-pentatonic* mode also appears occasionally:

Ex. 26   Stamping Feet

Sar - kan-tyúd zö- rög-jön, Fé-nyes pat-kód dö - rög-jön,

Acute and obtuse pentatony. "*Ti* and *fa* do not exist in the pentatonic system!" is heard everywhere. This is true, but only in most cases. Let us not exclude these rare, but perhaps just for this reason more interesting events. First let us think through these instances analytically. Our diatonic system will accommodate the pentatonic order (of the same melody) in not only one, but in three places. In each case we correlate the examples to *C-major:*

Ex. 27   *ti!*   *fa!*

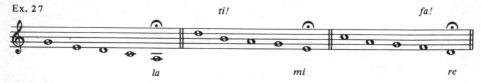

la   mi   re

In one case we hear a *ti* in place of *do.* We may call this *acute* pentatony. In the other case *fa* takes the place of *mi.* We may call this *obtuse* pentatony.

Although it is rare, we do meet these forms in our folksongs. The acute form is more frequent:

Ex. 28

Látod-e te babám, azt a szá-raz nyár-fát?   Az hol én el - me-gyek...

There aré those who would begin the solmization of this melody on *re*. While this is possible, if one examines the whole melody, it is not accurate. The beginning tones have an unmistakably *la* function. Let us not be afraid to call the 8–9–8 melodic degrees *la-ti-la!* In this way we may better express the double melodic system than if we were to give the same solmization to both halves of the melody. Thus:

Ex. 29

la - ti - la   mi,   re - mi - re   la

The second part of Ex. 29 corresponds perfectly to a piece of Bartók's in the key of *g = la:*

Ex. 30

Mint két egy-gyes   szív- nek   Egymástól   el - vál - ni.

The obtuse pentatony *(la-so-fa-re-do)* is much less frequent in our folk music. However examples do occur, if only as a motive here and there:

Ex. 31

'engem megát - ko-zott.   Hopp, hopp, zenge dob, mint a másé, zenge dob,

* Kodály: A magyar népzene, with examples added by Lajos Vargyas, 1952.
* * Corpus Musicae Popularis Hungaricae (Budapest, 1951.)

The following Bartók motives are based on $G\sharp = do$, thus the c$\sharp^2$ is the scale degree *fa* characteristic of obtuse pentatony:

Ex. 32

Nem szoktam, nem szoktam...   Csak szoktam, csak szoktam

The lower fifth-change is a construction so characteristically Hungarian that Bartók, especially when setting a folk text, could not refrain from using it:

Ex. 33

Thieving Bird

Ka- ra - héj-ja , héj - ja!   Ki-lenc pi-pénk híj - ja!

The second short line follows here in the tracks of the first. However, a more accurate quotation of our folksong form occurs when the lower half (two lines, not one) answers the upper half:

Ex. 34

The Wooing of a Girl

Mit ke-rü-löd, for-du-lod   Az én há-zam tá - ját:

Azt ke-rü-löm, for-du-lom   A te há-zad tá - ját:

An occassional *pien* tone does not obscure the pentatony, but rather, again as in the folk style, provides ornamentation. The final tone of the above example would probably be c^1. However, since we are not dealing with the end of the entire piece, the end of the answer opens onto the low *so* for the obvious sake of continuing.

There are even examples from our folk music—and from Bach!—of known *tonal answers*:

382

Ex. 35

Fel - sü - tött a   haj - nal - csil - lag,

The e^2-b^1 main fourth is answered by the b^1-e^1 main fifth. Moreover, the *re* and *so* of the second measures stand in a similar relation to each other!

Let us take leave of this group of themes with one of the most touching melodies of the volume:

Ex. 36   Had I Never Seen You

Is - ten ad - ta   vol - na,   Ne lát - ta - lak   vol - na,

Hí - re - det, ne - ve - det   Ne hal - lot - tam vol - na,

Each motive builds before our eyes (excuse me, before our ears) the entire pentatony from the primal cell, the pure fifth offered by nature. How? In the second motive a new tone appears the *so* ($b\flat^1$), the third motive presents the *do* ($e\flat^1$), and finally the fourth motive completes the scale by adding the *re* (f^1). At the same time the entire melody is itself a masterpiece: the arsis of the first part with its ascending octave, is answered by a delicate wave-like movement in the descending thesis line of the second part. Old style, new style folk song construction? It is at once both, out of which comes: Bartók!

Mikrokosmos

The child who studies piano may also come to know, through many examples, one of the most characteristic elements of our musical mother-tongue, the five-tone scale without half-steps. This example follows the construction of our fifth-changing melodies:

Ex. 37   Mikr. II, 66

p espr.

Related to this is No. 78 of the third volume. (Even its title = Five-tone scale.)

The "Transdanubian pentatony" with its raised seventh tone is heard in Melody in the mist:

Ex. 38   Mikr. IV, 107

We may compare the last line of this melody with the beginning of a folksong from Somogy county:

Ex. 39

Mi-kor gu-lás   bojtár vol - tam,

(Bartók published this melody as example 7/b in the volume *A magyar népdal* [Hungarian Folksong])

He also gives an example of the rarely found pentatony ending on *mi:*

Ex. 40   Mikr. V, 137

Let us also look for pentatonic elements in the following pieces of Mikrokosmos: Vol. I, 21 — Vol. III, 69, 78, 84 — Vol. IV, 103 — Vol. V, 125 — Vol. VI, 149, 151. It is characteristic of pieces which are otherwise not at all pentatonic to often have closing themes which are pentatonic. See for example the endings of Vol. III, 71, 80 — Vol. IV, 114, etc.

II. MELODIES BUILT ON PERFECT FOURTHS

Even though it falls within the realm of pentatony, this phenomenon is so special and so characteristic of Bartók that it deserves a separate chapter. To what do we refer?

The pentatonic scale may be derived from a five-membered chain of perfect fourths:

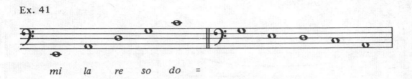

Ex. 41

mi   la   re   so   do   =

It is not as if these melodic passages so characteristic of Bartók are the only ones which present a series of perfect fourths built one upon the other. Such "step" melodies are not unknown in our folksongs:

Ex. 42   Bartók: Hungarian Folksong, 86

I- de   lát-szik   a   te - me-tő   szé - le,

Our composer found this melody in 1907 in the village of Felsőiregh, Tolna County. This type of melodic beginning, so different from Western tradition, certainly made a deep impression on Bartók. Relevant examples from the 27 Choruses:

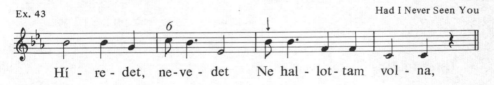

Ex. 43   Had I Never Seen You

Hí - re - det, ne - ve - det   Ne hal - lot - tam   vol - na,

The arsis motive of rising fourths is appropriately balanced by the answering thesis of descending fourths:

Ex. 44   Bread-baking

Ker- tem a - latt, ker-tem a - latt   a - rat há- rom var- nyú,

Ha ak-kor - ra nem jő, Bú- za- a - ra - tás - kor.

A melodic line similar to the above:

Ex. 46   The Sorrow of Love

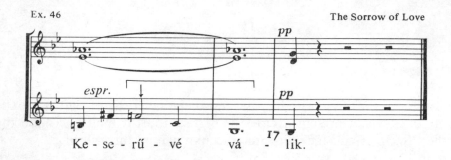

Ke - se - rű - vé   vá - lik.

In a lively manner, with recurring answers:

Ex. 47   Mocking of Girls

az el-ső,   az el- ső,   az el-ső,   az el-ső.

ső,   Ő lesz ott,   Ő lesz ott,   ő lesz ott,   ő lesz ott,

Three fourths one above the other:

Ex. 48   Bread-baking

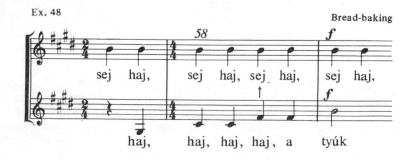

sej   haj,   sej   haj, sej haj,   sej haj,

haj,   haj, haj, haj, a   tyúk

386

(Caution!) The lower voice here must sing one of the fourths slightly larger so that the b^1 target-tone will fall exactly in line with that of the upper voice. Could this perhaps be done most practically on the leap of the middle fourth from $c\sharp^1$ to $f\sharp^1$? In the above examples (43–47) however, we must often take the seventh degree of the scale a hair lower, as indicated by a small arrow.

Mikrokosmos

Both the melody and the accompaniment of the piece entitled Boating begin with the "fourth upon fourth" formula:

Ex. 49

Mikr. V, 125

The beginning of the third melody of the piece entitled Ostinato:

Ex. 50

Mikr. VI, 146

A six-member column of fourths (to some extent with a harmonic influence as well):

Ex. 51

Mikr. V, 131

III. MODAL SCALES

Our folk music contains dorian, mixolydian, aeolian, and phrygian melodies in abundance. Bartók did not refrain from using these scales in his own unique way, while still remaining within the folk style.

Dorian. A melody corresponding to a four-line folksong, ending clearly on *re*:

Ex. 52   The Wooing of a Girl

Van né - ked, van né - ked Szép el - a - dó lá - nyod,

Szép el - a - dó lá - nyod, van né - ked, van né - ked, van,

Mixolydian. The lowered seventh degree distinguishes this line from the major. It almost seems as if pedagogical aims have caused this scale to appear in such an important position as the final cadence of the melody:

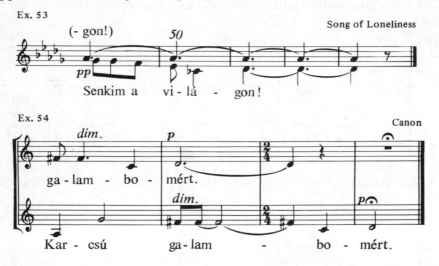

Ex. 53   Song of Loneliness

Senkim a vi - lá - gon!

Ex. 54   Canon

ga - lam - bo - mért.

Kar - csú ga - lam - bo - mért.

Phrygian. From point of view of the final phrases of the pieces, the phrygian mode, with its ending on *mi*, is the most common of the volume. We hear this quality sounding through even if the characteristic *fa* on the lowered second degree does not appear in the final measures:

Ex. 55 To My Homeland

so - ha sem - mi baj!
so - ha sem - mi baj!

due to the fact that the *fa* has previously been present in good measure. Further examples of phrygian-sounding pieces: Thieving Bird, The Fickle Girl, Only Tell Me!, Lonely Wanderer, Lament, The Sorrow of Love and Pillow Dance. (Many among these have a sad, lamenting character!)

Lydian. This is not a characteristic mode of our folk music. Scarcely a dozen lydian folksongs appear, almost by chance, among the several thousand melodies published to date. But we know that Bartók also undertook, with scholarly thoroughness, the collecting and investigation of neighboring Romanian, Ruthenian, and Slovak folk music. In this last category the lydian scale of the augmented fourth appears with significant frequency. It is as if, by giving such an important place to this scale, he had wanted to proclaim the brotherhood of the peoples. We immediately find an example in the principal melody and in the closing phrase of the very first children's choir:

Ex. 56 Don't Leave Me

visz - sza - jössz még!
Visz-sza, visz-sza - jössz még!

See also Spring, Michaelmas Greeting, perhaps the ending of Hussar also.

Locrian. The strangest, least common diatonic mode is the locrian, with its *ti*-ending and diminished fifth. It is similar to the phrygian, but even more suitable for expressing sorrow and complaint. How perfectly such an ending suits the text:

Mikrokosmos

We quote only a few among the many modal melodies. Among the dorian melodies, the beginning statement of the Study is especially worthy of our attention:

Ex. 58

♩=72

Mikr. III, 77

What should we know about the dorian? It is a scale of minor type, but with a major sixth. This is all stated immediately by the very first four tones of the above example.

In the same way, it is the pedagogue speaking in the lydian example:

Ex. 59

♩= 106

Mikr. II, 55

"Scale of the major type, but with an augmented fourth." The latter characteristic appears most clearly in the close of the motive.

There is even an example of that most uncommon scale, the locrian:

The first tones (relatively stressed) of each sixteenth-note pair delineate the characteristic diminished fifth from *c*♭ to *f*.

See also: II, 63 — III, Exercise 24 — IV, 116 — V, 123b (end) and the closing motive of our ex. 67. Further examples:

Dorian: Vol. I, 12, 14, 22, 31, 32 (title!) — Vol. II, 45, 53, 63 — Vol. III, 94 — Vol. IV, 100

Phrygian: Vol. I, 7, 34 (title!) — Vol. II, 44 — Vol. VI, 148 (end)

Mixolydian: Vol. I, 15 — Vol. II, 48 (title!) — Vol. III, 73, 75, 83, 85, 89, 93, 96 etc.

Lydian: Vol. I, 24 — Vol. II, 37 (title!)

IV. POLYMODAL CHROMATICISM

The term is Bartók's. By this he means that he readily accepts the existence of the twelve-tone system, but as often as not in such a way that integral parts of a melody sometimes move not in a chromatic order, but rather in a different diatonic mode. The combination of the two diatonic modes together produce the chromatic. For example:

Ex. 61

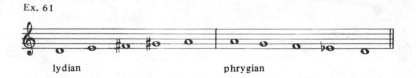

lydian   phrygian

If, as in the above example, a lydian pentachord is followed by a phrygian line based on the same initial tone, we hear the chromatic octachord *d-e*♭*-e-f-f*♯*-g-g*♯*-a*, even though the chromatic step of the augmented prime does not appear anywhere. Thus "duplex dos libelli", a two-fold benefit; the details of such an ordering are derived from folk music, but as a totality we find within it the maximum possibility of contemporary tonal order, the twelve-tone scale.

In the 27 Choruses the composer makes relatively infrequent use of this manner of weaving melodies. Nevertheless we do find significant examples. In modest measure:

The A-major or E-major outline of the first tetrachord is followed by an opening into the c-minor triad. Two separate diatonic parts, however g♯ and g, e and e♭ all appear within an organic unity.

An inter-twining of two two-measure motives:

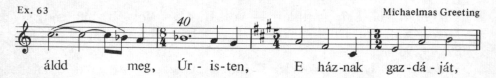

Three sharps after one flat, yet how smoothly the two motives, in seemingly unrelated keys, are joined to become one melody. The manoeuver is facilitated by the common-tone a which removes the possible difficulties of the b♭/b and c/c♯ chromatic conflict.

The volume's richest example of polymodal chromaticism:

From almost one measure to the next a different mode is heard. We sing b after, b♯, a after a♯, c after c♯, b♭ after b, g and f after g♯ and f♯ without ever having to trouble over the pure intonation of the chromatic step which causes so much difficulty, the direct augmented prime. Put into linear order, we hear each member of the c♯-c-b♯-b-b♭-a♯-a-g♯-g-f♯-f chromatic-enharmonic line. Nowhere is the difficulty of intonation more serious.

Mikrokosmos

Polymodal chromaticism is concisely displayed in the motives which appear at the end of the piece entitled Triplets. At first there is a lydian line, but then the final motive ascends on the major tetrachord and descends on the phrygian with the f^1 serving as a common tone:

Ex. 65
$\flat. = $ca.116
Mikr. IV, 118

The same thought in a more extended form:

Ex. 66
Mikr. VI, 151

Which mode do we hear in the ascending line, and which in the descending?

A complete folksong form:

Ex. 67
$\flat = 126$
Mikr. IV, 116

Can we determine for every two measures (or for every measure) the tonality which can be felt in the motives? How can we most readily solmizate each? What is the key of the closing pair of measures? Which tones of the 12-tone scale are missing over the entire melody?

V. SCALES WITH AUGMENTED SECONDS

Considered to be Hungarian by Liszt is the (gypsy) minor scale in which the fourth step is not *re* but rather *ri*. This forms an augmented second between the third and fourth degrees *(do-ri)*. In addition to this basic line, Liszt also deals with about a dozen other scales of similarly Eastern character. Bartók already knew that these are not the "Hungarian" scales. Nevertheless, he also dealt with such melodic turns. Was he perhaps in some way playing homage to Liszt? On the other hand such scales do occur in our folksongs. Moreover, these songs are precious and beautiful, even if only few in number.

These organum fifths:

fit exactly into Liszt's "Hungarian" *f*-minor.

Elsewhere we can hear the tones of the *g*-scale sounding in a musical sentence:

If we disregard the unstressed *b* passing tone, we find, quite clearly drawn, the beautifully named Hindu scale, the *kalindra,* which Liszt also used with some frequency:

394

If we hear the locrian closing motive together with its preceding phrase which contains a clearly stressed augmented second, we have an interesting new scale (a locrian with a major third):

Ex. 71   Had I Never Seen You

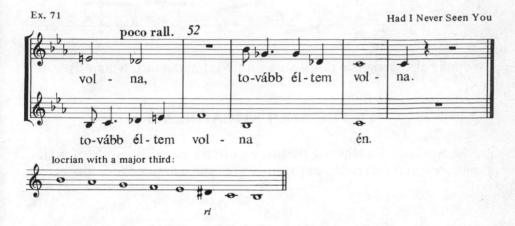

Mikrokosmos

An example of a dorian with an augmented fourth (tonal center is *g!*):

Ex. 72

$\downarrow = 100$ Mikr. IV, 98

Here the exposed tritone leap arrives at the significant *c♯*. (The piece continues with an upper fifth-change, giving an almost polymodal line to the melody.)

The very same scale ending on *a* is no longer a remembrance of Liszt, but rather resembles a melody in oriental style:

The *c♯* here is perceivable as the *si* and thus stresses the characteristic qualities of the scale: the augmented fourth and the augmented second.

Exercises 15a and 15b, found at the end of Vol. II, are also pertinent in this regard. Let us also study them!

The mixolydian scale of the Bourrée is given a special coloration:

Ex. 74   Mikr. IV, 117

(We may also designate this scale as a "Neapolitan mixolydian".)

VI. THE ACOUSTICAL SCALE

In the works of Kodály and Bartók we often meet with a scale of major type in which there is a raised fourth degree and a lowered seventh degree:

Ex. 75

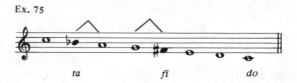

It unites within itself the characteristics of the three ancient major-third modes: the lydian fourth, the mixolydian seventh, the other five tones being taken from the ionian. We call this the *acoustical scale* as it most closely conforms the physical overtone series. (This scale had already been used in Debussy's time, and we even know several examples as well from the works of the greatest innovator of the 19th century, Liszt.)

The lower voice outlines precisely the scale beginning on *g:*

Ex. 76   The Sorrow of Love

Még az é - des méz is Ke - se - (rűvé)

An entire eight-measure open period:

Szép ma- dár a   fecs- ke, szé- pen is   szól,

Reg- gel, mi- kor har - mat hull az ág - ról.

Two voices, freely imitating each other, together shape the acoustical scale on *C:*

A - ki lán - got lát - ni a - kar, Hej, a - ki

A - ki lán - got, lán - got lát - ni a - kar,

lán - got lát - ni a - kar, Mind,

hej, lán- got lát - ni a - kar, mind,

397

In a three-voice piece:

Ex. 79   Pillow Dance

Rengő böl-cső-ben

(böl)-cső - ben   sí - ró

In the same manner on *B* :

Ex. 80   The Song-bird's Promise

Ha még ak-kor sem jő,

Mikrokosmos

Quite purposefully, as a pedagogical procedure, our composer, as early as in Vol II, has the student make friends with the very important acoustical scale:

Ex. 81   Mikr. II, 41

In the original, the *c* ♯ appears not as an occasional alteration—which is the way we have written it above for our descriptive purposes—but rather as a key signature valid for the entire piece!

Our composer repeatedly and concisely drives his point before us: the two characteristics of this (major type) scale are the augmented fourth and the minor seventh. Let them then be heard together:

It is commonly supposed that Bartók became acquainted with this scale and grew fond of it through the bagpipe folk music. (The bagpipe is capable of sounding only natural overtones.) An example of typical bagpipe music:

Ex. 83

Mikr. VI, 146

The high $f\sharp$ does indeed stand out conspicuously in this acoustical scale on g, but the bagpipe at times also gives out such "shrieking" tones. (If this example is played on the piano by two people, the upper, syncopated left-hand chords should be played by the person playing the accompaniment.)

We know that this scale is related to the major, the lydian, and the mixolydian scales. Bartók occasionally links the acoustical scale with all three. Let us find the pertinent sections of Vol. II, 52, 55 and Vol. III, 74a!

VII. A SECOND SEVEN-TONE ORDER

The acoustical scale introduced above is not playable on the white keys of the piano in any transposition—which is a simple proof and demonstration of the fact that it is not diatonic. It belongs to another order of seven tones. It also has its own set of seven modes, just as the diatonic has: We may of course choose any scale degree as the starting tone. (Please try to do this!)

Among these modes only one appears in Bartók's 27 Choruses. This mode may be considered as a relative minor to the acoustical scale. That is, it begins on *la*, but likewise contains the *ta* and *fi*. (Of course other solmizations may also be used!) The two scales shown in parallel relation to one another:

Ex. 84

"How shall I name you?" Until someone suggests a final apt and brief name for this unique scale, we could say that it is a phrygian with a major sixth, or a phrygian dorian, or (because of the lowered second step) a Neapolitan dorian.

Examples from Bartók's volume:

Ex. 85   Thieving Bird

Ha nem a-dod   vissza,   Ne jöjj er-re   héj - ja!

In a plagal ambitus:

Ex. 86   The Sorrow of Love

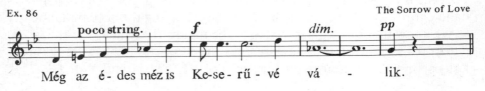

Még az é- des méz is Ke-se- rű - vé   vá - lik.

400

fi *ta*

Each of the two voices assumes responsibility for introducing one of the characteristic tones. The upper voice presents the *ta* (*f¹*), the lower voice the *fi* (c♯):

Ex. 87   The Fickle Girl

ic-ca-ri-ca te!   Van egy gyűrűm, ka-ri-ka,

ic-ca-ri-ca te!   Van egy gyű-rűm, ka-ri - ka,

fi   *ta*

Mikrokosmos

The very same phrygian-type dorian also appears toward the end of the Bourrée:

Ex. 88   Mikr. IV, 117

In rolling melodies, and in transposition:

Ex. 89   Mikr. IV, 118

a)   b)

By way of an exercise, let us determine separately in the course of a) and b) which of these tones belong to the melodic minor? Which to the acoustical scale?

Already in Vol. I, the student is introduced to yet another mode, the *kuruc*-scale:

Ex. 90

Mikr. I, Ex. 4

(legato)

The symmetrical quality of this scale:

Ex. 91

plagal

is used by Bartók, with the mirror imitation even being indicated in the title of Vol. I, 29:

Ex. 92

Imitation reflected

Let us study this piece to the end!

Two harmonies are sufficient for defining the "melodic major" scale:

Ex. 93

Mikr. V, 126

VII⁷   I

402

Let us add a *d* to the closing chords and then sing this scale placed in the *c-c'* octave!

Likewise, it is to the aeolian scale with *diminished-fifth:*

Ex. 94

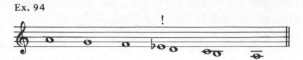

that our composer leads the children as early as the tenth(!) piece of the first volume. Here there is a key signature of *a♭* for a piece in *d* tonality. In the same way Vol. I, 25, with *b* as tonic, has a *c♯* key signature:

Ex. 95

Let us sing it with men's and women's voices in imitation. (If we begin on la, what syllable shall we use for the climatic *f* tone?)

Assignment. Play and sing the acoustical scale on a given tone. Then, beginning on each of the different tones of the same scale, do the same in turn with its other six modes. Identify the known modes (for example the *kuruc*-scale, the diminished-fifth aeolian, etc.) Write down the others and compare them to some known mode. (Such will appear, for example: locrian with diminished fifth, etc.)

Let us perform similar exercises starting from other related scales in place of the acoustical scale, for example

  a) from the melodic minor,
  b) from the *kuruc*-scale (*mi-fi-si*-etc.),
  c) from the melodic major which coincides with this (a *Do*-line but with lowered *la* and with *ta*),
  d) the diminished-fifth aeolian,
  e) the Neapolitan mixolydian.

VIII. CONFINALIS

In the collection of examples compiled by Lajos Vargyas which is appended to Zoltán Kodály's volume entitled The Folkmusic of Hungary, we find this Transylvanian minstrel song (No. 462):

Ex. 96

Por-ka ha-vak   e - se- deznek, de hó re - me   ró - ma,

How can we form an opinion concerning the tonality of this melody? We obviously feel that the tone *d* is the *do* even if the melody does not end on it but rather on the fifth above. In times past, before the system of closed tonality was established, such a melodic formation was not uncommon. Confinalis, a companion closing-tone, is the name given to that final tone which is heard on the fifth degree in place of the tonic which we, with our present feelings, now except to hear. We find examples of this in Gregorian and other old melodies, and in certain folk musics. Bartók does not exclude this either from his Mikrokosmos, his "little universe".

Mikrokosmos

Once again the pedagogue appears, and in this role Bartók, already in Vol. II, presents an example of this unusual type of melody:

Ex. 97

♩=120

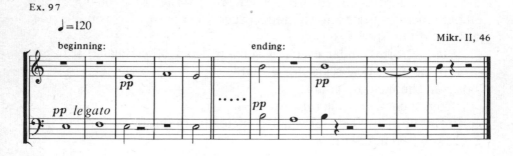

404

An *a♭* final tone above *d♭ = do:*

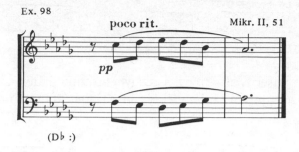

The piece entitled Big Fair concludes thus:

See also the endings of Vol. II, 37, 42, 48, 59, 60 — Vol. IV, 113 and Vol. VI, 139.

Look for examples of confinalis in the Exercises at the end of Vol. II!

IX. THE WHOLE-TONE SCALE

Of all the known tonal orders perhaps the Debussy–Ravel–Puccini type whole-tone (six degree) scale stands furthest removed from Bartók. It is exaggeratedly undefined in that each section is built on a uniform major second. Moreover it contains no perfect fifth which would serve to provide definition and tonal clarity. (Ernő Lendvai appropriately calls this the *omega* order thereby meaning that it is the furthest removed from the natural order.)

However, Bartók is a piano pedagogue as well, and, even if but briefly, makes the student acquainted with this musical element.

Mikrokosmos
In Vol. V we find the piece entitled Whole-tone Scale. Its theme:

Ex. 1·00   Mikr. V, 136

Yet the composer is also in evidence when, immediately following this, the left hand accompanies the melody in parallel minor thirds:

Ex. 101   Ibid.

(The above two lines of score are played together!) Being one of the most characteristic intervals of our pentatony, the minor third carries extraordinarily great significance in Bartók's music.

Let us sing each of these line, separately at first and then together. Thus, for example, the soprano and tenor sing the upper, the alto and bass sing the lower line (ommitting the held tones; we may add these later.)

X. DWARF TONALITY

We apply this name to the tonality of those melodies which move within the chromatic scale but only within a spread of about a half-octave. Furthermore, the altered tones are not, as in traditional music, changing or passing tones among diatonic degrees, but rather of entirely equal value to them.

Mikrokosmos

We meet with such melodies already in Vol. III:

Ex. 1·02

This melody in Bulgarian rhythms has an even narrower ambitus:

Ex. 103

Mikr. IV, 115

The melody of the lower voice may even fit into a perfect fourth:

Ex. 104

Mikr. V, 132

The rhythmic figure of the swineherd's dance also fits into this style:

Ex. 105

Mikr. VI, 146

Finally an entire period:

Ex. 106

Mikr. IV, 100

A useful and important assignment: sing these melodies a cappella with perfect intonation!

As a preparatory exercise sing major seconds in a chromatically sequential line as this is one of the characteristics of these melodies:

Ex. 107

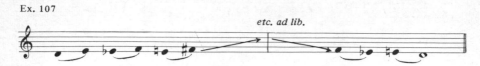

Look for such sections in examples 103, 104, and 106 which we have just quoted!

XI. SCALES OF ALTERNATING DISTANCES

As Ernő Lendvai has shown there is an important role given in Bartók's music to those new types of lines which are derived from the regular alternation of a half-step and one other interval. (I therefore suggest for these the term which appears in the chapter heading.) Within the span of a perfect octave there are three such scale possibilities:

Ex. 108

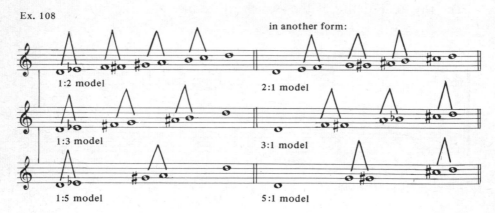

The terminology published here, which was given by Lendvai, is applied to the measurement of half-tones. In newer music there is often no difference between enharmonically spelled intervals. The composer may for example write a major third in one place, and elsewhere in the same motive may designate the same interval as a diminished fourth. The traditional intervalic names often break down, however it is all quite clear if we designate the size of an interval by the number of its half-steps.

While they may be rare in the volume of the 27 Choruses, examples of these arithmetically regulated scales do appear.

1:2 model. If we combine the tonal formulas of the two voices moving in thirds, we find a scale of eight degrees in the 2:1 version (mode):

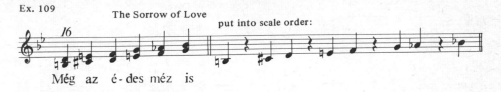

Ex. 109   The Sorrow of Love   put into scale order:

Még az é-des méz is

The main thought for each half-stanza in a unified melody:

Ex. 110   Canon

Meg-ha-lok Csur - gó-ért, De nem a vá - rá - ért,

in authentic range: in plagal range:

There is in all but one example of the *1:3 model*, and that appears in a more concealed manner. Let us leave out the unstressed passing eighth notes, and the more stressed tones then present the 3:1 formula, which is the second mode of the 1:3 model.

Ex. 111   Mocking of Girls

A tánc-he-lyen,   3   1   3

The *1:5 model* once again appears in a more clearly defined form. For example in the special melody of the word *keserűvé* (= turned to bitterness):

Ex. 112 — The Sorrow of Love

Ke- se- rű - vé   vá - lik

Two voices together bring forth the 1:5 model on an *e*-base at the change over the bar-line when the *f-bb* fourth opens to the *e-b* fifth:

Ex. 113 — Had I Never Seen You

szí - vem   Meg . . .

az én szívem   Meg . . .

The inversion of this, embedded in three voices:

Ex. 114 — The Song-bird's Promise

még ak - kor sem jő,   Tu - dom,

where after a *bb-f* fifth we hear a *b-e* fourth.

The surprising thing, and it is worthwhile for us to know it, is that these quite new types of lines were already used by Liszt.

Mikrokosmos

Let the young pianist learn the ways of new music as soon as possible! We may thank this pedagogical direction that already among the Exercises of Vol. II we find the following:

The hand of a small child spans only a fifth. However, we may complete the upper scale portion to the high *e* and the lower pentachord to the upper *g*♯. Then, have the women's and men's choirs sing the example according to the original score!

A period-form melody:

Ex. 116

Mikr. VI, 140

Let us sing the example, then line the tones up in scale order, beginning on the *c*, completing the line (with which tones?) to the upper *c*.

The major-minor double-third chord is derived from the 3:1 inversion of the 1:3 model:

Ex. 117

Mikr. III, 79

411

The main theme of the piece entitled Wrestling takes its shape from the same quaternion:

Ex. 118

Mikr. IV, 108

in which the *f♯* wrestles with the *f*.

There is a characteristic 1:5 beginning to the theme of the Chromatic Invention:

Ex. 119

Mikr. III, 91

Let us observe: realized within the melody is one of the principles of melodic structure of the Palestrina style, the *"motus interpositus"*. This means that interposed here and there in the course of the melody is an occurrence of one or another larger leap, following which those tones thus skipped then appear in the interest of closing, diversity, and completion. Let us notice how the first four and the following six tones of Bartók's melody compare in this regard!

Within the forms of its harmonies, a functional tension may arise among the members of this ordering:

Ex. 120

Mikr. IV, 111

Similar chord pairing occurs five times in the piece. Let us look for these, examining also their relation to the melody!

412

Interrelations. However diverse the building elements of these scales of alternating intervals may be, Bartók also understands well the surprising interrelations which exist among them.

If we put two different 1:5 models together:

Ex. 121   Mikr. IV, 109

we find a complete eight-degree 1:2 scale:

Ex. 122   right hand

left hand

There are also threefold combinations:

Ex. 123   Mikr. IV, 108

Let us examine the first melodic turn: we find in it the quaternion of a *d*-based 1:2 model. (Let us complete the entire scale!)

The continuation of this, starting from the same *f-f*♯ tone-pair, resolves to the double-third *D*-chord, together thus forming a 3:1 model on a *d*-base.

Lastly, if we compare the outer voices of the stressed beats, we find, just as in *Ex. 120,* that the tension of the *e*♭-*g*♯ arsis resolves to the closing *d-a* thesis.

The comparison of these models:

Ex. 124

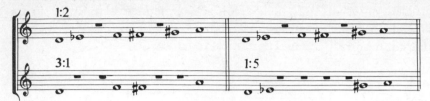

XII. MODAL CHORDS

Palestrina's characteristic chordal vocabulary (pure triads in modal lines) comes to life once again in the Romantic era, most prominently in the neo-modal style of Liszt. Bartók likewise followed this tendency. But in contrast to Liszt's modality which is quoted from the Renaissance masters, and which consequently shows characteristics of Western art music, our composer builds on Hungarian folk music, employing rather the modal triads of Eastern folk character.

He is even capable of giving an ionian character to the major when, in the manner of Liszt, he avoids the leading tone dominant in the cadence and give the final word to the plagal relationship of the II–I degrees:

Ex. 125

Lover's Farewell

Eny - nyi jót te - né - ked!

I II I

In a similar manner, a minor can be changed to an aeolian key, if the cadence does not include a *si* leading-tone but is formed instead with the subtonium (one whole-step below the finalis) on the natural VII degree:

Ex. 126

Stamping Feet

Ez az é-let gyöngy é - let!

VII I

We hear pure dorian turns in this section:

The very same appearing above the melody in the lower voice:

Similarly, the subtonium, the lowered VII degree, gives a mixolydian character to the pair of motives which otherwise are quite close to F♯ major:

This lydian cadence is reminiscent of Liszt's basic triads in the Palestrina style:

415

This lydian ending is however radically different, truly in Bartók's own style:

(Do we recognize the rarther old IV–V–I construction here?)

Excellently suited to sorrow and woe is the phrygian and its one remaining confinalis:

Once again the IV–V–I cadence appears in this other phrygian closing, here "enriched" with a seventh:

The picardian third, the *e* of the final chord, also reminds us of the old masters.

A locrian ending appears at the first introduction of the theme:

Ex. 134   5   Lament

Bok-ros bá - na - ta szí - vem-nek. jaj! jaj!

At the end of the piece the mode changes to phrygian, as we have seen in *Ex. 132*.

Here the closely related phrygian and locrian modes paint the hopelessness of the mood:

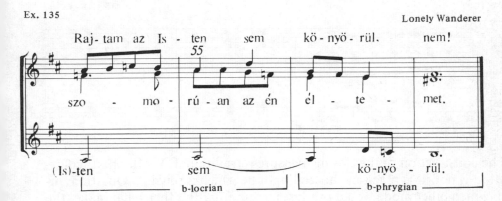

Ex. 135   Lonely Wanderer

Raj- tam az Is - ten   sem   kö - nyö - rül.   nem!

55

szo - mo - rú - an az én   él - te - met.

(Is)-ten   sem   kö-nyö - rül.

      b-locrian   b-phrygian

Thirds-pendulum. The old masters, and Liszt as well, readily employed a type of pendulum chord-alternation at the interval of a third. Nor did Bartók refrain from using this device:

Ex. 136   70   Spring

Sok min-den   szer - szá-mát,   e - ké-jét,   sar - ló-ját   Ő...

Modal cross-relations. We are likewise reminded of the Renaissance when a major third is shifted a distance of one minor third, thereby creating a cross-relation. For example $e + g\sharp$ after $g + b$, or $d + f\sharp$ after $f + a$ in the following section, likewise of third-pendulum type:

417

Choosing of a Girl

Fi -gye - lem - mel légy in - du - la. - tá - ra,

Mikrokosmos

Here also we find an abundance of modal harmonies.

a) This exercise has a pure dorian sound:

Ex. 138   Mikr. IV, Ex. 32

The construction of the closing measure is traditional (V⁷–I), but its color-ation is not. It is precisely the leading-tone which is missing. Question: in-to which other mode would this last measure fit? But then what makes the above excerpt dorian?

b) We find an aeolian cadence, here also a traditional construction, in the piece entitled Thirds:

Ex. 139   Mikr. III, 67

c) A regular V⁷–I cadence in phrygian:

A VII–I cadence in the style of Palestrina, i. e. with the subtonium, the whole-step preceding the final tone, also appears:

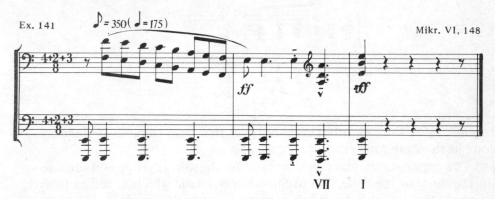

These combinations of seventh-chords present the phrygian mode:

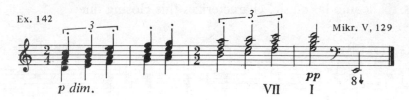

d) A single closing chord may present a mixolydian character (major type but with minor seventh):

Ex. 143

Mikr. VI, 153

but a series of chords may do the same:

Ex. 144   Mikr. III, 73

(Its close is on the $^6_4$ chord. This chord was first held capable of standing alone in the Romantic era.)

e) The lydian mode was much favored by Bartók. (Perhaps on the one hand because of the collection of Slovak folk music which he did early in his career, on the other hand is it perhaps because this mode is closely related to the acoustical scale?) The pendulum movement on I–II–I, known from Liszt's neomodal music, characterizes this closing line:

Ex. 145

Mikr. IV, Ex. 33

Richly sounding (strepitoso = noisy) chords of five tones begin immediately by presenting the lydian fourth:

420

Ex. 146

Mikr. V, 122

f) The locrian, perhaps the least common mode also receives its turn. Its tonic and characteristic diminished fifth are sounded simultaneously in the simplest manner (at the end of the exercise!):

Ex. 147

Mikr. III, Ex. 24

Chords broken into eighth-note pairs once again present a Palestrina-type construction:

Ex. 148

Mikr. V, 128

Simplified and sketched in white-key positions:

Ex. 149

VI⁷ VII⁷ I

XIII. MELODIES WITH HALF-CADENCE ENDINGS

There are melodies which, when judged by our feeling for traditional tonality, do not end on the expected basic tone, but rather on the second degree above. We find such tunes mostly among Serbian folk music. Several such examples also appear among the folksongs of Baranya County (Hungary), but here we may suspect the influence of the neighboring people:

Ex. 150

In János Nagy Berze's collection, Hungarian Folk Customs of Baranya County, we find (p. 291) a melody which appears to be in g-minor but which ends on *a (ti)*. (We may sing the *D* and *f♯* of the dominant under the final note!) If we consider half-melodies, we may place in this category melody No. 345 from the Kodály–Vargyas book (A szép leány aranybárány).

Mikrokosmos

Our composer, having made scholarly study of the music of neighboring peoples, already in Vol. I has the student playing such melodies as:

Ex. 151

After an *a*-minor bass line an ending on the *e-b* fifth:

422

Ex. 152

Mikr. IV, 103

We may presume the piece entitled In Yugoslav mode to be in *E*-mixo-lydian, but its end is on a half-cadence:

Ex. 153

Mikr. II, 40

We must note that within those cultures where this type of melody exists, such endings sound final and complete. It is only from the point of view of traditional Western music that we assume the designation half-cadence.

A similar ending:

Ex. 154

Mikr. II, Ex. 15

Further examples: Vol. II, 58, 62 as well as other exercises at the end of the volume.

XIV. POLAR RELATIONS

Let us draw the enharmonic circle of fifths: we find that $F\sharp = G\flat$ is the polar opposite to *C*. This augmented fourth or diminished fifth signifies the most distant relation in traditional styles. Just imagine after *C*-major an unexpected *f*♯-minor, or an *E*♭-major after *a*-minor... In the Romantic era (once again foremost in the works of Liszt!) these pairs of keys, or at least pairs of chords, come into a closer and closer relation. Later, with Bartók, the use of polar relations is already a common occurrence.

The *27 Choruses* provide relatively few such examples, but we do find some:

In the one example *f♯*-minor follows *C*-major, in the other *e*-minor follows *B♭*-major. (This was already seen in *Ex. 114* when we discussed the 1:5 model.)

The polar relation may also play a role in the form of a piece:

Here, in a piece whose beginning and recapitulation start with an *e♭*, the main cadence of the middle section presents the polar tone *a*.

In the same way, the principal dividing point (the end of the second of four pages) of the composition in *G*-major rests on the polar *c♯*:

Perhaps an even greater contrast is that which exists between the closing *c*-phrygian cadence and the *F♯*-major chords which prevail at the first return of the textual theme. Here we have the incisive sound of six sharps opposed by the bluntness of an ending in four flats:

424

Pusz-ta   ma-lom-ba   Cser-fa . . .   . . ma - lom.

Mikrokosmos

The two hands divide the polar-related $f\sharp$ and c pentachords, and the piece ends appropriately:

Ex. 159   Mikr. III, 86

Minor-type scale segments instead of major-type represent the $e\flat$ and a tonalities, with a polar sound at the close:

Ex. 160   Mikr. IV, 101

It is not rare for the arc of a single motive to stretch between the pillars of a diminished fifth or an augmented fourth. Let us examine *Exs. 102, 103, 116* and the lower voice of *Ex. 289* as well.

The basic organizational principle extending over an entire piece may also be a half-octave interval. The predominant key is *D*-major, but the middle section moves in *A♭*-major:

Ex. 161   Mikr. IV, 104

beginning: middle: ending:

XV. PENTATONIC HARMONIES

Chords constructed from a pentatonic scale appear in our art music since the time of Debussy. (Occasionally already in the works of Liszt). The possibilities for each basic form:

Ex. 162

The black noteheads indicate the most compressed form of one or another chord. The g) fourth-pillar occurs in yet one more place. Where? [We may read it from the j] group of five notes!)

Each of the above chords may be arranged in other types of voice order. One or another tone may appear in the low voice (inversion), and the others may change places above it (closed, open and mixed positions). Thus for chords of three tones there are 6 variations, for chords of four tones 24, and for the complete chords of five tones there are altogether 120 variations! (We should try to find these.)

Mikrokosmos

In the piano pieces we meet several times with the seventh chord (162f), which is indeed known among the secondary four-tone chords of traditional music, but then only as a dissonance to be resolved. In the new music it is already considered as consonant, and may even be a closing harmony to a piece:

Ex. 163

Mikr. III, 78

426

Bartók and Kodály both stated that since we often hear these four tones one after another in our folk music, they wished to draw them together into harmony as well. (See *Ex. 18.*)

Just such an ending is to be found in Vol. II, 66, Vol. III, 88, Vol. IV, 105 and 109.

Several further formulas:

Ex. 164 Mikr. III, 84 III, 83 V, 139 V, 122

a/ b/ c/ d/ e/

Let us determine from which basic forms of the table in *Ex. 162* do the above examples originate. (See also the end of Bagpipe Vol. V, 138!)

We can hear two separate chords in each measure of the following extract, but we may consider them rearrangements of one and the same chord:

Ex. 165 Mikr. VI, 149

XVI. THE DIMINISHED OCTAVE

The development of musical language over a thousand years—in our European art music—took in ever more narrow intervals of simultaneously sounding tones. At first these appear as ornamental dissonances, later, through usage, they become consonances. In ancient times (as today in our folksongs), men's and women's voices sounded in a perfect octave. Then approximately one thousand years ago, the fifth appeared, followed by the fourth and the third. Since Monteverdi the seventh becomes a part of chords, consequently the second as well, but for almost three hundred years still as a dissonance moving toward resolution. Already in Debussy's music the second, primarily the major second, is also consonant. Finally the composers of our century include among their devices all possible sound combinations offered by the tonal system.

Ever newer stimuli, the search for ever greater tension, placed in the foreground the most dissonant sounds (according to older sensibility). On the extreme edge stands the half-step interval, either as minor second or as augmented prime. Its inversions are the diminished octave, or in its more extended form, the augmented octave. There are three basic forms to this chromatic interval:

Ex. 166

Along with his contemporaries, Bartók also used these intervals amply. He was well aware that the singing voice, especially the child's voice, is not as capable of such challenges as an instrument of any type would be. Therefore the diminished octave is used only with a certain cautiousness in his choruses. However he does indeed use it so that children may become used to it in their singing.

It appears as a *changing tone* in the minor third of the melody under a sustained major third:

Ex. 167   Lover's Farewell

Is-ten ve-led, ró-zsám

and in the same way three measures later a bb-minor motive appears grating against a $B\flat$-major chord.

As a *passing tone* it is easily singable within the context of its own direct line. Therefore the b appearing in the scale does not cause any difficulty under the sustained $b\flat^1$:

428

Ex. 168   Michaelmas Greeting

Úr   -   is - ten

Áldd   meg.   Úr - is -   ten

E   ház - nak gaz - dá - ját.

A double passing tone, each voice separately maintaining its own natural melodic movement ("target-counterpoint"):

Ex. 169
                                    Pillow Dance
                                    85

Jaj, ren - gő   böl - csőm,

The $g\sharp$-g^1 diminished octave appears in a freer manner in the following example:

Ex. 170   Song of the Bird

                    39   !

II.

en - ni,   Gyöngy - harma -   tot in -   ni   gyöngy-

I.
III.

A possible explanation: the tone c^2 which dominates the melody may also be harmonized by the a-minor triad, as can be seen in the first and last measures of the extract. The natural change of this harmony is the dominant sounding above the $g\sharp$ leading tone. The harmonization thus does not follow the melody note for note, as it does for example in the chorale style, but rather views each three-measure motive as a larger unity. In this way both foreign (decorative) and chord tones appear ("target harmonization").

Mikrokosmos

In addition to the singing child, Bartók also acquaints the piano student with the diminished octave. Once again we stand in amazement at the pedagogical skill, when he thus brings forward the interval:

Ex. 171

Mikr. I, 27

As the *g* is for the time being a ticd note, the *g♯* then is not heard with such harshness on the piano as were we to strike the two tones simultaneously.

But already among the exercises of the first volume we find such:

Ex. 172

Mikr. I, Ex. 2

The volumes of the opus indeed offer many examples of the diminished and augmented octave. (Let us see who can find more?) We quote here only one more characteristic cadence:

Ex. 173

Mikr. V, 125

the *d-d♭* (together with the neighboring tones *f*, *a♭*, *c*) represent the dominant, while the *b-b♭* belong to the closing *G* major-minor chord.

430

XVII. CHORDS BUILT ON SECONDS AND FOURTHS

In chapter XV we already examined pentatonic intervals of seconds and fourths as chord building elements. In the preceding chapter we presented examples of the diminished octave. In addition to all this, the new music has claimed possession of all possibilities of the tempered chromatic-enharmonic 12-degree system, up to and including the simultaneously sounding chord of all twelve tones.

Within this, seconds and fourths have come to play a significant role as chord components.

This group of seven fourths enlarges the order of fourths which is closely related to the pentatonic:

Ex. 174

Mikr. V, 131

A judicious handling of voices: from the tower of fourths is missing precisely that $e\flat$ which then becomes the tone of resolution. (The dominant does not "shoot down" the tonic!) Let us determine which tones of this chord of fourths belong to the $e\flat$-minor pentatonic system and which are additions to it!

This section (in schematic form) of the piece entitled Syncopation presents, practically speaking, an evolutionary development of an agglomeration of seconds:

Ex. 175

Mikr. V, 133

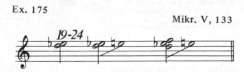

Let us examine the quoted segment in its original entirety as well! (The notation of the simultaneously sounding $e\flat$-e type of tone-pairs led composers to the use of the unusual "cherrystem".)

A minor second and (as its inversion) a major seventh may even form a closing consonance in this style:

431

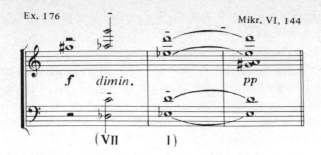

Ex. 176   Mikr. VI, 144

The *estam*-rhythm[3] of the stinging ternions is well suited for the Village Joke:

Ex. 177   Mikr. V, 130

The sounds of various seconds are entwined around the constantly ringing f-$f\sharp$ tone-pair:

Ex. 178   Mikr. VI, 144

Taking this section "under the magnifying glass", let us play the harmony of every single quarter note value separately, always striking the tied notes again as well. The best means of identification is the number of half-steps: let us measure the distance with which the neighboring chord-tones follow above each other. The numbers are given under the first measure—let us continue! (For example, on the second quarter of the second measure we

3 Characterised by stressed off-beats: ♫ ♩ ♩ ♫

432

hear the $e\flat$-f-$f\sharp$-$g\sharp$ quaternion, and we may analyze: two-one-two.) The pattern for the entire work is, however, the extensively varied use of seconds and sevenths.

See also *Exs. 104, 118, 123, 146, 187* and *279*.

XVIII. CHORDS FORMED FROM NEIGHBOR TONES

The occurrence of chords with neighbor tones, although related to the question of the diminished octave, is worthy of a separate chapter since we are now speaking of chords rather than intervals. That a neighboring foreign tone may decorate one or two tones of a chord is an old matter. A further development occurs in the newer music when we often meet with three or even more simultaneous neighbor tones. In this case we speak of changing chords. An example of their variety: for a simple triad there are no less than 64 possible changing chords—if we consider only those neighbor tones of a minor or a major second distance. That is to say, each chord tone may have an upper and a lower neighbor tone, and these may be either a half-tone or a whole-tone distant:

Ex. 179

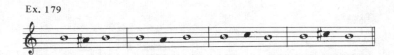

Since the same may be applied to each member of the chord, the number of possible three-voice altered chords is $4 \times 4 \times 4 = 64$. We find among them the most different types, from those entirely consonant to those which are strongly dissonant. (Please write these all out and try them!)

Bartók presents examples of these in his 27 Choruses. Let us quote those containing the diminished octave:

Ex. 180   Spring

For practice let us dissect this one chord into individual tones:

Ex. 181

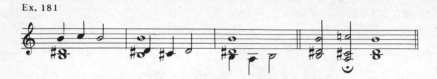

now "altogether"—stopping longer on the changing chord so that our singers may recognize and become used to its more daring sound.

In the following example, even though the d^1 of the lower voice is a passing tone, it is nevertheless a neighbor tone of the subsequent c^1:

Ex. 182   ! Enchanting Song

csin - gi-lin - gi - ling

It is worthwhile to prepare an exercise from this as well:

Ex. 183

(At a lower pitch, perhaps, for singing.)

Mikrokosmos

There are naturally many more possibilities on the keyboard for altered chords than there are in choral works of only several voices. As early as Vol. II we meet with such unusual sounds:

Ex. 184   Mikr. II, Ex. 17/b

Let us take note of the voice-leading logic which accounts for the simultaneous sounding of the note pairs *g♭-g♯* and *d♭-d♯*! What kind of intervals are these? What kind of interval is the *a♭-c♯*, the *d♭-g♯*?

Let us find the augmented and diminished octaves among the changing chords of the following section:

Ex. 185   ♩= ca 124   Mikr. V, 131

We perceive chord b) as a pentatonic changing chord, because it remains exactly within the *e♭*-based *la*-pentatonic.

The measure which repeatedly interrupts the melody:

Ex. 186   ♩= 108   Mikr. III, 83

f   *risoluto e pesante*

is heard in two ways. In the eighth-note pairs either the first chord is the main chord and the less accented one is the alternate, or the other way round. That this is a justifiable point of view is supported by the composer himself in measure 12 and 13 of the piece.

In a similar manner, a gently flickering soundscape depicts the Melody in the mist:

Ex. 187   ♩.= 46   Mikr. IV, 107

p

Next to the four pentatonic tones on the white keys, the changing chord is given entirely on black keys. (Just as in *Ex. 184*.) In the last line of the piece the two chords are also sounded simultaneously (the contours are washed together by the fog...).

Finally, several cadences in which the changing chords play a quasi-dominant role:

Ex. 188

The very last chord (*c-e-g-b*)—known also in older music—is the major-seventh harmony which Bartók was so fond of using as his "calling card". (Ernő Lendvai calls this chord the *hypermajor*—and its variant of the minor-type, the *c-e♭-g-b* type chord, the *hyperminor*.)

XIX. BITONALITY

The altered chords are considered to belong among the commonly recognized devices of classical music. If, for example, Bach or Mozart reinforces a melodic tone c^2, as the *do* of *C*-major, with $A♭$-$e♭$-$f♯$ voices, not one of the accompaniment tones belongs within the given key. Almost as if it were an extension and a consummation of this is that procedure of the new music by which, for some shorter or longer section of a piece, or throughout the duration of the entire piece, the voices move in two different keys.

For the most part, we can establish four classifications for the different types of bitonality (= of two keys):

A) *variant* scales (of the same name, on the same base) sound together;

B) *functionally identical*, but not on the same base, the two scales are related at a distance of one or two minor thirds (see Chapter XXI, Axis Order, in this regard);

C) *functionally different*, two scales still more distant from one another sound together;

D) *complementary scales* are joined, with no common tones occurring between the two scales.

436

Mikrokosmos

In each of the piano pieces examined so far—no small number!—an example appears.

Type A) Most modestly already in Vol. I, 33, the Slow Dance. Here, beneath the *G*-major pentachord of the right hand, the left hand is drawn from a *G*-lydian five-tone line. More colorful is Vol. II, 59, in which the two voices keep interchanging the *f*-minor and *F*-lydian pentachords. The same occurs at the end of the Bourrée when *d*-minor and *D*-lydian sound together:

Ex. 189   Mikr. IV, 117

Type B) We have already seen an example of parallel keys in the whole-tone scale piece *(Exs. 100, 101).*

A minor-third relation exists between the *e*-minor and *g*-minor pentachords also:

Ex. 190

Mikr. II, 64

Two minor-thirds create a diminished fifth. Thus the polar interval implies a functional identity, so to speak, in a "cousin-type" relationship. In this way the *F*♯ and *C* tonalities met in *Ex. 159,* and the *e*♭ and *a* tonalities in *Ex. 160.* See Mikr. III, 86!

Type C) There is a distance of a major-third between the *B*-do of the left hand and the upper *G*-do:

Ex. 191

Mikr. IV, 105

Type D) Our composer readily employs the most complete bitonality which arises from complementary scales. In these piano pieces the one hand does not "meddle" in the affairs of the other: each one moves in an entirely different tonal area.

The *d*-minor and *F♯*-major pentachords share no common tones:

Ex. 192

Mikr. III, 70

These two scales logically create the hypermajor closing chord.

The piece entitled Crossed hands brings two diminished pentachords to the two voices:

Ex. 193

Mikr. IV, 99

(Let us read these tones consecutively: what scale do we find?)

Contrasting areas of white and black keys are offered ready-made by the piano keyboard. Our composer makes use of this many times in the Mikrokosmos. For example in Playsong:

The tones sing and twang, the title of the piece speaks:

(with half-pedal throughout)

Let us examine once more *Ex. 49,* and then also the famous piece From the diary of a fly (Mikr. VI, 142).

XX. OSTINATO

In contrast to the widely billowing, generally grand gesticulations of Romantic music, the composers of our century, perhaps most often Stravinsky and Bartók, readily set up an ostinato: the stubborn repetition of one or another shorter formula. Here we may think of the influence of primitive folk music as well as the manifestation of the machine age.

Mikrokosmos
The ostinato is also given its place in these piano pieces. Most simply with the bagpipe-type exchange of tonic and dominant tones, throughout an entire piece. (See In Yugoslav mode, Vol. II, 40—we quoted its ending in our *Ex. 153.*)

A quaternion of lydian character accompanies the pentatonic melody:

Ex. 196

The composer of the new era even accompanies the characteristically traditional melody honoring the memory of Schumann with an ostinato:

Ex. 197

Furthermore, let us examine the last two lines of the Hungarian Song (Mikr. III, 74), and then, in its entirety, the piece appropriately entitled Ostinato (VI, 146).

XXI. AXIS ORDER

In order that we may arrive at the most Bartók-like application of the diminished octave, the so-called alpha chords, we must first reach back to a question rooted in traditional music.

It is an axiomatic, firm principle of the study of classical harmony that chords standing in relation to one another at the interval of a minor third have identical functions. Surely such chords most resemble one another having altogether a difference of only one tone between them:

Ex. 198

	T		S		D	
I	VI	IV	II	V	III	

On the tonic plane (on the "ground floor") lies the *do*-triad and the parallel *la*-chord. The subdominant degrees IV and II represent the deeper level, the "cellar", while we find the dominant *so*-major and *mi*-minor triads on the sharper, higher level, on the "first floor".

Ernő Lendvai has demonstrated that in Bartók's music, however far it may fall from the traditional style, functional relations have not ceased to exist. Moreover, in a logical expansion, they appear to present a validity to the entire 12-tone system.

The train of thought is:

a) in addition to the relative chords, the variant chords (chords of the same name) naturally have identical functions, for example *C*-major and *c*-minor, or *F*-major and *f*-minor, etc.

b) Consequently, chords at a distance of a minor-third from one another have identical functions, regardless of their major or minor coloration. For example, in *C*-major not only does the *a*-minor triad have a tonic function, but the *A*-major triad as well.

c) However, since *A*-major similarly is a functional relative of the *f♯*-minor and the *F♯*-major triads, these latter chords also have an identical function with *C*-major.

d) Final step: *F♯* also has a relative at the lower minor-third, the triad built on *d♯* or *e♭*. Thus the circle has been completed, since from here once again we reach the initial *C* with one further downward step of a minor-third:

Ex. 199

tonics of C-major:

441

We shall designate this group of four functionally identical basic tones (chain of minor thirds), once again with a term of Ernő Lendvai, as an *axis*.

The axis principle presents melodic, harmonic, and formal manifestations as well. Examples of the last:

The variant of *D*-major is *d*-minor, whose relative key is *F*-major. Therefore we may say that the theme in measure 13 also appears in a tonic key, albeit varied.

Conversely, the lower minor-third relation is demonstrated in this example through the use of the previously mentioned *C-a-A* connection:

(The theme as found in measure 18 indeed strongly varies the principal motive, but from the "fourth down—fourth up" contour we may still easily recognize that we are still dealing with the same musical thought.)

This chapter is in itself necessary not only for the understanding of Bartók's style, but also essential for an understanding of the following chapter as well.

Mikrokosmos

We have already cited the minor-third parallels in the piece Whole-tone scale *(Exs. 100, 101)*. But let us look further to see how the game continues from the $e\flat$-$g\flat$ starting tones. The a-c-$e\flat$-$g\flat$ chain of minor thirds, which is namely the functional axis, is thus completed.

Exactly the same four tones provide the skeleton for one section of the fourth Bulgarian Dance:

Ex. 202

First we find the tones *c-e♭-f♯* in the melody, and then in the middle voice (as the bases of the $^6_4$ chords) the *a-f♯-d♯*.

Let us look for the appearance of the very same *A-c...* axis in Exer. 22a of Vol. III, and also in the second half of Vol. IV, 100! (It is worthy of note that upon this same *C-F♯* axis is built the tonality of such large-scale Bartók works as the Wooden Prince, Bluebeard's Castle, the Sonata for Two Pianos and Percussion, and the Music for Strings, Percussion and Celesta.)

The chromatically compressed variation of Vol. IV, 112 (see Chapter XXIII on projection) receives just such an axis-imitation at the lower minor-third:

Ex. 203

XXII. ALPHA CHORDS

We may now join the previous chapters to the questions of the axis-system and the diminished octave.

Once again we may thank the investigations of Ernő Lendvai for the clarification and identification of a family of chords especially characteristic of Bartók: his alpha chords.

According to this: we may observe that—in the development of European art music over many centuries—tones belonging to the *dominant* axis most naturally reinforce the harmonization of a *tonic* tone:

Ex. 204

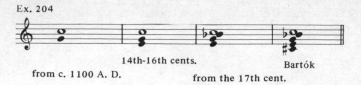

14th-16th cents.

from c. 1100 A. D.

from the 17th cent.

Bartók

which obviously rests on the acoustical overtone series. (The closest relative to *C* is *g,* and so forth.)

If Bartók then adds the fourth member of the dominant-family (the *c♯*) to the supporting tones, or elsewhere reinforces the melodic main tone, here the *c²*, with the tones of the upper axis-relativites:

Ex. 205

beta   gamma   delta

then is he not perhaps, with the strictest historical logic, simply completing the structure which has been taking shape in our art music since the era of organum one thousand years ago? Thus the diminished octave on the one hand has deep roots in tradition, and on the other hand it accords the maximum tension demanded by its own era!

The 27 Choruses, with their modest number of voices, naturally do not lend themselves to the full sounding of such multi-voiced chords. However, these structures do appear in broken form, and through them the child of school age becomes accustomed to Bartók's music and to the musical language of the day. At least it is a preparation for the later complete acceptance of such sounds.

Such a diminished-octave chord does shape the construction of at least one melody:

Ex. 206

Lover's Farewell

Is-ten ve-led, ró-zsám, szi-ved ví- gan   él - jen,   a♭ -gamma

Two voices divide between themselves the members of the *c*-gamma chord in a pure harmonic figuration with no foreign-tone decoration:

444

Ex. 207 — Had I Never Seen You

To- vább él - tem vol - na,

To - vább él - tem

c-gamma

Here decorated with passing- and altered-tones:

Ex. 208 — The Fickle Girl

Két aszt-ra - kán bun - dám lesz,

i - ca- ri - ca, Két aszt-ra - kán

a-gamma

The $e\flat^2$ and e^1 tones appear in close proximity to each other, giving the characteristic gamma sound to the group of chords which are in themselves simple:

Ex. 209 — Spring

ő - fel - sé - ge meg is áld - ja,

(incomplete)
c-gamma

But the $g\sharp$-g^1 octave is actually heard simultaneously:

Ex. 210 — The Song-bird's Promise

tu-dom, sohasem ... nem!

nem jő.

e-gamma

There are also examples of delta chords in broken form as a melody:

Ex. 211 Song of Loneliness

Csen- des fo-lyó víz - nek Csak zú - gá - sát hal - lom. d-delta

Considering the starred $e\flat^1$ as a changing-tone, the *d*-delta chord is clearly outlined.

Another delta chord is heard with an $f\sharp^1$-f^2 ambitus without any foreign-tones:

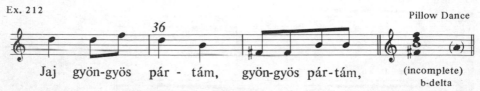

Ex. 212 Pillow Dance

Jaj gyön-gyös pár - tám, gyön-gyös pár-tám, (incomplete)
b-delta

(A useful experiment: let us sing the example replacing the f^2 of the first measure with an $f\sharp^2$. The *b*-minor broken chord thus formed seems so commonplace and insignificant! Then let us replace the f^2 and perhaps we may even better appreciate Bartók's flavor.)

Before we discuss examples from the piano pieces, it will be useful to survey the various incomplete forms of the alpha-chords, at least those that appear compressed within the frame of the diminished octave:

Ex. 213

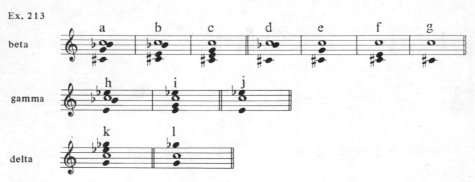

beta

gamma

delta

What is the common element which may not be omitted from any of these? The diminished octave. (It is sometimes notated as a major-seventh, for example $d\flat$ instead of $c\sharp$. On the piano the sound is identical.)

And how do we recognize the principal tone? From those tones which form a dominant minor-third chain sounding below it: from the perfect

446

fourth *(Ex. 213 a, d, e, i, k, l),* or from the major-second below *(Ex. 213 a, b, d, h),* and in some cases from the minor-sixth below *(Ex. 213 f, j).* This may be clearly verified when the principal tone is also reinforced by the upper chain of minor-thirds, since we then hear several diminished octaves (major sevenths). Let us identify these in the following complete forms:

Ex. 214

beta   gamma   delta

(In one instance above we intentionally write *f*♯ instead of *g*♭, since Bartók freely employed enharmonically interchangeable tones in his notation. The major seventh is thus equivalent here to the diminished octave.)

Mikrokosmos

Among the piano pieces we meet most often with the gamma inversion. Each measure presents the very same chord in broken form:

Ex. 215

Mikr. VI, 151

Passing-tones do not conceal the chord, they only ornament the motive:

Ex. 216

Mikr. II, 62

In the following example, let us determine which tones belong to the *d*-gamma chord, and which are the foreign-tones:

Ex. 217

Mikr. IV, 106

447

The two voices seem to present two different gamma chords:

Ex. 218

Mikr. VI, 143

The upper voice is a characteristic *a*-gamma, the lower an *f♯*-gamma. However, the pedal joins the tones into one chord. How do we know this: A perfect fourth sounds in both the upper and lower voices. An *a*-gamma is not possible, because the *f♯* below it is sounding, even though under the principal tone only the axis-tones of its dominant may be used. We are therefore dealing with a rich *f♯*-gamma chord from which only the upper-most member of the *f♯* axis, the *e♭* (*d♯*), is missing.

Let us locate the outline of the *beta*-chord in this section of the Inter-mezzo:

Ex. 219

Mikr. IV, 111

even if it is only heard for a duration of one or two beats.

Examples of the delta-inversion:

Ex. 220

Mikr. VI, 143

A characteristic blending arises when the minor thirds (augmented seconds) change function, in some places belonging to the relative domi-

nant axis below the melody tones, elsewhere belonging to the tonic group
above the principal tone:

Ex. 221

♩ = ca 86

Mikr. VI, 143

Let us determine the fundamental tone and the type of each chord of the
bracketed groups *a, b,* and *c.*

This piece (Broken Arpeggios) provides an abundant store of examples
of Bartók's harmonies, from pentatonic tetrachords—through other altered chords—to the rich alpha-chords. It is worthwhile to make a complete study of it!

XXIII. VARIATION AND PROJECTION TECHNIQUE

Bartók was known to have stated that where a theme is repeated or
brought back in a work, he does not like to copy it exactly, but is more inclined to vary it. This represents enormous compositional energy, for
surely it is easier to use an unvaried recapitulation. With inexhaustible
abundance our composer provides newer and newer variations for his
themes. This may cause some difficulty, for a child learns a slightly different form of a known melody less easily than he would a new melody.
But it has advantages: the further development of the chorus, and the
assertion of the particularly classical duality of "unity and diversity".

We quote only a few of the extraordinarily large number of examples.

The tripodic (three-measure) motive, in its second appearance, has a
mixolydian instead of a major character:

Ex. 222

Enchanting Song

Nőj - jön   fű   e - lőt - tük,   Baj   ne   jár - jon   köz - tük

449

The major theme appears in aeolian form at the beginning of the second verse:

Ex. 223   Hussar

Ez a   fa-lu   be va-gyon ke-rít - ve,   haj,

18

Hu-szá - ros - san   ü-lök a nye-reg-be,   haj,

(Originally in *d*-aeolian, it is here written in the common g^1 tonality for purposes of comparison. The same will be done elsewhere.)

The acoustical scale is simplified to the major:

Ex. 224   Spring

Szép ma-dár a   fecs - ke, szé-pen is   szól,

23

É - rez min-den   ál - lat vi-dá - mu - lást,

In the above examples the intervalic structure (second, third, etc.) remains the same, only the coloration (minor-second, major-second) is changed. The variation is more extensive when the structure also changes. It is sometimes a matter of only one tone, yet the prosody gains so much by the marked elevation of the word *édes* (= sweet):

Ex. 225   The Sorrow of Love

Köny-nyebb a   kő-szik - lát Lágy i - szap-pá   ten - ni,

9

Mert   ha két   é - des szív Egymás-tól meg - vá - lik,

450

The four-note melody is always slightly varied:

Ex. 226   Lament

ke - ser - vem - nek, Né - kem so - ha, víg - ság,

Fel - sü - tött a, Né - kem so - ha, Bú - val é - lem,

There is not one piece of the collection in which we cannot abundantly find a similar richness of variation. (In studying the pieces it is useful to place these sections next to each other and to consciously note the differences.)

Projection technique

Musical variation has a special facet which we call projection. What do we mean by this? From a photograph we are able to recognize the original subject—or, in reverse, the subject of the larger picture when a diapositive slide is projected—because even if the measurements are changed, the proportions and the directions remain the same. This can serve as the definition by which we understand projection in music.

It is true that enlargement or reduction of an interval belongs within the scope of the examples which we have previously examined. But it is of more interest if at least two consecutive intervals appear subsequently projected to a different size. Let us reserve the word projection for such cases.

We may examine a few of the many examples from the 27 Choruses. Seconds are widened to become thirds:

Ex. 227   Michaelmas Greeting

áldd   meg,

451

In reverse, thirds become seconds after three measures:

The descending group of four tones becomes narrower not only in space, but also in time (diminution):

Similarly, each third narrows to a second:

Thirds change into seconds, a fifth into a third:

Third-second-third following each other, each one widening to the next larger interval:

452

Ex. 232   Canon

Csak e-gyik uc-cá - ért;
De nem az uc - cá - ért,

Several additional examples readily lending themselves to analysis:

Ex. 233
a)   Bread-baking

Ker-tem a - latt,ker-tem a - latt, a - rat há-rom var - nyú,

Tücsök gyűj-ti, tücsök gyűj-ti, Szú-nyog kö-ti ké - vét,

c)   Bread-baking

ez itt szi - tál, ez itt szi - tál, az meg ros-tál, az meg ros-tál,

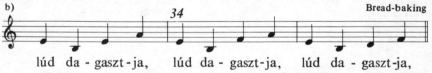

b)   Bread-baking

lúd da - gaszt-ja, lúd da - gaszt-ja, lúd da - gaszt-ja,

A change of direction intensifies the impact of the projection variant:

Ex. 234   Song of Loneliness

Er-dő - ben la - ká - som,

Er - - dő-ben la - ká - som,

A threefold appearance of one measure continuously widening, organically augmenting in form:

Ex. 235   To My Homeland

a szü- le- i há - zat, Hí -res kis fa- lu- mat, szép magyar hazá - mat,

An amazing order dominates this motive, similarly heard three times:

Ex. 236   Pillow Dance

Pusz - ta   ma- lom - ba

Cser - fa   ge -ren - da

Raj - ta   sé - ti - kál

The syncopa falls by five, then four, and finally by three half-steps. It is as if Bagoly asszonyka (= little Miss Owl) were "walking" up the overtone ladder:

Ex. 237

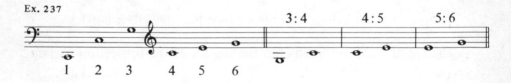

3:4   4:5   5:6

1   2   3   4   5   6

At the same time, the initial tones of the motive act similarly: comparing each one to the previous, they rise at first by a major-second and then by a half-step only *(Ex. 236).*

The reader would not regret the effort were he to write out and compare each of the two-measure motives as they appear in Elment a madárka (measures 1, 5, 7, 21, and 27). Six times the same mounded shape appears, but not twice is it uniform!

Mikrokosmos

These volumes abound in the most differentiated manifestations of variation. We can only cite a few examples here. "Variatio per arsin et thesin" could be the name for the alteration of stress-changes quoted here from the opening and closing sections of the famous piece "From the Isle of Bali":

Ex. 238 Mikr. IV, 109

Let us describe in order what happens to the tones written one beneath the other. (The first tone of the group of these eighth-notes is relatively stressed, the other two unstressed.) Let us begin thus: the previously stressed *g♯* has become unstressed, the unstressed *a* following it has become stressed, and so forth.

Among the countless other types of variation, the use of projection is particularly characteristic. The piece written in memory of Bach provides a copious store of examples. In true Bach-like style, the four-member sixteenth-note formulas spin forth, continuously taking ever different shapes. The excerpted sections:

Ex. 239 Mikr. III, 79

project the first harmonic figure into the diatonic, then further compressed into the chromatic. (Following this the motive gradually widens back to the original chord in thirds. See our *Ex. 117* for the end of the piece.)

Our composer does not specify, but it is quite possible that the theme of the Chromatic Invention is a variant of the first line of a commonly known folksong:

455

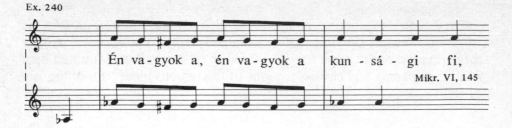

Ex. 240

Én va‑gyok a, én va‑gyok a | kun‑sá‑gi fi,

Mikr. VI, 145

The second variation also projects a folksong from diatonic to chromatic:

Ex. 241

Mikr. IV, 112

The rhythm is also subject to variation! And what are those upward-leaping minor-thirds seeking in the second of each two measures? Are they simply further enrichments after the major-seconds of the theme and the half-steps of the variation? Or are they at the same time finely disguised remembrances of the original tones of the theme, at least in the first two instances: $f=f$, $e=e$?

Practice. Let us improvise further projection variations on the melody of this children's song, using the following quaternions in order:

Ex. 242

| Major seventh | minor seventh | 3:1 | 5:1 | tower of fourths |

then other formulas according to your taste, for example the tower of sevenths divided between the two hands, etc. (Either by free choice, or with given agglomerations.) We may also choose other melodies. The simplest are those in which step-wise seconds predominate, for example Virág Erzsi (Mikr. III, 74), etc.

XXIV. SYMMETRY

The diversity of motivic work may also be served by the inversion of the melodic line, that is by symmetrical mirroring. It is an old device, in use for perhaps half a millennium, especially in the hands of the masters of polyphony. But after Bach, it seems to have lost significance. In our century, however, playing with inversions has been revived. And perhaps no other master employed it as readily as did Bartók. It is, to be sure, related to his well-known inclination toward mathematics and logic, i. e. the beauty of ordér.

Ambos, two-voiced formulas, also appear often in symmetrical mirror-inversion:

Ex. 243   The Fickle Girl

Sej, Haj, ic-ca te, ric-ca te, ic-ca-ri-ca te!

In a freer melody:

Ex. 244   Stamping Feet

38

Hej, é - let, gyöngy - é - let,

70

Hej, é - let, gyöngy-é - let,

457

The descending second (flexa) is answered both times in an ascending (podatus) form.

The overlapping imitation truly makes the inversion of seconds "Play"-ful:

Ex. 245

Candle Song

There is similar answering in the two outer voices, enriched by the balance of the middle voice:

Ex. 246

Lover's Farewell

Figurative contrary motion in the accompanying voices is more sharply effective, than if the voices were to repeat in place:

Ex. 247

Mocking of Youth

Fourths may also mirror each other:

Ex. 248   Bread-baking

e - szi.   sze -di,   e - szi,

(An additional observation: the closed-open-closed order of the three words is also symmetrical! Along with this goes the consonant-dissonant-consonant qualities, or, expressed in yet another way, the static-dynamic-static qualities.)

Two types of mirroring: within the first measure the half-measures reverse the sharp leap of the fourth—the third measure, however, reverses the second measure in its entirety:

Ex. 249   Bread-baking

+ 4   - 4   + 4   - 4

Ker-tem a-latt, ker-tem a-latt | a - rat há- rom var- nyú,

- 4   + 4

a - rat há- rom var- nyú

32

Lúd,   lúd,   lúd   da - gaszt - ja,

The goose later kneads the dough in augmentation...

Fourths, syncopated and in mirror-inversion:

Ex. 250   Pillow Dance

32

Hogy   is   ne   sír - nék,   Hogy is   ne,

Hogy is   ne   sír - nál,   Hogy is   ne   sír - nál,

459

The imitative contrary-motion of the two lower voices coincides with the opposition of the two persons involved (sírnék = I would cry; sírnál = you would cry).

Free contrary motion of thirds and fourths between the outer voices:

Ex. 251   Lover's Farewell

Annyi,   annyi,   annyi jót   kí - vá-nok   né - ked,   te-né - ked,

Ternions. Among three-membered formulas there is often a circular figuration of a principal tone with its upper and lower neighbors:

Ex. 252   The Fickle Girl   Enchanting Song

ic-ca - ri - ca   te!   csin- gi-lin- gi   lán - ga,

In a similar manner, in a complaining minor:

Ex. 253   Lonely Wanderer

Szől - lőm   volt,   el - pusz - tult,   saj - ná - lom,

Another favored ternion of our composer is the tri-chord in forward-and-back movement. (A folksong model for this could be the beginning of *Ex. 240,* Én vagyok a, én vagyok a kunsági fi...) In such a case the symmetry is double: in one voice the direction is successively changed—at the same time another voice simultaneously mirrors the melody. (Successive and simultaneous mirroring.)

460

The two lower voices compressed into a narrow space:

Ex. 254 — The Wooing of a Girl

el — se men-nék lány (nélkül)

Starting from a prime, but widening in range:

Ex. 255 — Candle Song

Ég — a gyertya, ég

Ég — a gyertya, ég

The two outer voices, within the range of an octave:

Ex. 256 — Enchanting Song

Hadd í-gér-je-nek sok szá-zig

In imitation, a richer picture:

Ex. 257 — Enchanting Song

Lán-cot a küszöb-re, csingi-lin-gi lán-ga

Lán-cot a kü-szöb-re, csin-gi-lin-gi lán-

There is further symmetry in that the answer begins from the lower fifth between measures 1 and 2, while between measures 3 and 4 it begins from symmetrically widened fifth, the major seventh. In other words, the order of the critical motivic tones, rearranging the imitation to an unusual simultaneity:

Ex. 258

(It is however truly by chance that the outlined picture is placed within the space of the five-line staff in an entirely symmetrical manner. But then who knows?...)

The mirror-image of the upper voice is quite freely varied rhythmically in the lower voice:

Ex. 259

But there are also other types of ternions. The mirror-image of the valley-delineation (porrectus) is the hill-delineation (torculus). They may appear successively as here in the second and fourth measures:

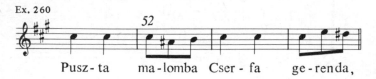

Ex. 260

or they may sound together in combination with an interval-reducing projection:

Ex. 261
The Wooing of a Girl

ne - ked a - dom, ne - ked a - dom,

meg is kap-tam, meg is kap-tam,

In exact contrary motion, a chromatic ternion joins together and bridges the *C* and the *B♭ + d:*

Ex. 262
Lover's Farewell

fér - jen,   Bá - nat-nak ár-nyé- ka

Quaternions. The simplest among them, the tetrachord, may also be mirrored:

Ex. 263
Bread-baking

hangya morzsát sze - di,

In harmonic simultaneity:

Ex. 264
The Wooing of a Girl

Kár-csú a de - re - ka, Pi - ros is a szá - ja

(The tone indicated with a star is not bb^1, as in the current edition, but rather a^1. Please correct this error!)

Tetrachords, followed by the previously discussed circular figuration of seconds (appearing within brackets):

Ex. 265

Spring

É - rez min-den ál - lat vi- dá - mu-lást,

Inversion in imitation, while at the same time each voice, in the second measure, presents its own lower fifth-answer:

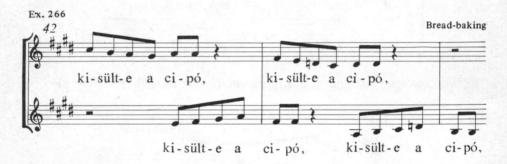

Ex. 266

Bread-baking

ki - sült-e a ci-pó, ki - sült-e a ci-pó,

ki - sült- e a ci- pó, ki-sült- e a ci- pó,

Quinternions. Simple pentachords:

Ex. 267

Spring

É- rez minden ál - lat...

Az ap-ró ma - dár - kák...

The pentachord in the lower voice and the pentatonic line in the upper voice stand opposite to each other:

464

Ex. 268

18 Stamping Feet

hej, é - let, gyöngyélet,

(The two previously mentioned Greek technical terms may be used to clearly describe the variant mirroring.)

The volume's richest example of mirror-symmetry: the first six measures of the lament. It is worth our while to look this up!

Crab-inversion, crab-mirror. All previous examples in this chapter may be considered as inversions around a level axis. But there is yet another type of symmetry. Let us also read the motive backwards: we find a crab-line. We may also combine the two types of symmetry and we find the crab-mirror inversion of the basic form. A diagram showing these elements:

Ex. 269

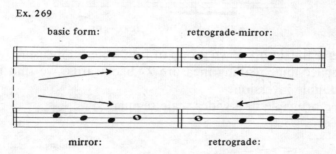

basic form: retrograde-mirror:

mirror: retrograde:

We may also say that mirroring is symmetrical in an area-axis (the lower answers the upper and vice versa), whereas crab-inversion is symmetrical on a time-axis (exchange of previous-subsequent). The crab-mirror unites the two.

We also find crab-lines in Bartók's choruses (see *Ex. 270*).

We find the up-up-down quaternion of meas. 33 in crab-inversion if we read the melody of meas. 35 backwards. (The simple two-note formulas of the second measure may be conceived both as mirroring and as crab-line.)

Ex. 270

Mocking of Youth

As- se bú-za - o - csú,

ha-nem csak zab - o - csú,

We also find examples of composite crab-mirror symmetry in the collection:

Ex. 271

Song of the Bird

Csi-nál - ta-tok né - ked

ka-lic- ká -ban lak - ni,

Let us reverse the up-up-down group of four notes of measure five in both time and space and, reading measure 27 backwards, we find the down-down-up double inversion.

The same principle in a wider scale segment:

Ex. 272

The Wooing of a Girl

Sár - arany a ha-ja, Szemöl-döke bar-na,

Symmetry of harmonies. We have so far discussed the symmetrical treatment of melodic elements. There are, however, instances when the symmetry appears not from the melodic line, but rather from the (broken) chords outlined by it. Thus, for example, from the pentatonic four-note harmonic grouping:

466

Taking the harmony in a wider, Bartók-like sense, other pentatonic formulas also display symmetry:

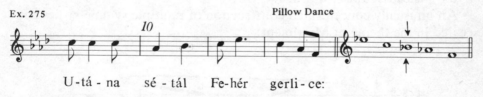

The entire *la*-pentaton is itself symmetrical (from the *re*):

Mikrokosmos

The child who studies piano is introduced to mirror-symmetry in the first weeks:

Ex. 276

Mikr. I, 12

♩=100

re

thus our two hands certainly find their place on the keys.

On the other hand, Bartók also knew—as the masters of the old polyphonic style already knew—that our diatonic system, seen from the *re,* is symmetrical, which we may read from the fifth-order:

FA DO SO RE LA MI TI

Consecutive mirroring instead of simultaneous mirroring:

Ex. 277

Mikr. II, 55

"Tonal mirroring" could be the name for this procedure, since it is not the exact half-step measure which is being used here (this would be the "real" mirroring), but rather the structural order remaining in the key. (The inversion begins with a minor third instead of the major third, etc.) A possible exercise: let us play the second part of the period in real mirroring, according to the exact half-step measurements, beginning with the c^2-$a\flat^1$ instead of the c^2-a^1 third!

An unusually concentrated construction of multiple symmetry lies concealed in the theme of Merriment:

Ex. 278

Mikr. III, 84

a) in the melodic line of each measure: octave down, octave up in the obtuse pentatonic ($d = fa$ instead of $c\sharp = mi!$);

b) in the rhythm of each half-measure (♪♪♩ after ♩♪♪ in the first measure);

c) in the intervalic measurement of each half-measure (the pentatonic ternion in 3:2 half-step ratio answers the 2:3 half-step ratio).

Even the dragons dance in symmetrical movement. Let us examine the inner voices between the tied outer tones:

468

Mikr. III, 72

they also maintain the same distance from the outer tones.

The chord-picture is often mirrored symmetrically as well:

Ex. 280

Mikr. VI, 143

The group of four pentatonic tones indicated in half notes is the basic chord, which is arranged symmetrically divided by the two hands (stems down and stems up). Along with this appears the previous chord of arsis tension, whose two outer altered tones again mirror each other. (All of this sounds one tritone higher in the original. Let us practice finding this in other transpositions, taking the major third between the two thumbs as the basis—the *f-a* pair of tones in our diagram.)

As one of the most abundant examples, it is worthwhile to thoroughly analyze measures 20–25 of the piece Divided Arpeggios, Vol VI, 143 (the last line of the first page)! At the same time we shall also recognize a series of six-tone chords.

Finally, a small collection of Bartók's symmetrical formulas:

Ex. 281

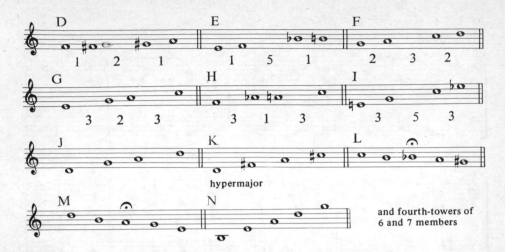

Several examples of the above from the material of this study:

A: *Exs. 243, 246, 252* — B: *Exs. 212, 260* — C: *Exs. 43, 46, 223, 249* —
D: *Ex. 110* — E: *Exs. 112, 114, 118–123*—in the 5:1 inversion, *Ex. 178* —
F: *Exs. 15, 16, 34, 164c, 274* — G: *Exs. 273 a, b* — H: *Exs. 111, 123* — I:
Exs. 209–215 — J: *Exs. 164b, 248* — K: *Exs. 188c, 192* — L: *Ex. 262* —
M: *Ex. 275* — N: *Ex. 51*.

An assignment: complete the above diagram with further symmetrical formulas found in this study (perhaps in other Bartók works as well), indicating where we have found them.

XXV. THE GOLDEN SECTION

We may once again thank the research of Ernő Lendvai for the recognition of the very important role played by the golden section in Bartók's works, especially the larger ones.

What does this term mean? It is the division into two parts of any whole in such a way that the whole is in the same proportion to the larger part as the larger is to the smaller. If, for example, we thus divide in two a whole comprised of 1000 units, we obtain measured parts of 618 + 382. Rounding this off slightly, we may say that the larger part is 62%, the smaller 38% of the whole. This unique proportion may also be found in numerous forms of nature, and to some degree in artistic creation as well (beginning with the pyramids of Egypt!). But there is no composer whose works may be described in terms of the golden section to such an extent as those of Bartók.

470

If we go further, what does the golden section mean in the case of a four-part whole? If we take 100% as our total area, then each quarter is 25%. And where does the 62% point in question occur? In the middle of the third quarter:

Ex. 282

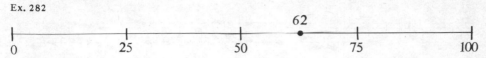

This clearly explains the great preponderance of AABA forms, and also, however enigmatic it may be, the instinctive fondness inculcated in us for the golden section (GS).

Bartók's 27 Choruses, in comparison to his other works, present the regularity of the GS rather infrequently. (Perhaps the texts tie the musical form to other types of construction?) Yet we do have some examples of it.

Melodically relevant here are those pentatonic ternions which divide the perfect fourth extending over 5 half-steps into $2+3$, or rather $3+2$ half-steps:

Ex. 283

An example of the first type, among others, is the beginning of Song of the Bird *(Ex. 10),* of the second type the beginning of Michaelmas Greeting *(Ex. 8).*

Harmonically: according to its proportions, the GS creates a major $^6_3$ triad, and if inverted, a minor $^6_4$ triad:

Ex. 284

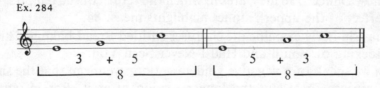

Examples of the first type are meas. 19 (the middle cadence) of the Loafer's Song — Spring *(Ex. 209):* — meas. 13 of the Michaelmas Greeting — meas. 53 of Lover's Farewell, etc. There are far fewer examples of the minor $^6_4$. In melodic broken form see our *Ex. 20.*

In form: the noteworthy principle of "the third among four" is upheld in more instances, and in greater variety. Something conspicuous happens in the third of four measures: see *Ex. 136 (e♭²!)* — *Ex. 253* (long, stressed tones) — *Ex. 273* (a new tone, the *so*), — *Ex. 275* (climatic point), etc. The third of four motives presents the high point:

Ex. 285   Don't Leave Me

itt   hagysz

Here the consequent leap of the sixth downward also throws the c^2 high point indirectly into prominence. (It is excellently suited to the words itt hagysz = here you leave!)

Not only the climactic tone, but the higher placement of an entire motive throws the third quarter of the GS into prominence:

Ex. 286   The Fickle Girl

Pieces showing GS form over their entire extent:

a) To My Homeland: 39 measures, beginning in meas. 25, after a sharp break, the closing section with the words "Szíveteket soha" (= your hearts never)...

b) Choosing of a Girl: 48 measures, beginning in meas. 29—here also after a strong break—with the words "Figyelemmel légy" (= pay attention)... is the positive, the preceding "Ne nézz, ne hajolj" (= Don't look, don't bend) begins the negative golden section.

c) The Sorrow of Love: 20 measures, in meas. 13 "Még az édes méz is" (= even the sweet honey) begins the concluding closing section.

d) Pillow Dance: 136 measures in which the return of the tempo and climactic effect of the upper f^2 tones highlights meas. 84.

We may similarly examine the choruses entitled Bread-baking, Thieving Bird, Mocking of Youth and Had I Never Seen You.

When we speak of a negative golden section, we mean that the shorter section appears first, and the longer section after it. For instance, in *Ex. 283* one formula is negative in comparison to the other, depending on whether we read them from bottom to top or from top to bottom. Formwise, the unexpected appearance in meas. 51 of the Allegretto dissects the 136 measures of the Pillow Dance, the principal key of C-major being related to the polar F♯-major triad. The main stanza "Puszta malomba" returns here.

472

The golden section is *double* if the positive and negative forms are interwoven. See the table *Ex. 281,* formulas F, G, and I.

Mikrokosmos
The piano pieces provide abundant examples of the golden section with equal respect to melody, form, and harmony.

Bartók especially favors that form of the double golden section in which two major-seconds surround a minor-third. This is understandable since pentatony, the golden section, and symmetry are all present.

From the point of view of key function, four variants of this quaternion present themselves:

Ex. 287

from a common starting tone:

Ex. 288

(By way of reminder: in the obtuse pentatony *fa* appears in place of *mi*, and in the acute pentatony *ti* is heard in place of *do*.)

Let us look for these forms in the following examples:

15, 16, 34, 35, 37, 38, 99, 163, 164, 186, 187, 191, 192, 194, 195, 196, 244, 274. Also in the Mikrokosmos: Vol. II, 51 — Vol. III, 78 — Vol. VI, 141 (in both voices of the lower line on the second page). Let us determine, wherever possible: of the above four types, into which do the four tones of the "Peacock" motive belong! *Ex. 288/a)*

Golden section in form. In four-line melodies, it is the third line which is often stressed. This is the manifestation of the GS. There are numerous folksongs of this type. We find such examples also in the Mikrokosmos. Let us analyse the closed four-line sections of the following pieces:

Vol. I, 31 (in its entirety) — Vol. II, 65 (entirely) — Vol. III, 69 (measures 3–18), 84 (measures 4–7), 94 (measures 1–19) — Vol. IV, 104 (entirely), 109 (measures 12–16), 113 (within the repeat signs) — Vol. V, 136 (measures 1–26).

The character of the third line may appear to differ in yet other ways. For example, in the A, A, b + b, A type, in which, in contrast to the larger

473

arc of the other line, the third line is divided in half: it consists of two shorter motives. (See for example: A csitári hegyek alatt...) *(Ex. 288/b)* Several relevant examples from the piano volumes:

Vol. I, 13, 15 — Vol. II, 54 — Vol. III, 68 (measures 1–8) — Vol. IV, 87 (measures 1–13), Vol. 114 (measures 3–6) — Vol. V, 130 (measures 1–14).

Looking over the entire work, approximately one-half of the 153 pieces in the Mikrokosmos show a GS form. Let us list several, indicating in parentheses the number of measures into which the sections are divided by the GS.

In Vol. III: 67 $(9+7)$ — 74 $(21+13)$ — 75 $(19+11)$ — 76 $(12+18)$ — 78 $(19+11)$ — 79 $(10+7)$ — 82 $(16+9)$ — 83 $(11+7)$ — 91 $(11+6)$ — 92 $(19+13)$ — 93 $(10+6)$.

In Vol. IV: 103 $(28+16)$ — 106 $(26+18)$ — 107 $(27+17)$ — 110 $(46+27)$ — 111 $(35+20)$ — 116 $(27+16)$ — 119 $(18+11)$.

Let us determine what happens at the point of intersection? What indications of form, tempo, or dynamic mark these places?

XXVI. FOLKSONG-TYPE FORMS

The great bards of the new Hungarian music are at the same time also scholars of our folk music. In the works of Kodály and Bartók, we often find such constructions which would not have come into existence without the given elements of our folksongs. The first which come to mind are those four-line closed melodies which mirror the formal concept of our folk music, without, however, being simple copies of one or another of our folksongs.

We list such Bartók melodies in the following section. Let us study and analyze these from the usual points of view of folk-music study, even if we do not examine each melody from every standpoint: constructional formula, style (old, new or a mixed classification), number of syllables per line, cadences, the shape and number of measures per line, the often stressed role of the third line (perhaps its division into two motives), scale, ambitus, rhythm, etc.

Let us have a contest to see who can find the folksong which most resembles each Bartók melody.

For a good number of the pieces listed, we will find variations of the principal melody, often in the second or third verse. Let us find these and compare them to the theme!

From the collection of the 27 Choruses let us study the following:

Don't Leave Me! (measures 1–12, the second part of the melody being repeated within this section)

Hussar (measures 1–17, with a similar type repetition as in the preceding piece)

Candle Song (measures 1–17)

Song of Loneliness (measures 1–14)

Thieving Bird (measures 1–12)

Bread-baking (measures 26–29)

The Fickle Girl (measures 7–14)

Only Tell Me! (measures 1–12)

Lonely Wanderer (measures 5–21, lower voice)

Choosing of a Girl (measures 1–16)

Enchanting Song (measures 1–16)

The Wooing of a Girl (measures 1–8)

Spring (measures 1–22)

Mocking of Youth (measures 1–12 ending in the lower voice)

Had I Never Seen You (measures 1–8)

The Sorrow of Love (measures 1–8)

The Song-bird's Promise (measures 1–8 ending in the middle voice)

Stamping Feet (measures 5–13 in the middle voice)

Michaelmas Greeting (measures 1–4)

Lover's Farewell! (measures 1–18 continuing in the middle voice and ending in the lower voice).

Mikrokosmos

In the preceding examples it is the text which usually determines the four-line construction. Our composer's propensity for this is even more pronounced in the piano pieces, even though the creative construction is here not bound by a verse form.

From this point on we will no longer give the measure numbers of the melody in question—the search for these may now serve a higher degree of investigation. The following pieces are offered for study:

Vol. I: 2a and b, 3, 4, 5, 7, 10, 13, 15, 18, 19, 23, 31;

Vol. II: 31, 38, 42, 45 (pentapodic lines alternate between right and left hand, as if written for women's and men's voices), 52, 53, 55 (measures 1–8, see our *Ex. 277*), 56, 61, 62, 65, 66 (our *Ex. 37*);

Vol. III: 69, 72 (our *Ex. 279*), 78, 83, 84, 87, 94, 95;

Vol. IV: 97 (the final melodic line in the bass), 98, 106, 107 (our *Ex. 38*), 109 (the first four measures of the quick middle section), 110 (our *Ex. 106*), 113, 114, 115 (reading the melody of the first six and the final two measures together), 116 (our *Ex. 67*);

Vol. V: 126, 128, 130, 131 (measures 1–16), 136 (measures 1–26), 138, 139;

Vol. VI: 140 (our *Exs. 290* and *116* as a theme and its variant), 146 (measures 8–16, then measures 32–41, 96–103, and 108–116), 148, 149 (the bass in measures 4–7), 150 (measures 6–19, the lower voice moving in octaves), 151 (a small four-measure period), 153.

Let us mention separately Vol. V, 137. We may compare the principal melody with the following folksong:

Ex. 289

(We may view the soprano-alto exchanges of the principal melody as a conversation.)

It would be desirable for these melodies of Bartók which are suitable for singing to sooner-or-later receive poetic texts, that they may later become common national treasures through textbooks, song collections etc.

XXVII. THE ELEMENTS IN COMBINATION

We may arrive at a thorough knowledge of a musical style only if we examine its elements separately, one by one. The preceding chapters have served this purpose. However, in living music, these elements are more-or-

476

less generally found together and overlap one another. (We have already, here and there in one chapter or in one example, been obliged to refer to several elements.)

We now present several examples for independent analysis according to each of the given points of view.

Mikrokosmos

1) The scale of the lower voice? The relation of the initial and final tones of the melodic period?

Ex. 290

Mikr. VI, 140

Exercise: from the above score, let us play the eight-measure melody at the piano in mirror inversion. We give the beginning and the end:

Ex. 291

We even find it in this form in measures 13–19 of the piece. A witty game with the held tone *a:* first the dominant of the tonic, then the tonic of the dominant? (This is also a type of inversion!)

2) Bitonality, symmetry, axis principle, pentatonic chord:

Ex. 293   Mikr. IV, 143

3) Gamma formulas, polar relation, a chord of two (major-minor) thirds, symmetry:

4) Closing group of four pentatonic tones, changing chords (what 8-tone scale is formed if all the tones are taken together?), symmetry, six-voice alpha chord:

Ex. 294 Mikr. IV, 109

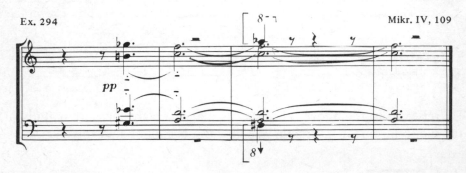

If we spell the first harmony enharmonically as $g\sharp$-b-$d\sharp$-$f\sharp$, we may then also ask in what relation it stands with the identically constructed closing chord?

5) Let us look back at *Ex. 49,* and we may find in it, besides the fourth-melody, bitonality, complementary sets of tones (i. e. sets of tones which together form one complete formula), pentatonic chords (in broken form of three eighth-notes each), pentatonic changing chords (quasi-dominant), and ostinato occurrences. (All this in the one illustration from Boating!)

6) What are all the elements which may be read from *Ex. 192?*

If for not other reason than that of the constraint imposed by a modest amount of material, the above does not nearly exhaust a complete knowledge of Bartók's style. But even a complete knowledge of all the pieces of the 27 Choruses and the Mikrokosmos would not achieve this. To the interested reader is entrusted further searching, examination, and analysis. Indispensible are the fundamental works of Ernő Lendvai: Bartók's Style (Bartók stílusa, Zeneműkiadó, 1955), Bartók's Dramaturgy (Bartók dramaturgiája, Zeneműkiadó, 1964), and Bartók's Poetic World (Bartók költői világa, Szépirodalmi Könyvkiadó, 1971), all published in Budapest.

Also: János Kárpáti's book On Bartók's String Quartets (Bartók vonós-négyeseiről, Zeneműkiadó, 1967), and József Ujfalussy's Book of Bartók (Bartók könyve, Gondolat, 1970). Of a different nature, but also a useful book Borsai–Csillag–Hegyi: On the Performance of Bartók's 27 Choruses for Women's and Children's Voices (Bartók egynemű kórusainak előadásáról, Zeneműkiadó, 1956).

Please complete the investigation by listening to as much of Bartók's music as possible. Let us arrive at the closest possible knowledge of our world-renowned composer. Surely, the better we understand something of value, the more we love it. And—as our main task—may we make this music better known and loved to those who put their trust in us.

(Népművelési Propaganda Iroda, 1972, Budapest)

ON STRAVINSKY'S SYMPHONY OF PSALMS

A SKETCH AND REMEMBRANCE

Stravinsky wrote this work in 1930 for the fifthieth anniversary of the founding of the Boston Symphony Orchestra ("composée à la gloire de DIEU").

The work is scored for mixed choir,[1] winds (without clarinet), brass, timpani, harp, two pianos and strings—but without violins and violas!

The psalm texts are taken from the Vulgate, and the composer's foreword specifies that they are to be sung in Latin.

The work consists of three movements. Three movements = three different worlds. Let us take them in order, even though here we may mention only the most significant, most important aspects of the music's great richness.

THE FIRST MOVEMENT

"Hear my prayer, O Lord!" (Psalm 38). Some very ancient voice calls to us from this movement.[2] It is as if the imploring half-steps recall the time from which the psalms issued forth:

Ex. 1

1 The score indicates that the soprano and alto voices should be sung by a children's choir; women's choir may be substituted if necessary.

2 In the 1948 revised Boosey and Hawkes edition "ovationem" appears in place of "orationem". The amusing misprint repeatedly mentions acclamation instead of supplication...

480

Vaa, the lamentation word of ancient Greek tragedy, is brought to mind with the arching *fa-mi* tones, as are many other examples, enough to fill a large volume of the minor second's imploring, complaining character up to and including the lamentation chorus of the *Psalmus Hungaricus...*

The ostinato of the bass and middle voices also points to both a distant place and time. (Yet it does so in a twentieth-century manner—which is only natural!)

The minor thirds of the middle voice (in augmentation) rise in the bass line as the piece continues:

Ex. 2

An F bass under an E melody tone—an E bass under an F melody tone. The sharpest dissonance of our tonal system, the minor second (major seventh, minor ninth, diminished and augmented octave) appears here so clearly stressed that it may then accompany the entire work to its end.

The effect is enormously intensified toward the end of the movement:

"Forgive me before I depart from this world." The tenor now takes over the alto motive (see *Exs. 1* and *2!*), which, due to the well-known "acoustical illusion", appears to be an octave higher. The soprano also climbs to the level of the *e-f* lamentation. The supplication becomes an elemental force. From the third measure of the quoted section onward the tenor and soprano, the two penetratingly piercing voices, continually reiterate the *e-f*, *f-e* interval. This occurs both as a melodic succession and as a harmonic simultaneity.

At the same time the middle voice and the bass (as already in *Exs. 1* and

2) enrich the soundscape with writhing minor thirds, bringing at once a more restful and a more sharply moving construction.

Also worthy of mention are the polymetric interweavings of the instrumental figures—the octave parallels of the tenor and the orchestral bass line—as the soprano reaches its high point on the f^2 and the bass unexpectedly descends to *D,* thus widening the tonal ambitus, which indirectly stresses even more the melodic high point.

THE SECOND MOVEMENT

After small steps and ostinati: large intervals and melodies unfolding in large arcs. We find a slow tempo which is appropriate to traditional middle movements.

The expressive sound of the oboe begins the movement:

Ex. 4

What a different mood compared to the preceding movement. Only later does one realize that the first four tones quote the well-known minor thirds of the earlier three examples—only now with an entirely new profile due to the octave displacement of exactly one tone:

Ex. 5

A single tone lands elsewhere—and which one is it? naturally "the third among four"!

The identical *c-e♭-b-d* quaternion appears three times before the first (sixteenth) rest. Moreover, the new start after the rest brings back for the fourth time the expressive motive with its major seventh ambitus.

Of the four appearances the third (again?!) reaches upward for its beginning tone:

Ex. 6

Four times the same—and always different! The ostinato character has been dissolved—the phrasing, the rhythm, the metrical placement is ever changing. It is characteristic of our composer's way of weaving a melody.

The first notes of the measures following *Ex. 4,* with their Baroque chaconne-chromaticism *(c-b-b♭-a-a♭)*, modulate to the dominant key, *g*-minor, for the fugal answer. A surprising faithfulness to Bach—a surprising newness of execution.

In the next measures the dux (in *c*-minor) returns, then once again the comes (in *g*-minor), again played by flute and oboe.

All of this is, however, only an introduction and a garnish for the more important fugato in which the chorus declaims:

Ex. 7

"I waited patiently for the Lord, and he inclined unto me" (Psalm 39). After the writhing-imploring voice of the first movement: internal restfulness. (Slow eighth-notes!)

484

The alto presents a strict real answer. Then the tenor begins again on *e♭*, later the bass on *b♭*.

But let us not forget the countersubject sounding under the theme which is presented by the soprano. Behold, there is the melody (the beginning of the movement) which was introduced in *Ex. 4* now transformed to the accompanying bass. Our composer here reaches the contrapuntal splendor of the Bach chorale variations, but of course with his own voice. (The instrumental middle voices, omitted from our sketched examples, serve to establish the rich harmonies of the new style.)

And still a further detail in the Bach style: the old order of the harmonic functions. One half-measure tonic, one half-measure dominant, etc. Something new may be built upon a traditional base.

In the closing section of the movement—just as in Bach— the stretto appears in the orchestra:

Ex. 8

The trochaic dotted rhythm is also from the Baroque style. The text is here exalted to become the motto of the entire work: "And he hath put a new song in my mouth."[3]

Following this we find a constant intensification, an ever-increasing fullness of sound, so that a *subito piano* may then close the movement:

3 In the above mentioned edition another misprint changes the original text in a peculiar manner: instead of "immisit" we find "immisi" in all four voice parts. The meaning is thus: I took a new song to my mouth... Is this accidental? In any event it is also true.

"And shall trust in the Lord." The chorus—perhaps symbolically—firmly sustains the arrived at tonic. Above and below it is the beginning motive of the major seventh. The trumpet, in augmentation, in the opening key of the movement (c-minor), and the instrumental bassline in the relative principal key (E♭), constantly interchange the tonic and dominant with pendulum motion.

The entire movement as it were: Hommage à J. S. Bach.

THE THIRD MOVEMENT

The closing movement begins slowly and peacefully with a solemn alleluja. Yet it is in some way related to the preceding movement:

Ex. 10

The upward-reaching *G-c-g* ternion in the orchestra recalls the first three tones of the second movement—but the perfect octave resolves the former major seventh to a final consonance. The men's voices sing in measures of three half-notes, the women's voices (principal melody) sing the psalm in gentle thirds and expressive syncopation.

But then quite suddenly in dance-like tones a feeling of joy and thanksgiving bursts forth freely:

Ex. 11

Dancing? In the Psalms? Yes! The fourth verse of Psalm 150 sings: "Laudate eum in tympano et choro!" Praise him with drum and round-dancing! In ancient times—as today in the East—the art of movement was offered in ritual service.

Then the chords snap rhythmically in changing metrical formulas:

Ex. 12

In an unusual way, the chorus stresses several times the first syllable of the word Laudate, and only for the fourth time sings it with the proper Latin accentuation: lau-*da*-te. (Is this the ecstatic oblivion of the dancers?...)

The dissonances extending through the entire work give a unique flavor to the C-major chords. At times an *f♯*, at times an *a♭* grates against the *g* melody tone. Furthermore, the tones *F* and *G* give the throbbing basic rhythm under the E-major triads.

After the ample exertion of this music, the impulse gradually slows down and the solemn, touching closing statement of the work appears:

Ex. 13

Perhaps the back-and-forth swaying of the melody still reflects the movements of some ancient holy dance. But the chromaticism of the fourth and fifth measures already relates to the dance music of 1930! This opulently-felt motive is also stressed as the bass doubles the soprano line one octave below. (See the small-print notes of the example from the score.)

Polymetry makes this section, heard four times, even more Stravinsky-like: under the music in ³/₂, the swinging fourths in ⁴/₂ ring out in the kettle

488

drums, harp and piano. This ostinato lasts for 42 measures, stately and tirelessly. At the very end the quiet alleluja of the movement's opening again sounds forth, and the classical, eternally solemn C-major harmony puts the finishing touch to the end of the movement.

THE CYCLICAL WORK

What is it that holds these three different movements together? What is the constructional secret of the entire work?

I cannot free myself from that point of view which I have tried to sketch in the following table:

I	II	III
Psalm 38; 13, 14	Psalm 39; 2–4	Psalm 150
supplication	confidence	gratefulness
heterophony	polyphony	homophony
antiquity	BACH	the newest era
Asia	Europe	America

From movement to movement: rising from darkness toward the light —proceding from the oldest continent to the New World—progression from ancient times to our own era. Thus it is precisely in its diversity that the unity of the plan is made manifest, in its differentation lies its integration.

Thus it is proclaimed that the Book of Psalms, independent of time, place, race, language, is a treasure of world literature valid for eternity, a universal human value.

THE HUNGARIAN PREMIERE

The symphony, as we have already mentioned, was written in 1930. In 1931 László Lajtha brought it to my attention. We obtained the score, studied it, and in May, 1932 we premiered the work with the Palestrina Chorus and the Concert Orchestra.

But until we arrived at that point!...

The chorus—the country's leading oratorio chorus—had until then only dealt with traditional style. Its members most readily sang Bach, Mozart, Beethoven. At best they felt at home with the melodies of the Verdi Requiem. And then along comes a young conductor, with the "unsingable, ugly sounding" lines of a new work. What is more, the date marked Haydn's 200th birthday, therefore the Lord Nelson Mass was also programmed. In rehearsal we had to deal with Haydn and Stravinsky one after the other. With what discomfort, reluctance and opposition the new, difficult, strange music was received! So much so that a palace revolution was narrowly avoided, and the chorus directorship were ready to dismiss me. I implored them: please wait for the concert! We have put so much work into studying the piece! Besides, the posters are already printed... Wait for the performance, then we may discuss the matter afterward.

They resigned themselves with great difficulty. And then came the gigantic surprise. The interesting colors of the orchestra brought the singers closer to the work, the conductor also "gave it everything"—and miracle of miracles! the audience, with thunderous applause, demanded the entire work be encored. The singers stood on the stage in amazement. We did not believe our eyes and ears... The piece then sounded magically different. Now everyone sang with enthusiasm, from the heart.

Which is only the fitting for this masterpiece.

(In memoriam Igor Stravisnky, Budapest, 1972)

ACKNOWLEDGEMENTS

Musical examples from the following works are included by kind permission of the Publishers as shown:

BOOSEY AND HAWKES MUSIC PUBLISHERS LTD., LONDON:
(a) *For all countries of the world*:
  Bartók: Mikrokosmos, Women's Choruses (Bread-baking, Don't Leave Me, Enchanting Song, Hussar, Loafer, Mocking of Youth, Only Tell Me)
  Kodály: Concerto, Five Songs op. 9, Five Songs of the Mountain Tcheremis', Four Songs, Hymn to King Stephen, Media Vita, Organ Mass, Seven Songs op. 6, Symphony, The Peacock, Three Songs op. 14, Two Songs op. 5.
  Stravinsky: Symphony of Psalms
(b) *For all countries of the world except Hungary and the socialist countries (for these countries: Editio Musica Budapest)*
  Kodály: Arise, my Horse, Battle Song, Bicinia Hungarica, 15 Two-part Exercises, 22 Two-part Exercises, 33 Two-part Exercises, 44 Two-part Exercises, 66 Two-part Exercises, 77 Two-part Exercises, 333 Reading Exercises, Cease Your Bitter Weeping, Communion Anthem, Dirge, Eight Little Duets, Epigrams, Epigraph, Evening Song, False Spring, Fancy, Garden of Angels, God's Miracle, Grow Tresses, Hey, Büngözsdi Bandi, Hippity, Hoppity, Honey, Hymn of Zrínyi, Lament, 'Mid the Oak Trees, Minuetto Serio, Mole Marriage, Mountain Nights, National Song, Norvegian Girls, O Come, Come Emmanuel, Orphan Am I, Psalm 150, Seven Easy Children's Choruses, Six Humorous Canons, Soldier's Song, Song from Gömör, Song of Faith, Song of Peace, The Forgotten Song of Balassi, The Hungarian Nation, The Shepherd, The Son of an Enslaved Country, Those Who are Always Late, To the Székely People, Tricinia, Vejnemöjnen Makes Music.

UNIVERSAL EDITION A.G. WIEN:

Kodály: Angels and Shepherds, Ave Maria, Dances of Marosszék, Drinking Song, Duo op. 7, Evening, Háry János, Hungarian Folk Music, Jesus and the Traders, Mátra Pictures, Molnár Anna, Ode to Liszt, Psalmus Hungaricus, Serenade op. 12, Seven Piano Pieces, Sonata for Cello and Piano op. 4, String Quartet II, Székely Lament, Székely Spinning Room, Tantum Ergo, Te Deum of Budavár, The Aged, The Voice of Jesus, Two Folksongs from Zobor.